CRITICAL THEORIES OF ANTI-SEMITISM

NEW DIRECTIONS IN CRITICAL THEORY

NEW DIRECTIONS IN CRITICAL THEORY

Amy Allen, General Editor

New Directions in Critical Theory presents outstanding classic and contemporary texts in the tradition of critical social theory, broadly construed. The series aims to renew and advance the program of critical social theory, with a particular focus on theorizing contemporary struggles around gender, race, sexuality, class, and globalization and their complex interconnections.

Fascist Mythologies: The History and Politics of Unreason in Borges, Freud, and Schmitt, Federico Finchelstein

Crisis Under Critique: How People Assess, Transform, and Respond to Critical Situations, edited by Didier Fassin and Axel Honneth

Selected Writings on Media, Propaganda, and Political Communication, Siegfried Kracauer, edited by Jaeho Kang, Graeme Gilloch, and John Abromeit

Praxis and Revolution: A Theory of Social Transformation, Eva von Redecker

Recognition and Ambivalence, edited by Heikki Ikäheimo, Kristina Lepold, and Titus Stahl

Critique on the Couch: Why Critical Theory Needs Psychoanalysis, Amy Allen

Hermeneutics as Critique: Science, Politics, Race and Culture, Lorenzo C. Simpson

Capitalism on Edge: How Fighting Precarity Can Achieve Radical Change Without Crisis or Utopia, Albena Azmanova

Transitional Subjects: Critical Theory and Object Relations, edited by Amy Allen and Brian O'Connor

Contesting the Far Right: A Psychoanalytic Critical Theory Approach, Claudia Leeb

For a complete list of books in the series, please see the Columbia University Press website.

CRITICAL THEORIES OF ANTI-SEMITISM

Jonathan Judaken

Columbia University Press
New York

Columbia University Press
Publishers Since 1893
New York   Chichester, West Sussex
cup.columbia.edu
Copyright © 2024 Columbia University Press
All rights reserved
Library of Congress Cataloging-in-Publication Data
Names: Judaken, Jonathan, 1968- author.
Title: Critical theories of Anti-Semitism / Jonathan Judaken.
Description: New York : Columbia University Press, 2024. | Series: New directions in critical theory | Includes bibliographical references and index.
Identifiers: LCCN 2023039196 (print) | LCCN 2023039197 (ebook) | ISBN 9780231212922 (hardback) | ISBN 9780231212939 (trade paperback) | ISBN 9780231559638 (ebook)
Subjects: LCSH: Antisemitism—History.
Classification: LCC DS145 .J785 2024 (print) | LCC DS145 (ebook) | DDC 305.892/409—dc23/eng/20231214
LC record available at https://lccn.loc.gov/2023039196
LC ebook record available at https://lccn.loc.gov/2023039197

Cover design: Julia Kushnirsky
Cover image: Shutterstock

To my mentors, teachers, and students

For Ben Zoma said: Who is wise? He who learns from every man, as it is said: "From all who taught me have I gained understanding" (Psalms 119:99). —Pirke Avot 4:1

Contents

Acknowledgments ix

Introduction: Critical Theory and Judeophobia   1

1. Jean-Paul Sartre's Existentialist Antiracism   21

2. The Frankfurt School and the Anti-Semitic Question   45

3. Hannah Arendt, Anti-Semitism, and Her "Story" of History   73

4. The Sociology of Modern Anti-Semitism from Talcott Parsons to Zygmunt Bauman   101

5. Jean-François Lyotard, Postmodernism, and "the jews"   133

6. Léon Poliakov, the Origins of Holocaust Studies, and the Long History of Judeophobia   158

7. George Mosse on Modernity, Culture, and "the Jew"   189

8. Critical Theory and Post-Holocaust Judeophobia   218

Notes   249

Select Bibliography   311

Index   333

Acknowledgments

I recall the visit to the Secretary of Hebrew University in 1998. I was there to get a signature for the deferment of my student loans while a postdoctoral fellow, when somewhat bizarrely he proceeded to remind me of the biblical story of Saul looking for the lost donkeys only to find out that he was to be anointed king. The reference was his segue to telling me that he had just received word that I was given a second year as a postdoc. This was made possible by the support of Gabriel Motzkin, then Head of the Franz Rosenzweig Research Center for German-Jewish Literature and Cultural History, Dalia Ofer, then Head of the Vidal Sassoon International Center for the Study of Antisemitism, and Ezra Mendelsohn z"l, then head of the Institute of Contemporary Jewry, based on a proposal to start on this book.

Without the encouragement of Daniel Schroeter, I would not have ended up at Hebrew University. While there, I wrestled in the dust and drank with thirst the words of many scholars who steeped me in Jewish studies for the first time, not least Steven Aschheim and Robert Wistrich, even if so much of what I argue is a counterweight to Wistrich's approach to anti-Semitism. From there, this book progressed in fits and starts over many years.

I conducted some of the research for the chapter on Mosse with aid from the George L. Mosse Program in History Libraries Grant-in-Aid at the University of Wisconsin–Madison during a chilly spring in 2003. The book was further developed during a year as a scholar-in-residence at the United States Holocaust Memorial Museum in 2006–2007. The drafted chapters were completely rewritten to examine the entangled approach to anti-Semitism that I tout in these pages while on sabbatical at Rhodes College in 2017–2018. This is reflected in the introduction, based on my introduction to the roundtable, "Rethinking

Anti-Semitism," for the *American Historical Review* (October 2018), which went through five rounds of review and passed through the hands of many scholars.

Early versions of parts of several chapters were published previously, beginning with the chapter on Lyotard in *Studies in Contemporary Jewry* in 2000. Sections of the chapter on the Frankfurt School were published in Phyllis Lassner and Lara Trubowitz's *Antisemitism and Philosemitism in the Twentieth and Twenty-First Centuries*. Sections of the chapter on Arendt and on Adorno's contribution to the Frankfurt School were published as a chapter in Lars Rensmann and Samir Gandesha's *Arendt and Adorno*. The section on Talcott Parsons for the chapter on sociology was published in *Antisemitism and the Constitution of Sociology*, edited by Marcel Stoetzler. Sections of the chapter on Poliakov were published in *Post-Holocaust France and the Jews, 1945–1955*, edited by Seán Hand and Steven T. Katz and in the *Graduate Faculty Philosophy Journal* 35, nos. 1–2 (2014). The chapter on Sartre was published in *Sartre, Jews, and the Other*, edited by Manuela Consonni and Vivian Liska.

Vital rethinking of the field of anti-Semitism studies, which is the aim of this book, was carried out in solidarity with the organizing members of the International Consortium for Research on Antisemitism and Racism (ICRAR), a network of leading scholars from universities and research institutes across Europe, Israel, and the United States who share the common goal of revitalizing and reshaping the field.

Most of this work first passed the muster of the brilliant and always insightful Torbjörn Wandel. Beyond the names already mentioned, I am indebted to my academic brother Ethan Katz, Gooner David Feldman, Stefanie Schüler-Springorum, Maurice Samuels, Lisa Leff, Scott Ury, Samuel Moyn, and Sander Gilman, among many other mentors, teachers, and students over the years.

I am forever grateful to my wife, Jaynie Cohen, who has taught me more than anyone about how to treat all Others with kindness and dignity, and to my kids, Julia and Joelle, who test me daily to check on whether I have learned these lessons well.

CRITICAL THEORIES
OF ANTI-SEMITISM

Introduction

Critical Theory and Judeophobia

Anti-Semitism requires rethinking. Unlike anti-Black racism, nationalism, postcolonialism, or gender, for example, the study of anti-Semitism remains undertheorized.[1] Fundamental questions remain unresolved: How does one define anti-Semitism? Should the word be hyphenated? Can the term "anti-Semitism," which was coined in order to distinguish racialized and politicized Judeophobia from religious anti-Judaism, stand for the whole history of Jew hatred? Is hatred the core of anti-Semitism? Or is Judeophobia better understood in terms of ambivalence: a volatile combination of both anxiety and awe, fear and fascination? Is anti-Judaism a leitmotif for understanding the Western tradition?[2] If so, were ancient Judeophobia and medieval anti-Judaism animated by the same impulses as Nazi anti-Semitism, and how do these map onto anti-Zionism? How should one periodize Judeophobia? What accounts for its continuity? Is it unique in its persistence, severity, and consequences, differing substantially from Islamophobia or Negrophobia or xenophobia? Is it based on fantasies or grounded in socioeconomic realities, or both?

These vexed and foundational questions are difficult to answer because they are straightjacketed twice over: first, by the history of the Holocaust and its memory complex and the way this often imposes an exceptionalist, transhistorical teleology on studies of anti-Semitism. But also by the politics of the Israeli-Palestinian conflict, which often turn political debates about the Middle East into fodder for disputes about anti-Semitism.

Stacked on top of the Israeli-Palestinian question, how one understands anti-Semitism is now thoroughly wound into the debate about how Jews, Israel, and anti-Semitism fit into struggles about identity, power, and antiracist politics.

Despite being a small minority everywhere outside of Israel, Jews are rarely counted in programs for diversity, equity, and inclusion. How they fit into antiracist struggles is also challenged. This is the case despite the fact that hate crimes against Jews continue to be the highest among all religious minorities in the United States.[3]

Indifference to Jewish precarity is partly a function of how many simply perceive Jews as white. A group of scholars have shown, in Karen Brodkin's felicitous title, *How Jews Became White Folks and What That Says About Race in America*.[4] For too many on the Left, since Jews are white, they are part and parcel of hegemonic domination. But this view is amnesic. It entirely represses non-Ashkenazic Jews: those Sephardic or Mizrahi Jews from North Africa or the Middle East or Jews from Ethiopia; these groups constitute a huge percentage of Jews in Israel and France. It also neglects Jews of color in the United States.[5] Even in America, it forgets the second part of Brodkin's title. It represses what Matthew Jacobson discusses as the complex relationship between "anti-Semitism and the racial odyssey of Jews in the United States," which was "neither wholly divisible from nor wholly dependent upon the history of whiteness and its vicissitudes in American political culture."[6]

Indeed, whiteness, for those Jews who present as such, has often been provisional and contested. For white Christian nationalists today, for example, Jews are a racial enemy, the puppeteers of white genocide, the masterminds of the great replacement.[7] For the Nazis, Jews were white negros.[8] Historically, Jews' place within the elastic category of whiteness was hotly disputed. Nonetheless, in recent melees concerning the Israeli-Palestinian conflict, pro-Palestinian activists often depict Israel as the embodiment of a colonial, racial, apartheid state and Zionism as a byword for white supremacy. On the other side of the barricade, some Jews consequently complain that they are maliciously harassed for their defense of Israel and Zionism. On college campuses in the United States, this has resulted in several Title VI lawsuits claiming civil rights violations against Jews.[9] Contesting the definition of anti-Semitism is central to these clashes. There are powerful watchdog organizations that monitor these turf wars, and off-campus agitators who aid and abet the combatants on both sides. On one side, the theory of intersectionality is sometimes drawn upon to represent Jews as the embodiment of power and privilege, preempting their inclusion in antiracist struggles.[10] Meanwhile, those on the other side often insist upon the disconnections between Judeophobia and Islamophobia, Negrophobia, homophobia, and xenophobia, staking their claims around the uniqueness of anti-Semitism and the imperiled state of Jews.

Contemporary discussions about anti-Semitism have consequently become a battlefield, with scholarship caught in the crossfire. It is time to pan back to widen the purview, reflecting on a metalevel about how to think about how we think about anti-Semitism. In doing so, I maintain that writing about Judeophobia today demands greater interrogation of our terms, methods, narratives, and epistemologies. It requires that we appreciate the connections between anti-Semitism and colonialism, immigration, and xenophobia; the links between gender and Jewishness, and between Jews and Muslims and other "Others"; and the ties between the postcolonial condition shaped by slavery and imperialism, and the experiences of other genocides and the Holocaust. In short, I argue against exceptionalism, eternalism, teleology, apologetics, and theoretical naïveté in how scholars approach anti-Semitism.

I call instead for an entangled history of anti-Semitism. By this, I mean four things. First, scholarship on anti-Semitism requires the same kind of attention to its categories of analysis that has been applied to the concepts of class, gender, race, religion, and nation.[11] This must begin with the concept that defines the field because "anti-Semitism" has meant different things to different people at different times. Second, I suggest that the oft-claimed uniqueness of anti-Semitism must cede to comparative frames, and ultimately to a history of interlaced pasts. Only through an assessment of the parallels and overlaps with other targeted groups can the singularities of Judeophobia emerge with clarity. Third, we must consider how the plasticity of anti-Jewish images rests upon a fundamental ambivalence. This helps account simultaneously for Jewish persecution and survival. It also enables an appreciation of the overdetermined nature of stereotypes about Jews. The concept of the Jew shapeshifts. These shifts help explain how myths about Jews have had different meanings at different moments or have signified differently to different people in the same era. Fourth, I urge that studies of anti-Semitism more deeply engage the theoretical and methodological considerations that have characterized work in cognate areas, such as critical race, postcolonial, and decolonial theorizing, and plumb more deeply the theoretical work within the field of anti-Semitism studies. Theory provides a language, ways of thinking, and methods that permit scholars to reflect at the metalevel on precisely the kinds of impasses that define the study of anti-Semitism at present.

THE HYPHEN

The dilemma of whether to hyphenate anti-Semitism provides an example. If you type "antisemitism" into your word processor it will perhaps autocorrect. This is because in most English dictionaries it is spelled with a hyphen. But the preponderant position among scholars of anti-Semitism is that this is wrong.[12] They give two main reasons. As Shmuel Almog puts it, "If you use the hyphenated form, you consider the words 'Semitism,' 'Semite,' 'Semitic' as meaningful. They supposedly convey an image of a real substance, of a real group of people—the Semites, who are said to be a race. This is a misnomer: firstly, because 'Semitic' or 'Aryan' were originally language groups, not people; but mainly because in antisemitic parlance, 'Semites' really stands for Jews, just that."[13]

The original German term *Antisemitismus* was not hyphenated when political activist and pamphleteer Wilhelm Marr popularized the neologism around 1879.[14] Marr sought to distinguish his position from the tradition of religious anti-Judaism by deploying a modern, secular, scientific construct based on racial theory.[15] Marr's term derived from the field of comparative philology, which grouped together Semitic languages. In the early nineteenth century, linguists, anthropologists, philosophers, and Orientalists not only opposed "Semitic" to "Aryan" languages, they also maintained that languages encapsulated the indelible racial spirit of the people who used them.[16] But since both Jews and Arabs were implicated by the construct "Semites," Edward Said provocatively noted in *Orientalism*, "I have found myself writing the history of a strange, secret sharer of Western anti-Semitism."[17] The work of Gil Anidjar has helped unlock this shared secret not only by suggesting its long history but also by indicating how and when it became a secret. As Anidjar puts it, "Once equally Semites, Jews and Arabs were both race and religion in a secular political world—fantasmatic and imaginary as the latter was and remains.... Today, and since Nazism at least, one can divide them again."[18]

Anidjar developed this insight in *The Jew, the Arab: A History of the Enemy*, where he maintained that European self-constructions long depended upon a two-headed hydra: the Jew as the internal enemy, the theological enemy, and the Saracen, the Moor, the Turk, the Arab, the Muslim, or Islam as differing names that served as the external enemy, the political enemy.[19] Developing Anidjar's point, Ivan Kalmar has traced a dialectic of doubled demonization in the cultural history of representations of Jews and Muslims in the West.[20] Jointly stigmatized by medieval Christianity, the construct "Semites" racialized this representation in the nineteenth century. Some stopping points along the way reveal how they were entangled: their fates were intertwined in the Crusades, which gave rise to the first mass killings of Jews en route to liberating the holy sites held by the Saracens in Jerusalem; the Fourth Lateran Council (1215) mandated marking not only Jewish but also Muslim clothing; the Spanish Inquisition targeted not only Jews but Moors. Postexpulsion, many Jews escaped Christendom by living under the crescent of Islam, with coexistence lasting into the Ottoman period. This resulted in the repeated trope of depicting Jews in Turkish garb in Renaissance art, as in many paintings by Rembrandt. By the nineteenth century, in works like *Tancred*, where Benjamin Disraeli claimed that "all is race," he nonetheless insisted that the Jews were an "Arabian tribe" and "Arabs are simply Jews on horseback."[21]

The conjoined history of "Semites" was erased around the time that "Judeo-Christian" was popularized in the 1930s as a means to enjoin Christian support for the struggle against Nazism.[22] "Judeo-Christian" was used by organizations like the National Conference of Christians and Jews, and championed by prominent theologians like Reinhold Niebuhr, Jacques Maritain, Paul Tillich, and Emmanuel Levinas. Marc Chagall provided the visual iconography in a series of images of Jesus crucified, but clearly wearing Jewish garb, like a Jewish prayer shawl (i.e., *tallit*). Its use continued following the Holocaust, with early efforts at interfaith dialogue, the creation of the State of Israel, and the onset of the Cold War.[23]

According to the myth as it developed post-Holocaust, what underpinned Western, liberal, democratic society was so-called Judeo-Christian civilization once under threat by Nazism, but now besieged by Soviet barbarism, materialism, and atheism.[24] It was during the Cold War that what Arthur A. Cohen terms "the myth of the Judeo-Christian tradition" and what Marshall Grossman calls "the violence of the hyphen in Judeo-Christian" solidified.[25] "Judeo-Christian" became a pillar of Western civilization and European and American democracy, implicitly negating the contributions of Islamic civilizations to "the West." What made the decoupling of Jews and Muslims definitive was that beginning in the 1930s, spurred by the burgeoning Arab-Israeli conflict, and accelerating to the present day, the demonization of Jews became more common in the Islamic world, drawing upon the European anti-Semitic arsenal, at the same time that anti-Arab racism spread among Jews. The two heads of the

European enemy now turned on one another, effacing their earlier entangled past.

This brief sketch only hints at the complicated story of the linkages and disconnects between Judeophobia and Islamophobia.[26] It makes plain, however, that the choice about the hyphen is and always has been both epistemological and political. To *consciously hyphenate* "anti-Semitism" today—by drawing attention to this grammatical mark as signifying a conjoined history—is to point to the forgotten intersections and interactions between Jews and Muslims, while remarking upon the history of the myth of "the Semite" that underpins the origins of the term.[27] Doing so also rebuffs the assertion of the unique targeting of Jews made by those who refuse to hyphenate "anti-Semitism."[28] The choice to hyphenate is particularly significant in a political frame where Jews and Muslims often are figured as perpetual enemies despite the historical scholarship that shows otherwise.[29]

DEFINING ANTI-SEMITISM

The seemingly small matter of the hyphen consequently encapsulates a host of bigger, entangled problems. These include the definition of anti-Semitism, which remains nebulous. "Anti-Semitism" covers everything from personal prejudices to murderous genocide.[30] As is the case with the overexpansive use of the term "racism," this equivocation stifles discussion and leads to misunderstandings.[31] A more refined conceptual palette that makes distinctions between terms could clear these up. *Stereotypes*—enduring mythic images of Jews and Judaism—do not necessarily entail the internalization of these representations, which form the basis of prejudicial views about groups of people.[32] Likewise, *prejudice*— "attitude, affective-imaginary disposition, linked to ethnic stereotypes"—does not necessarily lead to *discrimination*.[33] This necessitates behavioral, social, or legal means of enforcing certain practices. Discrimination, in turn, does not necessarily depend upon a racial ideology: a world view or doctrine that contains an interpretation of history and a metaphysics of identity built upon systems of racial classification. So not all forms of discrimination are *racist*.[34] None of these entails *genocide* (i.e., organized group annihilation).[35] But when "anti-Semitism" is used to label all these differing attitudes and actions, reiterating an anti-Jewish stereotype suddenly conjures images of Nazi storm troopers, even as this leap often misconstrues past and present cases of Judeophobia.

In 1990, Gavin Langmuir sought to provide some necessary clarity to this confusion in "Towards a Definition of Antisemitism."[36] He considered the then-available social scientific literature, parsing definitions of ethnocentrism, bias/bigotry/prejudice, discrimination, xenophobia, and anti-Semitism. Critiquing the notion of "eternal antisemitism," he insisted on a radical disjuncture between anti-Judaism and anti-Semitism, defining the latter as "socially significant chimerical hostility against Jews." In doing so, he articulated three modes of responding to outgroups: (1) realistic hostility, (2) xenophobic hostility, and (3) chimerical hostility.[37] The first response is based upon the rational competition for scarce goods and incommensurable values that Langmuir associated with ancient Judeophobia and early Christian-Jewish enmity. The second is the result of projecting a series of stereotypes onto a scapegoat because of perceived threats faced by a community. This is done not so much because of ignorance of the Other, but because of the ignorance by the in-group of the real social conditions that plague them. Theodor Adorno had earlier made this point when he maintained that stereotypes personify social conditions for those without an adequate language to express them otherwise.[38] Inspired by the new cultural history, Shulamit Volkov has influentially called the clusters in which these stereotypes come "a cultural code" for articulating social crises.[39] Unlike realistic and xenophobic hostility, Langmuir contended that anti-Semitism is entirely unamenable to reality: "In contrast ... chimeric assertions present fantasies, figments of the imagination, monsters which ... have no 'kernel of truth.' This is the contrast which distinguishes the hostility that produced Auschwitz from that manifested against Jews in ancient Alexandria."[40] A medievalist, Langmuir maintained that it was in the twelfth to thirteenth centuries that anti-Judaism turned into anti-Semitism. His prime example of a "socially significant chimerical assertion" was the charge of ritual murder. Like the other anti-Jewish medieval myths, specifically host desecration and well poisoning, ritual murder implicated Jews in a conspiracy against Christendom. What Langmuir does not address, however, is that chimerical assertions about Muslims were also bandied about in the centuries of the Crusades, as were such delusions apparent in the history of the witch hunts in following centuries, and monstrous fantasies of Blacks circulated in the era of Jim Crow lynching. Yet none of these led to Auschwitz.

In *Judeophobia: Attitudes Towards the Jews in the Ancient World*, Peter Schäfer pushed backed against Langmuir in the other temporal direction. He insists that chimerical assertions were integral to the pagan anti-Jewish diatribes in ancient Alexandria, most saliently in the charge of Jewish "ritual cannibalism."[41] Langmuir's theoretical model consequently does not help us to demarcate anti-Semitism.

> His crucial chimerical fantasies are part and parcel of ancient hostility, but not only against Jews. If his model is not altogether worthless, one should opt for a much more dynamic interplay of its components (realistic, xenophobic, chimerical), instead of his linear pattern of development. There is obviously no clear-cut, absolute point in history at which anti-Judaism turns into anti-Semitism. The transitions between the different components are fluid, and this applies to all periods of history, certainly to the ancient world.[42]

Schäfer's suggestion about the adaptable interplay of realistic, xenophobic, and chimerical components is spot on and problematizes the chronological unfolding of anti-Semitism suggested by Langmuir. The neat divides between these varieties not only break down in the ancient world but also falter in contemporary discourse around the Israeli-Palestinian conflict. Moreover, recent scholarship shows that racism was widespread within Christianity by the nineteenth century, if not earlier, so a categorical divide between anti-Judaism and anti-Semitism fails there as well.[43]

Given these problems of when, where, and how to locate "anti-Semitism," David Engel suggests eschewing the term in the interest of better scholarship. He explains that one cannot simply postulate the historical links between anti-Jewish animus and persecution: "No necessary relation among particular instances of violence, hostile depiction, agitation, discrimination, and private unfriendly feeling across time and space can be assumed," he writes.[44] Like Langmuir and Volkov, who sought to undercut a notion of anti-Semitism as eternal or teleologically culminating in the Nazi genocide, Engel insists that transhistorical causality must be demonstrated in connecting the various iterations of Judeophobia. They cannot just hang together tautologically in the construct "anti-Semitism" that unifies what historians need not only to describe but also to analyze. Hence, he endorses avoiding the term in the interest of scholarly attention to the frameworks and contexts where these differing elements arise.

Kenneth L. Marcus's *The Definition of Anti-Semitism* demurs as he tackles these nested problems.[45] The strength of eternalist approaches, Marcus claims, is their emphasis on continuities in assessing what Robert Wistrich dubbed "the longest hatred."[46] But ultimately, as Hannah Arendt pointed out, eternalists answer the question "Why the Jews?" with the question-begging reply: eternal hostility.[47] Following Arendt, historicists accordingly either view anti-Semitism as uniquely modern, or they consider its historical episodes as "discrete, socially embedded and contingent."[48]

Wanting to move beyond this deadlock, Marcus advocates what I would dub a *cyclical eternalism*, which he calls "anti-Semitism as repetition." He acknowledges that the recurrence of Judeophobia "involves continuities and discontinuities, evolutions and transformations, increases and diminutions, latencies and eruptions," hence freeing us "from the double-bind in which Jew-hatred is either eternal and immutable or else culturally specific and disconnected."[49] But rather than embrace this dynamic understanding, Marcus just gives eternalism a cyclical makeover. He insists that protoracism already existed even when racial categories and the science that underpinned them had yet to emerge. He vacillates on whether there are objective factors that define anti-Semitism or whether perceived threats by Jews are justifications for claims of anti-Semitism. In the end, he acknowledges that the various definitions of anti-Semitism he discusses are all provisional and depend upon what researchers seek to include in the classifications they adopt.

For his own purposes, Marcus claims that Israel today is the collective Jew, that anti-Zionism consequently slips easily into anti-Semitism, and that the so-called new anti-Semitism that targets Israel and Zionism rather than Jews and Judaism, including in the Boycott, Sanctions, and Divestment (BDS) movement against Israel, is nothing but the latest repetition of an eternal cycle that has perpetually plagued Jews, triggered by the same set of causes. In fact, the concept of "the new anti-Semitism" already indicates an eternalist bias. Whether transhistorical or cyclical, it is always already teleological.

Consequently, contra Marcus and all eternalists, historicists like me are right to insist that anti-Semitism per se depended upon science, mass politics, secularity, and modernity. Without the development of scientific theories of race, mass political organization, the secularization brought about by modernity, the shifts in populations from rural to urban spaces, and the rise of literacy and mass media, events like the Dreyfus affair are inexplicable. These were factors that did not exist in the premodern world. Likewise, the assumption that occurrences like blood libel charges meant the same thing in twelfth-century England as they do in the modern Middle East simply does not make sense. What has endured are persisting images, tropes, myths, scripts, or fantasies about Jews developed over the long history of anti-Judaism.[50] But these representations were reworked in different ways in different periods to serve different ends. Most importantly, the social forces, political frameworks and institutions, technological factors, and economic conditions that have periodically spurred the revival of these persisting myths are not the same in dissimilar contexts. Accordingly, different eruptions of Judeophobia require different explanations. For this reason, cyclical eternalism, like its twin, transhistorical anti-Semitism, does not advance our understanding.

Marcus's theoretical reflections on how to define anti-Semitism are underpinned by his zealous endorsement of the International Holocaust Remembrance Alliance's (IHRA) working definition of anti-Semitism.[51] The IHRA definition is now enshrined in policy and law by numerous governments, universities, and civic organizations, despite the fact that it was developed as a heuristic device for data collection on incidents of Judeophobia, not for use in enforcing legislation. This is why Kenneth Stern, who is more responsible for developing the definition than anyone else, opposes its utilization as a legal tool, for example, in the proposed "Antisemitism Awareness Act," and in Trump's executive order in 2019 that adopts the definition for Title VI purposes.[52]

Moreover, as David Feldman, director of the Birkbeck Institute for the Study of Antisemitism, has remarked, the IHRA definition is "bewilderingly imprecise."[53] Examining the three parts of the definition proves Feldman's point. The first part offers a generic definition: "Antisemitism is a certain perception of Jews, which may be expressed as hatred towards Jews." But what is meant by "a certain perception of Jews"? Is it precisely the perception that gets "expressed as hatred toward Jews"?

The focus on "perception" centers the discussion on attitudes, ideas, myths, images, and *misperceptions* of Jews. This places the emphasis of the IHRA definition on the intentions of those charged, which are notoriously difficult to prove. How is one to dissect the ostensible anti-Semitism of a student who draws an analogy between policies of the Nazis and those of the Israeli state, for example; or a group of students who create a swastika out of plastic beer glasses and then give it the Nazi salute while engaged in underage drinking? To assess these cases requires an analysis of the context. The emphasis on prejudices or biases as opposed to outcomes leads down a blind alley, as many scholars of racism now concur. Nonetheless, if this generic definition is corralled to enforce civil rights law within educational institutions, "the overall effect will place the onus on Israel's critics to demonstrate they are not antisemitic," creating a situation that Judith Butler has called censorship "in effect, if not in intent."[54]

The second part of the IHRA definition provides a much more helpful focus since it is leveled at actions, albeit in a convoluted way: "Rhetorical and physical manifestations of anti-Semitism," the definition continues, "are directed toward Jewish or non-Jewish individuals and/or their property, toward Jewish community institutions and religious facilities." The aim is now on anti-Semitic rhetoric and acts that target either Jewish individuals or their property, or Jewish communal institutions or religious facilities. That part is crystal clear. But it also includes acts or language directed against non-Jewish individuals and their property. In the latter case, what makes them anti-Semitic must ultimately rely on the nebulous first part of the definition.

To aid in deciphering cases that remain unclear, IHRA shifts genre from a definition to a memo that makes up a third part. It lists eleven potential examples of anti-Semitism, seven of which deal with criticism of Israel gone astray. These debatably include comparing Israeli policy to the Nazis, which is a problem since analogies to the Nazis are commonplace on both sides of the Israeli-Palestinian conflict; claiming that the State of Israel is racist, which neuters charges of Israeli racism a priori; and applying double standards by requiring Israel to behave in ways that are not expected or demanded of other democratic states, which is a claim easy to throw around willy-nilly. Ultimately, the IHRA definition is unclear and incoherent: it focuses on the ostensible intentions of those accused of anti-Semitism and not on the outcomes of actions, and most perniciously, it threatens to quell debate about Israel/Palestine and even to legally sanction the BDS movement and the speech acts and actions of many supporters of Palestinian liberation.

In response, a group of scholars sponsored by the Van Leer Institute in Jerusalem penned the Jerusalem Declaration on Antisemitism (JDA) to more acutely define anti-Semitism and to more clearly demarcate the line between criticism of Zionism and Israel and Judeophobic discourse.[55] The JDA includes a preamble, which locates its approach to the problem of defining anti-Semitism within the UN Declaration of Human Rights, the 1969 International Convention on

Elimination of All Forms of Racial Discrimination, the 2000 Declaration of the Stockholm International Forum on the Holocaust, and the 2005 UN Resolution on Holocaust Remembrance. It maintains that the struggle against anti-Semitism has some distinctive features but "the fight against it is inseparable from the overall fight against all forms of racial, ethnic, cultural, religious, and gender discrimination." It also stipulates that the goal of the JDA is to provide a sounder core definition of anti-Semitism and to provide sharper guidelines, especially on issues of political speech about Israel/Palestine. As a cosigner of the working definition of the JDA, I concur that it provides an important set of correctives to the IHRA working definition.

The JDA core definition states that "antisemitism is discrimination, prejudice, hostility or violence against Jews as Jews (or Jewish institutions as Jewish)." This is a far clearer core definition than IHRA's. When the JDA turns to its guidelines about how to apply this definition, as is the case with the IHRA definition, most of the focus is on when criticisms of Zionism and Israel become anti-Semitic. Here the JDA overlaps with IHRA in a number of ways: examples include claims associating Israel and Zionism with evil; or tarring Israel with classic Judeophobic tropes; or holding all Jews responsible for Israel's conduct; or forcing Jews to publicly condemn Israel or Zionism as a political litmus test; or assuming that non-Israeli Jews are more loyal to Israel than to their countries of citizenship; or denying the right of the State of Israel to exist. Where the two documents differ is in the enumeration by the JDA of what is *not anti-Semitic*, including support for Palestinian demands that are recognized by international law, critiquing Zionism, or insisting upon equal rights for all those "between the river and the sea," as well as all *evidenced-based* criticism of Israel as a state, and most controversially, calls for boycott, divestment, and sanctions.

However, the JDA has received its own share of criticism. Several of the signatories to the JDA have rightfully been spotlighted as themselves blameworthy of the provisions articulated in the JDA, including Sergio Luzzatto, who has suggested the medieval blood libel is true, Richard Falk, a 9/11 truther, and Yvonne Ridley, who once said that "the Zionists have tentacles everywhere." More germane and damning, David Schraub has consequently argued that the JDA is primarily embraced by those who seek to use it "as a tool for *denying* things are anti-semitic."[56] Michael Walzer, an original cosigner of the JDA, who supported it in order to "create a little distance ... between antisemitism and the Israel/Palestine battles" appreciates that these can and do overlap. He now insists that rescinding the IHRA definition or "replacing it with a definition perceived as more permissive" undermines the fight against anti-Semitism.[57] The most widespread critique, however, maintains that the JDA and the Nexus Document,[58] which also seeks to refine definitional approaches to fighting contemporary Judeophobia and shares much in common with the JDA, divide the struggle against anti-Semitism today. These critics maintain that this struggle is consequently best served by supporting the international and legal enforcement of the IHRA definition. Ultimately, for scholars of anti-Semitism, the political struggle over these contemporary definitions hinders rather than helps how they approach their subject.

FROM ANTI-SEMITISM TO JUDEOPHOBIA

Perhaps, therefore, it is time to adopt a different vocabulary that will nuance our understanding and thereby sharpen the tools in the struggle. "Judeophobia" offers a better overarching term for the field for at least three reasons. First, it defamiliarizes readers, which allows for the conceptual reflection I am calling for. Judeophobia, as I define it,[59] encompasses the *denigration* of Judaism, *defamation* of the Jewish character, *discrimination* against Jews, their *racialization*, and at its extreme, efforts at *destruction* of the Jewish people. This core definition should be understood to cover the five modes of Judeophobic discourse and anti-Jewish practices that I have distinguished: stereotypes, prejudice, discrimination, racialization, and murder. Embracing a Foucauldian lexicon by studying the Judeophobic discourses and practices at work in differing social contexts will allow for a more nuanced and pointed analysis that will not equivocate, as the term "anti-Semitism" does. Using Judeophobia as an overarching category in this way not only taps into the more refined conceptual palette I have delineated, but does so without the anachronistic associations that the term "anti-Semitism" often provokes. Ultimately, it is the distinctive modes of Judeophobic discourses and practices in their particular contexts that scholars need to describe and analyze.

Secondly, "Judeophobia" lends itself more readily to periodization that is attentive to social, political, economic, technological, and cultural shifts. This is a key way in which it differs from the term "anti-Semitism." Judeophobia has been transformed by changes in social mores, customs, and institutional formations, and in the modern and postcolonial periods by reactionary responses to antiracist activism. We can and should distinguish five main epochs. The ancient Judeophobia studied by Schäfer was characterized by important contextual differences from the early Christian Judeophobia of the Adversus Judaeos tradition. This anti-Judaism was transformed by the era of the Crusades and the High Middle Ages, when the new fantasies about Jews that are the focus of Langmuir's work emerged. Modern racism developed out of the theological heritage of the Spanish Inquisition, the conquest of the Americas, transatlantic slavery, Enlightenment systems of categorization, and the rise of nationalism in the wake of Napoleon. Post-Holocaust Judeophobia has taken new forms in a postcolonial era defined by globalization.

"Anti-Semitism" *sensu stricto* should not be discarded but more precisely circumscribed. The term should be delimited in its use only to the era of modern racism when it was coined, reaching its climax with the Holocaust. "What was new and menacingly different about antisemitism," Richard Levy astutely claimed, was "its politicization and embodiment in permanent political parties, voluntary associations, and publishing ventures—in short, its institutionalization."[60] Anti-Semitism was racialized and programmatic.[61] In these uniquely modern institutions in an era of mass politics, anti-Semitism developed into a world view by reworking "pre-and early Christian writings, medieval iconography, and modern literary expressions, pithy folk sayings, cartoons, and doggerel songs" that were based upon a reservoir of anti-Jewish figures, formulas, and myths.[62] Today's *post-Holocaust Judeophobia* has once again morphed. It is about cultural and political conflict, not about an ostensible racial conflict between Aryans and Semites, and it is unprecedentedly global. Moreover, today the State of Israel, acting as the Jewish state, is often central to both Judeophobic discourse and to the fight against it. The context has changed. If our vocabulary changed as well, the terminological morass that hinges on drawing a line or an equal sign between anti-Zionism and anti-Semitism might abate in discussions of contemporary Judeophobia.

A third reason to adopt the term "Judeophobia" is that it readily links what Frantz Fanon aptly designated "phobogenic" objects itemized in his studies of Negrophobia with instances of Islamophobia, xenophobia, homophobia, or gynophobia. These each name subjects of anxiety or unsubstantiated fear or resentment, but also fascination or envy.[63] To grasp this ambiguity, Bryan Cheyette refers to "semitic discourse" as a way to understand the ambivalences and slippages in figuring Jews in modern literature: "The radical emptiness and lack of a fixed meaning in the constructions of 'semitic' difference," he writes, "results in the 'the Jew' being made to occupy an incommensurable number of subject positions which traverse a range of contradictory discourses."[64] The social theorist Zygmunt Bauman took this insight furthest in his reassessment of Judeophobia. He borrowed and developed Artur Sandauer's concept of *allosemitism*, derived from *allos*, the Greek word for "other." Bauman uses this construct to highlight "the [problematic] practice of setting the Jews apart as people radically different from all the others, needing separate concepts to describe and comprehend them, and special treatment in all or most social intercourse."[65] Allosemitism, he maintained, is the root of both anti-Semitism and philo-Semitism. Bauman claims that we need a new vocabulary to capture this ambivalence because Jew hatred is not the core of what fuels anti-Jewish thought and practice.

Judeophobia is often treated as a case of *heterophobia*: the resentment or fear of the Other that provokes anxiety.[66] Bauman averred that it ought also to be understood as a form of *proteophobia*.[67] Proteophobia aims its venom at the figures who disrupt "the structure of the orderly world," who "[do] not fall easily into any of the established categories," who send out "contradictory signals as to proper conduct" and are "behaviorally confusing."[68] Judeophobes, concludes Bauman, fear the anxiety produced by Jews because Jews blur borderlines, disrupting systems of categorization and signification often defined through binary formulas.

In making this argument, Bauman picked up on threads running through postwar French theory. Thinkers from Jean-Paul Sartre to Jacques Derrida drew attention to the perpetually morphing "figural Jew."[69] Building on the social theory from Sartre, Arendt, and the Frankfurt School to post-structuralism and into contemporary sociology à la Bauman, along with historians of anti-Semitism, and drawing upon critical race, postcolonial, and decolonial theorists, this study aims to introduce ways of thinking about discourses and practices that scholars of Judeophobia have yet to take up adequately. The full depth and insight of these critical theories of anti-Semitism have never been considered together. This book aims to revitalize the field by doing so, and in the process, to write a history of the major theories and theorists of anti-Semitism, while bringing critical theories of anti-Semitism into dialogue with critical race theorizing.

PARADIGMS FOR EXPLAINING JUDEOPHOBIA

There are seven paradigms that we will explore. Each provides an overarching explanation of anti-Semitism. Indeed, my claim is that these are the major explanations that scholars have developed to account for the history of Judeophobia. In the concluding chapter of the book, we will examine their relevance to contemporary Judeophobia.

Prior to the rise of the Nazis, four key paradigms existed for explaining Judeophobia: Rabbinic, Christian, liberal, and Zionist.[70] What they each shared was the notion that to overcome Judeophobia, it would be necessary to change Jewish values, beliefs, or actions. Consequently, each of these approaches focused on the object of contempt—Jews—and not on the subjects who demonized them.

Even the *Hazal* (the Jewish sages) adopted this viewpoint. Martin Lockshin has surveyed the normative rabbinic view on Judeophobia by examining how the rabbis understood the concept of *sinat Yisrael* (hatred of Israel), which was their notion for encapsulating Judeophobia. He shows that it is difficult to pin down biblical and classical Talmudic views on anti-Jewish animus. But when the key medieval commentator, Rabbi Shlomo Yitzhaki (1040–1105), better known by his acronym Rashi, included Rabbi Shimon bar Yohai's once-obscure remark that "it is well known that Esau hates Jacob" (*halakhah be-yadu'a Esau soneh le-Ya'akov*), it led to its wide circulation as a formula.[71] The quote was significant since many rabbinic texts used "Esau" as a code for Romans or Christians or even all gentiles. This *halakhah* or rule was reinforced in the prayer Vehi She-'Amdah from the Passover Haggadah that includes the line that "in every generation they stand up against us to destroy us, and the Holy One, blessed be He, saves us from their hand."

Other scattered Talmudic passages and especially the biblical story of Esther reinforced the point. As Elaine Rose Glickman notes in her portrait of rabbinic literature interpreting the book of Esther, "In the figure of Haman, we have come to see not only Haman, a single person, but a paradigm: Haman as would-be destroyer, Haman as evil schemer, Haman as merciless enemy."[72] The medieval rabbinic perspective thus concluded that Judeophobia was inevitable, universal, and transhistorical. The rabbis thereby suggested that Judeophobia is eternal, at least until the messiah comes and the tears of Esau are dried.[73] Given the portrait of Jacob-Israel in the Bible, a significant measure of culpability is ascribed to

Jews in this affair. After all, Jacob-Israel stole the birthright of Esau, as well as his father's blessing on his deathbed. This is the cause of Esau's tears. In short, it was Jewish sin that was responsible for Jewish suffering.

If this was the traditional rabbinic perspective, in the Christian world before the modern period the range of attitudes to Judeophobia veered from ambivalence to hostility. Everyone from Augustine to Chrysostom agreed that Jews existed in a state of subordination as a sign of their spiritual blindness.[74] This Jewish failure legitimated the hostility, oppression, and persecution of Jews, even if violence against them was ostensibly condemned, at least theologically, if not in practice. I use the church fathers Augustine and Chrysostom here to name two key strands within the tradition of Christian anti-Judaism: Augustine stands for the dominant position, at least until the Crusades, characterized by the ambivalence that legitimated subjection but that limited violence. Chrysostom is a placeholder for anti-Jewish Christian hostility, animated by the goal of separation, segregation, and eventually expulsion, with the goal of eliminating Judaizing, if not Jewishness.

Hostility toward Jews as a problem that Western civilization needed to address about itself really only emerged in the Enlightenment and was phrased as the so-called Jewish Question.[75] The solution to this question for liberals of the eighteenth and nineteenth century was to advocate tolerance for Jewish religious difference and equal civic and political rights. This was intended to lead to Jewish "regeneration" or even assimilation. On the more radical extreme of liberalism, socialists were convinced that the Jewish problem would disappear with the victory of the social revolution. When they were not complicit in reworking anti-Jewish venom as a basis for their critique of capitalism (as was the case with Pierre-Joseph Proudhon, Charles Fourier, and Karl Marx), they regarded anti-Semitism, in August Bebel's words, as "the socialism of fools," a "stratagem to distract the toiling masses from fighting their real enemies—the exploiters, capitalism, and the reactionaries."[76]

Even the response to anti-Semitism by political Zionists in the nineteenth century concurred that Jews needed to change if they were to avert anti-Jewish discrimination. The Zionist solution to the Jewish Question was that the transformation of the Jews affected by having a nation like all other nation-states would normalize their status and end anti-Semitism. The quotidian existence of diaspora Jews was still the problem.[77] So thought Leon Pinsker when he coined the term "Judeophobia." Writing in the immediate aftermath of the pogroms in Russia in 1881, Pinsker's anonymously published *Auto-Emancipation* was one of the seminal texts of modern Zionism and arguably defined the Zionist position on Judeophobia.[78] Lacking a nation-state, Pinsker claimed, Jews had fallen into "decay," a destructive lack of "self-respect," living only in "the uncanny form of one of the dead walking among the living.... A people without unity or organization, without land or other bonds of unity, no longer alive, and yet walking among the living—this spectral form ... could but strangely affect the imagination of the nations."[79]

The anomalous Jewish condition resulted in Judeophobia, "an hereditary form of demonopathy," "an inherited aberration of the human mind."[80] Pinsker, a medical doctor, depicted anti-Jewish animus as a perpetual disease. In making this claim, his political Zionism constituted a secularization of the rabbinic understanding of eternal anti-Semitism, maintaining that prejudice against Jews was an inherited psychological condition woven into the cultural code of the nations of Europe. "Jews are not *the chosen people*," he wrote, but "the people chosen for universal hatred."[81] Pinsker echoed the anti-Semites' claim about the pathologies of Jewish life; where Pinsker differed was in the belief that if Jews apprehended the destitution of their condition they could change, emancipating themselves through Jewish nationalism.

The first histories of Judeophobia incorporated aspects of these four paradigms of Judeophobia and were roughly concomitant with the first Zionist manifestoes, written as they were in response to the rise of political anti-Semitism.[82] The radicalization of anti-Semitism that followed World War I led to the first theories of how race and nation were intertwined and addressed the role played by anti-Semitism in defining European nationalisms. But it was only with the rise of the Nazis in the 1930s that a new critical philosophy and social scientific approach emerged on the topic of anti-Semitism that focused on trying to understand the phenomenon by explaining the reasons anti-Semites focused their contempt on Jews.[83] It was also only then that the term "racism" was popularized to name this problem.[84]

As such, by *critical theories of anti-Semitism*, I mean two things. First, it was not until the rise of the Nazis that scholars fully turned from focusing on Jews and Judaism as the objects of condescension toward the subjects who castigated them in an effort to offer a critical analysis of what accounted for anti-Semitism. Second, and more obviously, the social theorists I will consider are all part of the broader tradition of critical theory, as this term is understood in the American academy, and their work is usefully supplemented by the historians I consider.[85]

On an international scale, individuals and teams of scholars took up the topic and proposed causes. I highlight and explicate the most influential of these approaches. We begin this book in France, focused on the existentialist writing of Jean-Paul Sartre in the late 1930s and then more comprehensively following the Holocaust. Across the Rhine and then across the Atlantic, the work undertaken to explain the sociopsychological etiology of anti-Semitism was led by the Institute for Social Research, first in Frankfurt and later sponsored by the American Jewish Committee in the United States, which would prove crucially important to this development. The psychologists Erich Fromm, Marie Jahoda, Bruno Bettelheim, Daniel Levinson, and Ernest Simmel, and the historian Paul Massing and political scientist Franz Neumann significantly abetted this undertaking.[86] Hannah Arendt's own itinerary crossed similar paths but disputed the existentialist and socio-psychoanalytic theories of Sartre and the Frankfurt School. In her case, she fled from Germany to France and then fled from her internment there to America, where she produced her magnum opus, *The Origins of Totalitarianism*, offering what I will term her interactionist approach. Contesting American isolationism, Talcott Parsons's opposition to Nazism spurred his synthesis of modern sociological insights on anti-Semitism during the Second World War. His modernist understanding was later challenged by Zygmunt Bauman's postmodern sociological approach. In articulating his position, Bauman brought together the Frankfurt School and Arendt alongside French postmodernism. Jean-François Lyotard developed the most robust postmodern analysis, inspired in part by the massive historical erudition in the multivolume works of historian Léon Poliakov. I turn, finally, to another pioneering historian of modernity, George Mosse.

In short, the heart of this book is seven chapters that focus respectively on Jean-Paul Sartre, the Frankfurt School, Hannah Arendt, the sociological approaches of Talcott Parsons and Zygmunt Bauman, Jean-François Lyotard's postmodernism, and the work of two major historians, Léon Poliakov and George Mosse. Each of these figures represents one of the paradigms that have provided the major explanatory frameworks for accounting for anti-Semitism: existentialist, interactionist, socio-psychoanalytic, sociological, postmodern, and historical (over the *longue durée* in the case of Poliakov and focused on modernity in Mosse's work). I discuss how each of these theories incorporates an analysis of religious anti-Judaism, scientific or cultural racism, economic and class factors, exclusionary nationalism and nation-state politics, the relations of power between majorities and minorities, and scapegoating. My main principle of selection in choosing these thinkers, however, is to isolate key representatives of defining approaches that were taken to understand anti-Semitism after the rise of Nazism and in the wake of the Holocaust. I also want to examine important representatives of the French, German, English, and American intellectual traditions, including both Jewish and non-Jewish thinkers.

Through brief biographical vignettes, I locate each of these theorists in their sociocultural context. Then I engage in a critical reading of their work: after reconstructing the central concepts, narratives, and theoretical models that structure how these scholars came to think about anti-Semitism, I examine the limits and possibilities of their approaches. My interpretations focus on how their political perspectives shape and were shaped by their approach to Judeophobia; how many of these critics of anti-Semitism nonetheless reiterate Judeophobic tropes and what this means for race thinking and its deconstruction;[87] and how each understands the links between anti-Semitism and modernity.

Thus, I consider Sartre's phenomenological existentialism and how his views on racism changed with his developing Marxism (chapter 1); Arendt's insistence on historicizing anti-Semitism by focusing on the role of Jews in relation to developments in the modern nation-state system, the rise of imperialism, and the death camps as the laboratories of totalitarianism (chapter 2); the Frankfurt School's application of psychoanalytic, Weberian, and Marxist categories to society and culture (chapter 3); Parsons's synthesis of modernist sociological theory and the critique of this viewpoint in Bauman's postmodern sociological theory (chapter 4); Lyotard's discussion of how alterity has been excluded, repressed, or marginalized within the Western tradition (chapter 5); how these postmodern approaches were shaped by a moment of French Judeophilia in the late 1970s and early 1980s when the work of historian Léon Poliakov was finally recognized for the role he played in considerations of the Holocaust, racism, and anti-Semitism over the course of Western culture (chapter 6); and the influential oeuvre of George Mosse, who linked the cultural history of Nazi ideology, volkish thought, studies of nationalism and masculinity, fascism, bourgeois norms, and the ongoing forms of religious life in his understanding of secular modernity (chapter 7). These are, I submit, the seven major overarching paradigms we have developed for understanding Judeophobia. I conclude with a chapter discussing how these major theories and theorists offer key insights to understanding post-Holocaust Judeophobia, which is once more morphing in the new millennium.

CHAPTER 1

Jean-Paul Sartre's Existentialist Antiracism

In *Le Spectateur engagé* (*The Committed Observer*), Raymond Aron mentions a conversation he had with Sartre in 1945 about why there was nothing in the French press concerning the Jews returning from the death camps.[1] For Aron, "The profound reason for this silence was because one had in a sense effaced what had happened.... The French settled down again in their France as if the Jews had never been cast out."[2] Aron broached the matter with Sartre because his philosophical tract, *Réflexions sur la question juive* (translated as *Anti-Semite and Jew*) was an exception to what Emmanuel Mounier called the "strange silence" on the Jewish Question in the aftermath of the Liberation.[3] Sartre clearly sought to shatter this silence by openly confronting the indigenous French tradition of anti-Semitism that had reigned during the Vichy years.[4] "*Réflexions* is famous for turning the tables on the antisemites," notes Maurice Samuels, "subjecting them to the same kind of scrutiny to which they long subjected the Jews."[5] This chapter considers how Sartre's *Réflexions* theorized anti-Semitism and how he developed his theory about it into a full-blown multidirectional antiracism.[6]

What distinguished Sartre's contribution to critical theories of anti-Semitism was his existential analysis. "The most striking feature of Sartre's fight resides less in his victory than in the new weapons he deploys. They are wholly new," Emmanuel Levinas proclaimed in applauding Sartre's essay, since "antisemitism is attacked with existentialist arguments."[7] The key axiom of Sartre's reflections was that anti-Semitism has its basis in fear and anxiety. There were five postulates that Sartre developed that followed from this: first, that there is no biological, cultural, or metaphysical reality to the anti-Semitic fantasy of "the Jews"; it is a social construct.[8] Existentialism thus became the basis for theories about the social construction of race. Second, Sartre was nonetheless aware that "the Jew" for the anti-Semite serves as an Archimedean point for an all-encompassing ideology. As such, he called anti-Semitism a "passion" whose "bad faith" is akin to religious faith and therefore not amenable to any rational evidence that opposes the anti-Semites' Manichean, binary thinking. Third, Sartre's *Réflexions* also castigated what he labeled the "politics of assimilation"—the Enlightenment, liberal tradition that defines French Republicanism—contending that it ultimately eliminated Jewishness through its universal and abstract principles that did not recognize Jewish difference. As such, the liberal, Enlightenment tradition was the shadow of anti-Semitism, still desiring the elimination of Jews and Judaism, but by means of their absorption. Sartre thus decried any polity or policy based upon homogeneity, normalization, or what goes by the name today in France of *intégration*. Fourth, Sartre announced that the fight against anti-Semitism must be waged in the name of liberty, based not on the abstract axioms of liberalism (i.e., human rights, constitutionalism, equality of opportunity, equality before the law, etc.), but rather on the existential conception of freedom at the root of human existence. He called for a "concrete liberalism" capable of recognizing and celebrating human difference. Jews were given intellectual license to embrace their Jewishness with pride, which he dubbed "authenticity." And finally, Sartre maintained that the primary responsibility to combat anti-Semitism lay with the dominant culture whose own freedom was contingent upon the freedom of all in their midst. "Not one Frenchman will be free," he thundered at the conclusion of his *Réflexions*, "so long as the Jews do not enjoy the fullness of their rights."[9]

In drawing out the key axioms of Sartre's existential analysis of anti-Semitism, I develop five main points: first, that Sartre had explicitly sketched out the basic arguments that he developed in *Anti-Semite and Jew* in *Being and Nothingness*. Secondly, I broaden Sartre's existentialist portrait of the anti-Semite by showing how Simone de Beauvoir's *The Ethics of Ambiguity* elaborates Sartre's insights. Third, I underline the critique of the liberal-democratic response to anti-Semitism in the short second section of the *Réflexions*. Fourth, I then thread Sartre's critique of liberalism into his Marxist-inflected antiracism, outlining the links he drew between anti-Semitism and colonial racism. Lastly, I consider how Sartre squared the circle between his commitments to opposing postcolonial racism (i.e., "the new racism") and anti-Zionist "neo-anti-Semitism" (i.e., post-Holocaust Judeophobia), and his interventions into the Arab-Israeli conflict.

A PORTRAIT OF SARTRE AND HIS "PORTRAIT OF THE ANTI-SEMITE"

Sartre's anti-anti-Semitism stemmed from his existential phenomenology, which he developed over the course of the 1930s, a period when Judeophobic discourse on the Right was precipitously on the rise.[10] Sartre was then in his twenties. Born in Paris on June 21, 1905, Sartre's life was shaped by the death of his father when he was only fifteen months old. His grandfather, a supporter of Alfred Dreyfus, an educator and author of German-language instructional books, home-schooled him and helped raise him alongside his doting mother. He completed his education at two elite preparatory schools in Paris, the Lycées Henri IV and Louis-le-Grand. He then entered the École normale supérieure (ENS) in 1924, alongside several others who would emerge as famous writers from his generation, including Aron and his closest friend, Paul Nizan. He also met his lifelong partner at this time, Beauvoir, who was studying at the Sorbonne since women were not yet admitted to the ENS.

Graduating at the top of his class, Sartre became a high school professor. He was already publishing philosophical treatises on the role of the imagination and perception in consciousness when in 1933-34 he spent the academic year in Germany just as Hitler rose to power. He went to Germany to study phenomenology at the font. He returned to a France increasingly polarized over fascism and anti-Semitism. Scandals like the Stavinsky affair and the riots of February 6, 1934, indicated the rising tide of the extreme Right. The Left responded by unifying and electing the antifascist Popular Front (1936-38), headed by the first socialist and Jewish premier, Léon Blum. Blum served as the ultimate symbol for the opponents of the Popular Front to tar the French Republic with a series of interchangeable epithets, exemplified by fascist Jacques Doriot's condemning what he called the "pluto-Judeo-Bolshevik coalition" that he claimed ruled France.[11]

Sartre's response to this widespread anti-Semitic discourse was his first overtly politicized work, the novella *L'Enfance d'un chef* ("The Childhood of a Leader," 1938). Included in his collection of short stories, *The Wall*, it is an ironic *Bildungsroman* of a boy who believes he finds his true identity as a member of the Action Française's shock troops, the Camelots du roi, the extreme-Right incubator for French fascism. They defined their Frenchness against the abject image of "the Jew."[12] The protagonist of the story, Lucien Fleurier, floats through the existential anguish of his youth determined to root his identity, which he eventually does by echoing the Judeophobic slurs of the youth group.

The literary portrait of Lucien Fleurier, the would-be *chef* of the story and an archetype of the "bad faith" of the anti-Semite, would reach theoretical fruition in his philosophical essay, *Réflexions sur la question juive*. The first long section of the book, "Portrait de l'antisémite," Sartre's phenomenological description of the racial oppressor, was the earliest concrete application of the key existential axioms regarding the relation of Self and Other articulated in *L'Être et le néant* (*Being and Nothingness*, 1943).[13]

BEING AND NOTHINGNESS

The core elements of his existentialist analysis of anti-Semitism were already embedded in *Being and Nothingness*. There, Sartre enumerated the philosophical underpinnings of his existential-phenomenological critique of anti-Semitism and racism: his ontological description of human freedom; his existential analysis of responsibility; and his concepts of "bad faith," "the situation," and the dialectic of human recognition between Self and Other engendered by "the gaze."

The first half of *Being and Nothingness* defines the central categories of Sartre's ontology through an elaboration of the distinction between the object world, which Sartre calls the in-itself (*être-en-soi*), and the perceiving subject, which he names the for-itself (*être-pour-soi*). There is also a third kind of being that Sartre discusses, which occupies the second half of *Being and Nothingness*, being-for-others (*être-pour-autrui*).

The gaze determines our being-for-others. We seek to define ourselves in response to how others perceive us. I see others and see them seeing me and I know that they judge my choices. The Other's gaze turns me into an object in her world, a character in her life drama. She thereby takes away my freedom to determine my own essence, just as I do hers. On the basis of this struggle for recognition, Sartre describes all relations with others as conflict-ridden. There is no judgment-free zone for Sartre. Indifference is impossible: it is a mode of self-deception that refuses to acknowledge that others look at me, a refusal to accept that I am alienated from my own essence. My desire for an essence—my wish to objectify myself—and my objectification by others are each the fundaments of self-deception that Sartre terms *mauvaise foi* (bad faith). Each is a denial of the ontological freedom constitutive of human beings.

Toward the end of *Being and Nothingness*, Sartre concretizes this discussion more explicitly around the relation between the anti-Semitic gaze and the Jewish Other. Sartre's illustration takes place in the context of a larger discussion about "freedom and facticity: the situation." It should be remembered that the book was published in 1943 under the German occupation, with the genocidal assault on Jews in full force. Sartre makes clear that the conception of freedom that he is developing is not an abstract freedom divorced from the strictures upon individual choices. Freedom is always situated and conditioned. There are specific factors that shape one's situation: a person's *place* in the world, their *past*, the *environment*, and all *others* that impinge upon our choices.

In the subsection on "my fellowman" Sartre explicitly uses the example of the relation between the anti-Semite and "the Jew" to explicate the struggle for recognition and the objective limits of freedom in a situation. He explains what was apparent at the time: a limit of the Jewish situation is the gaze of the anti-Semitic Other, who defines "the Jew" by essentializing their being-a-Jew. Jews can refuse this designation. What "the Jew" cannot deny is that the anti-Semite perceives her as a Jew, forcing her to wrestle with the meaning of her being and how she defines her identity.

Sartre goes on to tackle the question: "How then shall I experience the objective limits of my being: Jew[?]" The objectification of your being does not define who you are for-yourself. These labels conferred upon us by others require "an interiorization and a subjectivizing."[14] Every essence ascribed to us by others, Sartre categorically insists, must be conferred with a meaning by us. In short, "a Jew is not a Jew *first* in order to be *subsequently* ashamed or proud; it is his pride of being a Jew, his shame, or his indifference which will reveal to him his being-a-Jew; and this being-a-Jew is nothing outside the free manner of adopting it."[15] The Jewish situation—never more so than during the Holocaust—thus magnifies the human condition. For all of us, there are objective conditions that structure our choices—class, race, place, the body, and the gaze of the Other. We each have the responsibility for assuming what these will mean for us and how we will navigate them as individuals. But we are in self-denial when we deny the objective structures that delimit our situation.

While Sartre's mention of Jews and Judaism are relatively scant in the body of his enormous ontological description of the human condition in *Being and*

Nothingness, he is explicit about its implications for the anti-Semite and draws some provisional conclusions for Jews. Sartre argues that the anti-Semite embodies the quintessence of "bad faith" by seeking to found his essence in his sadistic domination of "the Jew," which at its extreme leads to a violent hatred not only of Jews, but ultimately of all alterity. Jews, on the other hand, must respond to their situation by defining the meaning of their Jewishness, alongside their humanity—always a double responsibility. Life is the perpetual struggle with situations like this, Sartre avers, and the situation of Jews caught in the trap of how they are perceived by anti-Semites makes Sartre's point.

ANTI-SEMITE AND JEW

Anti-Semite and Jew would elaborate in great detail what he had sketched in *Being and Nothingness*, applying his existentialist categories to the hostile situation faced by Jews in France at the time of its writing.[16] His insightful essay acknowledged many differing modalities of anti-Semitism that each merit further attention than I will give them here. He recognized the importance of Christian anti-Judaism where Jews were persecuted as "the assassin[s] of Christ."[17] He discussed French cultural racism à la Maurras and Barrès, where cultural *traditions* function as an analogue to blood in biological racism. He highlighted the psychology of the anti-Semitic perpetrator: his cowardice and herd mentality, so powerfully ridiculed by Nietzsche. As often underlined in sociological approaches to anti-Semitism, he foregrounded the shock of peasants who moved to cities and, overwhelmed by their new urban environments, displaced and often disgraced, projected their displeasure onto Jews who became the personalized form of the cause of their anguish and despair. Sartre also closed the book with a Marxist, economically and class-based assessment that contended Jews were nothing but scapegoats, serving to blind the working class to the systems that oppressed them. But he ultimately argued that anti-Semitism does not rest upon economic, sociological, cultural, religious, or political foundations. It demands an existential analysis.

In undertaking this examination, he argued that the fundamental cause of anti-Semitism is the *mauvaise foi* (bad faith) of the anti-Semite: his response to his fears and anxiety. Rather than face his own finitude and freedom, the anti-Semite, like Lucien in "The Childhood of a Leader," adopts in advance a "certain idea of the Jew, of his nature and of his role in society."[18] Through a process of projection, he chooses himself through this reified image. In accord with a binary or Manichean logic, the anti-Semite defines himself through abjection. He opposes his identity to what he deems the impurity and depravity, corruption and pollution, impiety and deviance, ugliness and untruth, or the urbanity and foreignness of "the Jew." Through a constellation of negative and essentialized images, the anti-Semite explains his experience of the world. With this model of the degraded and perverse Other, he "is under no necessity to look for his personality within himself. He has chosen... to be nothing save the fear he inspires in others."[19] Anti-Semitism consequently boils down to a "basic fear of oneself and of truth," a fear of all humans' fundamental ontological freedom.[20] "Antisemitism, in short," writes Sartre in conclusion, "is fear of the human condition. The antisemite is a man who wishes to be a pitiless stone, a furious torrent, a devastating thunderbolt—anything except a man."[21]

ANXIETY AND ANTI-SEMITISM

The distinction developed by Martin Heidegger between fear and anxiety helps to illuminate Sartre's analysis of anti-Semitism.[22] Heidegger developed this thematic in both *Being and Time* (1927) and in "What Is Metaphysics?" (1929). Fear, Heidegger insists, has a fixed object: we fear the mugger who assaults us, for example. With fear, "we are always afraid of this or that definite thing," Heidegger asserts. We fear something "which threatens us in this or that definite way."[23] But anxiety is free-floating: it is provoked by the groundlessness of our being. In *Being and Time*, Heidegger contends, "*That about which one has* Angst *is being-in-the world as such.*"[24] Angst is the recognition of the fact that human beings are "thrown" into a world that they did not make—a world with a past, facticity, and a repository of institutions and discourses those individuals did not create themselves. Heidegger insists in "What Is Metaphysics?" that anxiety or *angst* differs wholly from fear because it is unnamable, unfixed, and consequently makes us feel uncanny. When we tune into this anxiety—which Sartre termed "contingency," or, using a concept he shared with Albert Camus, "absurdity"—it manifests bodily as queasiness: the sickly taste of our ontological freedom, explored by him in his modernist masterpiece *Nausea*.

In arguing that anti-Semitism is a fear of the human condition, Sartre conflates this distinction. But what he was clearly suggesting is that anti-Semites displaced the anxiety of being "condemned to be free"—a Sartrean reformulation and translation of Heidegger's being-in-the-world—by objectifying "the Jew."[25] All the forces that constitute the anti-Semite's "being-in-the-world" in ways that make life uneasy, uncomfortable, or unreasonable are fixed on the very being of "the Jew" in the form of a paranoid fear. The unnamable, unfixed, and shifting forces of anxiety then can take a concrete form. By a necessary and dangerously tautological logic, eliminating the purported source of danger and fear—(i.e., "the Jew,")—would therefore result in the elimination of anxiety.

THE ETHICS OF AMBIGUITY

In *The Ethics of Ambiguity* (1948), Simone de Beauvoir would elaborate on Sartre's existential analysis of anti-Jewish racism. Her second chapter, on "Personal Freedom and Others," has never before been considered in this way. But in it she explored four different anti-Semitic personalities that expand Sartre's portrait, nuancing his analysis. Conceptualizing these types, she itemized the psychology of "sub-men," "serious men," "nihilistic men," and "adventurous men." In each case, Beauvoir names not only concrete examples of anti-Semites and fascists but also colonialists and misogynists. Her analysis is broader and more abstract than Sartre's focused assessment of the anti-Semite and Jew, helping to illuminate the multidirectional tendency at work in their theorizing of anti-Semitism.

In discussing "*sub-men,*" Beauvoir specifically evokes Hermann Goering, second in power only to Hitler within the Nazi Party and founder of the Gestapo, who eventually committed suicide before his sentence at the Nuremberg trial.[26] Her term for this type turns the tables on the likes of Goering, for she argues that sub-men are those that deny that human beings are freedom. She elaborates:

> In lynchings, in pogroms, in all the great bloody movements organized by the fanaticism of seriousness and passion ... those who do the actual dirty work are recruited from among the sub-men. That is why every man who wills himself free within a human world fashioned by free men will be so disgusted by the sub-men. Ethics is the triumph of freedom over facticity, and the sub-man feels only the facticity of his existence.[27]

Sub-men are those who deny the freedom of others. They refuse to acknowledge that what defines each person is their freedom to shape their own destiny. Sub-men treat other humans as objects. They engage in what Aimé Cesaire in *Discourse on Colonialism* termed the "thingification" of others.[28]

If sub-men are those who deny the freedom of others, then the *"serious men"* are those who deny their own freedom. Beauvoir suggests that the *serious men* account for a significant amount of the support for Nazism. Today, the serious men might be termed the Orangemen, the foot soldiers of Trump's MAGA-nation, the army of supporters who galvanize behind authoritarian populists. Serious men submerge their identity through any form of determinism, whether religious absolutes, social Darwinism, essentialist nationalism, or any form of metaphysical, cultural, or biological racism that denies that "existence precedes essence." This can take the form of not questioning social conventions and thereby turning oneself into nothing but the murmurer of rumors and conspiracism.[29] "The serious man gets rid of his freedom by claiming to subordinate it to values which would be unconditioned.... Shielded with 'rights,' he fulfills himself as a *being* who is escaping from the stress of existence," Beauvoir writes.[30] Lucien Fleurier is the archetype of the *serious man*. The serious man is infantile, she continues, for like a child, he believes that values are absolute and identities are predefined and prescribed. The serious man is also a "mythomaniac," who denies individual freedom through the deification of the leader and his mythic narratives.[31] This, of course, can take the form of the self-mythologization of the leader, including through the use of the propaganda mechanisms of the state. The serious man puts "nothing into question" and not only denies his own freedom, but, like the sub-man, also "ignores the values of the subjectivity and the freedom of others."[32] Beauvoir thus concludes that "Nazism was in the service of petit bourgeois seriousness."[33]

A third kind of anti-Semite in Beauvoir's set of portraits is the *"nihilistic man."* Her representative of the type is Drieu la Rochelle, drawing explicitly from the article on Drieu that Sartre had published in the underground press in 1943.[34] Drieu was an intellectual supporter of Jacques Doriot's fascist Parti Populaire Français (PPF), the most right-wing, pro-Nazi party in France, whose blue shirts directly aided in the mass roundup of Jews.[35] Drieu's anti-Semitism, according to Beauvoir, was nihilistic because he was aware that "the world *possesses* no justification and that he himself *is* nothing."[36] Drieu demonstrated this in his first novel, whose title sums it up: *The Empty Suitcase*. In it, he tells the story of a young man "who acutely felt the fact of existing as a lack of being."[37] As did Sartre, Beauvoir argues that Drieu's novel *Gilles* represented his flight from the realization of the anxiety that comes with the responsibility of freedom. Collaborationists like Drieu, Sartre had argued at length in his underground article and later in "Qu'est-ce qu'un collaborateur?" (What is a collaborator?), flee their own freedom. They hate themselves for it. And they cannot abide a France that provides this freedom. So they want to transform society into an ironclad hierarchy of rules and norms, draped in flags, and decorated with the symbols of militarism. Ultimately, they want to annihilate the humanity in people: the principle of liberty itself. Their inhumanity, which is the product of their fear of the human condition, is what leads to their anti-Semitism.

Beauvoir also portrays a fourth type of anti-Semite, "*the adventurer*" who "likes action for its own sake." The bad faith of the adventurer is that they pursue "a freedom which remains indifferent to its content."[38] The content of freedom, for both Sartre and Beauvoir, is action that leads to liberation not only of the self but also of all others. This entails that every action must also respect "this end through the means" that are used to attain it.[39] Freedom's end is the freedom of all and it can only be achieved through acknowledging the freedom of both Self and Other.

The anti-Semitism of the adventurer can take the form of the pursuit of "fortune or glory," which Beauvoir suggests was at the heart of the "collaborationists in '41."[40] The adventurer is "indifferent to the ends they set up for themselves, [and] they were still more indifferent to the means of attaining them; they cared only for their pleasure or their glory," she writes.[41] The root cause of the adventurer's bad faith is narcissism, egoism, and self-satisfaction that denies the freedom of others. The adventurer's "fault," Beauvoir continues, "is believing that one can do something for oneself without others and even against them."[42] There is thus "a dialectical necessity," Beauvoir avers, which leads the adventurer to becoming a "tyrant or hangman" at the worst, or feckless toward regimes that "defend the privilege of a class or a party, and more particularly authoritarian regimes and fascism."[43]

Between Beauvoir and Sartre, then, the portraits of diverse types of anti-Semites—each variations on the theme that anti-Semitism is a fear of the human condition—provide us with a complex phenomenological description of the anti-Semitic personality. This existential analysis of anti-Semitism drew out the consequences of Sartre's early ontological description of the Self/Other dialectic by illuminating the anti-Semitic gaze in accord with a set of existential precepts.

SARTRE'S CRITIQUE OF LIBERALISM

These postulates were critical of liberal responses to anti-Semitism as well. "The Jews have one friend," notes Sartre about the liberal, "but he is a feeble protector."[44] The French liberalism Sartre discusses has its basis in the Enlightenment and its principles of toleration and equal rights summarized in the Declaration of the Rights of Man and Citizen and platforms like the League for the Rights of Man, formed in 1898 at the height of the Dreyfus affair. Within a liberal-democratic framework, the social body is defined as a collection of individuals and the individual is defined as the incarnation of the traits that constitute the universal in human nature, like the rights of man. The liberal democrat can thus only save the Jew as the incarnation of the universal, never save him in his particularity. "It follows that his defense of the Jew saves the latter as man and annihilates him as Jew," says Sartre.[45] Moreover, the liberal "wants to separate the Jew from his religion, from his family, from his ethnic community, in order to plunge him into the democratic crucible when he will emerge naked and alone, an individual and solitary particle like all the other particles."[46] The problem with the liberal response to the Jewish Question is that the anti-Semite does not attack the Jew as an individual, but as a group.

The liberal denies Jews precisely the religious, cultural, and communal factors that provide sanctuary and solidarity in the struggle against their denigration and demonization. The republican universalism that Sartre derided denies Jews "all forms of Jewish collective political and social organization," that the French today term *communautarisme*.[47] This is what Sartre decries about the "politics of assimilation" since it is the hinge that ties the liberal to the Judeophobe. While the anti-Semite and the liberal unquestionably have a different political framework and agenda for Jews and Judaism, they converge insofar as "the former wishes to destroy him as a man and leave nothing in him but the Jew, the pariah, the untouchable; the latter wishes to destroy him as a Jew and leave nothing in him but the man, the abstract and universal subject of the rights of man and the rights of the citizen."[48] The difference between the anti-Semite and the liberal is that the former rebukes the Jew for *being* Jewish, while the liberal reviles Jewry's consideration of itself as different. "Thus there may be detected in the most liberal democrat a tinge of anti-Semitism," notes Sartre, for "he is hostile to the Jew to the extent that the latter thinks of himself as a Jew."[49] This led Sartre to pursue a path of "concrete liberalism" that simultaneously debunked liberalism and anti-Semitism, assimilation and persecution.

SARTRE'S MULTIDIRECTIONAL ANTIRACISM

Beyond the occasional references to his *Réflexions*, and his involvement in the Arab/Israeli conflict, Sartre would write little about the Jewish Question in the period from 1945-65.[50] He was more focused on anti-Black racism and colonial oppression. But his antiracist interventions were still significantly indebted to his critique of anti-Semitism. "Replace the Jew with the Black, the anti-Semite with the supporter of slavery," he claimed, "and there would be nothing essential to be cut from my book [on the Jewish Question]."[51] Sartre's anticolonialist essays written in the two decades following the Holocaust indicate an expanded approach to racism. In his writings on Blacks in America (1945), in his play *The Respectful Prostitute* (1946), in his excursus on "The Oppression of Blacks in the United States," in *Notebooks for an Ethics*, in "Présence noir" (1947), "Black Orpheus," (1948), and in most of his writings on colonialism gathered in *Situations V* (*Colonialism and Neo-Colonialism*, 1964), Sartre developed a multipronged critical theory of racism that went beyond his earlier existentialist critique of fascist anti-Semitism in France.[52]

Sartre continued to maintain that racism depends upon the bad faith of a Medusa-like gaze, reifying others, turning them into objects as a way of defining one's own subjectivity. But in accord with his critique of liberalism, he doubled down on the imperative that the freedom of individuals is dependent upon the freedom of all. Beauvoir used a quote from Dostoevsky as an epigraph to her novel *The Blood of Others* that acutely summarized Sartre's view: "Each of us is responsible for everything and to every human being."[53] This formulation encapsulates the notion of "metaphysical guilt" that the founder of German *Existenzphilosophie*, Karl Jaspers, developed in his 1947 essay *Die Schuldfrage* (*The Question of German Guilt*): "There exists a solidarity among men as human beings," wrote Jaspers, "that makes each co-responsible for every wrong and every injustice in the world, especially for crimes committed in his presence or with his knowledge."[54] Sartre frequently reworked this idea, that he termed "collective responsibility" in his post-Holocaust reflections on colonial racism.[55] In doing so, he developed a key axiom in *L'Existentialisme est un humanisme* (*Existentialism Is a Humanism*, 1946) where he maintained, "if existence really does precede essence, man is responsible for what he is ... and when we say that a man is responsible for himself, we do not only mean that he is responsible for his own individuality, but that he is responsible for all men."[56] This was the universal principle registered in the concluding lines of *Anti-Semite and Jew*.

Sartre thus drew upon his analysis of anti-Semitism in his critique of the racial oppression of Blacks. He continued to focus on dismantling racist structures of perception, as is apparent in "Black Orpheus," his famous celebration of negritude poetry written as a preface to Léopold Sédar Senghor's *Anthologie de la nouvelle poésie nègre et malgache de langue française* (Anthology of African and West Indian poets writing in French).[57] As "Black Orpheus" makes plain, much of his early writing on colonialism would continue to revolve around the same conflict that he characterized for Jews: the struggle with how the dominant culture imposes itself, how this is internalized, and how colonial subjects can liberate themselves. In "Black Orpheus," however, he does take a more definitive step in the direction of the argument that defined his politics in the postwar period: the demand that the writer reveal the world from the perspective of the oppressed. The standpoint of "the Jew," "the African," the colonized, and the worker offers a critical lens through which to view the system of oppression.

One of the radically new theorems of "Black Orpheus" is that if Blacks have nothing to lose but their chains, this will depend upon negritude writers deconstructing how Blackness is figured within the semiotic system of the West. Sartre's semiology of the racialized Other as a sign within the system of colonial oppression thereby anticipated deconstructive and postcolonial analyses. But just as was the case with his writing on Jewishness, where he recycles certain anti-Semitic motifs, Sartre echoes stereotypical conceptions of Blackness and Africa.[58] As Stuart Zane Charmé perceptively charges, "Repeating the same strategy that had produced *Antisemite and Jew*, Sartre remained on the level of myth or symbol rather than history. Like the Jew, the black's primary mythic function was to embody simultaneously the victimization by, and the negation of, white European culture and the colonialism it supported."[59] Sartre's depiction of Blackness as the negation of white supremacy serves to destabilize white,

European, bourgeois hegemony. In the process, however, he reinscribes typological constructs of Blackness that figure for him the negativity of European values.[60] He thus identifies "the Black" with primitivism. He resorts to images of Blacks as natural man and unchaste woman whose identification with nature and Eros have an emancipatory function not only for Blacks but also for repressed Europeans. Sartre says, for example, that the Blacks' "wild and free looks that judge our world"[61] do so by plunging "man back into the seething breast of Nature."[62] Blacks have "timeless instincts, a simple manifestation of universal and eternal fecundity."[63] He justifies his identification of Blacks with nature, sexuality, a phallic order, instinct, creation, and rhythm as a necessary stage within what he calls "Universal History."

Frantz Fanon's first published article sharply criticized Sartre for failing to condemn some of these hackneyed images of Blackness, even as Fanon drew upon Sartre's earlier critique of anti-Semitism. Fanon's evaluation was woven into his first published piece, "The Lived Experience of the Black," which appeared in May 1951 in *Esprit*, the rival Catholic journal that vied with Sartre's *Les Temps Modernes* as the prime mover of Left-Bank cultural analysis in the postwar years.[64] Fanon's early approach to anti-Black colonial racism was akin to Sartre's *Anti-Semite and Jew* since Fanon's considerations are generated by his encounter with the racist gaze that objectified him as Black. In reflecting on the genesis of his thinking, Fanon recollected how his teacher, Aimé Cesaire, who coined the term "negritude" as a badge of pride and was a foundational theorist of the movement, had warned his student about the connections between Judeophobia and Negrophobia: "At first glance it seems strange that the attitude of the anti-Semite can be equated with that of the negrophobe," wrote Fanon. "It was my philosophy teacher from the Antilles who reminded me one day: 'When you hear someone insulting the Jews, pay attention; he is talking about you.' And I believed at the time he was universally right, meaning that I was responsible in my body and my soul for the fate reserved for my brother. Since then, I have understood that what he meant quite simply was the anti-Semite is inevitably a negrophobe."[65] But Fanon also distanced himself from Sartre and distinguished the Black experience of racial subjugation from the Jewish experience. He dismissively suggested, for example, that the Holocaust was a "family quarrel" and that unlike Blacks, Jews could readily assimilate into white culture.

Most importantly, Sartre's preface to Senghor's anthology, Fanon suggested, was too enthusiastic about embracing tropes of Blackness that identified Blacks with nature, timeless instincts, rhythm, and fecundity, even if these were used tactically as a moment in what Sartre dubbed the dialectic of "antiracist racism."⁶⁶ As Abiola Irele incisively puts it, "Sartre's term ["antiracist racism"] therefore meant a negro racial pride designed to destroy racialism itself."⁶⁷ If this was its intent, V. Y. Mudimbé nevertheless derides Sartre, "[Senghor] asked for a cloak to celebrate négritude; he was given a shroud."⁶⁸ Fanon understood that Sartre was parroting Senghor in the essay, who is likewise critiqued. Fanon faults not only the abstraction of the Hegelian dialectic employed by Sartre, which denies the lived experience of Blackness, but also criticizes both Sartre's and Senghor's romanticized, homogenized valorization of the song and dance of African culture, and their idealized veneration of African customs, as its own form of essentializing produced by the lens of European primitivism.⁶⁹

Fanon's essay was later included as the renowned fifth chapter of *Black Skin, White Masks*, a book where Fanon did for Negrophobia what Sartre had done for Judeophobia. He wanted to show how Blacks, like Jews, were phobogenic objects, producing the anxiety that racists sought to contain by essentializing and objectifying them. But Fanon also began to explore the material and institutional formations that constitute racism. The impact of Fanon's critique, as well as Sartre's deepening Marxist understanding of colonial racism as a result of his involvement in the French-Algerian war, was clear in his preface to Albert Memmi's *The Colonizer and the Colonized*.⁷⁰

Memmi's *Portrait du colonisé, précédé du portrait du colonisateur* (*The Colonizer and the Colonized*, 1957) was consecrated by the preface Sartre wrote. Originally written as a critical review, but subsequently permanently attached to Memmi's text, Sartre's preface helped to establish *The Colonizer and the Colonized* as a classic anticolonial tract. In it, Sartre commended Memmi's inquiry since Memmi's biography—between colonizer and colonized, Jew and Arab, Occident and Orient—clearly allowed him to appreciate both the dominator and the dominated from the inside.⁷¹ Memmi's analysis is modeled on Sartre's intersubjective dialectic of the gaze. He translates this via two ideal types depicted as two portraits locked in a struggle: "Portrait of the Colonizer," and "Portrait of the Colonized." Drawing on the same Hegelian heritage of the master-slave dialectic, *Anti-Semite and Jew* remained foundational for the two portraits Memmi draws: the colonizer is a kindred type to the anti-Semite and the situation of the colonized overlaps with Sartre's portrait of "the Jew."

Sartre is nevertheless critical of Memmi's subtle depiction of the relationship within colonization and how this results in the interiorization of colonial hegemony. As Lia Brozgal points out, Sartre's critique is based on three points: "First, whereas Sartre views racism as implicit in the system of colonialism that creates benefits for the colonizer to the detriment of the colonized, for Memmi, racism is located within individuals and is mobilized by the colonizer in order to justify the colonial enterprise and his place within it."[72] Second, Sartre's Marxist emphasis prioritizes an economic assessment of colonialism. The third point is definitely hammered home by Sartre: "The whole difference between us arises," Sartre asserts, "because he sees a situation where I see a system."[73] Sartre had made this shift in his thinking by the time of his speech "Colonialism Is a System," which reflected the subsuming of his existential-phenomenological analysis within his developing existential Marxist framework.[74]

In his preface to Memmi's *The Colonizer and the Colonized*, Sartre made clear that racist rationales are a function of a system of exploitation, rather than a matter of individual prejudice: "Colonialism denies human rights to human beings whom it has subdued by violence, and keeps them by force in a state of misery and ignorance that Marx would rightly call a subhuman condition. Racism is ingrained in action, institutions, and in the nature of the colonialist methods of production and exchange."[75] While racism operates psychically, conditioning how we perceive and receive the Other, serving to dehumanize colonial and racialized subjects so that human rights and equality need not be extended to them, Sartre's point now is unequivocally that racism is enmeshed in the power structure and material system of oppression itself.

Discrimination functions not only cognitively and intersubjectively, but within institutions and everyday practices and policies. Racism is not only an idea but an ideology. The racist colonial system "is embodied in a million colonists, children and grandchildren of colonists, who have been shaped by colonialism and who think, speak and act according to the very principles of the colonial system," wrote Sartre.[76] The racist system therefore shaped both the colonized and the colonizer, infecting all "with its racism."[77]

THE *CRITIQUE OF DIALECTICAL REASON* AND "NEO-ANTI-SEMITISM"

By the late 1950s, Sartre conceived of racism not as a mythical blinder that legitimates oppression; he argued that it is a central pillar in the structure of colonial exploitation. The theoretical elaboration of his existentialist Marxist position was most developed in *Critique de la raison dialectique* (*Critique of Dialectical Reason*, 1960), where a new series of concepts governed Sartre's analysis: dialectical history, praxis, the practico-inert, totalization, and seriality.[78] The *Critique* sought to explain how humans make history and in turn are made by that history. Developing what he called after Henri Lefebvre the "progressive-regressive method," dialectical history moved back and forth between the social totality and the individual in search of the mediations that could account for historical configurations. Humans are always set in specific situations, which they interpret and act upon. This "subjective process of self-definition through action in the world" defines praxis, which, as Martin Jay explains, translates Sartre's notion of the for-itself in *Being and Nothingness* into the terms of the *Critique*. The accumulated result of human action is the practico-inert. "Like Marx's concept of capital as dead labor or Sartre's own earlier notion of the in-itself," Jay elaborates, "the practico-inert confronts man as an irreducible other, despite his role in its creation."[79] Most people thus lead atomized, alienated lives, an existence that Herbert Marcuse called the life of "one-dimensional man," where they do little more than satisfy themselves as the reified incarnation of prescripted social messages. Collective existence is thus dominated by what Sartre called seriality. "'Serial' collectives are agglomerations of human beings," William McBride explains, "engaged in some enterprise to which a common name can be given but which far from unifying them, reinforces their isolation."[80] Racism, Sartre maintains, is a part of "a *praxis* illuminated by a 'theory' ('biological,' 'social,' or empirical racism, it does not matter which) aiming to keep the masses in a state of molecular aggregation."[81]

Abstracting from his specific interventions into the Algerian conflict, but also reflecting on Nazi and Stalinist anti-Semitism, Sartre tried to elucidate what he now called "the seriality of racism."[82] Internal to the supraexploitation of colonialism was violence and appropriation that was justified through the self-reinforcing logic of racism. In the terms of the *Critique*, Sartre enumerated its unfolding: it begins as a "structure of alienation in the *practico-inert*, it is actualized as *praxis* in colonization; and its (temporary) victory presents itself as the objectification of the practical ensemble (army, capitalists, commodity merchants, colonialists) in a *practico-inert* system where it represents the fundamental structure of reciprocity between the colonialists and the colonized."[83] This "serial exis" is engraved in the practices and institutions of the lived world, where the colonialist or anti-Semite "lives on an 'Island of Doctor Moreau,' surrounded by terrifying beasts created in the image of man, but botched."[84] The racial oppressor lives constantly with a paranoid vision that these sub-humans—demonized and bestialized to justify anti-Semitism or colonial oppression—are deemed dangerous and violent. He thereby legitimates the everyday violence of the racial system as well as any extreme measures that might become necessary as a reasonable self-defense.

In the second volume of his *Critique de la raison dialectique*, never finished and published posthumously, Sartre developed this analysis as a critique of Stalinist anti-Zionism, which persecuted Jews all the while avowing that it was antiracist.[85] This Sartre termed "neo-antisemitisme." While "anti-Semitism in its basic form as *racism* . . . was obviously condemned by Marxist ideology," Sartre wrote, Stalinist anti-Zionism "became racist anti-Semitism through an inexorable dialectic." Neo-antisemitism sprang from "the old anti-Semitic racism," via a feedback loop between the Soviet regime and populist fear and anxiety about the Jews. Stalin's Judeophobia was new in that it reworked the nineteenth-century Jewish exclusion from the nation-state into an argument about how Jewish cosmopolitanism linked Soviet Jews, American Jews, and Israelis into the "Jewish International." This evil conspiracy of Jewish cosmopolitans led by Zionists was ostensibly a key enemy to the communist international. Sartre consequently reasoned that the assault on Zionism in the Soviet Union ultimately "seeks to preserve racism while claiming to transcend it."[86] He thus demonstrated that "Stalin and his collaborators were retotalized as racists by the masses" and this transformation of "neo-anti-Semitism into racism" was "at once free and inevitable."[87] Sartre's analysis in the second volume of his *Critique de la raison dialectique* is clearly applicable to what David Myers has termed the "unprincipled" anti-Zionist post-Holocaust Judeophobia today.[88]

"THE NEW RACISM"

But Sartre's analysis of Soviet-style anti-Zionist Judeophobia was never segregated. His critique of neo-anti-Semitism was part and parcel of his commitment to oppose all forms of what Sartre termed "the new racism." By the mid-1960s, he began to assess how racism was morphing in postcolonial contexts. He developed his core insights in his opposition to apartheid South Africa. In a press conference and public gathering he participated in on November 9, 1966, organized by the Comité de liaison contre l'apartheid, Sartre fulminated against what he said "is today a cancer that risks becoming in a short period of time a generalized cancer: it is apartheid practiced systematically by South Africa."[89] As Jacques Derrida would suggest later in "Racism's Last Word," apartheid was both something specific, but it was also something general: a social arrangement of ideas, practices, and institutions that could spread globally.[90]

Subsequent interventions would clarify the parallels Sartre found between the racism akin to that in South Africa and what he began to label the "interior colonies" of capitalist countries. For example, on the occasion of the appearance in 1970 of *Livre des travailleurs africains en France*, prefaced by Albert Memmi, a debate was organized under the title, "Le Tiers-monde commence en banlieue" (The third world begins in the suburbs). Sartre's intervention, "Les Pays capitalistes et leurs colonies intérieures," made evident the connection between postcolonial immigration—legal and illegal—and colonialism. Like a black hole, capitalist metropoles pull in immigrants. Often no matter how skilled, they are confined to jobs that European or American workers are loath to take. As such, rather than being integrated as a class, they were rejected as a group. "This is how," Sartre explained, "one developed a racism that is very useful to capital."[91] While many in France derided the racism in the United States, claiming that Americans had de facto colonies in their country, France, Sartre cautioned, was "in the midst of trying to reconstitute within her borders the colonies she had lost."[92] He explicitly compared Blacks in the United States and the North African and West African immigrants of Muslim heritage in France as members of the *lumpenproletariat* who suffered from the iniquities of deplorable housing conditions, low salaries, and racist discrimination, segregated in ghettos, defined by systemic unemployment, educational failure, and criminalized solutions to poverty. His focus on the "interior colonies" that characterize the metropolitan centers of late capitalism thus highlighted the generalizable structures of apartheid.

According to Michel Contat and Michel Rybalka, between January 1970 and July 1971 alone, Sartre participated in fifteen meetings, press conferences, demonstrations, or delegations, signed twelve petitions, messages, or telegrams of solidarity, testified at four trials of immigrant militants, and wrote short circumstantial articles, communiqués, or public declarations about immigrant workers in France.[93] Defending these immigrant populations was one of his last significant political initiatives while he was physically able. These interventions never resulted in a major article on how racism continued to function in an era of mobile labor and production. But perhaps the most enduring statement Sartre made on the subject was in an article written in 1973 called "Le Nouveau racisme," an intervention in response to the killing of Mohamad Diab by a French police sergeant. In it, Sartre declared,

> another colonialism has been established on our own soil. We bring in workers... to do the unpleasant work the French workers no longer want to do. Underpaid, threatened with expulsion if they protest, and crowded into filthy lodgings, it has been necessary to justify their overexploitation which is now an important cog in the machine of French capitalism. Thus a new racism has been born which would like the immigrants to live in terror, and to rob them of the desire to protest against the living conditions that have been forced upon them.[94]

SARTRE, ISRAEL, AND THE POSTCOLONIAL TURN

Sartre sought to square the circle between his commitments to fighting postcolonial racism (i.e., the new racism) and anti-Zionist neo-anti-Semitism (i.e., post-Holocaust Judeophobia) in his interventions into the Arab-Israeli conflict. To gauge his viewpoint, we have to understand how his position on the Israeli-Palestinian conflict shifted from *Anti-Semite and Jew* in 1946, when he understood Zionism as an anticolonial movement, through to his last statements on the topic in 1979, by which time Israel was an island within the postcolonial Middle East.

Sartre's *Anti-Semite and Jew* provided the philosophical grounding for his interventions on behalf of Israel. He maintained that one authentic response Jews might adopt in response to anti-Jewish persecution was to embrace Zionism as the national liberation struggle of the Jewish people.[95] This is the same position Memmi took in works such as *The Liberation of the Jew*.[96] Sartre reiterated this position in the concluding section of *What Is Literature?*, and in his testimony in the trial of Robert Misrahi, who was accused of hiding explosives for the Stern Gang (i.e., Lehi), as well as in a statement to *Hillel* following the May 14, 1948, Declaration of Independence of the State of Israel.[97] While embracing Zionism as proximate with other anticolonial struggles, Sartre also understood that this put the Jews who remained in France in a bind. They would invariably be accused by anti-Semites of double loyalty and of being "a nation within a nation." These inexorable tensions indicated the limits of his existential analysis in part 3 of *Anti-Semite and Jew*. Sartre therefore suggested in the last section that the Jewish Question could ultimately only be solved on the political level and in accord with the universalism of a socialist approach.

As Sartre drifted into his years as a fellow traveler of the French Communist Party (1952–56), *Les Temps Modernes* nonetheless condemned the destruction of Jewish culture in the USSR and Sartre personally made several interventions at the Soviet embassy on behalf of dissident Jews, many of whom sought refuge in Israel.[98] These were also years when as a result of his commitments to the Algerian struggle, Sartre's awareness deepened about the Arab-Israeli conflict.

By the middle of the 1960s, Sartre called the Arab-Israeli conflict the "différend judéo-arabe,"[99] employing the term in precisely the sense that Jean-François Lyotard would later, when he articulated the task of the postmodern thinker as that of "bearing witness to the différend."[100] "As distinguished from a litigation," Lyotard wrote, "a differend [*différend*] would be a case of conflict, between (at least) two parties that cannot be equitably resolved for lack of a rule of judgment applicable to both arguments. *One side's legitimacy does not imply the other's lack of legitimacy.*"[101] A differend entails two competing and irreconcilable narratives both of which are legitimate. For Lyotard, conflicts over these irreconcilable differences are inevitable and the postmodern condition is such that there is no universal discourse that can provide a final arbitration of disputes.[102] This is very similar to what Sartre suggests about the Arab-Israeli conflict. He therefore maintained that his role was to reveal the inherent differences in each side's positions and how their underlying presuppositions are incompatible and lead to conflict.

As Foucault would suggest about the specific intellectual, Sartre sought to use his position as an intellectual star in order to open a space for the parties involved in the Arab-Israeli conflict to express their differences, which he hoped might open a dialogue between Arab leftists and Israeli leftists.[103] To this end, *Les Temps Modernes* conceived a massive special issue to coincide with Sartre and Beauvoir's voyage to the Middle East in February–March 1967. During his visit to Egypt and Israel Sartre avoided general pronouncements, insisting that he came to learn from his interlocutors, not to offer his own solutions. After the Six-Day War in 1967 and through the 1970s, he continued to actively bear witness to the

Judeo-Arab differend. He echoed the narratives he heard from both sides, insisted upon the justice of both positions, and urged leftists on both sides to negotiate with each other, recognizing that both their claims were inherently justified and in conflict.

But when it came to blanket statements about Zionism or positions that questioned the legitimacy of the State of Israel, Sartre demurred. Even when blind and enfeebled in the last years of his life, Sartre made this plain. For instance, on November 7, 1976, Sartre accepted a degree of *honoris causa* in philosophy from the Hebrew University of Jerusalem. This was remarkable from the man who refused the Nobel Prize and other honors because he said he did not want to become frozen as an institution. However, on this occasion, Sartre insisted that to accept this honor could justifiably be "interpreted as a political choice."[104] He accepted his honorary degree one year after UN Resolution 3379 maintained that "Zionism is a form of racism and racial discrimination." In his acceptance speech, Sartre explicitly castigated those who made such a claim, since he argued that those who submit to the simple equation that "Zionism is racism" align themselves with racial anti-Semitism for they imply that "the Jews are in their eyes a race."

As we have seen, Sartre's multidirectional antiracism aligned him with many in the pantheon of the decolonial struggle: Césaire, Fanon, and Memmi, for example, and made him a precursor to Foucault, who also explicitly decried the UN resolution that "Zionism is racism" in 1976 as "shameful."[105] But Sartre's framing of the Arab-Israeli conflict as a "différend judéo-arabe" would provoke ire from some decolonial and postcolonial corners. Just after Fanon's death, his wife Josie wrote an acerbic article titled, "À propos de Frantz Fanon, Sartre, le racisme et les Arabes," in *El Moudjahid*, published on June 10, 1967. She accused Sartre of joining the "camp of the assassins" and asked François Maspero to retract Sartre's preface from all future editions of *The Wretched of the Earth* explicitly because of his position on Israel taken during the crisis leading up to the Six-Day War.[106]

Edward Said was just as vituperative about Sartre's position on Israel. To the end and despite his decaying health, Sartre continued to hope that dialogue between Arabs and Israelis would lead to their mutual recognition. In March 1979, he and Simone de Beauvoir supported a colloquium called by Benny Lévy that was convened in Foucault's apartment, financed by *Les Temps Modernes*, that brought together Israeli, Palestinian, and Arab scholars and intellectuals. Said was there. His retrospective analysis of the gathering published in the *London Review of Books* encapsulates his bitter disappointment with Sartre's views on Zionism and Israel. "For reasons that we still cannot know for certain, Sartre did indeed remain constant in his fundamental pro-Zionism," Said wrote. "Whether that was because he was afraid of seeming anti-semitic, or because he felt guilt about the Holocaust, or because he allowed himself no deep appreciation of the Palestinians as victims of and fighters against Israel's injustice, or for some other reason, I shall never know." He had hoped Sartre would address "Israeli settler-colonialism," but this was to no avail. Despite his genuine admiration for Sartre, Said concluded that when it came to Israel/Palestine, Sartre was "a bitter disappointment to every (non-Algerian) Arab who admired him."[107] As Annie Cohen-Solal notes in opening her biography of Sartre, Said's sentiments were widely shared in the Arab world and they would be adopted by many of Said's postcolonial acolytes.[108]

Said surely skewed Sartre's stance, however. Rather than advocating unwavering support for Israel, Sartre was committed to advancing mutual recognition between Palestinians and Israelis. Take the case of Sartre's response to the Munich massacre in 1972 when Palestinian terrorists kidnapped and killed eleven Olympic athletes. In this instance, Sartre was to the left of the New Left, including the Trotskyists and Maoists, when he maintained in *La Cause du peuple-J'Accuse* that the Munich massacre was a success, since it put the Palestinian struggle on the global radar, affirming his notion that terrorism was the weapon of the weak: "In this war, the only weapon the Palestinians have at their disposal is terrorism. It is a terrible weapon but the oppressed poor have no other," he wrote.[109]

Sartre's advocacy of terrorist or revolutionary violence like that carried out in the Munich massacre or advocated by Fanon in *The Wretched of the Earth* must be set against his other analyses of how violence could become serialized, institutionalized, and ultimately counter-revolutionary.[110] But on the whole, Sartre's existentialist multidirectional antiracism remains a model for confronting the global racisms of the present. Beginning with *Anti-Semite and Jew*, Sartre laid out a set of theorems that remain powerful to thinking about Judeophobia and Negrophobia and Islamophobia today. These begin with understanding the process of Othering at the heart of racism, which originates in claims of essentialism. These claims stem from fear and anxiety that emerge from the desire to control and dominate others, the refusal to recognize their freedom, or from flight from our responsibility to make choices that lead not only to our own freedom, as in liberalism, but to the freedom of all others. As he drifted toward existential Marxism, Sartre developed the axioms he articulated in his opposition to fascist anti-Semitism into a more encompassing understanding of institutional and structural racism in his ruminations on anti-Black and anticolonial racism. In doing so, he was critical of communist dogmatism, including Stalin's Judeophobic anti-Zionism whereby antiracism could dialectically morph into "the new racism." By 1973, Sartre was blind and debilitated, but still clung to a faint hope that the Israeli-Palestinian conflict could be resolved if the two sides could recognize the legitimacy of the other's narrative and aspirations for national liberation. This was foreclosed when Zionism was simply decried as a form of racism and when resistance by terrorism, which could become serialized, simply legitimated further state violence, subjugation, and expropriation. Sartre died in 1980 just as the Israeli occupation of the West Bank was deepening and the success of the Iranian revolution spurred jihadi terrorism. But his global, multidirectional antiracism left us critical resources for the ongoing struggle today.

CHAPTER 2

The Frankfurt School and the Anti-Semitic Question

The critical theory articulated by the group of scholars known as the Frankfurt School is as foundational to German theorizing about anti-Semitism as Sartre is to French theorizing. Their work was on the cusp of efforts to rethink the links between modernity and anti-Semitism, not as opposing tendencies, but as mutually reinforcing. They wove together Freudian and Marxist approaches with social scientific insights from both European sociology and American social psychology to produce their insights. This chapter is an account of the key theorists, texts, and arguments within the Frankfurt School's multifaceted approach as they developed it during World War II and its immediate aftermath.[1]

Despite being forced into exile by the Nazis, members of the group did not directly confront anti-Semitism until Max Horkheimer's "The Jews and Europe" appeared in 1939. Horkheimer's emphasis was on a materialist account of social domination as it had shifted under monopoly capitalism and fascist authoritarianism. Still blind to the depth of Nazi anti-Semitism, Horkheimer analyzed Judeophobia within a Marxist framework as a scapegoat tactic to divert the masses from the real cause of oppression: exploitation under capitalism. But "The Jews and Europe" was a promissory note that opened the way to the extraordinary insights of the Frankfurt School's socio-psychoanalytic account of anti-Semitism. The fullest development of this approach was the chapter on the "Elements of Anti-Semitism" added in 1947 as the conclusion to one of the masterworks of the twentieth century, *Dialectic of Enlightenment*.

Earlier statements included those of Franz Neumann within his seminal work on the Nazi state, *Behemoth*, whose publishing history between 1942 and 1944 indicates the shifts in how the group was transcending classical Marxist approaches. By 1944, Neumann definitively rejected scapegoat theories in favor of what he termed the "spearhead theory of anti-Semitism," arguing that anti-Jewish discourse and practice was merely a rehearsal for a totalitarian order aimed at destroying modern democracy.[2] Under the direction of Horkheimer and with funding from the American Jewish Committee, a set of groundbreaking analyses were undertaken, culminating in the Studies in Prejudice series, comprising five books that investigated the origins of racial anti-Semitism in Germany, the rhetoric of American profascist anti-Semites of the 1930s and 1940s, a couple of explicitly psychoanalytic accounts—*Dynamics of Prejudice* and *Anti-Semitism and Emotional Disorder*—and the influential study, *The Authoritarian Personality*.

Along the way, key principles were enumerated. First, to understand anti-Semitism, it must be located in its social context and understood as a mechanism of social domination. Second, while anti-Semitism serves as a diversion from social conflict for elites, it also functions as a distorted means of expressing that conflict for the exploited. Third, since standardization and mass production are the engines of modernity, stereotyping is endemic within modern culture. Fourth, stereotypes and conspiracy theories are social codes or narratives about social processes for people without adequate analytic tools to otherwise express their social discontents and the social causes of their oppression and exploitation. Fifth, anti-Semitic discourse is a convenient and effective tool of mass deception because it personalizes social frustration, providing a clear target for resentment. Sixth, the tools of psychoanalysis are key to decoding anti-Semitic discourse because it expresses unconscious desires and internal psychic conflicts, which rational analyses easily overlook. Seventh, the forms of expression and dissemination—what Horkheimer and Adorno termed "the culture industry"—are equally central to assess as the content of anti-Semitic hate speech. And finally, projection is a key mechanism to understand prejudice. These axioms are the core of the Frankfurt School's socio-psychoanalytic approach to understanding anti-Semitism.

Despite the development of these foundational precepts for critical approaches to prejudice and racism, postcolonial and decolonial critics have accused the Frankfurt School of blindness to imperialist racism in their understanding of discrimination. Edward Said is unequivocal: "Frankfurt School critical theory, despite its seminal insights into the relationship between domination, modern society, and the opportunities for redemption through art as critique, is stunningly silent on racist theory, anti-imperialist resistance, and oppositional practice in the empire."[3] Espen Hammer also derides Adorno's "blunt Eurocentrism" that is "virtually oblivious to the concerns of post-colonialism, including racism, discrimination, and imperialism."[4] As a result, contemporary exponents of the Frankfurt School have sought to redress this oversight. Thomas McCarthy in *Race, Empire and the Idea of Human Development* has written an important critical history of developmental schemas at work in racism and imperialism centered on the concepts of "enlightenment, civilization, progress, social evolution, economic growth, modernization, and so forth."[5] More recently, Amy Allen in *The End of Progress: Decolonizing the Normative Foundations of Critical Theory*, aims explicitly to show "how and why Frankfurt School critical theory remains wedded to problematically Eurocentric and/or foundationalist strategies for grounding normativity" in order to open up the strands between the Frankfurt School and post- and decolonial critical theory.[6] Her criticism is focused primarily on contemporary Frankfurt School theorists like Jurgen Habermas, Axel Honneth, and Rainer Forst. Indeed, she draws upon the early Frankfurt School, especially Adorno, and specifically the *Dialectic of Enlightenment*, to articulate an imminent critique.

Despite Allen's thoroughgoing meta-analysis, she never makes the point that part of the postcolonial critique rests upon an undue split between anti-Jewish and other racisms, since the optic of the early Frankfurt School was primarily anti-Semitism. As this chapter will show, however, there is a vast body of work to mine for critical race theories in general. Moreover, the charge of Eurocentrism is odd, since clearly the Frankfurt School contributed significant work to understanding racism in America, as well as to considering post-Holocaust Judeophobia that was anti-Israel. Their acuity for considerations of contemporary Judeophobia will be addressed in my conclusion.[7]

Indeed, in reconstructing the seminal work of how the early Frankfurt School understood racialization, I show that they never had only one target (i.e., Jews) in mind. They were clear from the outset that the links between forms of oppression targeting minoritized social groups were key to understanding social domination. Most significantly, what Frankfurt School theorists illuminate about anti-Jewish persecution and subjugation largely translates into the experience of colonized subjects, since Jews were one of Europe's internal colonial Others.[8] At the same time, the unexamined assumptions and reiterated stereotypes about Jews and Judaism one finds within Horkheimer's and Adorno's work reveal why decolonial and postcolonial theorists should continue to revise and update the Frankfurt School's landmark efforts alongside other critical theorists.

A PORTRAIT OF THE INSTITUTE FOR SOCIAL RESEARCH

The Frankfurt School is a coterie of intellectuals affiliated with the Institut für Sozialforschung (Institute of Social Research).[9] It was founded in Frankfurt am Main in 1923 with the backing of millionaire Jewish grain merchant Hermann Weil. Weil was perhaps convinced to fund this interdisciplinary group of dissident Marxist researchers committed to the overthrow of capitalism because his son Felix, a disciple of Karl Korsch, appealed to his father by suggesting that the group would be committed to analyzing the worker's movement and to studying anti-Semitism.[10] The critical viewpoint of the group, as Martin Jay explains, came from their brilliant integration of "cultural mandarinism, aesthetic modernism, Jewish self-awareness, psychoanalysis, [and] Weberian rationalization theory," which supplemented their rethinking of Marxism in light of the socioeconomic and political transformations of the twentieth century.[11] The building that housed the Institut exuded the school's purpose and Frankfurt's post-World War I ambience with its modernist, *Neue Sachlichkeit* (New Objectivity) architecture that rejected the Wilhelminian past.[12]

As a city with a long history in international trade, Frankfurt was a center of liberalism and innovation. This was evident in its daily newspaper, the *Frankfurter Zeitung*; Radio Frankfurt, which broadcast modernist music, radio plays, and challenging lectures; the creation of one of the earliest psychoanalytic institutes; and the establishment of the new Frankfurt University in 1914, funded privately and in significant measure by Jewish philanthropists, to which the Institut was formally attached. Frankfurt's Jewish community was second only to Berlin's in importance, comprising about 30,000 members. Many participated in the courses offered by the innovative Freie Jüdische Lehrhaus (Free Jewish School), founded in 1920 under the leadership of Franz Rosenzweig and his key collaborator Martin Buber, including many early affiliates of the Institut, like Leo Löwenthal, Siegfried Kracauer, and Erich Fromm.[13]

The overwhelming majority of the first generation of those associated with the Institut were both Jewish and Marxist, including the Institut's first director Carl Grünberg, early members Henryk Grossmann, Friedrich Pollock, Fromm, and Löwenthal. Max Horkheimer became the Institut's director in 1931. He oversaw a group of the Frankfurt School's most famous initiates, Theodor Adorno and Herbert Marcuse, and affiliates like Walter Benjamin and Franz Neumann. As Jews and Marxists, they were early targets of the Nazis, and consequently forced into exile. The core members of the Institut initially resettled at Columbia University via Geneva in 1934. Over the course of World War II, the group became more dispersed. Horkheimer and Adorno, for example, moved to Southern California in 1941, joining a community of exiles from Weimer Germany that included Thomas Mann and Arnold Schoenberg, until they returned permanently to Frankfurt in the early 1950s.

"THE JEWS AND EUROPE"

Despite their founding promise to study the problem of anti-Semitism and the fact that the first phases of anti-Jewish persecution were enacted in Nazi Germany, including the boycott of Jewish businesses and legislation against Jewish professionals in 1933, the Nuremberg laws of 1935, and the Kristallnacht pogrom of 1938, throughout the 1930s, the members of the Institut did not directly analyze anti-Semitism. According to Friedrich Pollock, Institut members did not want to "advertise" the Jewish Question nor were they willing "to draw unnecessary attention to the overwhelming Jewish origins" of the Institut's members.[14] In fact, writes Jay, "If one were to characterize the Institut's general attitude towards the 'Jewish question,' it would have to be seen as similar to that expressed by another radical Jew almost a century before, Karl Marx. In both cases the religious or ethnic issue was clearly subordinated to the social."[15] The particularity of Jewish persecution was deemphasized in the interest of highlighting social domination more generally. Their Jewish or ethnic backgrounds were almost entirely repressed from their work in the 1930s.[16]

Writing in 1944 at the tail end of the war, Horkheimer states, "As early as 1930, I became aware of the gravity of the problem of anti-Semitism, which even then was a real menace in Germany and in the rest of the world."[17] Scholars have now shown, in fact, that his earliest writings penned during World War I already reckoned anti-Semitism as a concern.[18] Nonetheless, the first significant analysis of anti-Semitism by the Institut was Horkheimer's essay "The Jews and Europe," published *only* in 1939.[19] In the essay, the problem is still subsumed under the rubric of class conflict and largely assessed according to a paradigm established by the Comintern press that saw fascism as monopoly capitalism in its final phase. For all of the insights of Horkheimer's essay that go beyond orthodox Marxism (and there are many!),[20] his article was congruent with the failures of Marxist thinkers in assessing what was new and unique about Nazism in the interwar period.[21] This is because, as Gershom Scholem put it in the last letter he sent to Benjamin, "the Jews interest him not as Jews but only from the standpoint of the fate of the economic category that they represent for him."[22]

Horkheimer's basic premises are that "the new antisemitism is the emissary of the totalitarian order, which has developed from the liberal one"; that "whoever is not willing to talk about capitalism should also keep quiet about fascism"; that "fascist ideology conceals the same relationship as the old harmonizing ideology: domination by a minority on the basis of actual possession of the tools of production"; that "the totalitarian order differs from its bourgeois predecessor only in that it has lost its inhibitions"; and that "class rule has taken the form of the 'folk community' [Volksgemeinschaft]."[23]

In the process of developing this critique, Horkheimer himself sometimes reiterates leftist anti-Jewish tropes developed by the utopian socialists through Marx and beyond in their representations of the role of Jews within capitalism.[24] He argues that since the Jews are "money's representatives" and that "the Jews are [now] stripped of power as agents of circulation" they have become "the first victims of the ruling group."[25] Horkheimer is justly critical of the attitudes of Jews who "curse ... with the Aryans ... his coreligionists coming across the border,"[26] but flirts with anti-Semitic constructions when he suggests that "nouveau riche Jews and Aryans ... have always acquiesced in the impoverishment of other social and national groups, [and in the] ... mass poverty in mother countries and colonies."[27] In making these claims, Horkheimer was building upon premises about the Jewish bourgeoisie he had already articulated in *Dämmerung*, published in 1934:

> Jewish capitalists become terribly excited about anti-Semitism. They say that what they hold most sacred is under attack. But I believe that their unspeakable annoyance merely comes from the fact that something about them is being threatened which yields no profit, yet cannot possibly be changed.... Among bourgeois Jews, the hierarchy of goods is neither Jewish nor Christian but bourgeois. The Jewish capitalist brings sacrifices to power, just like his Aryan class colleague.[28]

Horkheimer thus suggests that the Jewish bourgeoisie bear responsibility for the exploitation and domination of the bourgeois mode of production because it serves their class interests. Anti-Semitism is assessed as little more than a screen for deflecting the class antagonisms wrought by capitalist exploitation.

In light of this tendency in the essay, the concluding note of the article is interesting in that it weaves together the Jewish and Hegelian Marxist traditions on the issue of social justice, as Horkheimer enjoins Jews and non-Jews to resist the system of domination imposed by the fascists and National Socialists: "The Jews were once proud of abstract monotheism, their rejection of idolatry, their refusal to make something finite an absolute. Their distress points them back. Disrespect for anything mortal that puffs itself up as a god is the religion of those who cannot resist devoting their life to the preparation of something better, even in the Europe of the Iron Heel." His conclusion thus encourages the resistance to fascism in the name of specific Jewish values: monotheism calls for a universal unity; the "rejection of idolatry," the castigation of anyone who poses as a god. Horkheimer suggests an ideology critique that refuses to accept the finite and particular for the absolute and he also intimates the affirmation of a messianic or revolutionary hope for "something better." But he was embarrassed enough about the article to exclude it from his collection of writings, *Kritische Theorie*.[29]

RESEARCH PROJECTS ON ANTI-SEMITISM

The concluding note and passing insights of Horkheimer's essay confirm Jack Jacobs's contention that "The Jews of Europe" was a transitional piece that reflected the Institut's groping toward a more substantive and complex analysis of anti-Semitism.[30] If the Frankfurt School had largely neglected the problem in the 1930s, by the early 1940s it had developed into a major concern. As early as August 1940, for example, Adorno wrote to Horkheimer that he could not "stop thinking about the fate of the Jews any more. It often seems that everything that we used to see from the point of view of the proletariat has been concentrated today with frightful force upon the Jews."[31]

In 1939, the same year as his essay "The Jews and Europe" appeared, Horkheimer began to discuss the possibility of a large collective research project on anti-Semitism to be directed by himself and Adorno. An early version of this plan was drafted by Adorno as the "Research Project on Anti-Semitism" and published in the spring of 1941 in *Studies in Philosophy and Social Science*, the English-language continuation of the *Zeitschrift für Sozialforschung*, now published in New York. The project was to show the saturation of anti-Semitism within Western culture historically and to develop research methodologies for measuring its contemporary forms.[32] As Thomas Wheatland maintains in summarizing it, "The first anti-Semitism proposal arrived at a hypothetical theory of prejudice that reinforced the Institute's pessimistic assessments of European humanism, enlightened Reason, totalitarian, and mass culture."[33] This remained a core strand of their theorizing, even as it was mediated by the search for funding in America.

As early as September 1940, Adorno began to send Horkheimer a sample of his early theoretical ruminations on anti-Semitism as they were developing. As was the case with Horkheimer's first efforts, these unpublished reflections indicate how Adorno assigns Jews to conceptual categories that recycle well-worn typologies, even as this is what enabled him to unpack the socio-psychic structures of anti-Semitism.[34] He opened by picking up on the old trope of the wandering Jew, the perpetual peripatetic, as both at the origin of anti-Semitism but also its ultimate victim. "The survival of nomadism among the Jews might provide not only an explanation for the nature of the Jew himself, but even more an explanation for anti-Semitism," he wrote to Horkheimer. Jewish nomadism, Adorno claimed, constituted Jewish nature, or, at least, so Jews are constructed in the anti-Semitic imagination.

He put this association to work by offering it as a twist on Freud's claim in *Moses and Monotheism*. Freud had argued that anti-Jewish hatred was a function of the association of Jews with the difficult ethical imperatives of monotheism, which elicited wrathful loathing by those who agreed with these ideals, but could not fulfill them personally. Providing a Marxian turn, Adorno shifts the terms from ethics to labor, but the Freudian insight remains: the Jewish identification with the quality of nomadism elicits contempt from those condemned by monopoly capitalism to sludge through the daily grind and misery of work, which is a by-product of settlement. "The Jews are the ones who have not allowed themselves to be 'civilized' and subjected to the priority of work," he claimed. "This ban is the origin of anti-Semitism, the expulsions of the Jews, and the attempt to complete or imitate the expulsion from Paradise."[35] Jewish exclusion and the image of the Jewish parasite and the Jewish miser are invoked and explained at a stroke.

The insight is powerful. For on the basis of this simple set of assumptions, Adorno provides an account as well of why Jews were a key antitype for nationalists and empire builders in the nineteenth century. He also explains why Jews are the targets of those whose lives are strained by the conditions of the modes of production in late modernity. The cultural and the economic imperatives at work behind this image of the Jew are illuminated. But to offer the interpretation, Adorno echoes the claim that Jews are condemned to exile and wandering, even if this is only in the cultural unconscious of the West. Adorno's conceptual Jew as nomad is naturalized by his gloss on why this captures the fascist's imagination and what it explains in their lives. This way of conceptualizing anti-Semitism by reiterating Judeophobic tropes of Jews would repeat itself in the more developed works by Adorno as well.

Anti-Semitism: A Social Disease

These would only reach full fruition after the war. Writing in the preface to *The Authoritarian Personality*, Horkheimer noted that the research project on anti-Semitism initiated in 1939 combined with "a series of discussions with the late Dr. Ernst Simmel and Professor R. Nevitt Sanford of the University of California [five years later that] laid the basis for the present project."[36] The conference that Horkheimer alludes to took place in San Francisco in June 1944. Convened under the auspices of the San Francisco Psychoanalytic Society—the California constituent society of the American Psychoanalytic Association—it was arranged by Ernst Simmel. A psychoanalyst who had emigrated from Germany, Simmel had been practicing in Los Angeles since 1934. He sought to "invite a group of scientists to participate in a symposium on anti-Semitism."[37] The results were published in 1946 in a work Simmel edited and introduced: *Anti-Semitism: A Social Disease*. In the acknowledgements, he expresses his "special thanks" to "Dr. T.W. Adorno, who gave me the benefit of his experience in arranging the material of this volume."[38]

Adorno's contribution "Anti-Semitism and Fascist Propaganda" was the bookend to Horkheimer's opening chapter, "Sociological Background of the Psychoanalytic Approach." Horkheimer and Adorno were invited as sociologists, since the symposium sought "the collaboration of sociologists and research psychologists who accepted the basic psychoanalytic concepts." It also included Otto Fenichel, another psychoanalyst who had fled Germany in 1933, whose paper on the "Elements of a Psychoanalytic Theory of Anti-Semitism" would influence Horkheimer and Adorno's "Elements of Anti-Semitism" in the *Dialectic of Enlightenment*. Also represented at the symposium were Else Frenkel-Brunswik and Sanford, the core of the Berkeley experimental psychologists who were the key partners in developing *The Authoritarian Personality*. Their joint paper was a research report tellingly titled "The Anti-Semitic Personality."[39]

Horkheimer's chapter served as an introduction to the guiding principle of the symposium, which argued that psychoanalysis was a necessary element in any approach to anti-Semitism. "A mere appeal to the conscious mind does not suffice," Horkheimer insisted, "because anti-Semitism and the susceptibility to anti-Semitic propaganda spring from the unconscious." What experimental social psychology could contribute, therefore, was "the character structures of anti-Semites" and a set of anti-Semitic types, including "religious and philosophical anti-Semitism," "the paranoid," "the vanquished competitor," "the Jew baiter," and the streamlined, up-to-date "fascist anti-Semite."[40]

It was the fascist anti-Semite that was the focus of Adorno's chapter. His observations were based on studies by Institut affiliates Leo Löwenthal and Norbert Guterman, who worked alongside him on West Coast anti-Semitic agitators, examining the rhetoric in their pamphlets, weekly publications, and radio addresses. In this analysis of fascist discourse, Adorno makes the remarkable claim that it is the fascist mode of propaganda that makes this discourse fascist rather than an economic plan or mode of politics. And he itemizes three key mechanisms that are at the heart of fascist anti-Semitic propaganda: (1) "It is *personalized* propaganda," (2) "all these demagogues substitute means for ends," and (3) "propaganda functions as a kind of *wish-fulfillment*."[41]

Personalized propaganda operates in a number of ways. "Fascist propaganda attacks bogies rather than real opponents," Adorno avows. "That is to say, it builds up an *imagery* of the Jew, or of the Communist, and tears it to pieces, without caring much how this imagery is related to reality."[42] In accord with the volume's title, Adorno concurs that anti-Semitism is a social disease. But its origins are psychic. It is a form of neurosis that has been transformed into a commodity and marketed with propaganda. As such, Adorno terms it "a kind of psychotechnics" that is reminiscent of how other mass commodities are packaged in movies, sporting events, and other forms of mass entertainment. In short, what was new about fascist anti-Semitic propaganda was that it was product of the culture industry where what was produced was a bogeyman that could personalize social resentment and could be burned in effigy as such.

Adorno also put great emphasis on the ritualistic aspects of fascist propaganda, which he suggests was only a version of the administered production of all products that are created by the culture industry. The ceremony of the ritual operates through the crowd "having their own minds expressed to them." It depends upon a politics of identity: the follower identifies with the leader who embodies "a kind of institutionalized redemption of their own inarticulateness through the speaker's verbosity." Fascist discourse is also bifurcated, based upon the Schmittian "dichotomy of black and white, foe and friend."[43] These binaries are trotted out as formulas that are laced together to shape the ideology.

This ideology is built upon wish fulfillment, the concept Freud developed to explain dreams. It is the form of fascist propaganda that is ultimately so gratifying, Adorno continues. For it provides the enchanted dream that is the basis of the fascist world view. Moreover, Adorno maintains that "at the hub of the fascist, anti-Semitic ritual is the desire for ritual murder": sacrifice that is made sacrosanct. It is made sacred through the sacraments of fascist propaganda. Adorno consequently concludes that "psychologically, all fascist propaganda is simply a system of such symbols.... The unconscious psychological desire for self-annihilation faithfully reproduces the structure of a political movement which ultimately transforms its followers into victims."[44]

Behemoth

The full development of these lines of analysis would eventually culminate in Adorno's contributions to *The Authoritarian Personality*, alongside the other volumes of the five-volume Studies in Prejudice series.[45] This whole endeavor was made possible because in March 1943 the Institut was funded by the American Jewish Committee (AJC) to support their multifaceted research project on anti-Semitism on the basis of a proposal rewritten by Herbert Marcuse and Franz Neumann.[46]

Neumann's revision of the proposal to the AJC late in 1941, alongside his stubborn advocacy for the project, helped to secure the AJC's support.[47] It was fortuitous that when he met with the AJC in the summer of 1942 to make a final appeal, joined by Isacque Graeber, the AJC's organ, *Contemporary Jewish Record*, had just published a review of Neumann's groundbreaking study, *Behemoth: The Structure and Practice of National Socialism, 1933–1944*.[48] *Behemoth* was, in Rolf Wiggershaus's words, the Institut's "principal analysis of Nazism" at the time.[49] *Behemoth* combined a foundational analysis of the Nazi state with a *Sonderweg* argument about German anti-Semitism. Neumann sought to prove that Nazi policies were opportunistic, ultimately reflecting the competition between four power bases: the Nazi party, the German state bureaucracy, the military, and big business. The book was organized into three parts that analyzed Nazi politics, economics, and society, reflecting Neumann's Marxist methodology. As Peter Hayes notes in his new introduction, however, "the effects of his angle of vision as a German, a lawyer cum political scientist, and a leftist" skew Neumann's account in three key areas: "the existence and importance of Nazi ideology, the impulse behind Nazi anti-Semitism, and the role of big business in the Nazi economic system."[50]

Neumann was insightful in maintaining that Hitlerism was inchoate. But he went too far in declaring that it "consisted of nothing but shifting aims and goals" that served the purpose of obscuring Nazi economic exploitation.[51] His commitment to a Marxist framework failed him when it came to understanding the centrality of race and space in integrating the Nazi viewpoint. He did understand that a racial ethnonationalism was "deeply embedded in the history of German thought."[52] Racial imperialism, he noted, took the form of anti-Semitism, since the "whole history of German intellectual life is shot through with Jew-baiting, and Anti-Semitic organizations played a leading part even during the imperial period."[53] Neumann traced this lineage from Luther to Hitler. But he blindly insisted that "although Anti-Semitism was nowhere so actively propagated as in Germany, it failed to strike root in the population," least of all among the worker's movement, which "remained immune from it."[54] In his 1942 version of the book he claimed, "Spontaneous, popular Anti-Semitism is still weak in Germany," preposterously maintaining, "The writer's personal conviction, paradoxical as it may seem, is that the German people are the least Anti-Semitic of all."[55]

To account for this paradox, Neumann distinguished between anti-Semitism and hard-core Nazi totalitarian ideology, which identified Jews with "the incarnation of evil in Germany" and was ultimately "magic and beyond discussion."[56] Pretotalitarian anti-Semitism, Neumann suggested, appealed to religious anti-Judaism, but even more powerfully spoke to economic, social, and political discontent. It was an "outlet for resentment" expressing the gripes of the older and newer middle classes (the free professions, university teachers, farmers, white-collar workers, artisans, shopkeepers, and civil servants) dislocated by capitalist modernity. Modernity was personified by Jews, explains Neumann: "The modern theater, atonal music, expressionism in painting and literature, functional architecture, all these seemed to constitute a threat to the conservatives whose cultural outlook was basically rural, and who thus came to identify the city and its culture, its economics, and its politics with the Jew."[57] So rather than a fundamental outlook, anti-Semitism was a screen and Jews a scapegoat that masked deeper social resentment about the forces of modernity. The Nazis manipulated this when it was useful. Summing up his views in 1942, Neumann claimed that three factors played a role in Nazi practices: "First, racism and Anti-Semitism are substitutes for the class struggle.... Secondly, Anti-Semitism provides a justification for eastern expansion.... Finally, Anti-Semitism in Germany is an expression of the rejection of Christianity and all it stands for."[58]

When Neumann revised his book for a second publication in 1944, he added an appendix with a section titled "Anti-Semitism." The tone of the writing is totally different, since he now knew that he erred when he previously claimed, "The internal political value of Anti-Semitism will, therefore, never allow a complete extermination of the Jews. The foe cannot and must not disappear; he must always be held in readiness as a scapegoat for all the evils originating in the socio-political system."[59] In 1944, Neumann flatly rejected "the scapegoat theory according to which the Jews are used as scapegoats for all evils of society." Instead, he advanced a "spearhead theory of Anti-Semitism," arguing that the Jews are "guinea pigs" for an "all-comprehensive terrorist machine. The denunciation of bolshevism, socialism, democracy, liberalism, capitalism as Jewish, together with the planned extermination of the Jews." This served to foster a totalitarian society that persecuted all groups that were not subservient to the Nazi system.[60] Anti-Semitism was consequently the spearhead for a broader totalitarian assault on democracy. These shifts in Neumann's approach to anti-Semitism reflected in the publishing history of *Behemoth* indicate that between 1942 and 1944 the spearhead theory was becoming more pronounced by Frankfurt School theorists, and it was certainly central to selling the Frankfurt School's projects to the AJC.[61]

STUDIES IN PREJUDICE

The key outcome of the AJC-funded work was the Studies in Prejudice series of five books. These were the result of a set of interdisciplinary and multi-institutional efforts. All were published by 1950. They made an important contribution to the study of racism and discrimination with an integrated set of works intended to "constitute one unit."[62] The analysis with the most enduring impact was *The Authoritarian Personality*, but the series included Paul Massing's description of the genesis and development of anti-Semitism in Germany before World War I in *Rehearsal for Destruction* and Leo Löwenthal and Norbert Guterman's *Prophets of Deceit*, which was the full-length analysis of the techniques of mass persuasion and manipulation by the West Coast agitators that Adorno had discussed in 1946. The other two volumes extended the experiments with psychoanalysis, considering the psychological elements that predispose individuals to prejudice and racial hatred.[63] They were less directly a product of the Frankfurt School's analysis of anti-Semitism, so I will not discuss them. In toto, this enormous endeavor sought to broaden the categories for conceptualizing prejudice, racism, and anti-Semitism by incorporating psychoanalytic elements into Marxist social theory.

Rehearsal for Destruction

If Neumann's focus was on the Nazi state in *Behemoth*, his Frankfurt School colleague Paul Massing wrote a straightforward historical analysis of the preamble to Nazi anti-Semitism in *Rehearsal for Destruction: A Study of Political Anti-Semitism in Imperial Germany*. It was one of the earliest analyses of politicized and racialized anti-Semitism in Germany, situating it within its social context.[64] Massing's four parts begin with anti-Semitism in Bismarck's Reich, continue with the rise of racial anti-Semitism, then discuss anti-Semitism and imperialism, and end with a section on socialist labor and anti-Semitism. Massing located German anti-Semitism within German modernity following Jewish emancipation and up until World War I: "Anti-Semitism was inextricably tied to German nineteenth-century nationalism; its destructive nature derived from the peculiar social and political crises through which Germany struggled,"[65] states Samuel Flowers in introducing the work. According to Massing's version of the *Sonderweg* thesis, the failure of Germany to institutionalize bourgeois liberalism on the Western model combined with class tensions were what shaped Germany's imperial-era anti-Semitism. Summing this up, he writes, "The old ruling powers and the *Mittelstand* shared an antipathy to the kind of liberalism sponsored by the middle classes, and all these strata combined shared the fear of rising labor. Anti-Semitism became part of the ensuing sociopolitical configuration."[66] Within this configuration, Massing argues that anti-Semitism served two key purposes: as "a political tool" of the ruling elite and "a confused expression of social protest."[67]

Prophets of Deceit

If Massing's study analyzed the context that led to the Nazi assault and Neumann's *Behemoth* analyzed the Nazi state, then Leo Löwenthal and Norbert Guterman's *Prophets of Deceit: A Study of the Techniques of the American Agitator* broadened the analysis of anti-Semitism to consider it in the American context. While generally well received when it was published in 1949, *Prophets of Deceit* has had little enduring influence since it analyzed the rhetoric of a now-forgotten set of political agitators. A coterie of a dozen primarily anti-Semitic cranks and profascist populists in the 1930s and 1940s who never came to power, their influence was nonetheless quite widespread at the time. They included Father Charles Coughlin, whose radio broadcasts reached millions, and Gerald L. K. Smith, who founded the America First Party.

The echoes of this tradition in the age of Donald Trump and his ilk across the globe are uncanny. Reading *Prophets of Deceit* today is like discovering their secret playbook, since it provides an encompassing rhetorical analysis of contemporary right-wing populist authoritarian discourse. Deepening the analysis in Adorno's 1943 trial study, *The Psychological Technique of Martin Luther Thomas' Radio Addresses*, as well as Adorno's paper on "Anti-Semitism and Fascist Propaganda," Löwenthal and Guterman analyzed the ideological content and interconnected themes mobilized by these American agitators.[68]

Do not try to understand the themes of the agitator's rhetoric by its surface content, Löwenthal and Guterman countenance. Rather, you have to demystify their "secret psychological language," they explain. Otherwise, you might "wave it aside as a kind of mania or a mere tissue of lies and nonsense."[69] To plumb the manifest content of the agitators' speech and pamphlets, Löwenthal and Guterman open by distinguishing "agitators" from "reformers" and "revolutionaries." They explain how the agitator's discourse differs from conservatives, liberals, and radicals. This is because *agitators have no specific agenda for change*. They seduce by becoming ciphers for resentment and fear. If liberals and conservatives speak about *what* causes social problems, the key to the rhetoric of the agitator is *who* causes "social malaise."

"Social malaise" is a term of art that Löwenthal and Guterman borrow from sociologists, which encapsulates the objective causes of their listener's anxiety and disillusionment that are triggered by the forces of global capitalism, which include "the replacement of the class of small independent producers by gigantic industrial bureaucracies, the decay of the patriarchal family, the breakdown of primary personal ties between individuals in an increasingly mechanized world, the compartmentalization and atomization of group life, and the substitution of mass culture for traditional patterns."[70] The response for many left behind by these abstract forces is a welter of feelings of distrust, abandonment, and exclusion. Global capitalism results in a bundle of economic, political, cultural, and moral grievances. Those who suffer from social malaise are desperate to pour their hearts out.

The agitator is their mouthpiece and megaphone. He feigns the bravery to speak out against political correctness, to utter publicly what many think privately. When he does so, he *personifies* their grievances and targets their origins by pointing to the "ruthless enemies" of America. The agitators of the 1930s pointed to Jews, whereas Trump targets Mexicans and the Chinese or follows many populist authoritarians in Europe who focus on Muslim immigrants; the 1930s agitators focused on communists, whereas today's authoritarians berate liberals; the agitators decried the plutocrats of predatory capital, whereas today's prophets of deceit target globalization and free trade agreements. But just like the agitators of the 1930s, today's populists rail about refugees, corrupt government, and dangerous foreigners, including foreign entanglements, the key theme of Smith's America First platform. "The alien," Löwenthal and Guterman write, "is thus connected with the disturbing aspects of contemporary life, while the nostalgic image of the 'good old days' suggests a pristine and uncontaminated era of security."[71] Brandishing a quiver of stereotypes, the agitator often slings his arrows in a Morse code that his listeners know how to decode. The scapegoated enemies are many, but always powerless. Yet they are magnified to appear powerful and threatening.

Brilliantly, *Prophets of Deceit* shows how an emotional substratum of grievances is fixed onto a conspiracy narrative with these enemies as its engine. Feelings of distrust are warranted, the agitator explains, because ordinary

Americans are duped. The prophet of deceit encourages his followers to admit that they are cheated and disillusioned. Conspiracies are stoked on the basis of this admission. Conspiracies depend upon unverified and unverifiable accounts of anonymous social forces. They ultimately divert from attempts to explain objective social processes by providing a story of dark forces operating behind the scenes to advance their own benefits. Conspiracies appease people without the analytic tools to explicate the causes of their frustration. For this reason, the well-worn figure of the Jew lurks behind much of the discourse of the agitator: "The Jew becomes the symbol on which [the agitator] centers the projections of his own impotent rage against the restraints of civilization."[72] The agitator constantly harps on how elites are allowed to enjoy "forbidden fruit" while simple Americans suffer by upholding moral virtue. The agitator repetitively extols simple folk and their instincts over intellectuality. Social Darwinian to the core, the agitator downplays dialogue and compromise, which only thwart the struggle for self-preservation, which is a central motif.

The agitator pretends that his tale is not only negative. He offers an alternative set of values and goals. But what is valued is ultimately Manichean: us-versus-them virtues that are warranted by depicting life as shaped by inexorable conflict. For this reason, the military and police are celebrated. The agitator's goals are shaped by the discourse of housecleaning and hygiene, purification and cleanliness. Key to the success of the narrative is to highlight the contradictions between a set of American ideals and values, and how these are violated. Framing the whole narrative is a pall of gloom that reinforces a constant sense of danger. Ultimately, the effect is to trick his audience into accepting the situation that causes social malaise, reinforcing the status quo. This is accomplished because the agitator's followers are underdogs—or individuals who are worried that their status is jeopardized—who are converted into "watchdogs of order": "They are invited, not to organize rational responses, but to act out their impulses."[73] The agitator dangles the promise of access to the centers of social power. His unbridled narcissism appeals to people used to self-denial since they are ready for identification with uninhibited ego gratification. The agitator offers nothing but incessant debate about the fearless leader. For his adherents, his provocations offer the constant discharge of their emotions and reactions. It is an unending rehearsal for violence. What they most desire is for the complexity of the world to end and for a return to bygone days when, like children, their desires would be satisfied by the agitator's authoritarian personality.

The Authoritarian Personality

Certainly the most ambitious undertaking of the Studies in Prejudice series was *The Authoritarian Personality*. The title linked it terminologically to the work of Erich Fromm in the Institut's first collective publication, *Studies on Authority and the Family*, where "the concept of the 'authoritarian personality' was put forward as a link between psychological dispositions and political leanings."[74] Institutionally, *The Authoritarian Personality* was a joint undertaking of the Berkeley Public Opinion Study Group and the Institute of Social Research, combining Berkeley's experimental and empirical academic social psychology with the Institut's sociological and philosophical bent. The Berkeley group included Else Frenkel-Brunswik, a Polish-born, Vienna-trained psychoanalyst, who was a refugee from Nazi Germany; R. Nevitt Sanford, a Berkeley professor of psychology; and Daniel J. Levinson, a research student at Berkeley who became a professor of psychology at Yale.[75] Adorno represented the Institut.

As the authors noted in their opening lines:

> The research to be reported in this volume was guided by the following major hypothesis: that the political, economic, and social convictions of an individual often form a broad and coherent pattern, as if bound together by a "mentality" or "spirit," and that this pattern is an expression of deep-lying trends in his personality.
>
> The major concern was with the *potentially fascistic* individual, one whose structure is such as to render him particularly susceptible to anti-democratic propaganda.[76]

To capture those who were susceptible to anti-Semitism, political conservatism, ethnocentrism, and fascism, the researchers designed a series of questionnaires that were answered by 2,099 subjects. Their responses were mapped onto four separate scales: the A-S Scale (measuring anti-Semitism), the E-Scale (ethnocentrism), the Politico-Economic Conservatism scale, and the F-Scale, measuring propensity to fascism. The F-Scale was supposed to provide the key measure of "authoritarianism," a syndrome that had nine features: "conventionalism" (i.e., conformity to middle-class value systems); "authoritarian submission" (to the moral authorities of the ingroup); "authoritarian aggression" (toward those who are perceived to violate conventional norms); "anti-intraception" (or opposition to those sensitive to alternate solutions to social questions); "superstition and stereotypy" ("the belief in mystical determinants of the individual's fate" and "the disposition to think in rigid categories"); infatuation with "power and 'toughness,'"; "destructiveness and cynicism"; "projectivity" (i.e., "the projection outwards of unconscious emotional impulses"); and "an exaggerated concern with sexual 'goings-on.'"[77] *The Authoritarian Personality* combined quantitative and qualitative analysis with theoretical reflection, which made it a landmark study in empirical social psychology with a massive influence.[78]

Adorno's chapters within the larger study, however, indicate his divergence with the conclusions drawn by the study. As Peter Gordon incisively puts it, "Adorno's collaboration with [these] American social scientists exposed lines of tension that were never fully resolved."[79] If the Berkeley group emphasized the root of the problem in personality types, Adorno sought to emphasize how these were a product of social forces. Adorno was specifically responsible for formulating the "sociological dimensions related to personality factors and characterological concepts concomitant with authoritarianism," as well as analyzing qualitatively the ideological dimensions of the interview material in the study.[80]

In doing so, Adorno addressed head on the challenges of the work in his methodological chapter on "Types and Syndromes." For he was keenly aware that to suggest that there was an "authoritarian personality" risked collapsing the problem into an essentialism that located the origins of anti-Semitism in the personality type encapsulated in the title of the volume. Any doctrine of types, wrote Adorno, could "tend towards pigeonholing and transform highly flexible traits into static, quasi-biological characteristics" just as fascist typologies tended to do.[81] Nonetheless, it is certainly the case that at times Adorno and the other contributors did box their interpretations into the categories of their analysis.[82]

But the drive to locate the etiology of the authoritarian personality and its correlate types—the anti-Semite, the fascist, and the xenophobe—was justified according to Adorno, since the social conditions of modernity inherently produce typecasting. All the social processes of modernity tend toward standardization and mass production, including the personality types of individuals. "Only by identifying stereotypical traits in modern humans, and not by denying their existence," Adorno therefore averred, "can the pernicious tendency towards all-pervasive classification and subsumption be challenged."[83] Social types were the products of social rubber stamps.

How these rubber stamps were constituted as socially produced phenomena was the basis of Adorno's specific anthropology of anti-Semitism in the three substantive chapters he authored in *The Authoritarian Personality*. In these chapters, Adorno's first principle for understanding anti-Semitism as a social disease was to appreciate that the object of prejudice—that is, "the Jews"—is *not* what provokes the syndrome. This is precisely why Adorno insisted upon "the 'functional' character of anti-Semitism." The social functionality of the stereotype depends upon what Adorno termed "stereotypy" and "ticket thinking": the social production of the stereotype, which is itself linked to psychological needs that are created by the "cold, alienated, and largely ununderstandable world" of modernity.[84]

The psychological motor of stereotypy is projection. The key mechanism that prompts stereotypy is the defamation of other groups as a way to code one's own status. When it comes to the paranoid delusions that shape anti-Semitism, Adorno suggests that "the whole complex of the Jew is a kind of recognized redlight district of legitimatized psychotic distortions."[85] The social functionality of anti-Semitism is that it serves as compensation for social alienation. Also key is that anti-Semitism is a means to personalize an explanation of the complicated contradictions that engender social and psychological discomfort and unrest that are the outcome of alienation. The ineloquence or confusion of social life can be unraveled in an instant through a set of stock images. "The stereotypes just discussed," proclaims Adorno, "have been interpreted as means for pseudo-orientation in an estranged world, and at the same time as devices for 'mastering' this world by being able completely to pigeonhole its negative aspects."[86]

Adorno also suggested that part of how anti-Semitism functions is to serve as the site for the internal contradictions of individuals: the inner conflicts between id and superego. Stereotypes are the externalization of these inner conflicts, which are themselves the internalization of the contradictions of global capitalism. This is why many positive stereotypes are closely linked to their negative shadow side. For example, the contention that Jews are solidly entrenched in family values has its double in the assertion of Jewish clannishness. This double set of values ascribed to the stereotyping of Jews fits Adorno's "basic hypothesis": "the largely projective character of anti-Semitism," whereby "the Jews are blamed, in social terms, for those properties which by their existence, sociologically ambiguous though it may be, impinge on sensitive spots in ... class identification."[87] In contrast, those subjects who were low scorers on the various scales of prejudice measured by the Berkeley group intuitively understood that prejudice was a mechanism of social organization and thus focused their critique not on the object of hatred—the Jews, the Blacks, the Japanese, the communists, etc.—but on the social conditions that produced the stereotype itself. The core ideas that Adorno developed in his contribution to *The Authoritarian Personality* were based on ideas he had developed with Horkheimer in writing the *Dialectic of Enlightenment*.

THE *DIALECTIC OF ENLIGHTENMENT*

Horkheimer and Adorno's *Dialectic of Enlightenment*, insists Gunzelin Schmid Noerr, "is undoubtedly the most influential publication of the Critical Theory of the Frankfurt School, and one of its most compressed theoretical statements."[88] Written during the Second World War, "when the end of the National Socialist terror was in sight," it was first published in 1944 in a limited-edition hectographic typescript and dedicated to Friedrich Pollock on his fiftieth birthday.[89] It was republished in 1947 in Amsterdam in a printed edition by Querido, a leading publisher of German writers in exile, with the addition of the final, seventh section of "Elements of Anti-Semitism." It was republished again in 1969 with minor changes and rededicated for Pollock's seventy-fifth birthday.[90] The concluding chapter of the book, "Elements of Anti-Semitism: The Limits of Enlightenment" is composed of seven intertwined sections, the first three of which were written in collaboration with Leo Löwenthal. The first five sections were completed in 1943, the sixth section was completed for the first publication in 1944, and the seventh was written after World War II and published in 1947. As Lars Rensmann notes, this chapter offers the Frankfurt School's "most focused, theoretically rich, and complex account of antisemitism."[91]

Dialectic of Enlightenment considers anti-Semitism within the development of Western civilization, instrumental rationality, and the administered society of modernity. Horkheimer and Adorno argue that Western rationality is dialectically entwined with ideological obfuscation (i.e., myth), in particular, in the domination of nature. In five loosely connected chapters or "Philosophical Fragments" as the subtitle puts it, with a collection of "Notes and Drafts" as a postscript, they trace this imbrication from ancient Greece through the Enlightenment and into the mass culture of modernity. Against this long-term theoretical and historical backdrop, they culminate with "Elements of Anti-Semitism." The seven sections of this final chapter present a constellation or "force field," with each exploring different facets of anti-Semitism. "Force field" is used here in the sense developed by Martin Jay, based on the ideas of Walter Benjamin and Adorno, to suggest "a nontotalized juxtaposition of changing elements, a dynamic interplay of attractions and aversions, without a generative first principle, common denominator, or inherent essence."[92]

The first section of "Elements of Anti-Semitism" proffers that Jews are the antitype to fascism, and as such are slated for destruction (while Negroes are slated to remain "where they belong" as a subjugated group within the social hierarchy). This is the case because Adorno and Horkheimer argue that within the fascist creed, Jews are depicted as "the embodiment of the negative principle" and as "absolute evil." Since the fascist world view is inherently projective, "the portrait of the Jews that the nationalists offer to the world is in fact their own self-portrait."[93] If the paranoid, conspiratorial world view of Hitlerism is haunted by the threat of Jewish domination, this is because Nazis desire total domination and unlimited power that is then projected onto the Jewish Other. This is a key insight of "Elements of Anti-Semitism": projection is a central concept for understanding how anti-Semitism works.

Horkheimer and Adorno, like Sartre, also peel apart liberalism, arguing that it "serves as [an] apology for the existing order."[94] They skewer the assimilationist impulse of Jews who sought to ride the tide of liberalism to take their place among the modern bourgeoisie. In doing so, like Sartre, Horkheimer and Adorno blame the Jewish victims for having become the target of fascist domination because their "inflexible adherence to their own order of life has brought the Jews into an uncertain relationship with the dominant order."[95] In fact, as we will see, a thread through the chapter is that the persecution of Jews is linked to a system of domination for which Jews have some culpability.

The second section is a set of reflections on the relationship between populist, anti-Semitic, nationalist movements and the mob. It anticipates some of the ideas developed in *Prophets of Deceit* and by Adorno in *The Authoritarian Personality* and his other writings on fascist anti-Semitism. On the one hand, Horkheimer and Adorno claim that anti-Semitism "is an obvious asset to the ruling clique. It is used as a diversion."[96] On the other hand, the anti-Semitism of pogroms and plunder is not really amenable to "rational, economic, and political explanations and counter-arguments,"⁹⁷ not least because "rationality itself, through its link to power, is submerged in the same malady."⁹⁸

While Nazism defined itself in opposition to the Social Democrats and their principle of equality, what enthuses the mob about anti-Semitic violence is the voyeuristic and participatory pleasure of "seeing others robbed of all they possess" because it enables ordinary people to see the Other suffer their ordinary fate.⁹⁹ Anti-Semitism is consequently tied to the politics of outrage and as a form of release. This is a "deeply imprinted schema, a ritual of civilization" that has targeted an exchangeable list of victims:¹⁰⁰ "Rage is vented on those who are both conspicuous and unprotected.... the victims are interchangeable: Negroes, Mexican wrestling clubs, vagrants, Jews, Protestants, Catholics, so each of them can replace the murderer, in the same blind lust for killing, as soon as he feels the power of repressing the norm. There is no authentic anti-Semitism, and certainly no born anti-Semite."¹⁰¹ The source of mob frustration, Horkheimer and Adorno maintain, is that liberalism and capitalism promise happiness, but this is often perpetually deferred for the masses. The stereotype of Jewish bankers and intellectuals reaping the rewards of money and the leisure to think without the "sweat of toil and physical effort" personifies what is assured but denied to the mob, who vent their "destructive lust" on the Jews who have ostensibly gained at their expense.¹⁰²

Moving on from fascist anti-Semitism and the links between populist movements and the mob, the third section focuses on "bourgeois anti-Semitism," which "has a specific economic purpose: the concealment of domination in production."¹⁰³ Clearly inspired by a classic Marxist retake, as Jacobs notes, their development of this precept is "reminiscent of the position propounded by Horkheimer in 'The Jews of Europe.'"¹⁰⁴ But Horkheimer and Adorno are clearer in *Dialectic of Enlightenment* that "Jews are the scapegoats" for capitalist modernity, which is inherently a system of commodification and exploitation wherein Jews are denigrated as embodying the materialism and huckstering of the system.¹⁰⁵

In section 4, inspired now by Freud, they explore the religious origin of anti-Semitism, wherein "the adherents of the religion of the Father are hated by those who support the religion of the Son."¹⁰⁶ They also consider how nationalist anti-Semitism is a sublimation of religious aspirations. This is because nationalism transformed religious feelings and rites in its rituals and symbols, creating a civic religion, at the same time that religion became a commodified product of the culture industry: "In this way religion as an institution is partly meshed directly into the system and partly transposed into the pomp of mass culture and parades."[107]

But in passages within sections 3 and 4, Horkheimer and Adorno present a troubling dialectical unfolding of how Jewish history placed the Jews in the unique historical position of simultaneously playing a key role in the dialectic of civilization and ending up as the victims of this dialectic. They represent Jews as both the origin and end of this dialectic. They explain this in a dense historical overview of the dialectic of religion within civilization that echoes Max Weber's *Ancient Judaism* without ever referencing it.[108] Within this dialectic, God simultaneously represents liberation from nature and what explains the mythical forces of nature. In the unfolding of the dialectical relationship with God, pagan ritual sacrifice is transmogrified by Judaism. Christianity then spiritualized and universalized this process, which was further transformed to determine the division of labor under capitalism: "Its new form went on to determine the labor process. Sacrifice is rationalized on this basis. The taboo becomes the rational organization of the labor process."[109] Adorno and Horkheimer thus argue that the capitalist mode of production is the *Aufhebung* of ritual sacrifice. What is sacrificed in this modern "ritual of civilization" is the surplus labor of industrial workers. In this sweeping dialectical movement, therefore, Jews and Judaism constitute the source of the domination of the capitalist mode of production and its exploitation—their transmutation of ritual sacrifice is the root of the ritual sacrifice that constitutes modern capitalism.

Adorno and Horkheimer's argument that anti-Semitism is the culmination of Western civilization's instrumental rationality reaches its apotheosis in section 5, where they argue that civilization has progressed by organizing and controlling through mimesis. Mimesis began as the imitation of nature in order to control nature. It developed by copying nature "to ward off what is feared," transforming into mimicry in the mode of appropriation.[110] Civilization has advanced through mimesis while repressing the connection to nature. Horkheimer and Adorno thus twist Freud's *Civilization and Its Discontents* to account for fascist anti-Semitism. The principle of the mimetic impulse is "the absorption of the different by the same."[111] The scientific gaze that orders the world according to a process of observed regularity exemplifies the mimetic impulse in the modern period. "Science is repetition, refined into observed regularity, and preserved in stereotypes," they write.[112] Scientific reification inherently functions to stereotype—to order through classification, compartmentalization, reducing humanity to one-dimensionality. The Nazi racial state with its emphasis on mental and physical hygiene and purity is the zenith of society ordered by the technological logic of this scientific gaze.

Adorno and Horkheimer contend that anti-Semitism is "the mimesis of mimesis": "There is no anti-Semite who does not basically want to imitate his mental image of the Jew, which is composed of mimetic ciphers."[113] The anti-Semite is accordingly the mimetic double of his image of "the Jew." Every aspect of this mental image corresponds with the conscious or unconscious desires of the fascist: "The fantasies of Jewish crimes, infanticide and sadistic excess, poisoning of the nation, and international conspiracy, accurately define the anti-Semitic dream."[114] Every aspect of the image of the body of "the Jew" is the anti-Semite's own desires embodied by the Jew: the nose "the physiognomic *principium individuationis* [principle of individuation]," the smell, a "longing for the lower forms of existence, for direct unification with circumambient nature, with the earth and mud."[115] The same is the case with the voice of "the Jew," the hand gestures, all of which are mimetically reproduced by the fascist. In fact, the whole apparatus of the fascist order—the fascist formulas, the ritual discipline, and the uniforms—are the quintessence of mimetic behavior, the construction of community around "monotonous repetition." Horkheimer and Adorno explain, "This machinery needs the Jews," or "gypsies," or Blacks because our collective propensity to mimicry is so repressed that it can only be experienced through projection onto Others who personify the taboos.[116] "The screamers deliberately use the wail of the victim," Horkheimer and Adorno write, whether "Negro, [or] Jew" to "reproduce within themselves the insatiability of the power of which they are afraid."[117] In sum, Nazism detested Jews while ceaselessly imitating its stereotype of Jews.

Section 6 elaborates by exposing the deep psychology of totalitarian anti-Semitism, which functions as a paranoid projection onto "the Jew" of the narcissistic, megalomaniacal impulses that unite the hysterical and compulsive fascist masses. "Anti-Semitism is based on a false projection," Horkheimer and Adorno note in their opening line.[118] If "all perception is projection," individuals are taught to control, refine, and inhibit this. They learn through the civilizing process to distinguish their own thoughts from others, which is essential for detachment, self-consciousness, and conscience. But anti-Semitism is a special case of paranoid delusion that preempts such self-reflexivity, self-regulation, or sense of discernment: "Instead of the voice of conscience, it hears voices; instead of inwardly examining itself in order to draw up a protocol of its own lust for power, it attributes to others the Protocols of the Elders of Zion."[119] Anti-Semitism consequently results in a politics of paranoia or a paranoid politics, whereby the fascist believes that they are being persecuted by an objective enemy that is actually created by their own imagination. Most racists, Adorno and Horkheimer teach us, therefore see themselves as victims and the objects of their persecution as the persecutors.

But despite the acuity of this analysis, in the course of developing their take on fascist racism, Horkheimer and Adorno project onto women, the effeminate, and homosexuals acquiescence to the politics of paranoia, reiterating gendered stereotypes, as did Sartre.[120] Their point is that false projection cannot make distinctions between inside and outside, individual fate and the social law, appearance and essence. Individual wish thus becomes a collective fantasy.

Education and culture should preempt these projections, instructing individuals that these are delusions. But cultural education has become another facet of bourgeois property, "a commodity disseminated as information."[121] Too often people are "half-educated" (as opposed to uneducated), and fail to make connections:

> Thought becomes short winded.... The present order of life allows the self no scope to draw intellectual or spiritual conclusions. Thought, stripped down to knowledge, is neutralized, harnessed merely to qualifying its practitioner for specific labor markets and heightening the commodity value of the personality. In this way the self-reflection of the mind, which counteracts paranoia, is disabled.[122]

In the totalitarian phase of domination, delusion becomes systematized via propaganda, spoon-fed to the masses who are already primed by the culture industry. Under fascist rule, the conscience, which is the ability to take account of the true interests of others, is waylaid in the name of "blind compliance" and conformity. Here Horkheimer and Adorno anticipate Hannah Arendt's analysis of the "banality of evil." Late capitalism embroiders these values into the rhythm of daily production, "eroding the basis of moral decisions."[123]

The Jews are ready-made objects for the paranoiac projection because their image is what fascism defines itself against: "happiness without power, reward without work, a homeland without frontiers, religion without myth."[124] Emancipation from domination entails liberation of thought from power, renunciation of violence, and the recognition of Jews (and other abject subjects) as human beings. In lines that powerfully conclude the original 1944 version, Horkheimer and Adorno state: "The individual and social emancipation from domination is the countermovement to false projection, and no longer would Jews seek, by resembling it, to appease the evil senselessly visited on them as on all the persecuted, whether animals or human beings."[125]

But the acuity and panache of the phrase also reveal the place of Jews within the dialectic that Horkheimer and Adorno develop. It is precisely because "the Jews themselves have taken part in this process for thousands of years" that they become its victims. They are "the oldest surviving patriarchate... who transformed taboos into civilizing maxims when others still clung to magic... they defused magic by its own power—turned against itself as ritual service of God."[126] Jews are therefore accused of something that they "were the first to overcome: the lure of base instincts, reversion to animality and to the ground, the service of images."[127] Once again, the Jewish civilizing impulse, which is the negativity that is itself the ur-moment in the dialectic of enlightenment, is responsible for the victimization of the Jews. In short, anti-Semitism as the ultimate result of the logic of the dialectic of enlightenment and reflective of the limits of enlightenment simultaneously has its origins and its end in a Jewish impulse.

Horkheimer and Adorno's complicated argument can be reduced to its basic dialectical principles: (1) mimesis (i.e., imitation of nature for control over nature) is the central impulse of civilization; (2) Jewish civilization is at the origins of mimesis; (3) anti-Semitism is the mimesis of mimesis and the anti-Semite equals the mimetic double of his image of "the Jew." According to this dialectical logic, Jews and Judaism are fatefully linked as the starting point and the deadly outcome of mimesis. At crucial moments in the text, then, rather than critically undermine the image of "the Jew" and Judaism within Western civilization, Adorno and Horkheimer reinforce it by repeating the negative construction of Jews that facilitated their destruction.

Adorno's and the Frankfurt School's anti-anti-Semitism itself emerged out of their silence in the 1930s. When they did intervene, "the Jews," in their analysis, were caught not only between the Scylla and Charybdis of Western history and anti-Semitism, but within the double binds of Adorno and Horkheimer's own dialectical unfolding of that history. In the process of this dialectic, Jews are defined not only with a nature that is dominated but also as the "colonizers for progress"[128] and identified with dominating civilization. In the end, the aspects of Jewish tradition and Jewish history that are outside or an alternative to Western civilization are erased as "the Jew" becomes the very negativity that animates the dialectic: the principle of nonidentity itself. "The Jew" functioning as the placeholder of nonidentity is a quintessential case of the conceptual Jew: a site for thinking about the role of Jews and Judaism in history. It places Jews and Judaism at the origin and at the end of the dialectic of enlightenment, in a parallel fashion to the story that Hannah Arendt tells about the role of Jews in modernity. While certainly not anti-Semitic—indeed the point is that the conceptual move is made to think anti-Semitism—it does assign Jews to a rather damning position. Jews come to function typologically. This can have the unhappy consequence of leading to the reiteration of anti-Semitic motifs, reproducing a paranoid image of Judaism and Jews who are culpable for the pathologies that ultimately result in their victimization.

Despite these shortcomings, the Frankfurt School's various socio-psychoanalytic projects to understand anti-Semitism pioneered new approaches to the topic. At the intersection of their works, they laid out a set of novel axioms that provide a fulsome account of how anti-Semitism festers within the discontents necessarily engendered by global capitalism. While her interactionist, perspectival historicism differed significantly from the Frankfurt School, Arendt also identified how capitalist modernity fostered a ripe environment for seething Judeophobia to flourish, even as she placed far more emphasis on the place that imperialism played within this process.

CHAPTER 3

Hannah Arendt, Anti-Semitism, and Her "Story" of History

Hannah Arendt was a biting critic of existential approaches to anti-Semitism like Sartre's,[1] as well as accounts like those advanced by the Frankfurt School that emphasize psychoanalytic concepts like projection.[2] She was an even more trenchant critic of scapegoat theories, or worst of all, the notion of an eternal anti-Semitism. Each of these approaches, she claimed, misconstrues anti-Semitism because each fails to examine the intertwined history of Jews, anti-Semitism, and the Jewish Question within a more general history of modern Europe. This is what makes Arendt's approach to anti-Semitism distinctive among critical theorists: her *interactionist* understanding of it as the story of the role of Jews in relation to non-Jewish society over the course of modernity. Consequently, Arendt's most significant contribution to the theorization of anti-Semitism is her insistence on its historicization.

Since Arendt insists on history as pivotal to gaining an understanding of anti-Semitism, I examine the relationship between Arendt's theory of history as "storytelling," and the story that she tells about the history of modern anti-Semitism. Doing so reveals a number of the key guidelines of her approach to Judeophobia. Above all, Arendt derides eternalist narratives that postulate that Jews are transhistorically hated and abused. This eternalism is inherently ahistorical. Moreover, it postulates the myth of Jewish innocence and victimization in place of the comprehension Arendt insists upon, which demands an appreciation of the discontinuities and disjunctures within the history of anti-Semitism. Arendt is also critical of apologetics, causal teleology, and exceptionalist narratives (i.e., claims about the uniqueness of anti-Semitism compared to other racisms). Contra scapegoat theories, which propose that any weak or marginal group might be victimized or persecuted, Arendt insists that historicization must provide an account of why Jews are a chosen object of contempt, defamation, or destruction. In opposition to Jewish apologetics that bolster a sense of Jewish identity as a form of resistance to anti-Semitism, Arendt maintains that the purpose of writing about the history of anti-Jewish persecution is not to memorialize it, but ultimately to subvert it. In contrast to causal teleology, Arendt created a complex theory of "storytelling" as a methodology for writing such a history. In the process, akin to Sartre, she develops an approach to history that Michael Rothberg has usefully called "multidirectional" and a mode of thinking about racism that Bryan Cheyette terms "metaphorical," whereby she connects often dissimilar, but nonetheless jointed strands, linking Judeophobia to Negrophobia and genocide in Africa to the Holocaust in Europe.[3] This is clear in the three parts of *The Origins of Totalitarianism* that examine the connections between anti-Semitism, imperialism, and totalitarianism. These Arendtian precepts all disrupt and problematize exceptionalist accounts while enabling her to address the components of racism that are particular to the Jewish experience.

Unlike the Frankfurt School or Sartre, for whom Jews are a projection or construct of the anti-Semite, Arendt insists that the specific history of Jews and their interactions with non-Jews are key to understanding Judeophobia. It is this story that Arendt tells in the first third of *The Origins of Totalitarianism* that is the heart of this chapter. Reconstructing it allows us to highlight her theoretical insights about it. But it also reveals that Arendt reiterates a number of stereotypes about Jews and other imperiled groups, like Blacks and homosexuals, that emerge in the course of her larger history.

Arendt's interactionist approach inherently entails this risk of blaming the victim. But it also gives powerful agency to the ostracized and subjugated, since Arendt demands that they take responsibility for their historical fate. She is consequently engaged in a double project: at once condemning anti-Semitism and simultaneously assuming the role of the "conscious pariah" committed to an internal critique of the Jewish elite for their complicity in aiding the destruction of European Jewry.[4] Hence, in working through the story of anti-Semitism that Arendt recounts, I suggest some of what remains problematic in her account, while at the same time clarifying the acuity of her approach that proves critical in our axiological and epistemological "dark times."[5]

HER-STORY: HANNAH ARENDT IN DARK TIMES

Born in Hanover in 1906 into an "a-religious" German Jewish family that moved to Königsburg when she was three, she left home at eighteen to study theology with Rudolf Bultmann in Marburg, and philosophy with Martin Heidegger in Freiburg and with Karl Jaspers in Heidelberg.[6] Having completed her dissertation, *Der Liebersbegriff bei Augustin* (*Love and St. Augustine*, 1929), she moved to Frankfurt with her first husband, Günter (Stern) Anders, who was another of Heidegger's Jewish students.[7] Theodor Adorno rejected Stern's dissertation, dashing his hopes for a job at the University of Frankfurt, sparking a lifelong friction between Adorno and Arendt. The couple then moved to Berlin where they were soon swept into the maelstrom of Hitler's early roundups.

Triggered by the assault on European Jewry, Arendt had already begun to affirm her Jewish identity. She later famously insisted, "If one is attacked as a Jew, one must defend oneself as a Jew. Not as a German, not as a world-citizen, not as an upholder of the Rights of Man."[8] She had already been drifting toward "a Zionist critique of assimilation" in writing her *Habilitationsschrift* about Rahel Varnhagen,[9] when in spring of 1933, her friend Kurt Blumenfeld, head of the German Zionist Organization, asked her to do some illegal work documenting the Nazi's anti-Semitic activities. Returning from a day's research in the Prussian State Library, she was arrested by the Gestapo and interrogated for eight days. After her release, she and her mother fled to Paris, where Arendt worked for several Jewish agencies. In 1936, she met her soul mate: the anti-Heidegger, Heinrich Blücher, a self-educated German gentile and communist activist.

In 1940, like thousands of "enemy aliens," she and Heinrich were interned in camps. In her article "We Refugees" (January 1943), Arendt later quipped that fugitives like her were "put in concentration camps by their foes and in internment camps by their friends."[10] In the chaos of the Nazi assault on France in the summer of 1940, she escaped and found refuge with a friend in Montauban, where she reconnected with Heinrich and her mother. From there, they fled to Lisbon. They then booked passage to America, where Arendt would begin writing in Jewish journals such as *Aufbau*, *The Menorah Journal*, and *Jewish Social Studies*, slowly laying the groundwork for her masterpiece, *The Origins of Totalitarianism* (1951). It instantly became a key reference in debates about totalitarianism during the Cold War and in postwar discussions of anti-Semitism and the Holocaust. Her analysis of Adolf Eichmann, based on attending his trial in 1961, first published in the *New Yorker* and later as *Eichmann in Jerusalem: A Report on the Banality of Evil* (1963), was far more controversial and helped ignite key debates in the emerging field of Holocaust studies.[11]

If *Origins* and *Eichmann* defined her early acclaim, by the time of her death in 1975, Arendt was read more as a political theorist, exemplified in her books *The Human Condition* (1958) and *On Revolution* (1963), rather than by the issues considered in *The Origins of Totalitarianism*.[12] But starting with Ron H. Feldman's 1978 collection of Arendt's Jewish essays, *The Jew as Pariah*, and followed by Elisabeth Young-Bruehl's magisterial biography, *Hannah Arendt: For Love of the World* (1982), a new generation of scholars came to appreciate the depth and breadth of Arendt's engagement with Jewish history, Zionism, the State of Israel, and anti-Semitism, and to debate Arendt's understanding of these issues.[13] The same period gave rise to Shiraz Dossa's 1980 essay, "Human Status and Politics: Hannah Arendt on the Holocaust," which raised the "ethnocentric strain" in Arendt's thought by considering how she parroted primitivism in her depictions of colonized sub-Saharan Africans in *The Origins of Totalitarianism*.[14] Central to this charge was Arendt's reading of Joseph Conrad's *Heart of Darkness*, a work famously indicted as racist by Chinua Achebe, but that Arendt claims in contrast "is the most illuminating work on actual race experience in Africa."[15] George Kateb's brief account "On Racism in Africa" in his *Hannah Arendt* quashed Dossa's insight by insisting that Arendt did not share European colonial and racial attitudes; she merely sought to describe the effects of racism.[16] Kateb thereby inaugurated what has emerged as an ongoing quandary in treatments of Arendt's writing: how to pull apart her descriptions of others' work from her own perspective.

The 1990s saw a deepening rift around these interpretative issues. Anne Norton pointed not only to Arendt's attitudes toward Africans, but toward African American activists in her "Reflections on Little Rock," as further evidence of Arendt's deprecation of Blacks.[17] In the article, Arendt decried the public legislation of social discrimination that was the foundation of Jim Crow segregation. But she insisted that children should not bear the burden of correcting the "original crime in America's history," and maintained that forced integration of schools was wrong. She also defended states' rights as an important principle since it is core to the checks and balances of American republicanism.[18] In her letter responding to the critics of her article, she speaks to Black parents in a superior tone that anticipated the row caused by her haughtiness in *Eichmann in Jerusalem*, the text that remains a lightning rod in critiques of Arendt's views on Jews.[19] Agreeing with Dossa and Norton about Arendt's views of Blacks was Hannah Pitkin, who stated that Arendt "simply shares the European prejudice against so-called primitive culture as somehow less cultured or more natural—in a pejorative sense—than the European."[20] Seyla Benhabib's response to these charges was similar to Kateb's, indicating that these claims about her prejudices were reductive of Arendt's views.[21] Benhabib's defense of Arendt appeared amid a new wave of works depicting her as a paragon of the experience of German Jewish Weimar intellectuals who became permanent exiles after the rise of National Socialism.[22]

More recently, a slate of postcolonial theorists, historians, and some critical philosophers of race have moved beyond the dichotomies of earlier Arendt scholarship, recognizing the shortcomings of her work, but nonetheless deploying *The Origins of Totalitarianism* as a site for connecting the histories of anti-Semitism, racism, imperialism, Nazism, and genocide.[23] It is not surprising to find these shifts in the reception of her oeuvre, if Ernst Gellner's insight about Arendt as "a parable, not just of our age, but of several centuries of European thought and experience" is apposite.[24] According to Gellner's reading of Arendt, her story is an allegory of the Enlightenment and the Romantic reaction, a moral fable of the strictures entailed by Jewish emancipation and its entwinement in modern European history. Arendt's story is about someone who not only personally experienced that history, but who tried to comprehend its significance as "the burden of our time."[25]

Arendt would have appreciated the depiction of her life as a parable of both German Jewish and modern European history not only because this was at the heart of her understanding of anti-Semitism but because in her own biographical essays she constructed the individual and her-story as a hinge that might open the meaning of the past to consideration and confrontation in the present. In *Men in Dark Times*, Arendt holds, "It is rather as though the colorless light of historical time were forced through and refracted by the prism of a great character so that in the resulting spectrum a complete unity of life and world is achieved."[26] Taking this to the metalevel, in *The Human Condition*, she suggests, "That every individual life between birth and death can eventually be told as a story with beginning and end is the prepolitical and prehistoric condition of history, the great story without beginning and end."[27]

HANNAH ARENDT'S METHODOLOGY: HISTORY AS "STORYTELLING"

The story of Arendt's methodological contributions to understanding the past is seldom highlighted because she felt that such disclosure was self-indulgent and irrelevant to contemporary political problems, which were consistently the priority of her thought.[28] As such, those scholars who have developed her thought on this question have done so in order to extrapolate the fecundity of her approach for political theory. But just as Arendt's *Origins* has become pivotal to understanding her political theory, appreciating Arendt's historical methodology is central to fully comprehending *The Origins of Totalitarianism*.[29] For Arendt, writing the history of totalitarianism and its elements poses unique methodological problems.[30] She explicitly says of anti-Semitism that historians "had to write the history of a subject which they did not want to conserve; they had to write in a destructive way and to write history for purposes of destruction," which "is somehow a contradiction in terms."[31]

The way out of this dilemma was often to examine the events from the viewpoint of the victims, which for Arendt has "resulted in apologetics," which she derisively states "is no history at all."[32] Given her rejection of victimology and apologetic approaches to the history of Judeophobia, Arendt spurns conventional historiography in favor of what she calls "storytelling." She is critical of any historical determinism that posits laws of development in history, especially those predicated upon class or race as the keys to history, which she sees as part of the latent logic that resulted in the disasters of the twentieth century. She condemns causality as the deduction of the unprecedented from precedents. She critiques analogic thinking as the reduction of the dissimilar to sameness.[33] And she derides universalization from particular examples as the seed of ideological thinking.[34] Rather, inspired most profoundly by both Walter Benjamin and Heidegger, Arendt conceives of history as the weaving of discrete stories by the historian attempting to comprehend events. The historian is a storyteller who rescues the past from oblivion, illuminating the dark times of human existence with meaning-making narratives.

While never elaborated systematically, Arendt's theoretical and methodological assumptions about history are widely dispersed in her work. The most condensed statement of her approach is her "Reply" to Eric Voegelin's review of *The Origins of Totalitarianism* in January 1953. Voegelin read *The Origins of Totalitarianism* as a chronological, causal history that describes the origins of the transformation of nation-state societies into the superfluous masses of modernity who form both the populist base of totalitarian movements and their brutal victims.[35] In Arendt's reply to Voegelin, she repudiates the title of her book, signifying the differences between her approach to history and its depiction in Voegelin's review: "The book... does not really deal with the 'origins' of totalitarianism—as its title unfortunately claims—but gives a historical account of the elements which crystallized into totalitarianism."[36]

Arendt's reply argues that the *origins* in her title does not accurately represent her practice if what is implied by "origins" is an evolutionary narrative about causally related events. She makes this point clearly in a draft for her essay "Understanding and Politics," where she writes that "the elements of totalitarianism form its origins if by origins we do not understand 'causes.'... Elements by themselves never cause anything. They become origins of events if and when they suddenly crystallize into fixed and definitive forms."[37] She decries causal history because it arranges what she provocatively calls "phenomenal differences" (i.e., what are more commonly referred to as facts) into a narrative of "essential sameness."[38] Causal history is built on explaining what is new or "original" through analogies and chains of previously understood causes and influences.[39] Thus, for Arendt "causality is... [a] falsifying category in the historical sciences. Not only does the actual meaning of every event always transcend any number of past 'causes' which we may assign to it... this past itself comes into being only with the event itself.... The event illuminates its own past; it can never be deduced from it."[40]

There are other ways of conceiving of "origins," however, that are important to understanding Arendt's approach, the first deriving from the fragmentary historiography of Benjamin and the second from the *Ursprungsphilosophie* of Heidegger.[41] Arendt's debt to Benjamin is made clear in the following passage from her introduction to the volume *Illuminations* that she edited in English and that includes his "Theses on History," which were part of the cache of manuscripts given to her to preserve just before Benjamin's suicide at Portbou on the night of September 25, 1940:

> Like a pearl diver who descends to the bottom of the sea, not to excavate the bottom and bring it to light but to pry loose the rich and the strange, the pearls and the coral in the depths, and to carry them to the surface, this

thinking [of Benjamin] delves into the depths of the past—but not in order to resuscitate it to the way it was and to contribute to the renewal of extinct ages. What guides this thinking is the conviction that although the living is subject to the ruin of time, the process of decay is at the same time a process of crystallization, that in the depth of the sea, into which sinks and is dissolved what once was alive, some things "suffer a sea-change" and survive in new crystallized forms and shapes that remain immune to the elements, as though they waited only for the pearl diver who one day will come down to them and bring them up into the world of the living—as "thought fragments," as something "rich and strange," and perhaps even as everlasting *Urphäenomene*.[42]

In this version of the search for origins qua *Urphäenomene*, the historian's task is to reveal those crystallized elements of the past that will illuminate the present because as thought fragments they enable us to apprehend what has past and help to orient us to what may befall us in the future.

The search for origins as *Urphäenomene* is also evident in what Arendt borrows from Heidegger. Heidegger's *Destruktion* of the Western metaphysical tradition depended upon a radical hermeneutics that sought to uncover the original meaning of philosophical categories by unconcealing them from their historically constructed and distorting encrustations. In Arendt's method of writing history as a configuration of etiological tales,[43] there is a poesis to storytelling that enables history to reveal the "inner truth of the event."[44] In this version of history-as-storytelling, the task of the historian is to uncover a crystalline point in the past that serves as a hinge to open the present to questioning its own foundations.

In accord with both the Heideggerian and Benjaminian notions of history, Arendt is critical of Enlightenment and Hegelian notions of historical *progress* as necessary and determined by a causal process, as well as historical narratives whose *telos* is determined by a story of inevitable *decline* or destruction.[45] In the preface to the first edition of *Origins*, she warns that "progress and Doom are two sides of the same medal."[46] Since historical writing must preserve the contingency of history, what requires understanding is precisely the disparity between cause and effect in history. A multiplicity of stories that are mutually exclusive can account for the same event.[47] In short, Arendt suggests that historical meaning is always underdetermined because historical events are overdetermined.[48]

In her reply to Voegelin, Arendt further argues that the epistemological considerations she has raised about the writing of history have another side that "presents itself as a problem of 'style.'"[49] Under the rubric of "style," Arendt raises three interrelated problems with the historiographical tradition: the problem of objectivity, the importance of locution, and the form and content of the historical narrative.

Arendt dismisses the pursuit of objectivity as a noble dream for historians of anti-Semitism and racism: "I parted quite consciously with the tradition of *sine ira et studio* of whose greatness I was fully aware, and to me this was a methodological necessity closely connected with my particular subject matter," she states.[50] In her essay "The Concept of History: Ancient and Modern," she elaborates on why she attacks detachment. Objectivity, she explains, was developed as the gold standard in the Rankean approach to history: "Objectivity [meant] the 'extinction of the self' as the condition of 'pure vision' (*das reine Sehen der Dinge*—Ranke) [and it] meant the historian's abstention from bestowing either praise or blame, together with an attitude of perfect distance with which he would follow the course of events as they were revealed in the documentary sources."[51] The conditions of objectivity—elimination of the knowing subject and a refusal to judge the past—are built on the separation of fact and value. But blind adherence to facts is meaningless without an axiology that gives it significance and condemnation of racism is intrinsic to its evaluation and destruction. Arendt thus dismisses what, following Droysen, she calls "eunuchic-objectivity" in favor of an approach to history built on impartiality.

Impartiality, she maintains, began with Homer singing the praises of the Trojans no less than the Achaeans, reached its apotheosis with Greek historians like Thucydides and Herodotus, and "is still the highest type of objectivity we know."[52] Arendtian "impartiality" resists the abstract, neutral, "objective" view of history from everywhere and nowhere in favor of storytelling from a committed ethical and political perspective. Lisa Ditsch has provocatively called "this critical vantage point, not from outside but from within the plurality of contesting standpoints, . . . 'situated impartiality,'" after Donna Haraway's "situated knowledges."[53] Situated impartiality built upon Arendt's concept of plurality, which rests upon the notion that "the world we have in common is usually regarded from an infinite number of different standpoints, to which correspond the most diverse points of view.[54] The insistence on a multiplicity of perspectives in and on history enables one to judge history not from the "eunuchic" detachment of the Rankean historian, but like an umpire in the heat of the game.[55] The result is a history that aims not at the "objective" truth of the past, but at a situated perspective that enables the historian to write a history that facilitates looking upon the same world from another's standpoint,[56] recreating the world as it appeared to others, thus putting the reader in others' shoes (which is not the same as putting yourself in the Other's shoes).

The tone of Arendt's writing is also different from the neutral and "objective" language of more traditional historical narrators. She embraces passion and commitment in historical narratives.[57] She uses emotionally and ethically loaded language to express outrage and moral condemnation. She insists on thinking against the grain, wanting to discomfort her readers, pointing beyond conventional thinking.[58] Through writing rich in metaphoric resonance, through the use of oxymoronic expressions like "death factory" to describe the death camps, and through hyperbole and irony, Arendt searches for an idiom that matches the object of her analysis.[59] She maintains that "to describe the concentration camps *sine ira* is not to be 'objective' but to condone them"[60] and furthermore "that a description of the camps as hell on earth is [actually] more 'objective.'"[61]

Both the form and content of Arendt's style of writing history are innovative. Her focus on the fragmentation of the past results in a methodology that emphasizes rupture and discontinuity. Perhaps the most well-known example of this is her insistence on the radical disjuncture between political anti-Semitism and religious Jew-hatred in the opening line to her preface to the section on "Antisemitism."[62] She also emphasizes discontinuities between colonialism and imperialism and race thinking and racism.[63] Dismissing what Lyotard would later call "metanarratives," she concentrates on retelling *petites histoires*.[64] These stories are made up of the lives and works and quotations of individuals enmeshed in "dark times."[65] But she is wary of any practice of storytelling whose narrative is structured by a teleological or eschatological endpoint because this fails to preserve the indeterminacy of historical actors and of historians in the present. In the case of anti-Semitism, Arendt sought to comprehend racism pre-Auschwitz without falling into the trap of recounting how the story she tells inevitably leads to the Holocaust.

Hence, rather than presenting a conventional historical narrative that begins with the purported origins of the historical event at some point in the past, Arendt's historical writing re-presents a mobile of individual stories that help describe and analyze the past.[66] She uses the stories of individuals like Rahel

Varnhagen or Adolf Eichmann, and events like the Dreyfus affair to illuminate various breaks in the past. She also uses fiction like Conrad, Kipling, and Proust as important evidence of different historical junctures. Individual aphorisms and events are taken as distillations of pivotal stages in a historical configuration. David Luban has described the pastiche produced by Arendt's microhistories as kaleidoscopic, revealing crystallizing and dissipating patterns.[67]

Arendt's metahistorical critique of Archimedean thinking was extended in her work to a critique of the Western metaphysical tradition. This is how she closes her unfinished last book, *The Life of the Mind*:

> I have clearly joined the ranks of those who for some time now have been attempting to dismantle metaphysics and philosophy with all its categories, as we have known them from their beginning in Greece until today. Such dismantling is possible only on the assumption that the thread of tradition is broken and that we shall not be able to renew it.... What you then are left with is still the past, but a *fragmented* past, which has lost its certainty of evaluation.[68]

In Arendt's hands, history as a story told in the gap between past and present becomes pivotal to the dismantling of a tradition permanently damaged "after Auschwitz."[69] Arendt substitutes for Hegel's owl of Minerva the image of Penelope's weaving, where what is thought historically consistently needs to be rethought:[70] "The business of thinking is like the veil of Penelope: it undoes every morning what it had finished the night before."[71]

Arendt's approach is thus neither objectivism nor relativism, neither a historicism nor a presentism, but a plural and perspectival approach to history that seeks to recreate the past as a shared world where the historian should never re-present only one view on that past. Historical events are made by a plurality of individual stories that form a complex matrix of meaning. Since Arendt insists on multiple perspectives (both within events and in reflecting on events) there are also many versions of historical truth. Therefore, situated impartiality is neither objectivity nor relativism precisely because it depends upon "perspectival differences [being] raised, contested, and situated in reference to each other."[72]

Arendt's approach to history is also critical of the "politicization of memory" that Lyotard has called the "memorialization of the past."[73] As Seyla Benhabib has argued, what is foregrounded in her analysis is "the *politics of memory* and the *morality of historiography.*"[74] Arendt presciently helps us to theorize a perspectival approach to history as "storytelling" and offers us multiple exemplary exercises in this approach to the past. Arendtian history as storytelling analyzes individuals, memorials, anecdotes, concepts, incidents, and institutions. She practices a *Begriffsgeschichte*[75] that locates instances of rupture in the past in order to rethink through remembering, using the ruins of the past as the shards of history that enable us to forge the weapons of thought in the present. Arendtian storytelling thus makes history a praxis "whose purpose is not to defend abstract principles or objective facts but to tell provocative stories that invite contestation from rival perspectives."[76] The ambiguous space of historical writing thus serves to encourage permanent contestation and reinterpretation that make situated impartiality and plurality possible to begin with.[77]

ARENDT'S STORY OF MODERN ANTI-SEMITISM

Having elucidated Arendt's metahistorical assumptions in light of her response to Eric Voegelin's reading of *Origins*, in what remains of this chapter, I focus on the narrative that opens *Origins* and how it threads through the rest of the book: Arendt's story of modern anti-Semitism. Here, I examine what in Arendt's text entitles Voegelin's reading. Or put differently, I show that the story of modern Jewish history that Arendt tells provides the glue that binds together *Origins*. At the same time, I underscore how appreciating Arendt's methodology is key to understanding the history of anti-Semitism that Arendt tells. Read in light of her theory of storytelling, her narrative of anti-Semitism as it shifted over the course of modernity proves to be at once a complex and ambiguous, sometimes troubling, account.

Clearly Voegelin understood origins, causes, and the relation of the parts of the book to the whole differently from Arendt. But his brief interpretation of her multifaceted, hybridized text is quite acute, even though as a review it only emphasizes the central strand in her tapestry of stories. He opens his article by stating that *Origins* "is an attempt to make contemporary phenomena intelligible by tracing their origin back to the eighteenth century."[78] Voegelin thus suggests that Arendt's work is a genealogy of totalitarianism, anticipating Foucault's deployment of this Nietzschean methodology, since its point of departure is a history of the present. He argues that while the three parts of the text are roughly chronological, they overlap in time:

> Anti-Semitism begins to rear its head in the Age of Enlightenment; the imperialist expansion and the pan-movements reach from the middle of the nineteenth century to the present; and the totalitarian movements belong to the twentieth century. The sequence is, furthermore, an order of increasing intensity and ferocity in the growth of totalitarian features toward the climax in the atrocities of the concentration camps.[79]

He indicates quite rightly that the center that animates Arendt's discussion is the destruction of European Jewry.

Voeglin proceeds to elucidate the governing theme as the rise and fall of the nation-state in the nineteenth century until its virtual dissolution created the mass society of the twentieth century. With every transformation, new sections of society become superfluous and their legal, social, and economic status is therefore threatened: centralization of the nation-state and the rise of bureaucracy makes the aristocracy superfluous; growth of industrialization and new sources of revenue makes Jews as bankers superfluous; every industrial crisis creates superfluous human beings through unemployment. In the twentieth century, and still today, wars and totalitarian regimes create millions of refugees, which Arendt called the "stateless": those who were unmoored from their communities by the processes of modernity and war, becoming what Georgio Agamben terms "bare life," the rightless "scum" whose only logical place ultimately became the internment and slave labor of the concentration camps, which are the laboratories of "total domination."[80]

Arendt brilliantly showed that fascism and communism were a new form of tyranny fostered by an atomized, alienated mass society. Totalitarian regimes organized the masses through the cult of the leader and the civic religion of the movement. For those not entranced by the propaganda, there was the terror of the secret police and the camps, coupled to the demonization of the enemy. Imperialism was the training ground for total domination, creating the bureaucratic methods of new forms of rule beyond the bounds of the nation-state, where racism replaced citizenship, marking those included from those excluded. Inside Europe, the imperial order also marked the shift from the anti-Semitism of the nineteenth century, which soldered together national identity, to the imperialist anti-Semitism of pan-Germanism and pan-Slavism that was the heartbeat of totalitarian anti-Semitism as a political ideology. The sections on "Antisemitism" and "Imperialism" are the necessary, although not sufficient conditions, for the future synchronic structure of "Totalitarianism," which is what Arendt ultimately sought to comprehend. Voegelin even insightfully suggests that Arendt's method is best likened to Thucydides, who also spans an arc "from the presently moving events to their origins,"[81] and whose impartiality Arendt so admired.

The arc covered in Arendt's book seeks to understand what on the surface appears to her as an enigma: "It must be possible to face and understand the outrageous fact that so small (and, in world politics, so unimportant) a phenomenon as the Jewish question and anti-Semitism could become the catalytic agent for first, the Nazi movement, then a world war, and finally the establishment of death factories."[82] The story of modern Jewish history thus proves to be the innermost story of the twentieth century. The book is consequently an attempt to comprehend the incomprehensible: how the Jewish Question emerged as the central pivot of modern European history and an elemental basis of totalitarianism.[83]

In chapter 1, "Anti-Semitism as an Outrage to Common Sense," Arendt laid down her critique of the scapegoat theory, apologetics, and eternal anti-Semitism. In contrast, she presents her own thesis that it is the history of the Jews' relation to the nation-state that is the basis of anti-Semitism in the nineteenth century. As such, her approach is *interactionist*. In accord with her metahistory, she suggests that the so-called Jewish problem constitutes a reversal of cause and effect and as such was as an outrage to common sense:

> There is hardly an aspect of contemporary history more irritating and mystifying than the fact that of all the great unsolved political questions of our century, it should have been this seemingly small and unimportant Jewish problem that had the dubious honor of setting the whole infernal machine in motion. Such discrepancies between cause and effect outrage our common sense, to say nothing of the historian's sense of balance and harmony. Compared with the events themselves, all explanations of anti-Semitism look as if they had been hastily and hazardously contrived, to cover up an issue which so gravely threatens our sense of proportion and our hope for sanity.[84]

Three approaches to dealing with anti-Semitism have masked this outrageous history more than others: the scapegoat theory, apologetics, and eternal anti-Semitism.

Arendt refutes the scapegoat theory because it implies that there could have been another scapegoat and thereby denies the particular history that resulted in the persecution and extermination of Jews. In a good example of her argumentative style, she derides scapegoat theories with a joke that functions as a reductio ad absurdum: "An antisemite claimed that the Jews had caused the war; the reply was: Yes, the Jews and the bicyclists. Why the bicyclists? asks the one. Why the Jews? asks the other."[85] She maintains that whenever one tries to explain something by the scapegoat theory one must begin to reconstruct the historical events, leaving behind the scapegoat in its abstraction, and one becomes "involved in the usual historical research—where nothing is ever discovered except that history is made by many groups and that for certain reasons one group was singled out." In addition to its inherent ahistoricism, Arendt also repudiates the scapegoat theory because "it upholds the perfect innocence of the victim," in this case making the Jewish scapegoat blameless, which thereby "discharges the victim of responsibility."[86]

Scapegoat theories have their historiographic parallel in the apologetic tenor of much scholarship on anti-Semitism. The field of the study of anti-Semitism, Arendt maintains, is largely reactionary, spurred in response to the new forms of Judeophobia that have emerged in different periods: "It was Jewish historiography, with its strong polemical and apologetical bias," she writes, "that undertook to trace the record of Jew-hatred in Christian history, while it was left to the anti-Semites to trace an intellectually not too dissimilar record."[87] There are two takeaways from this quote. First, Arendt highlights the emotional passion connected to the identity politics that underpin the polemics in so much work in the field. In a lengthy unpublished manuscript, "Antisemitism," that served as a draft for the section in *Origins*, she explicitly called out two schools of Jewish historiography for their apologetics: assimilationists and nationalists. Assimilationist apologetics insist that Jews were no different from all others, except religiously, and so turn the story of Jews into a "*history of the injustice* inflicted on us," emphasizing how Jews, despite their maltreatment, contributed to the culture and institutional life of the places where they found themselves.[88] Zionists, on the other hand, insist that Jews were racially different from those they lived among, "*foreign* to and despised by that other people on the basis of its inalterable substance."[89] Both of these approaches fail to adequately account for Jewish identity because they downplay the wide divergences among Jews and differing Jewish interests. They consequently also downplay the interactions between Jews and non-Jews as a precipitating factor in Judeophobia. As a result, "both types of Jewish historiography are characterized by their inability to come to terms with *antisemitism*."[90]

Arendt's second takeaway is connected to her broader skewering of eternal antisemitism. All eternalist accounts reinforce the anti-Semitic narrative that Jews are despised everywhere they have lived; if this is so, it buttresses the essential claim of anti-Semites that there must be something endemic in the Jews or Jewish culture that has led to this aversion. Eternal anti-Semitism naturalizes anti-Jewish hate, making it "a normal and natural reaction to which history gives only more or less opportunity."[91] This transhistorical claim is, therefore, actually unhistorical. As noted in the introduction, eternal anti-Semitism answers the question "why the Jews?" with the question-begging reply, "eternal hostility."[92] It is thus tautological and essentializing. But Arendt suggests that Jews nonetheless use eternal anti-Semitism as a means of cohering Jewish identity, since at the same moment as anti-Semitism arose, Jews were threatened from without and from within and anti-Semitism emerged as a way to keep Jews together.[93] Eternal anti-Semitism paradoxically enables both anti-Semites and Jews to remain blameless for anti-Semitism by making themselves into victims in their shared narrative. What ties together Arendt's critique of the scapegoat theory, apologetics, and eternal anti-Semitism is the failure of Jews to take political responsibility for their situation within modern European history. Thus, inspired by Salo Baron's critique of Jewish history as a "lachrymose" history, Arendt rejected eternalist narratives.[94]

This becomes clearer when Arendt articulates her interactionist understanding of modern anti-Semitism. Her core thesis is clear: "Modern antisemitism must be seen in the more general framework of the development of the nation-state, and at the same time its source must be found in certain aspects of Jewish history and specifically in Jewish functions during the last centuries."[95] It was for both theoretical and empirical reasons, then, that Arendt suggested that the origins of anti-Semitism must be understood in the patterns of Jewish history, which her following chapters sketch.

In chapter 2, "The Jews, the Nation-State, and the Birth of Antisemitism," Arendt locates the source of modern anti-Semitism in the underlying double binds at the origin of debates about citizenship and Jewish emancipation (i.e., Jewish equal civil rights). There are two aspects to Arendt's argument. First, she maintains that there are latent tensions between nation and state in the notion of the nation-state. These strains became manifest in the equivocality of Jewish emancipation:

> At the height of its development in the nineteenth century, the nation state granted its Jewish inhabitants equality of rights. Deeper, older and more fateful contradictions are hidden behind the abstract and palpable inconsistency that Jews received their citizenship from governments which in the process of centuries had made nationality a prerequisite for citizenship and homogeneity of population the outstanding characteristic of the body politic.[96]

Zygmunt Bauman astutely rearticulated this Arendtian argument, explaining that the nation-state order established in modern Europe "involved political powers waging cultural crusades against ethnic minorities, regional customs and local dialects, so that the myth of national self-sameness could be made into the legitimizing formula of political powers. Into this Europe of . . . nation-states . . . Jews did not fit . . . [since they were] a non-national nation, and so cast a shadow on the fundamental principle of modern European order."[97]

Drawing from her own experience of statelessness, Arendt elaborates this point in chapter 9, "The Decline of the Nation-State and the End of the Rights of Man." She explains that the rights of citizens and the rule of law depended upon belonging to a nation. Human rights were unenforceable separate from citizenship. Therefore, if states purged certain citizens or when states disintegrated, as they did during the wars of the twentieth century, and as they continue to do today, the stateless are relegated to the status of undesirables. Statelessness thus became "the newest mass phenomenon in contemporary history,"[98] highlighting the ongoing problem of "a right to have rights."[99] Arendt underlines that both as a national minority "and in the formation of stateless people, Jews have played a significant role . . . as the *minorité par excellence.*"[100]

While Arendt's point is an insightful critique of the liberal, rights-based tradition that was the foundation of Jewish emancipation, the second aspect of her narrative is more troubling. In a sweeping historical account, she maintains that Jewish rights were always purchased at a price. It was Jewish finance from the seventeenth century that was central to the development of the nation-state, starting with the pivotal role played by the court Jews and later by Jewish bankers and financiers. While her narrative has the merit of conferring Jews with agency in their civil rights struggle, Arendt also ends up recycling an image of the "Rothschild Jew" prevalent in the nineteenth century.[101] But her key claim is perceptive: that "emancipation of the Jews, therefore, as granted by the national state system in Europe during the nineteenth century, had a double origin and an ever-present equivocal meaning."[102] Arendt's elucidation of this "double origin" and "equivocal meaning" constitutes the ambivalent causal factor that runs through her story of modern anti-Semitism. In this story, there is a consistent interplay in the relationship of the Jewish community to the state. It is determined by privileges bought for financial favors granted by the state that in turn aided state development. The result was the simultaneous waning of Jewish communal life and the rise of wealthy Jewish individuals as the nation-state declined and the imperialist order replaced it.

Arendt clearly outlines the four phases of her story. First, in the seventeenth and eighteenth century, the nation-state developed under absolute monarchs with the financial aid of court Jews. Second, after the French Revolution the nation-state required far more capital, which individuals could no longer provide. This necessitated the combined wealth of western and central European Jewry in the form of Jewish bankers. This assistance of the Jewish community was then rewarded with the privileges of emancipation being extended from a few privileged individuals to the community as a whole. The third phase is characterized by the decline of the nation-state and the rise of imperialist capitalist development. Imperialism marked the transition from the nation-state's domination of power to its domination by capital interests, which were no longer linked to the Jewish community. As Jewish communal wealth became superfluous, political anti-Semitism rose, since Jews were increasingly regarded as "the power behind the power."[103] The Jews served as a universal target of hatred because of their prior identity with the state and financial capitalism. All social groups at odds with the state or distressed by capitalist transformation turned their wrath on the Jews: "Jews became the symbols of Society as such and the objects of hatred for all those whom society did not accept."[104] In the fourth and final stage, Jews declined as a group in the period before World War I. This decline was characterized by Jewish atomization "into a herd of wealthy individuals." As a result, "the non-national, inter-European Jewish element became an object of universal hatred because of its useless wealth, and of contempt because of its lack of power."[105]

In this socioeconomic and political history of anti-Semitism in the nineteenth century, Jews were doubly burdened: both cause and effect of their oppression. Jews were benefactors of the drive toward equality and assimilation and victims of their own separation and exclusion, caught between the underprivileged and overprivileged, positioned between what Arendt terms, after Bernard Lazare and Max Weber, the "pariah" and the "parvenu." The ambivalent position of Jews also corresponds to two types of anti-Semitism that Arendt distinguishes—social discrimination and political anti-Semitism. The first is caused by the growing equality of Jews with all other groups and the second is caused by the ongoing legacy of Jewish separatism and difference. Political anti-Semitism was a reaction against Jewish legal equality, while social discrimination is a function of the liberal failure to achieve genuine political emancipation. Arendt never believed social discrimination could be eliminated; it was part of her reticence about the role of the state in Black integration in cases like Little Rock. But social discrimination was wholly different from the political anti-Semitism that arose in the imperial age when a new kind of "tribal nationalism" emerged with exterminationist tendencies that were a product of the orchestrated fantasies embodied by totalitarian ideology.[106]

If Arendt's chapter on the nation-state and the origin of anti-Semitism focuses on the political and socioeconomic factors that account for exclusionary, nationalist anti-Semitism, chapter 3, "The Jews and Society" is a cultural history of the Jewish condition in the modern period. It is an effort to uncover and assess the *mentalités* and cultural meanings that were accorded to Jewish assimilation and that haunted that process throughout modern European history. This is encapsulated in the strictures between pariah and parvenu. The modern Jewish situation produced a complex psychology that was tied to the ambiguities of assimilation: "Jews felt simultaneously the pariah's regret at not having become a parvenu and the parvenu's bad conscience at having betrayed his people and exchanged equal rights for personal privileges." Based on these antinomies, anti-Semites would construct the "'Jew in general,' 'the Jew everywhere and nowhere' with those qualities which the parvenu must acquire if he wants to arrive—inhumanity, greed, insolence, cringing servility, and determination to push ahead."[107]

As in Arendt's story of Rahel Varnhagen, whose last chapter was titled, "One Does Not Escape Jewishness," and her article on "The Jew as Pariah," she plumbs deeply the double binds of the project of emancipation, where even culturally integrated Jews were to maintain the appeal of their Jewishness:[108] "Jews were exhorted to be educated enough not to behave like ordinary Jews, but they were, on the on the other hand, accepted only because they were Jews, because of their foreign, exotic appeal."[109] Thus, Arendt conjoins her analysis of the precarious balance between society and state upon which the nation-state rested (depicted in chapter 2 and chapter 9) to the individual situation of Jews who were integrating. This meant "they always had to pay with political misery for social glory and with social insult for political success."[110] On an individual level, this meant mastering the paradoxical process of knowing "how to play the role of what one actually was."[111]

This playing-at-being-yourself underpins modern Jewish identity.[112] In a wonderful example of how Arendt explores a widespread social phenomenon that she wants to bring to light, the paradoxes of assimilation are crystallized in her reading of the quotation "to 'be a man in the street and a Jew at home'" from Judah Leib Gordon's Hebrew poem "Hakitzah 'ami" ("Awake, My People!"), which she takes as a "motto of assimilation." "This actually amounted to a feeling of being different from other men in the street because they were Jews, and different from other Jews at home because they were not like 'ordinary Jews,'" Arendt writes.[113] As Steven Aschheim has so aptly put it, while she "knew very little about the body of Judaism itself, [Arendt] was the great explicator of 'Jewishness' and its psychological machinations. She highlighted its ambivalences, multiple loyalties, fissures, breakdowns, and partial reconstitutions."[114]

According to Arendt, the result of the paradoxes of assimilation was a Jewish type, defined psychologically, rather than nationally or religiously, "the sum total of which was supposed to constitute 'Jewishness.' In other words, Judaism became a psychological quality and the Jewish question became an involved personal problem for every individual Jew."[115] It was this step from Judaism to Jewishness that made possible the next step to seeing Jewishness as a vice. As she had in her book on Rahel Varnhagen, Arendt decried assimilation as a vicious myth: "In a society on the whole hostile to the Jews—and that situation obtained in all countries in which Jews lived, down to the twentieth century—it is possible to assimilate only by assimilating to anti-Semitism also."[116] As micronarratives that illuminate this process, Arendt offers two examples in *Origins*: her section on Disraeli entitled "The Potent Wizard" and "Between Vice and Crime" that focuses on Proust.

Arendt uses Disraeli as her example of how race became the basis of Jewish identity in the context of Jewish secularization and assimilation (i.e., where there is no longer a shared religion, national identity, or memory of a common destiny for many Jews). She quotes extensively from Disraeli's own propagation of racialist discourse to show that Disraeli's "secularized self-representation as a 'chosen man of the chosen race' foreshadowed and outlined the lines along which Jewish self-interpretation was to take place," which crisscrossed anti-Semitic and racial lines.[117] Arendt sought to underscore how by the end of the nineteenth century, modern racism was rearticulating Jewish identity from religious into racial categories. This was the case among both Jews and non-Jews. In drawing from Disraeli's statements to make the case, Arendt emphasized how this was a product of an interactionist history.

The fin de siècle would mark the shift from exceptional Jews to ordinary Jews as objects of abject fascination.[118] The salons of Faubourg Saint-Germain illustrate her point about Jewish relations within the fin de siècle, which were the roots of "the Nazi brand of anti-Semitism."[119] This time it is Marcel Proust's account of Swann, Charlus, and the Guermantes in *Remembrance of Things Past* that illuminates this social world. Proust was like a prism, reflecting and refracting the transformations of the period. "Both Jewish and Catholic, neither one nor the other or perhaps both simultaneously," Julia Kristeva notes, "[Proust was] destined to live through the historical events that overwhelmed the turn of the century—the Dreyfus Affair and the First World War."[120] Proust's ambivalence made him an icon of the era for Arendt. She maintains that the fin de siècle marked a time of transition from the crime of Judaism, signified in Christian thought and practice by deicide and the Jews as the embodiment of the anti-Christ, into the racial vice of Jewishness. "As far as the Jews were concerned," writes Arendt, "the transformation of the 'crime' of Judaism into the fashionable 'vice' of Jewishness was dangerous in the extreme. Jews had been able to escape from Judaism into conversion; from Jewishness there was no escape. A crime, moreover, is met with punishment; a vice can only be exterminated."[121]

Proust was an example of the great vices of the period: "the greatest witness of dejudaized Judaism," she notes, he represented not only the racial vice of Jewishness but also the sexual vice of homosexuality.[122] Presciently, Arendt makes much of the overlaps between the sexual and the racial Other. The vice of Jewishness and the vice of homosexuality are compared to one another, where their reflection and individual reconsideration became very much alike indeed. What Eve

Kosovsky Sedgwick has called "the epistemology of the closet"[123] applies for Arendt equally to the racialized category of Jewishness and the sexualized category of what she calls "inverts":

> The complicated game of exposure and concealment, of half-confessions and lying distortions, of exaggerated humility and exaggerated arrogance, all of which were consequences of the fact that only one's Jewishness (or homosexuality) had opened the doors of the exclusive salons, which at the same time had made one's position extremely insecure. In this equivocal situation, Jewishness was for the individual Jew at once a physical stain and a mysterious personal privilege, both inherent in a "racial predestination."[124]

Arendt suggests that Jews and homosexuals, in their equivocal situations, had the same behavioral patterns: both felt different from the norm (in a superior or inferior way); both believed this difference was the result of birth; both justified not what they did but what they were; both wavered between an apologetic attitude and the claim that they were an elite; and both Jews and homosexuals embodied clannishness. So by the time that Arendt retold the story of the Dreyfus affair as "a foregleam of the twentieth century"[125] in the fourth and last chapter of her history of anti-Semitism, she had shown how anti-Semitism in the nineteenth century was the result of an interaction of Jews with the forces shaping the larger world of which they were a part: the economic transformations of capitalism, the rise and fall of the nation-state, and the social and cultural attitudes that found Jews dangling on the horns of the dilemmas involved in Jewish emancipation and assimilation. The Dreyfus affair constituted the moment of transformation between the nineteenth century and the twentieth century, between nationalist anti-Semitism and imperialist or totalitarian anti-Semitism, between social discrimination and the politicization of anti-Jewish racism, between race thinking and racism.[126]

ANTI-SEMITISM AS A POLITICAL IDEOLOGY

Arendt is clearest about the disjunctures between two types of anti-Semitism in a letter she penned to Jaspers in 1946:

I distinguish in modern times between two kinds of anti-Semitism. First comes anti-Semitism in the nation-state (beginning with the Wars of Liberation in Germany, ending with the Dreyfus affair in France), which came about because the Jews emerged as a group particularly useful to the state and receiving special protection from it. As a consequence of that, every group in the population that came into conflict with the state became anti-Semitic. Then comes the anti-Semitism of the imperial age (which began in the 1880s). This latter form was, from the outset, international in its organization.[127]

As Richard Bernstein highlights, the anti-Semitism of the imperial age melded together imperialist politics, racism, and political anti-Semitism, forging what was to become the exterminatory anti-Semitism of the Holocaust.[128] Arendt develops these connections in the central section of *The Origins of Totalitarianism*, "Imperialism."

Drawing on the work of J. A. Hobson spotlighting the role of Jewish financial capitalism in South Africa, Arendt contends that Jewish financiers were the pioneers, laying the ground for imperialist expansion that would then be taken over by the bourgeoisie, embodied by individuals like Cecil Rhodes. In making her case, she largely adopts Lenin's, Rosa Luxemburg's, and especially Hobson's accounts of imperialism as generated by the need to find new markets for "superfluous" capital in the context of European economic depression. Where Arendt is particularly insightful, however, is in stressing how the Marxists and radical liberals overlooked the rising centrality of racism in soldering together the new alliance "between mob and capital," "between the much-too-rich and the much-too-poor," that catalyzed imperialism. In this context, a new form of "tribal national and outright racism" emerged that fully embraced polygenesis, social Darwinism, and systems of racial classification, dividing humanity into white and Black, Aryan and Semite.[129]

Arendt then traces the intellectual history of "Race-Thinking Before Racism" (chapter 6) in order to establish how pre-imperialist racialism did not yet form a coherent ideology that possessed "the key to history, or the solution for all the 'riddles of the universe,' or the intimate knowledge of the hidden universal laws which are supposed to rule nature and man."[130] Racism as such an ideology was generated as an excuse for the brutal deeds committed by European rule abroad and as a mode of political organization within imperial bureaucracies that she outlines in chapter 7, "Race and Bureaucracy." Racism crystallized as a way of life in South Africa and a mode of governance in Algeria, Egypt, and India. It is in making these links that Arendt invokes Conrad's *Heart of Darkness* as a tale that encapsulates the implications of racial imperialism.

She then tells the story of Boer conquest in South Africa as her historical exemplar of how imperial racism and imperial anti-Semitism cohered. Dutch conquerors justified their exploitation and murder by claiming that like the Jews, they were the chosen people, even as their exploits were "financed, organized, and connected with the ordinary European economy through the accumulated superfluous wealth and with the help of Jewish financiers."[131] In what became a pattern, anti-Semites thus distorted Jewish self-representation as chosen in order to legitimate the contempt or defamation of Jews. In what was a progenitor of Nazi anti-Semitism and a precursor of Arendt's famous boomerang thesis, Afrikaaner anti-Semitism turned upon Jews as the symbols for their whole enterprise:

> Here for the first time Jews were driven into the midst of a race society and almost automatically singled out by the Boers from all other "white" people for special hatred, not only as the representatives of the whole enterprise but as a different "race," the embodiment of a devilish principle introduced into the normal world of "blacks" and "whites." This hatred was all the more violent as it was partly caused by the suspicion that the Jews with their own older and more authentic claim would be harder than anyone else to convince of the Boers' claim to chosenness.[132]

With the rise of imperialism, anti-Semitism as a political ideology severed antipathy for "the Jews" from the actual acts of Jews and became wholly ideological in the form of "tribal nationalism."[133] The anti-Semitism of tribal nationalism as purely ideological was potentially genocidal, going beyond the social discrimination of national patriotism or the integral nationalism of the anti-Dreyfusards or the Stoecker movement in Germany. Its origins were in figures like Georg von Schoenerer and in the pan-German and pan-Slavic movements, whose ideology was then fully actualized by Hitler. The national community was reconceptualized in volkish and mystical terms, appealing emotionally as a "surrogate of religion," appropriating the claim to chosenness.[134] As such, imperial anti-Semitism linked what happened in the empire to what would happen on the continent.

These movements were the bridge between imperialism and totalitarianism, eventually bringing together bureaucratic rule, state power, a propaganda machine, and a terror apparatus whose laboratories were the concentration camps, all welded together by the notion of the "objective enemy."[135] Arendt concludes *Origins*, in her chapter on "Ideology and Terror," by explicating the centrality of an ideology like anti-Semitism to totalitarianism, which explained everything by reference to a single idea or law, which was divorced from reality, but sought to mold reality in its image through propaganda and terror.

ARENDT'S JEWISH PROBLEM

Arendt has been lambasted for this story that she constructs in *Origins* about the development of anti-Semitism into full-throttle ideological racism. As noted, she has been taken to task for her primitivism and Eurocentrism in her account of imperialism in Africa. She has been derided for her failure to apply to Blacks the same insights that she applies to Jews, as well as for failing to distinguish adequately between these modes of racism.[136] When it comes to her story about Judeophobia, she is often faulted for what she did not include in her history. For example, in "Where Hannah Arendt Went Wrong," Shlomo Avineri reprimands her for failing to discuss eastern Europe, which had the largest population of Jews and was the heart of the blood lands during the Holocaust.[137] Despite applauding her for understanding that anti-Semitism requires historicization, Leon Wieseltier claimed that "Arendt blames the victim" because she placed too much emphasis on the relationship between Jews and non-Jews when what was required was an emphasis solely on the contexts of Russian, French, and German history.[138] Another article directly titled "Blame the Victim" by Bernard Wasserstein rightly rebukes Arendt for her reliance on anti-Semitic sources, like those of Hobson, which are so central to her account of South Africa, as well as her sympathetic use of Nazi sources, especially the work of Walter Frank.[139] In a penetrating summa of this literature, Peter Staudenmaier's critical appraisal of Arendt's *Origins* criticizes not only her repeated reliance on such problematic sources, but "her inconsistent analysis of assimilation, her overstated distinction between the social and political dimension of anti-Jewish sentiment, and her emphasis on partial Jewish responsibility for antisemitism," which indicate "fundamental problems with her interpretation of the historical record."[140]

Arendt's narrative, which ascribes to Jews an equivocal causal function, clearly does not always deconstruct the anti-Semitic system of thought that she assesses. In certain moments, she reinscribes Jews within prevalent Judeophobic stereotypes. Three brief examples make the point. First, the sameness that Arendt posits between homosexuality and Judaism verges on reiterating nineteenth-century images of "the Jew" as perverted, debauched, and feminized: in short, as the inversion of the norm. Arendt's point is to emphasize how the fin de siècle was focused on mass identities and that queers, whether Jews or homosexuals, were accepted because they were fascinating and exotic outsiders and as such their condition was precarious. But she reiterates the conflation of the stereotypes of these two queers rather than problematizes it. "It is true that to the recording onlooker the behavior of the Jewish clique showed the same obsession as the behavior patterns followed by inverts," she claims.[141]

In addition to Arendt's postulation of the queerness of Jewishness, she does not adequately undermine the notion that Jews were inherently a queer nation—the alien-nation, outsiders, foreigners, the nation within the nation—since she constantly identifies Jews as the paradigm of the supernational group, which the Boers and then the pan-movements imitated and envied. Jews were "an international element whose importance and usefulness lay precisely in their not being bound to any national cause," she asserts.[142] Arendt's position stems in part from her insistence that political anti-Semitism derived from the pan-movements of the imperial age. But she gives little credence to the hope of Jewish assimilationists, which is an example of the teleological history she decried: "The Jews very clearly were the only inter-European element in a national Europe. It seemed only logical that their enemies had to organize on the same principle, if they were to fight those who were supposed to be the secret manipulators of the political destiny of all nations."[143] Jewish assimilation thus appears as foreclosed not only as a result of the historical processes of nation-state formation but also because of Arendt's positing of Jews as inherently internationalist and cosmopolitan.

Finally, and most problematically, in her account of the Jewish role in fostering the economic activity of the state, Arendt suggests that financial alliances are the only bond that "ever tied a Jewish group to another stratum in society."[144] Pierre Birnbaum has thus suggested, "By adopting—strangely—the analyses of a Drumont which, as far as the role of the Jews is concerned, are akin in some respects to those of a Marx, Arendt postulates a purely economic interpretation of the Jews' place in the state." This, he argues, was a "flawed hunch," only partly valid with respect to Germany and questionable as a description of French history.[145] Like Marx's *Sur Judenfrage*, Arendt places the Jewish Question at the center of her early critique of modernity, too closely identifying Jews with financial capitalism and capitalism with the dissolution of politics, the state, and individuality, which threatened to degenerate into the atomistic, antagonistic individualism that, for Marx, destroys species-being, and for Arendt, produces the loss of world-being.[146]

These shortcomings are wound into the story of anti-Semitism that Arendt tells. Nonetheless, she helped to transform the historiography of anti-Semitism by warning against eternalism, scapegoat theories, apologetics, facile causality, and teleology. Arendt's unconventional narrative dared to analyze economic, political, and social factors "hidden under the surface of events, never perceived by the historian and recorded by the more penetrating and passionate force of poets or novelists." According to her, these are what one needs to appreciate in order to understand "the Jews' fateful journey to the storm center of events," which resulted in the "passion-driven hunt of the 'Jew in general,' the 'Jew everywhere and nowhere.'"[147] In insisting on the poesis of storytelling to unveil what is hidden, Arendt closes the hermeneutic circle of the story that I have sought to open by examining the relation between her metahistory as "storytelling" and the story she tells of anti-Semitism.

In her description and analysis of anti-Semitism, Jews are identified not only as symbols of what society does not accept, but at the origins of the degenerating influences of dominant society itself—financial capitalism, the nation-state, and the bourgeoisie. Jews are situated in the interstices of the fundamental bifurcations that constitute the central categories that structure her thinking: between past and future, state and nation, society and politics, tradition and innovation, the antimodern and modern. In short, Jews are caught in the double binds between the pariah and the parvenu, between being Jewish and assimilating into European society and culture. There is an ambivalence to the story that Arendt tells that makes it difficult to determine whether her account is caught within contradictions produced by her own distinctions, or those of the European tradition that she seeks to analyze. It is sometimes difficult to demarcate in

Arendt's story when she echoes the anti-Semitic (or anti-Black) tradition she wants to critique and when her analysis offers a nuanced description of the paradoxes of the Jewish condition in modernity. Arendt's insights traverse the dichotomies that structure her understanding of anti-Semitism, politics, and modernity, even as "the Jew" that underpins her interpretation ambivalently transgresses these distinctions, occupying an ambiguous, often contradictory situation.

Arendt noted of other thinkers that "fundamental and flagrant contradictions rarely occur in second-rate writers, in whom they can be discounted. In the work of great authors they lead into the very center of their work and are the most important clue to a true understanding of their problems and new insights."[148] Like Arendt's own story, which is itself fraught with the tensions and ambiguity of her own universality and particularity, Germanness and Jewishness, the relation between her theory of history as "storytelling" and the story of her history of anti-Semitism demands to be reevaluated and rethought. In the chiasma that I have traced between Arendt's perspectival approach to history and the perspectives she unfolds in her history of anti-Semitism, her account of the "double origins" and" equivocal meaning" of modern Jewish history opens her-story to internal contestation and reinterpretation.

CHAPTER 4

The Sociology of Modern Anti-Semitism from Talcott Parsons to Zygmunt Bauman

Zygmunt Bauman famously claimed in *Modernity and the Holocaust*, "Sociology is concerned with modern society, but has never come to terms with one of the most distinctive and horrific aspects of modernity—the Holocaust."[1] The Holocaust, he insists, was not just an upsurge of medieval barbarism in the form of modern anti-Semitism; it was at the heart of the sociological processes that define modernity. Accepting this demands a rethinking of sociological theory and sociology's understanding of anti-Semitism, which his work undertakes. In making this case, Bauman's *Modernity and the Holocaust* became an important touchstone for many scholars in Jewish cultural and literary studies, the sociology of genocide, and the history and theory of anti-Semitism for his rethinking of the Holocaust and anti-Semitism from a postmodern sociological perspective.

In this chapter, I set Bauman's work against one of the preeminent American sociologists of modernity, Talcott Parsons. While the numerous articles, radio broadcasts, speeches, addresses, and position papers dealing with Germany, National Socialism, fascism, and anti-Semitism written by Parsons between 1938–1945 never tackled the Holocaust per se, they do constitute a robust series of reflections on the constellation of forces that produced it by arguably the leading practitioner of American sociology in the middle of the twentieth century. Parsons's "The Sociology of Modern Anti-Semitism" (1942) and his other short sociological analyses of Hitlerism and fascism, so helpfully gathered together by Uta Gerhardt in her collection, *Talcott Parsons on National Socialism*, are not generally depicted as central theoretical works in his development. But World War II clearly marked a crucial moment of change in Parsons's evolution. The rise of the Nazis and the events of World War II were the context of the shift from Parsons's voluntarist theory of social action developed in his first major work, *The Structure of Social Action* (1937), to his structuralist-functionalist systems theory, which he elaborated primarily in *The Social System* (1951), *Toward a General Theory of Action* (1951), and *Economy and Society* (1956). This same period saw both a rise in sociological studies focused on anti-Semitism and an important influence of models drawn from the social sciences into the writing of social history and concomitantly into analyses of the history of anti-Semitism. An investigation of Parsons's work is therefore important to consider in evaluating the categories that underlie the social history of anti-Semitism as well the insights of sociological approaches to theorizing the underlying causes of anti-Semitism.

The first half of this chapter is an elucidation and critical analysis of Parsons's "The Sociology of Anti-Semitism." I locate this text within the unfolding discipline of sociology itself. As Marcel Stoetzler and Chad Alan Goldberg have shown, anti-Semitism and the discipline of sociology have traveled parallel paths.[2] Contra Bauman, one could trace the evolution of the field from the perspective of the different accounts of modernity and anti-Semitism that sociologists have offered over time. Part of the importance of Parsons's early theoretical work was that it translated and synthesized the classics of European sociological theory. Parsons then applied this to his analysis of Nazism and anti-Semitism. This places him, alongside Sartre, the Frankfurt School, and Arendt, on the cusp of the development of critical theories of anti-Semitism. Parsons was an important contributor to these pioneering works by indicating what social scientists could contribute.

In developing his understanding of anti-Semitism, Parsons drew from the work of Émile Durkheim, supplemented by Freudian theories of projection. But he was most significantly influenced by Max Weber's sociological analyses of Judaism. Consequently, like Weber, Parsons's theory of anti-Semitism is riddled with the problems of an ambivalent liberalism, albeit with a distinctively American twist. His commitment to a set of classical liberal values that ultimately did not affirm the historically embedded particularities of Jewish culture, religion, and rites led him to reiterate a series of typological constructions of Jews and Judaism despite his clear desire to contest and critique anti-Semitism and fascism.

The second half of the chapter then turns to the postmodern sociology of Zygmunt Bauman. Bauman reassessed the approach to social deviance and difference within modern sociology, exemplified by Parsons. He was influenced primarily by Georg Simmel's writing on "the stranger," and the work of the Frankfurt School and Arendt, alongside his translation of French post-structuralist theorists, and his adoption of Emmanuel Levinas's ethics of alterity. In so doing, Bauman insisted upon a fundamental conceptual shift to understanding anti-Jewish antipathy, which he augured was based not on hatred of Jews, but on ambivalence. As "ambivalence incarnate," Jews became potent foils within the modernist project, which Nazism racialized and amplified, highlighting certain inherent tendencies within modern state formations.

In outlining the approaches of Parsons and Bauman, this chapter underscores some of the key processes that modern sociology emphasizes to understand anti-Semitism. Borrowing Durkheim's term, Parsons maintained that anti-Semitism is a product of *anomie*, brought about by the social dislocations that resulted from modernization: that is, democratic revolutions, industrial capitalism, urbanization, and the shifting demographics, mobility, and heterogeneity of modern social life. These disruptions to social order result in insecurity, frustration, and resentment, which are often projected onto a symbolic object. Parsons thus offers a sociologically inflected scapegoat theory. Drawing from Weber, he furnished a narrative for why Jews were particularly suited to personify the processes of modernization. As other scholars have shown, Weber's account drew from cultural schemas rooted in Protestant theology.[3] The supersessionism of both Weber and then Parsons was a secularized version of liberal modernity that each sought to describe, analyze, and defend.

Bauman, in turn, rejected the notion that sociology should bolster liberal modernity and modern social systems. He instead offered a critical optic on modernity by examining the sociological processes that made the Holocaust and other genocides possible. Refusing supersessionism, he propounded in its place a historical account of how Christianity and later Enlightenment and modern European traditions defined themselves against the Jewish Other. Insisting upon the inherent ambivalence toward Jews and Judaism within these frameworks, he drew from French theorists a new vocabulary for conceptualizing this ambivalence. He also stressed how the bent for categorization within modern nationalism, science, and bureaucracy was threatened by the boundary-busting ambiguity that characterized Jews. Lastly, he emphasized the modern and postmodern tendency to abdicate ethical responsibility for strangers as a result of the task-oriented functionality so prevalent in modern life. Between Parsons and Bauman, then, we are offered some of the key insights that sociological approaches lend to our understanding of modern anti-Semitism.

PORTRAITS: PARSONS AND BAUMAN

Hailing from a line of Americans that went back to the founders, Talcott Parsons (1902–1979) was born in Colorado Springs, where his father, Edward Parsons, a graduate of Yale Divinity School, was then a professor of English and vice president at Colorado College, later to become president of Marietta College. A member of the Social Gospel movement that influenced the origins of sociology in the United States, père Parsons was the author of *The Social Message of Jesus* (1910), a liberal response to "the social question," that advocated "social solidarity," but that was critical of socialism.[4] In accord with family tradition, Parsons attended Amherst, where he intended to focus on a premed curriculum, but was exposed to social science and philosophy, changing his life path. He spent a year at the London School of Economics, where he met his wife and was influenced by the social anthropologist Bronislaw Malinowski. Parsons then seized upon the opportunity of a German exchange program and landed at the University of Heidelberg. There, under the direct tutelage of Max Weber's brother, Alfred, he was transformed by Weber's work, getting permission from his wife to translate *The Protestant Ethic and the Spirit of Capitalism*, the first of several translations of Weber's writings. After completing his PhD in Heidelberg in economics and sociology with a dissertation on "The Concept of Capitalism in Recent German Literature," which began with Marx, but focused on Werner Sombart and Weber, he taught for a year at Amherst before moving to Harvard in 1927, where he spent the remainder of his career.

Written against the backdrop of the Great Depression and the crisis of liberalism it occasioned, Parsons published his first major opus in 1937, *The Structure of Social Action*. It offered a synthesis of Marshall, Durkheim, Pareto, and Weber, all assembled to critique social Darwinism, behaviorism, utilitarianism, positivism, and Marxism in understanding how social systems shape human action. Parsons's acclaim slowly percolated over the war years. With the second printing in 1949, *The Structure of Social Action* became "mandatory reading in sociology courses" and by the 1960s, "a milestone of sociology's development as an academic discipline."[5] In 1944, Parsons became chair of the interdisciplinary Department of Social Relations, which, in addition to sociology, also included social anthropology and social and clinical psychology. He was elected president of the American Sociological Association in 1949 and with the publication of two major books in 1951, he was established at the apex of the discipline of sociology in the United States.

Zygmunt Bauman's (1925-2017) trajectory to becoming a leading Anglo-American sociologist could not have been more different from Parsons's itinerary.[6] Born into a poor Jewish family in Poznan in western Poland, Bauman's family suffered not only from poverty but also from anti-Semitism. When World War II began in 1939, they fled into the Soviet Union to survive. After attending a Russian university for two years, at eighteen Bauman joined the Polish army in Russia, becoming a junior officer. Wounded while serving in his artillery unit, he recovered in time to participate in the final battle of Berlin. As Keith Tester notes, "By the time he was twenty, Bauman had confronted anti-Semitism, Stalinism, Nazism and warfare."[7] Postwar, he was decorated with the Military Cross of Valor and he eventually rose to the rank of captain. He served from 1945-1953 in the Internal Security Corps (KBW), a unit established to fight anticommunist resistance in Poland. A communist patriot, Bauman was attracted to the cause because he believed "there would be no room for anti-Semitism, or any other racial hatred" and because "this fairest of social systems" would "guarantee full equality between human beings."[8] But at twenty-eight, in "a bolt from the blue," he was suddenly dishonorably discharged following his father's consult at the Israeli embassy in Warsaw about emigrating to Israel.[9]

Bauman had already begun to study sociology and philosophy, and by 1954 he had embarked on a second career as a junior lecturer in the Faculty of Philosophy and Social Sciences at the University of Warsaw. During his Polish period in sociology, he published numerous books that were critical of Stalinist orthodoxy and "actually existing socialism,"[10] including a treatise on Marxist sociology that was translated into Serb and Italian; he became head of the editorial committee of *Studia Socjologiczne* (Sociological studies); he visited abroad, including a year at the London School of Economics, during which he wrote a study on the British socialist movement; and in 1966 he was elected president of the executive committee of the Polish Sociological Association.[11] But following the Six Day War in 1967 and during the student protests in Poland in March 1968, he was among those targeted during a vicious "anti-Zionist" campaign, which claimed that "the leaders of the student unrest were Zionists and enemies of the Polish nation."[12]

Like Socrates, Bauman was charged with corrupting the youth, and at the end of March 1968, dismissed from his chair at the University of Warsaw. With his wife Janina and their children, he moved first to Tel Aviv, then, like wandering Jews, to Canada, the United States, and eventually in 1971 to Leeds University. There he embarked on a third career, publishing five books in the 1970s, and four in the 1980s, including his Amalfi Prize-winning *Modernity and the Holocaust* in 1989, which brought him international acclaim. He officially retired in 1990 but continued to publish at least one book each year until his death, thus establishing himself, according to Peter Beilharz, as the "greatest sociologist writing in English."[13]

SOCIOLOGY AND ANTI-SEMITISM

Parsons and Bauman were part of a lineage within the discipline of sociology that conceived of modernity in part through their representations of Jews or anti-Semitism. Several of the classical figures of sociology contributed major works assessing the place of Jews in society, the role of Judaism in modernity, and the consequent impact on being Jewish. One might even draw a red thread through many of the canonic figures of the discipline by how they accounted for Jewishness and anti-Semitism as a social phenomenon and in turn theoretically constructed their systems of social thought. This is certainly the case for Karl Marx, Émile Durkheim and the Durkheimians in France (Robert Hertz, Lucien Lévy-Bruhl, later Marcel Mauss), Werner Sombart, Georg Simmel, and Max Weber.[14] As Goldberg has shown, this was also true in the work of four major figures in the Chicago school when they were the ascendant institution within American sociology: William Isaac Thomas, Robert Ezra Park, Louis Wirth, and Everett Verner Stonequist.[15] As William Helmreich indicates in his brief overview of "The Sociological Study of Anti-Semitism in the United States," "there is no question that American sociologists have been aware of anti-Semitism as a social phenomenon throughout the history of the field."[16]

In *Geography of Hope*, historical sociologist Pierre Birnbaum has mapped just how widespread was the correlation between the development of the value-neutral, objective rationality and scientificity of the social sciences as they emerged in the late nineteenth and twentieth centuries and the relegation of Jewish subjects to the margins, especially for Jews aspiring to make it in the academy.[17] Nonetheless, many of the major canonical sociologists reflected on anti-Semitism, and consequently about Jews, Jewishness, and the Jewish Question as a jumping off point to their sociological theories. As Stoetzler documents, "The milieus and intellectual traditions out of which...antisemitism and positivism, and out of the latter, sociology, emerged, are closely related."[18] Indeed, Auguste Comte, who coined the term "sociology," defined his program partly by responding to utopian socialism, which personified the pathologies of modernity and capitalism by identifying them with Jews and Judaism. The genealogical lineage continued with Marx's "On the Jewish Question," Durkheim's "L'Individualisme et les intellectuels," through Weber's *Ancient Judaism* and *The Sociology of Religion*, into Sombart's *The Jews and Modern Capitalism*, through to Simmel's famous excursus on "The Stranger," and across the Atlantic in Robert Park's and his students' ruminations on the "marginal man."

Stoetzler's edited volume *Antisemitism and the Constitution of Sociology* shows that "the discipline of sociology emerged out of the liberal response to crisis phenomena of modern society, aiming at that society's consolidation, regeneration, and its defense" and that anti-Semitism was likewise a response to this same social situation, "offering in its phantasmagorias of 'the Jew' and 'Jewification' an explanation of its deficiencies and crises."[19] In fact, classical sociological theory and modern anti-Semitism have shared the same discursive space. Goldberg makes evident in his comparative study of classical sociology in France, Germany, and America that "regardless of which aspect of modernity they emphasized—democratization [France], capitalist development [Germany], or urbanization [America]—they turned repeatedly to the Jews as a touchstone for interpreting the new social order."[20]

In synthesizing the classics of the European sociological tradition, Parsons picked up on this sociological tradition that had long wrestled with anti-Semitism. The founding "sociologists developed a discourse that aimed to defend liberal society and modernization" while at the same time attacking the utilitarianism that they blamed for the dismal aspects of the emerging new society. During and after World War II, Parsons took up this mantle. As a result, "post–Second World War sociology, especially due to the influence of Talcott Parsons... successfully amalgamated its main traditions...into liberal, progressivist modernization theory," which he described through a set of binaries: democracy and fascism, liberalism and anti-Semitism.[21]

JEWS IN A GENTILE WORLD

Parsons's major contribution in this area was his essay "The Sociology of Modern Anti-Semitism," included in the voluminous and pioneering collection, *Jews in a Gentile World: The Problem of Anti-Semitism*, edited by Isacque Graeber and Steuart Henderson Britt. The volume was a groundbreaking early interdisciplinary effort to bring together eighteen sociologists, anthropologists, psychologists, political scientists, economists, and historians to "examine the problems of anti-Semitism in a dispassionate, objective manner."[22] Parsons's colleague, Harvard Professor of Government Carl Friedrich, who would gain fame as the leading postwar theorist of totalitarianism, introduced the volume. A non-Jewish German, Friedrich had emigrated to the United States in the 1920s and by the eve of the Holocaust he was a leading liberal activist, who continued this engagement into postwar fights for civil liberties and civil rights.[23] Following his introduction, the book then contained an open debate on whether Jews have a racial identity. This section included opposing views, with essays by Carleton Stevens Coon, the leading physical anthropologist of the day, whose helm at Harvard was a powerful soapbox for his biological justification of race-based theories, and Melville Jacobs, who vehemently opposed Coon's views. Also included was a section on "The Psychology of Anti-Semitism" with chapters by J. F. Brown and Ellis Freeman; a section on "The American Scene"; a section on "The Rhythm of Two Worlds" that included a summative statement of Stonequist's *The Marginal Man* focused on Jews, titled, "The Marginal Character of the Jews"; and a section on "The Mirage of the Economic Jew" by Jacob Lestchinsky and Miriam Beard, daughter of the famed historian Charles Beard, who rebuked anti-Semitism as the product of economic myths.

While eight sociologists contributed to the volume, only two chapters were included in the section on "The History and Sociology of Anti-Semitism": the essays by Parsons and by J. O. Hertzler. Hertzler itemized a series of social forces that accounted for anti-Semitism that many other scholars have developed. They included Jewish religious difference; the ire against the idea of Jews as a "chosen people"; their cultural isolation and "rigidity" that Hertzler termed "the ghetto influence"; Jewish internationalism and cosmopolitanism; Jewish dual loyalty; racial conflicts, which Hertzler maintained were real sociologically, even if they had no basis biologically; the objection of Jews to intermarriage; their minority status; economic competition; parvenu Jews whose ostentation was deemed obnoxious; and Jewish radicalism. Given the variety of these factors, for Hertzler Judeophobia was an eternal problem from "Haman to Hitler," and it would only change if Jews changed, which he maintained was not going to happen.

When the book was published, it was widely and positively reviewed. It was hailed as "a kind of encyclopedia on the Jewish question," given "the uniformly high quality of each of the essays."[24] One reviewer noted, "The history and sociology of anti-Semitism is done with great understanding by two non-Jews," while Robert Park singled out Parsons's contribution and two others "as of outstanding importance."[25]

Central to putting the volume together was the sociologist Isacque Graeber. Born in Congress Poland, he immigrated to the United States with his family, and then concluded his studies at the University of Paris. Upon his return to America, Graeber was an active antifascist aligned with the Communist Party USA–sponsored League of American Writers.[26] Long interested in the issue of anti-Semitism, he contacted Horkheimer after the publication of the Frankfurt School's research proposal in *Studies in Philosophy and Social Science* and, as I have already discussed, worked alongside Neumann to procure funding for their research. Graeber began work on *Jews in a Gentile World* as early as 1935, pulling together leading academics in a number of the social sciences to reflect on anti-Semitism as a social problem.

Graeber approached Parsons to participate in 1939 and Parsons wrote a manuscript that was over fifty pages long in early 1940. Parsons sent it to Eric Voegelin for his comments and then sent off the final draft to Graeber. Upon request at the end of the year, he would follow up with a short abstract of the argument. With no further communication between the two, Parsons received the galley proofs of his article, which had been shortened by Graeber.

Parsons was apparently horrified by the editorial intervention. Writing to Ben Halpern, who had served as an editorial assistant on *The Theory of Social Action*, Parsons declaimed: "Graeber, under the guise of shortening my manuscript, rewrote the article, and put in a great many statements to which I would not subscribe.... As it happens, that article represents the worst experience with editorial interference with an author's work I have ever encountered."[27] For his part, Graeber claimed that the editorial changes were a necessity imposed by the publisher's limits on the size of the book and in order to avoid the repetition of points made by the various authors. "I beg you not to castigate me for having cut your chapter," he beseeched Parsons. "In fact, I had instruction to rewrite yours as well as several others. Please believe that I did this—yours especially—with pains in my vitals."[28] Parsons responded by writing out eleven inserts that were supposed to be entered into the text, but of which Graeber only included two in the final version. And Graeber kept most of the changes he had made to the chapter. Parsons was apparently displeased enough by the final product that he would not have the article reprinted in any of the five collections of his essays edited after 1949. This is the only case of all of his published pieces from the war years to suffer this fate. Moreover, the article is today listed in the Harvard University Archives under "unpublished manuscripts," as if it had never appeared in print.

UTA GERHARDT ON ISACQUE GRAEBER

So, what accounts for Parsons's burying "The Sociology of Modern Anti-Semitism"? This was, after all, his only substantial theoretical contribution to what has undeniably been a major social phenomenon. Moreover, the essay was on the cutting edge of sociological work when it was published. On the basis of the account above, Uta Gerhardt suggests that Parsons was dismayed by the editorial changes made by Graeber, who ostensibly changed Parsons's own approach, insights, and conclusions.[29] In *Talcott Parsons on National Socialism*, which contains a collection of Parsons's published and unpublished articles from this period, she includes a version true to Parsons's original intent with the following footnote: "Chapter 4 of this volume omits these additions by Graeber and restores as much of the original of Parsons' text as could be reconstructed. The nine inserts unused in the printed article are put in. Where the manuscript from the Harvard University Archives deviates from the published version, the former is taken to be authentic."[30] Moreover, she maintains that the article bothered Parsons enough to warrant his writing a posthumously published postscript in 1978. In *Talcott Parsons: An Intellectual Biography*, Gerhardt states that the key difference between Graeber and Parsons was methodological: "What was the conflict about? The issue was whether condemnation of anti-Semitism as amoral should stand at the end of the article, as Graeber found and wrote into the manuscript, replacing Parsons's insisting on the primacy of scientific analysis rather than an attempt to press any particular policy."[31]

But none of Gerhardt's claims stand up to scrutiny. Most of the changes that were made by Graeber were cosmetic. There are some slight alterations of phrasing or sentence order. But not one single fundamental theorem of Parsons's analysis differs in the version published by Graeber and that published by Gerhardt. The postscript that Parsons wrote in 1978 served to contextualize the original article and primarily to update it, not to recant it. The article was written at the apex of Nazi power, Parsons explained, "after the fall of France and before the impact of Pearl Harbor and the American entry into the Second World War." It is important to note, as Parsons does, that "the Holocaust was not part of the historical record as early as that."[32] The focus of Parsons's postscript was a discussion of the ways in which the Jewish situation had changed in the intervening half century, not a refutation of his earlier published piece. There is nothing in his 1978 article indicating a fundamental disavowal of his earlier work as it had appeared.

As to Gerhardt's claim about moral condemnation versus scientific analysis, Parsons unequivocally decried anti-Semitism in moral and political terms within the article. He insists in the concluding section *included in Gerhardt's restored version*,

> The attitude expressed in what follows is to be taken only as a personal view, no scientific authority being claimed for it. The author considers anti-Semitism of the type discussed here a pernicious and undesirable phenomenon which should be reduced to a minimum. He has strong moral sentiments regarding the importance and desirability of the universalistic patterns of equality of opportunity, so important in modern economic life.[33]

Rather than the anecdotal and circumstantial evidence that Gerhardt provides, I maintain that what is troubling about Parsons's text stems directly from the theoretical axis that guides his orientation: his universalistic liberalism in the face of what he construes as Jewish particularity, intractable separateness, and difference. This was a position he shared, moreover, with Max Weber, whose work was his primary influence.[34] To get at this we have to enter the text.

"THE SOCIOLOGY OF MODERN ANTI-SEMITISM"

The "Sociology of Modern Anti-Semitism" is broken up into six sections, opening with an "Introductory Statement," and hinged together by a sociological account of the development of Judaism (called "The Character of the Jewish People"), moving into an analysis of "The Position of the Jews in the Modern World" that in turn is weighted against the "Chief Characteristics of Western Society." The clash between these antinomies—between Jewishness and modernity—plays out in "The Phenomenon of Anti-Semitism." The article concludes with a section on "Prognosis and Policy," a concern that runs through all of Parsons's work in this period.

Parsons's operative thesis in "The Sociology of Modern Anti-Semitism," is that "the most important source of virulent anti-Semitism is probably the projection on the Jew, as a symbol, of free-floating aggression, springing from insecurities and social disorganization."[35] Anti-Semitism thus results from social disaggregation. The breakdown of a social system with clearly defined values, goals, and expectations results from the processes unleashed by the shift from the *Gemeinschaft* (community) to the *Gesellschaft* (society), to use Ferdinand Tönnies's classic terms. This shift is created by the sociological processes of modernization—including urbanization, industrialization, the developing complexity and instability of the economy, increasing heterogeneity and mobility of the population, shifts in consumption patterns, the "'debunking' of traditional values and ideas," and the expansion of popular education and mass means of communication—that all result in the "large-scale incidence of anomie in Western society."[36]

Borrowing the notion of anomie from Durkheim's study on *Suicide*,[37] Parsons defines it as "the state where large numbers of individuals are to a serious degree lacking in the kind of integration with stable institutional patterns which is essential to their own personal stability and to the smooth functioning of the social system."[38] Anomie is a state of rootlessness, disconnection, and social alienation. It results from the breakdown of norms or cultural expectations that conflict with the social realities attendant upon the transformations brought about as a result of modernity. The effect of anomie is social and psychological insecurity, frustration, and resentment, which is often expressed as aggression. The more heightened the anxiety, the more "free-floating" the aggression. In these circumstances, people act out this frustration and insecurity on a symbolic object.

Parsons goes on to explain why it is that Jews constitute a particularly appropriate symbol, "on which to project aggressive attitudes generated by a large-scale state of *anomie* in modern society."[39] The reasons for this, according to Parsons, are deeply rooted in the character both of the Jewish people and of the wider society in which they live.

PARSONS AND WEBER

In order to explicate this "Jewish character," Parsons tells a historical narrative, largely based on Max Weber's writings on Jews and Judaism in *Ancient Judaism* and *The Sociology of Religion*. Indeed, Parsons includes a footnote to the section on "The Character of the Jewish People" that makes explicit that "the most important single source for the following sketch is Max Weber's study 'Das Antike Judentum,' in *Gesammelte Aufsätze zur Religionssoziologie* (Collected Essays on the Sociology of Religion), Vol. III."[40] And in his correspondence with Voegelin about the article, he indicates that in order to respond to the questions he had raised, he had reread Weber's *Ancient Judaism* three or four times.[41]

Both Weber's narrative and Parsons's echo of it are, of course, complex accounts. David Ellenson provides a useful summation of the key points of Weber's analysis, which were picked up wholesale by Parsons:

> The authors of the Bible, by positing belief in a single God who was simultaneously both the purposeful creator of the world and a transcendent agent apart from nature, were able to secularize the cosmos. The prophets, in particular, with their message of moral rationalism, directed worship toward this one sovereign God who was above and beyond the universe. Their teachings not only disenchanted the world by ridding it of other gods; they also led people to focus on the meaning and import of human activity. God was not arbitrary, and the divine could be pleased and the people thereby rewarded through observance of the deity's commandments. In this way, the prophets and the Jewish people of ancient days laid the foundation for the construction of a social ethic of activity within the world that could inform all dimensions of human life. This foundation allowed Judaism to develop ritual and social guidelines for a highly systematic mode of daily conduct based upon a devotion to rationally consistent procedures and rules in the areas of commandment and law.[42]

The heart of this historical narrative was Weber's contention that Jews were what he famously called "a pariah people":

> The Jews were a pariah people, which means ... that they were a guest people who were ritually separated, formally or de facto, from their social

surroundings. All the essential traits of Jewry's attitude toward the environment can be deduced from this pariah existence, especially its voluntary ghetto, long antedating compulsory internment, and the dualistic nature of its in-group and out-group morality.[43]

In the *Sociology of Religion*, Weber would develop this conception of Jewry into an ideal-typical construct. "'Pariah people' denotes a distinctive hereditary social group lacking autonomous political organization and characterized by prohibitions against commensality and intermarriage.... Two additional traits of a pariah people are political and social disprivilege and a far-reaching distinctiveness in economic functioning."[44]

Weber's "pariah people" thesis, as well as his history of Judaism, has been roundly critiqued. "Weber's analysis," writes Ephraim Schmueli, "disregards most relevant elements in Jewish history and accentuates a one-sided arrangement of the selected elements."[45] Freddy Raphael has derided Weber for oversimplifying Judaism's attitudes toward non-Jews.[46] Jay Holstein has taken Weber to task for relying on the skewed biblical scholarship of his era, steeped as it was in a set of cultural presuppositions about Jews.[47] In a more wholesale fashion, Gary Abraham's *Max Weber and the Jewish Question* has gutted Weber's writings on Jews and Judaism, showing how intrinsic they were to his whole sociological perspective.[48] Once more David Ellenson usefully summarizes the key point for our purposes:

> Weber himself was a liberal who desired the Jew to participate fully in the civic and cultural life of Germany. He desired full Jewish integration into the life of Germany's majority culture. The continued Jewish insistence upon particularity—Jewry's "self-segregation" as a "pariah people"—disturbed Weber, who felt that the most appropriate Jewish response to the modern setting ought to have been full assimilation into German society. His writings on Judaism and his characterizations of the Jews reflect his impatience with and disapproval of this stance on the part of modern Jewry.[49]

It is interesting to note that in his later introduction to the English translation of *The Sociology of Religion*, published in 1963, Parsons would slight Weber for his contention that "ritual segregation" was an essential feature of Jewry's pariah people status. For in "The Sociology of Modern Anti-Semitism" he was wholly congruent with Weber on this point as on others.⁵⁰ After "the loss of their territory and national independence and consequent dispersion" the Jews would intensify "their tendency to exclusiveness," Parsons writes, through placing greater emphasis on "the Law and on those ritual elements which served to mark off the Jew from the non-Jew."⁵¹

PARSONS'S TYPOLOGICAL CONSTRUCTIONS OF JEWS

Indeed, without referring to the Jews as a "pariah people" as such, like Weber, woven into the strands of Parsons's writing are a series of stereotypical images. Since they are "a people without a country,"⁵² they pose the threat of the nation within a nation. The result was that Jews developed "certain characteristics." Since Jews lived in humble circumstances, they puffed up their self-image with the arrogant pride of Jewish chosenness. This Parsons takes as a "natural" source of friction with gentiles. The Jews' diasporic identity was unified as a "People of the Book," Parsons maintains, preoccupied with the Law, resulting in a "certain kind of rationalism or rather intellectualism." This is the stereotype of the smart Jew. The strong predilection of Jews was for separatism and exclusiveness, Parsons insists. Moreover, he states that while Jews maintained ethical obligations toward other members of the Jewish community, "it was only natural ... that the Jews did not feel such responsibilities towards Gentiles," which he explains as "a transfer of the primitive in-group attitude, where outsiders are outside the law governing the group." Here Parsons reiterates the ancient image of "the Jew" as misanthrope or primitive or simply so clan-bound as to apply different standards to those inside and outside the group, a stereotype elaborated by Werner Sombart.⁵³

The evidence that Parsons offers for this last point is that Jews would not take interest from Jews, but they could take interest from heathens or idolaters. This figure of the Jew as usurer—the Shylock Jew—who exploits those outside his own tribe through interest on money, has damned Jews perhaps more than any other in modernity. It is interesting to note that Graeber and Britt insert an editorial footnote to Parsons's text indicating that "Maimonides, the great codifier of Jewish law and ritual, clearly differentiates between 'Non-Jew' and 'heathen,'" clearly distancing themselves from Parsons's take on this.⁵⁴

Parsons assuredly wanted to debunk the myth of Shylock and the Jewish huckster businessman. It was explicable for him by the fact that Jews were forced to live in urban environments and concentrate on trade. He attacked the pernicious trope that Jews control "our whole economic life." But in doing so, he assents to the notion that Jewish control of certain industries is "highly conspicuous ... [in] the motion-picture industry, department stores, and the clothing industry. The Jews [also] play a relatively prominent role in the press, in the theater business, as well as in some of the professions—notably law and medicine."[55] While he did not articulate it as such, Parsons was laboring—albeit stumbling over certain stereotypes in the process—to suggest that Jewish *visibility* in these sectors of the modern economy, rather than *control* of the economy by Jews, as anti-Semites maintained, made the Jewish situation precarious. As such, he was fully in accord with the liberal and Enlightenment tradition from Wilhelm Dohm forward that shaped Weber's approach to Jewish emancipation that so influenced Parsons. In accord with this liberal position, Parsons's suggestion was that "any policy which tends to make Jews as Jews more conspicuous and particularly those Jews who are at the same time vulnerable symbols in other respects would tend to be an invitation to anti-Semitic reaction."[56]

Parsons's position on anti-Semitism, it turns out, was in stark contrast to Graeber's at the time. Unlike Parsons, who focused a lot on Jewish behavior, Graeber placed full responsibility for anti-Semitism on the dominant culture. He maintained that anti-Semitism was deeply wound into the Christian tradition. The church, he wrote, had dehumanized the Jew as "a 'monster,' a theological abstraction of superhuman cunning and malice" and Christians were raised with the "hostile myth of the cruel, greedy, treacherous, Christ-killing, Christ-rejecting Jew."[57] In a postwar article, "An Examination of Theories of Race Prejudice," Graeber explicitly rejected what he termed the "frustration-aggression hypothesis" articulated by Parsons, honing more closely to the Frankfurt School's approach that explained racism as a justification for the material benefits it enabled in a competitive society: "Prejudice against the Negro, the Jew, the Oriental, the European immigrant," Graeber wrote, "improves the economic opportunity of the majority group, to whose obvious advantage it is to keep the prejudice alive."[58] Still, both Graeber and Parsons shared the view that what Nazism ultimately sought was to tear apart Western culture and that anti-Semitism was only a spearhead for a more general assault on democracy. For Parsons, the modern, democratic West sat on the precipice of liberalism.

PARSONS, NAZISM, AND LIBERAL MODERNITY

It is clear in the full gamut of Parsons's writings from 1938–1945 that he opposed Nazism and all forms of anti-Semitism on the grounds that they were a threat to the form of liberal democracy he was not only personally committed to defend, but that he saw as the culmination of Western modernity. In "The Sociology of Modern Anti-Semitism" he largely identifies the "Chief Characteristics of Western Society" with "liberal democracy" and "certain broad social values such as a modicum of equality of opportunity" and "a separation of church and state so that religion is a 'personal affair.'"[59]

His first effort to sound the alarm about the dangers of Nazism was a short article he published in the *Radcliffe News* just after the Kristallnacht pogrom of November 1938. In it, he augured that Hitlerism was something radically new that was "rapidly coming to be the most formidable threat to many of the institutional fundamentals of western civilization as a whole which has been seen for many centuries."[60] As such, anti-Semitism was the canary in the gold mine:

> Seen in this perspective the treatment of the Jews, tragic as it is for the victims, is only a small part of the significance of the movement, perhaps even more of symptomatic importance than itself the major danger. For various reasons they, the most widespread and at the same time persistently "unassimilated" cultural minority in Western society, are particularly vulnerable as a symbol and a scapegoat.[61]

In an unpublished article, "Academic Freedom," written in 1939, Parsons warned of the "tendency in the Nazi party to a basic anti-intellectualism which in principle questions the values of science." He argued that since professionalism depends upon liberality in the pursuit of knowledge, in certain circumstances an academic needs "to defend the liberal values which are essential to his own academic ethic, and to back up the forces in his society which maintain them."[62]

This commitment to a liberal vision of modernity guided Parsons's own involvement in a number of efforts from 1939 to 1945. These included his active role in the Harvard Defense Committee and his biweekly radio broadcasts to combat American isolationism, his efforts to urge intervention in the war after Pearl Harbor, and finally in his thoughts about how to create conditions in postwar

Germany that would foster a liberal democratic system to emerge from the ashes of the Nazi defeat. In accord with his liberalism, after the war, Parsons would consistently oppose right-wing politics: he was a vehement critic of McCarthyism, strongly supported the civil rights movement,[63] opposed the Vietnam War, and robustly condemned the Nixon administration. In short, as Jens Nielsen has convincingly concluded about Parsons, "It is safe to classify him as a Left liberalist."[64]

It is clear from his unbridled opposition against fascism and Hitlerism in terms of a set of democratic values that the axis of Parsons's perspective was his liberalism. But it must be emphasized that Parsons's views on liberalism were not those of a Pollyanna. He was not naïve about the tensions and antinomies of liberal modernity and the Enlightenment tradition that he embraced. He makes this evident in his article "Some Sociological Aspects of the Fascist Movements," originally given as his Presidential Address to the Eastern Sociological Society in 1942 and then published in *Social Forces*.

This article was an elaboration of the same argument that he had made in "The Sociology of Modern Anti-Semitism." Supplementing his Durkheimian theory of anti-Semitism as a response to anomie with a Weberian spin, he argued that the solvent of modernity was a critical rationality that began with a series of Enlightenment promises calling for a "new and magnificent social order, for freedom against tyranny, for enlightenment against ignorance and superstition, for equality and justice against privilege, for free enterprise against monopoly and the irrational restrictions of custom."[65] Akin to the Frankfurt School, he argued that over time, this Enlightenment program degenerated. As utilitarian measures were applied to more and more processes, Parsons asserted, this led to an overemphasis on market-driven processes and the concomitant reduction of social relations to transactions. The result has been an "underestimating [of] the role of what Pareto has called the 'non-logical' aspects of human behavior in society, of the sentiments and traditions of family and informal social relationships, of the refinements of social stratification, of the peculiarities of regional, ethnic or national culture—perhaps above all of religion." In response to these contradictions experienced socially and individually as anomie, certain key targets have emerged. Both capitalism and communism have been depicted as twin enemies and "the Jew serves as a convenient symbolic link between them."[66]

Most insightfully, as had Neumann, Parsons argues that in fascist discourse the processes of modernity are each understood as symptomatic of overarching problems with the modern order and each is identified with "the Jews": intellectualism; urbanism; economic, technological, and administrative rationalization;

cultural emancipation in literature and the arts; and the perception of moral emancipation. Each stand in fascist discourse as a proxy for Jews and Judaism. He put this succinctly and powerfully in "Democracy and Social Structure in Pre-Nazi Germany," another article from the same period: there is a "coincidence in Nazi ideology of the Jews, capitalism, bolshevism, anti-religious secularism, internationalism, moral laxity, and emancipation of women as a single class of things to be energetically combated." This approach is what Baum and Lechner call Parsons's "status insecurity and aggression theorem."[67]

Parsons went on to argue that specific groups experienced the social dislocations of modernity more intensely, specifically the lower-middle class because they are closest to achieving the promises of modernity. But the processes of rational-legal forms of rule combined with social stratification mean that only some actually achieve the goals of the social whole. Youth also suffer disproportionately from the "insecurities of competitive occupational adjustment," as do women.[68] Parsons had learned from his close colleague Edward Y. Hartshorne that these were some of the same groups that were more likely followers of the Nazi Party.[69]

In closing the article, Parsons perceptively suggested that nationalism is the ultimate incubator of the contradictions of modernity. On the one hand, the processes of state functions are a major engine of what Weber called simply "rationalization." But nationalism is also a repository of all the traditional sentiments that are melting into air in the cauldron of modernization. Parsons avers that transformational processes are always going to challenge certain vested interests. Fascism harnessed these discontents and was able at the same time to bring into the movement not only a traditional elite, but also the new business elite, since fascists were willing to fight organized labor on their behalf. Here and elsewhere in Parsons's wartime work, we thus see a robust sociological analysis of the structures that undergirded the Nazi movement and the role that anti-Semitism played in it. Parsons appreciated that these were internal not only to the development of Germany, but also to the contradictions of modernity itself, and that liberals needed to manage these counterforces.[70]

PARSONS ON RACISM

By 1945, Parsons had worked this material to the point of synthesizing his understanding of the dynamics of racism into a set of clear-cut propositions, best articulated in his article, "Racial and Religious Differences as Factors in Group

Tensions." Industrial modernity creates conditions of anomie, he stated, which lead to insecurity and aggression. To displace this aggression social groups either harness it or project it onto a pathologized out-group. As Parsons itemized it,

> There are (1) actually existent cultural and other differences between groups, creating barriers to communication and understanding. There are (2) elements of realistic conflict of value and interest. There are (3) internal tensions and insecurity in group life and structure, which create a need for the scapegoat reaction. There is (4) the relative adequacy or inadequacy of the other mechanisms of control or neutralization of the aggressive impulses generated by insecurity. There is (5) the symbolic appropriateness of an out-group as a scapegoat relative to particular tensions in the in-group. Finally, there are (6) the patterns of rationalization which justify scapegoating and make it subjectively acceptable to people.[71]

Parsons avows that these processes are as true for the Black/white dyad as for the relationship between Jews and non-Jews. But the situation of Jews was somewhat unique, he concluded:

> Their appropriateness as a scapegoat is to an important degree a function of their association with those areas of modern society most rapidly rationalized and "emancipated" from traditional values. Their actual concentration in metropolitan centers, in intellectual pursuits, in the literary and artistic world, and in some areas of business lend this association plausibility. If Jews could be evenly distributed through the total social structure, anti-Semitism would probably be greatly reduced.

Twenty years later, in the midst of Parsons's activism in the civil right struggle, we can see how his views had shifted, even as his commitment to liberal democracy continued. With the eruption of violence in Northern cities following the Civil Rights Bill in 1964, Parsons convinced the American Academy of Arts and Sciences, backed by the Ford Foundation, to engage in the most substantial analysis of the American Negro undertaken since the publication of Gunnar Myrdal's *An American Dilemma*. The result was a series of conferences that led to two groundbreaking issues of *Daedalus*, which in 1966 were edited together by Parsons and Kenneth B. Clark, with a foreword by President Johnson, as *The*

American Negro. Parsons's introduction "Why 'Freedom Now,' Not Yesterday?" drew together the contributors' insights to explain why the moment was fortuitous for the full inclusion of Negros as citizens.

Parsons's own contribution to the volume, "Full Citizenship for the Negro American? A Sociological Problem," drew on his updated theory of "societal community" to argue that African American citizenship required adherence to T. H. Marshall's threefold conception of citizenship. This entailed achievement of full civil, political, and social equality. Civil equality meant equal rights. Political equality involved not only the franchise but also the right to influence policy. These were necessary, but not sufficient to satisfy full citizenship, however.[72] The weight of Parsons's analysis consequently emphasized the social component, since liberal citizenship ultimately rested upon equality of opportunity, which required that discrimination be "abolished or minimized across a whole range" of areas, including employment, health, housing, and education.[73]

To make the case that this was possible for Blacks, Parsons assessed the processes that enabled ethnic white immigrants to integrate as full citizens, including Jews who confronted anti-Semitism in the United States. Since his attention was on American Judeophobia, which was historically quite different from its European manifestation, Parsons focused on how "snobbish anti-Semitism" was mostly about the articulation of status, thus resulting in the "exclusion of Jews from select clubs, college fraternities, residential neighborhoods, and resorts."[74] In his overview of Jewish integration into the United States, Parsons maintained that Jews showed a strong desire for inclusion, and Reform Judaism had eased Jewish self-segregation, which he continued to signal as an issue within Orthodox Jewish communities.[75]

A key factor distinguishing Parsons's approach in the 1960s from his earlier work was the emphasis he placed on pluralism, explicitly framing the article with a "clear distinction between *inclusion* and *assimilation*."[76] Pluralistic liberal democracy allowed for full inclusion of a diverse citizenry with the preservation of identity. The great test of this in America was whether the Negro American would achieve not only civil and political equality but also overcome social discrimination:

> This subcommunity of our pluralistic society [i.e., African Americans] has the opportunity to be *the* main symbolic spokesman of the possibility of achieving a racially, as well as religiously, nationally, and otherwise,

pluralistic world society in which some kind of integration among the racial groups can be developed without a loss of identity and in terms compatible with raising the previously inferior to the status of those fundamentally equal in world citizenship.[77]

The crucible of the civil rights struggle would test American democracy's capacity for achieving the normative values of modernity, claimed Parsons. He was engaged in the struggle to make sure they would, critiquing the separatism of Black nationalists in America just as he had that of ostensible Jewish separateness in Europe. But his pluralist emphasis on integration by the 1960s, rather than the assimilationist thrust in "The Sociology of Modern Anti-Semitism," showed that his viewpoint had shifted from his earlier writing.

PARSONS'S ALLOSEMITISM

Parsons's "The Sociology of Modern Anti-Semitism" ultimately depended upon what Zygmunt Bauman calls "allosemitism," which, as we have seen, he defined as "the practice of setting the Jews apart as people radically different from all the others, needing separate concepts to describe and comprehend them and special treatment in all or most social intercourse."[78] Indeed Parsons's allosemitism helps to reveal the limits of his liberal "anti-anti-Semitism." Like Weber's sociological analyses of Judaism, Parsons's early sociological theory of anti-Semitism was riddled with the problems of an ambivalent liberal universalism that ultimately did not affirm the historical particularities of Jewish culture, religion, and practices. Consequently, Parsons's solution to the Jewish Question was to caution against "any policy which tends to make Jews as Jews more conspicuous."

As we have seen, Sartre insightfully argued in *Anti-Semite and Jew*, written only a few years after Parsons's own reflections, that while the anti-Semite and the liberal unquestionably have a different political framework and agenda for Jews and Judaism, they converge insofar as "the former wishes to destroy him as a man and leave nothing in him but the Jew, the pariah, the untouchable; the latter wishes to destroy him as a Jew and leave nothing in him but the man, the abstract and universal subject of the rights of man and the rights of the citizen."[79] I conjecture, and one can do no more based on the evidence, that Parsons—like Sartre, Adorno and Horkheimer, and Arendt—came to recognize the limits of universalist liberalism in the aftermath of the Holocaust and that this accounts for why he buried "The Sociology of Modern Anti-Semitism" and shifted his approach in his later writings toward a more pluralist liberalism.

Still, Parsons's text, and the myriad of other works of sociology on the problem of anti-Semitism, gives lie to the boldness of Bauman's claim about sociology never wrestling with anti-Semitism as a motor not only of the Holocaust but of modernity, too.[80] It is wiser to think that Bauman built on a legacy that Parsons helped to establish. But Bauman's postmodern sociology of anti-Semitism does have the merit, where Parsons's approach did not, of orienting his understanding around an appreciation of Jewish alterity quite distinct from the liberal, Enlightenment, modernist tradition that undergirded Parsons's sociological imagination.

"'ANTISEMITISM' REASSESSED"

What Zygmunt Bauman did in his postmodern turn within sociological theory was to retheorize social differences and deviance, including anti-Semitism.[81] Bauman articulated the limits of prior approaches to sociology that sought to rescue and rehabilitate the modern social system through an analysis of its social structures and functions, explicitly calling out Parsons in an interview in *Telos*. Said Bauman, "The last great attempt to present the world as an orderly system was Talcott Parsons' theory—an attempt to impose on a disorganized world some sort of order, by selecting some aspects as normal and dismissing others as abnormal, deviations, pattern-breaking, etc."[82] Parsons's work, Bauman signaled, invariably reiterated the conceptual binaries of normality/abnormality and modernity/backwardness that Bauman maintained trapped Jews and other Others, reinforcing their marginalization, oppression, or persecution. Bauman's postmodern drift in sociological theory offered a new approach by reflexively examining some of the key assumptions and categories within modern sociology, in particular its treatment of alterity: how sociology understood the role of strangers, outsiders, the abnormal, and the dysfunctional, including Jews.

In Bauman's rethinking of Jews and Judaism, he drew from Simmel's sociology of the stranger,[83] alongside Horkheimer and Adorno's and Arendt's accounts of anti-Semitism, together with contemporary French postmodern insights drawn primarily from reflections on the work of Levinas and Derrida, in order to offer a postmodern sociological account of anti-Semitism. As such, his work is a new catalyst in social theory for reexamining cultural difference post-Holocaust. It was in his breakthrough duo of works, *Modernity and the Holocaust* (1989)[84] and *Modernity and Ambivalence* (1991),[85] that Bauman reconceptualized anti-Semitism as a part of his larger argument about the modernity of the Holocaust,[86] offering a new vocabulary and a different historical perspective on anti-Semitism.

Bauman distilled the core claims of his rethinking of anti-Semitism in a section of *Life in Fragments: Essays in Postmodern Morality* (1995), simply titled "'Antisemitism' Reassessed."[87] In this abbreviated version, Bauman brings together his reevaluation of modern sociology's approach to anti-Semitism developed in his earlier monographs by making four points: (1) the vocabulary of analysis needs to change; (2) this is because Jew-hatred is not the core of anti-Semitism; rather what fuels anti-Jewish thought and practice is ambivalence about Jews;[88] (3) this ambivalence is not timeless and unchanging; and (4) he offers his own historical account of how what he terms "allosemitism" has changed over time.

ALLOSEMITISM RECONSIDERED

Bauman's first intervention is to begin with terminology. He suggests that what must be understood is not "anti-Semitism," but *allosemitism*, "of which anti-semitism (alongside *philo*-semitism, as it were) is but an offshoot or a variety."[89] The Polish literary historian Artur Sandauer, Bauman explains, coined the term "allosemitism." *Allos* is the Greek word for *otherness*, and Bauman uses it as a framing category to understand the ways that Jews and Judaism are treated as the quintessence of difference, often embodying how all forms of alterity should be handled within a social system.[90] The shift in categories entailed by Bauman's vocabulary from "anti-Semitism" to "allosemitism" draws attention to an emphasis not on hatred, but on ambivalence toward Jews. Hatred is treated instead as a secondary emotion, rooted in the primordial confrontation with ambivalent feelings about Jews and Judaism.

This conception of allosemitism folds onto Bauman's second point, which is that anti-Semitism is often treated as a case of *heterophobia*—the resentment of differences that provoke anxiety.[91] Bauman maintains, however, that the heart of attitudes to Jews is not anti-Jewish hatred or contempt. Rather allosemitism is a form of *proteophobia*. To address the ambivalence that engenders the phobia of strangers, Bauman coins this term to name "the presence of multiform, allotropic phenomena which stubbornly elide assignment and sap the familiar classificatory grids."[92] Jews are not only disdained because they embody something that is "disquieting through otherness and unfamiliarity [i.e., heterophobia]." Instead, proteophobia aims its venom at the figures who disrupt the structure of the orderly world, "who do not fall easily into any of the established categories, who send out contradictory signals as to proper conduct and are behaviorally confusing."[93] Judeophobes, Bauman insists, fear the anxiety produced by Jews because they blur borderlines. They fear Jews as boundary busters who call into question the systems of reference for a modern world founded on categorization and classification often through binary formulas. Underlying this phobia is a mix of emotions ranging from hatred and contempt to envy and resentment.

What Bauman consequently thinks is at stake is not the hatred of Jewish otherness, but the contempt for forms of difference that cannot be neatly carved into categories. In suggesting this, Bauman reconceives Jewish alterity. He follows Simmel but with a Derridean drift, arguing in *Modernity and Ambivalence* that "strangers" are those who confuse the binaries of modernity, and that Jews are the paradigmatic strangers within Europe. Jews are "neither neighbours nor aliens, yet potentially (incongruously) both."[94] They are neither insiders nor outsiders, neither friends nor enemies, neither integrated nor repelled; they are liminal figures who straddle the borders of order.[95] The social figure of the stranger is always a social construction specific to differing social formations. Everywhere strangers are dangers not because of what they do but because they threaten to expose the social construction of nativity: the naturalness of other social categories like ethnicity and nationalism.[96]

THE HISTORY OF ALLOSEMITISM

Proteophobia is not free-floating in the cultural imagination, however. À la Durkheim and Parsons, for Bauman it is likewise engendered by social dislocation, the "dislike of situations in which one feels lost, confused, [and] disempowered."[97] These moments of social crisis have happened across time in different places for different reasons.

Bauman's third point consequently takes on the notion that anti-Semitism is timeless or of one block: "The history of the Jews is a subtle interplay of continuity and numerous discontinuities," he writes.[98] And "like all other 'special' histories, it is at each stage part and parcel of the currently prevailing type of society."[99] He critiques not only eternalist but also internalist histories of Jews and Judaism that only reflect on Jewish relations from within a Jewish perspective. Both impoverish or even bar the understanding of Judeophobia. Bauman concurs with Arendt that attitudes toward Jews cannot be severed from a broader comparative or interactionist lens.

Bauman's fourth move is to investigate the distinctive "shapes and causes of pre-modern, modern and postmodern allosemitism as a case of proteophobia."[100] He provides a historical account of the differences between these three epochs that he developed in greater detail in chapters 2 and 3 in *Modernity and the Holocaust*. In the first part of this historical overview, titled, "Jews Are Unlike the Others," Bauman advances the notion that under Christendom what defined attitudes and practices toward Jews is what Bauman terms *contestant enmity*: the antagonism generated by the practices of identity seeking and boundary drawing. Leveraging a reservoir of allosemitic stereotypes attached to Jews going back to the ancient world, Christianity augmented and reshaped these in developing its iconography, ultimately making the Jew the "virtual *alter ego* of the Christian church" since the identity of Christianity is "born of the rejection *by the Jews*."[101]

There were two aspects to this that Bauman underscores that are both innovative: first the "casting of Jews as the *embodiment of ambivalence*, that is of disorder" by Christian cultures. Jews were neither heathens nor heretics, but at the same time served as "the prototype and arch-pattern of all nonconformity, heterodoxy, anomaly and aberration," "the alternative to that order of things which had been defined, narrated and practiced by the Church."[102] Second was the construction of "the *abstract* Jew, the Jew as a concept located in a different discourse from practical knowledge of 'empirical' Jews."[103] The tyranny of the Cross consequently turned Jews into "that sworn enemy of the law of contradiction and the law of the excluded middle, those twin pillars of all order.... The Jew is ambivalence incarnate. And ambivalence is ambivalence mostly because it cannot be contemplated without ambivalent feelings: it is simultaneously attractive and repelling."[104] When the Christian world dominated the European world, Jews served as the world's "*alter ego*, marking the spatial and temporal boundaries of Christian civilization" where the "self-definition and boundary-drawing" was done around the idea of Jews.[105] Jews were thus the personification of the Christian uncanny.

Christian proteophobia, then, was defined by the anxiety of the Jew as a figure of ambivalence. Christendom constituted itself on the combined motifs of parricide and infanticide: "The Jews were the venerable ancestors of Christianity, who, however, refused to withdraw and to pass away once Christianity was born and took over, and having overstayed their time and outlived their divine mission continued to haunt the world as living fossils; and the Jews gave birth to Jesus only to reject, denigrate and disown Him."[106] In this formulation, Bauman ties together ideas of Freud, the Frankfurt School, and Leon Pinsker in positing his own theoretical claim about the contributions of Christian culture in its fixation on Jews as *ambivalence crucified*. In short, Bauman suggests that we do not correctly understand Christian Judeophobia as a form of heterophobia. Rather its murderous impulse is generated by contempt for the figure of Jews and Judaism it created in order to define itself—a figure of ambivalence itself.

Within premodern societies, Bauman contends, ambivalence was regulated primarily through religion. The key term was *sin*, which was seen as inevitable. Religion was a means of repentance from sin. Jews, however, were labeled as ontologically sinful: sin was sewn into their being. For this reason, Christian laws, regulations, social norms, and institutions could explode into crusades with Jewish targets, since sin and salvation were each connected to Jews through the drama of Christian redemption.

Following Pierre-André Taguieff, who draws from Claude-Levi Strauss's *Tristes tropiques*, Bauman further suggests that premodern cultures dealt with the threat of strangers primarily through an "*anthropophagic* strategy: they eat up, devour and digest (*biologically* incorporate and assimilate) the strangers who carry powerful, mysterious forces,"[107] hoping to absorb them. Premodern cultures seek to turn strangers into neighbors through conversation or assimilation. For Levi-Strauss, modern cultures, on the contrary, are *anthropoemic* (from the Greek, to vomit) evicting strangers or incarcerating them within bounds where they are sealed off. Strangers are constituted as aliens. All cultures oscillate in these *phagic* and *emic* strategies, insists Bauman. All societies are both inclusive and exclusive; all societies demand that one "conform or be damned"[108] as modes of social domination. Rules of admission are wedded to sanctions of expulsion and banishment. In the premodern world, the segregation of Jews was not an issue, since it was built into the order of things. But with modernity, when Jews left the ghetto walls, it was manufactured, rationally justified, technologically designed, administered, monitored, and managed.

JEWS AND MODERNITY

Modern modes of social engineering, therefore, shifted the terms and mechanisms of inclusion and expulsion. Modernity promised life free from sin (now renamed guilt). Modernity also promised a life free from ambivalence. The way this was carried out was by emphasizing individual moral responsibility more than rule following. Meta-ethical responsibility was assigned to specialists. As a result, instead of religious crusades, "modernity was the time of cultural crusades."[109] Invoking Louis Althusser and Michel Foucault, Bauman indicates that these were carried out through "schooling, therapy, jailing and universal surveillance"; the masters of this system were "medics, psychiatrists and jailers" who fought among themselves about what was abnormal—clamoring about whether it was medical, mental, or criminal.[110]

This was cashed out most emphatically on the bodies of colonial subjects abroad and on Jews in Europe. Central to Bauman's reevaluation of modernity and the Holocaust is his claim that genocide was not an accidental feature of the modern era. Instead, the modern world was founded on genocide after genocide.[111] He itemizes the extermination of Hottentots by the Boers, the Germans in South West Africa, Leopold II's Congo, and Vietnam. The genocide of European Jewry was part of a modern series. "What we learned in this century," he says, "is that modernity is not only about producing more and travelling faster, getting richer and moving around more freely. *It is also about—it has been about— fast and efficient killing, scientifically designed and administered genocide.*"[112]

In a reworking of some of the central arguments in *Modernity and the Holocaust* that link Bauman's reevaluation of anti-Semitism and the Holocaust, in *Life in Fragments* he discusses the three key features of modernity that facilitate genocidal murder: "(1) *The ability to act at a distance*, (2) *the neutralization of the moral constraints of action*, and (3) its 'gardening posture'—*the pursuit of artificial, rationally designed order.*"[113] I will treat these in reverse order.

The modern imagination treated the human habitat as a garden.[114] The social engineering of Hitler (and Stalin, for Bauman) was not a form of premodern barbarism, nor an example of "heterophobia—a resentment of everything strange, alien, unnatural and thus frightening."¹¹⁵ Nazis were antimodernist knights who drew upon modern science, eugenics, and biopower. What was unprecedented about the Nazi genocide from prior pogroms or cases of anti-Jewish mass slaughter was that it was planned and carried through in the name of social hygiene. Nazi anti-Semitism, Bauman insists, was social engineering on steroids. To make the point, he quotes Detlev Peukert's *Inside Nazi Germany*, which explains that Nazi Germany's social order, "was the racialist elimination of all elements that deviated from the norm.... It laid down criteria of assessment, categories of classification and norms of efficiency that were applicable to the population as a whole."¹¹⁶ Conveniently for the Nazis, Jews had already been defined as the embodiment of the deviant, the abnormal, the decadent, and the dysfunctional by Christendom. The Nazi project was to target those social types marked as degenerate, useless, and unhealthy.

Nazi legislation built upon the abstract Jew of Christendom to constitute the *metaphysical Jew* of Nazi propaganda, placing Jews legally and morally outside the "universe of obligation."¹¹⁷ Jews were weeds who defied the classificatory grids of the Nazi social landscape. Explicating Bauman, Sophia Marshman summarizes the point: "Put simply, once 'classified' as weeds, as people standing outside of (and in the way of) the 'perfect' order/utopia" Jews became superfluous to the ideal society, the ultimate threat to its existence.¹¹⁸ The Nazis sought to eliminate what Christianity had already constituted as the essence of ambivalence. As Bauman puts it in *Modernity and the Holocaust*, "All visions of society-as-garden define parts of the social habitat as human weeds. Like all other weeds, they [Jews] must be segregated, contained, prevented from spreading, and kept outside the society's boundaries; if all these means prove insufficient, they must be killed."¹¹⁹

Bauman avers that Nazi racism was thus different in nature, function, and mode of operation from either contestant enmity or heterophobia. As we have seen, early Christianity was defined by the identity seeking and boundary drawing that characterized the competition and contestation between Christianity and Judaism. In the later medieval period and through the early modern world, Christian heterophobia added antipathy and resentment to the activity of separation. With contestant enmity, segregation marks off an out-group clearly identified as alien and different. Heterophobia is more concerned with the enemy within. Nazi-style racism is different and specifically modern, connected to social engineering—a strategy of modern social organization that combines design, gardening, and medicine—to transform social reality into a utopian ideal by eliminating the undesirable elements of present reality: "Gardening and medicine supply the archetypes... while normality, health, or sanitation offered the archmetaphors for human tasks and strategies."[120] Hitler's racism was consumed with "disease, infection, infestations, putrefaction, [and] pestilence."[121] Parasitological paranoia cultivated anti-Jewish repellence that led to extermination as "an exercise in the rational management of society."[122] Exterminatory anti-Semitism is thus thoroughly modern in bringing together race, medicine, and social engineering.

Christian Judeophobia was a blueprint for why Jews were the primary target for the Nazis; but Nazi racism combined contestant enmity and heterophobia into a new form of redemptive racism. If Jews were the chosen targets, the twisted road to Auschwitz was built upon two additional aspects unique to modernity. First, a "moral *adiaphorisation* of action" was demanded.[123] In other words, killing must be rendered morally neutral.[124] Secondly, to accomplish this, killing needed to become a mediated action—a product of the "agentic state." Drawing from Raul Hilberg's historical work and Arendt's "banality of evil" thesis, Bauman maintains that each actor in the long chain of bureaucratic decisions was split from the process as a whole and only made decisions within their own narrow purview. This was how the modern bureaucracy, Weber's "iron cage of modernity," neutralized the moral questions entailed in following orders.

POSTMODERN ALLOSEMITISM

Bauman concludes his historical overview in "'Antisemitism' Reassessed" with a take on how allosemitism has morphed in the contemporary period. Postmodernity, or "liquid modernity" as Bauman's later writing would term it, is more fragmented and market dominated than the "solid modernity" of the short twentieth century. Bauman likes the term "liquid modernity" because liquids do not hold their shape, and the world we live in is one of constant flux and change. As Bauman cleverly puts it, modernity was characterized by a delay of *gratification*, while postmodernity is about a "*delay of payment*": "If the savings book was the epitome of modern life, the credit card is the paradigm of the postmodern one."[125]

Postmodern Judeophobia is consequently less about social engineering and statist projects than about the anxiety generated by the marketplace. Still, the long-enduring stereotype about an international Jewish cabal to achieve world domination is well suited to the fears engendered by globalization. But the globalized marketplace and the capitalist postindustrial order is Janus-faced. On the one hand (as is evident in Bauman's earlier and more optimistic writing on the postmodern), liquid modernity offers a diffuse social pluralism, where "every choice goes, providing it is a choice, and each order is good, providing it is one of many and does not exclude other orders." The liquidity of the postmodern thus opens a new hermeneutic for reevaluating the terms of Jewish difference about what generates the ambivalence about Jews and Judaism within the history of the West, evident in so much postmodern theorizing, as we will explore in the next chapter.[126]

On the other hand, and more ominously, our postmodern present is constituted by "the sectarian fury of neotribal self-assertion, the resurgence of violence as the principal instrument of order-building, the feverish search for home truths."[127] This is the face of the most lethal forms of populist authoritarianism and jihadi Judeophobia. This view, as Bauman puts it at one point, is based upon "'I shout, therefore I am,' which is the neotribal version of the *cogito*."[128] This is also evident in aspects of the post-Holocaust Judeophobia explored in detail in my conclusion.[129]

Most of Bauman's writing on postmodern strangers does not focus on Jews, however. The qualities identified with contestant enmity, heterophobia, the conceptual Jew, and the metaphysical Jew morphed to discussions that target other communities. The postmodern stranger is a privatized version of the modern stranger.[130] New social types embody postmodern strangers that Bauman terms in different places the "flawed consumer," the "non-voluntary traveler," "the undecidable," and especially, the "vagabonds" who make up the "new poor." These sociological categories are embodied by those people deemed worthless today who are denied entry visas to the corridors of postmodern power: "unemployed people, welfare mothers, homeless people, beggars, housing project tenants, illegal immigrants, refugees, and indigenous minorities, all carrying different religions, ethnicities and nationalities."[131] The challenge of conceptualizing Judeophobia in this changed social setting is to understand how the social location of Jews and Judaism comports with the racialized social formations affecting these other postmodern strangers. This challenge is taken up in my concluding chapter.

We have seen that Bauman both built upon a robust sociological tradition that developed in tandem with modern anti-Semitism and reconceptualized how that tradition should theorize Judeophobia. He provided a new vocabulary for understanding the shifts between early Christian contestant enmity and medieval and early modern heterophobia, and he articulated what was distinctive about the proteophobia that undergirded modern anti-Jewish racism. He insightfully showed that Judeophobia rests upon ambivalence, not unbridled hatred. Lastly, drawing upon Simmel's sociological ruminations on the stranger, he repositioned sociology not as a bulwark against those who opposed liberal modernity in the vein of Durkheim and Weber as synthesized by Parsons, but instead mined the resources of critical theory from Arendt, the Frankfurt School, and those French postmodern theorists who followed in Sartre's wake. None of these French theorists was more responsible for articulating a postmodern philosophical interpretation of anti-Semitism than Jean-François Lyotard.

CHAPTER 5

Jean-François Lyotard, Postmodernism, and "the jews"

Like Arendt who maintained that the Holocaust required a reconsideration of Western political theory, and Bauman who used it as a window to reexamine sociology, the French philosopher Jean-François Lyotard considered the Holocaust an event of such magnitude that it necessitated a reassessment of Western philosophy. As the thinker who gave the term "postmodernism" its philosophical meaning, Lyotard closely linked his understanding of the postmodern with rethinking the place of Jews, Judaism, and anti-Semitism within Western culture. He thus contributed to reformulating the way philosophers, literary critics, and historians talk and think about Auschwitz. In the process, he showed how Judeophobia serves to deconstruct Western philosophy and culture. For Judeophobia reveals the West's persistent repression, rejection, oppression, and persecution of Jewish difference: the primordial Other within the West.

This chapter traces Lyotard's intellectual trajectory, showing how it exemplifies some of the dominant themes of postmodernism, underscoring the pivotal significance connecting the history of Jews, Judaism, and the Jewish Question to the postmodern position.[1] These themes have a long history in Lyotard's work,[2] starting with his first published text, a review of Karl Jaspers's *The Question of German Guilt*, written just after World War II (1948). Lyotard picked up this thread in essays composed in the 1960s and 1970s on psychoanalysis in general and *Moses and Monotheism* in particular, drawing a parallel between the unconscious and the figure of "the Jew" in Western culture. He later extended these insights, arguing that "the Jew" signified an incomprehensible, unidentifiable alterity that the European tradition has consistently excluded, repressed, or otherwise forgotten. His philosophical magnum opus, *Le Différend* (*The Differend*,

1983)—Lyotard's concept for a dispute that can no longer be resolved with reference to a universal metanarrative—threaded its philosophical questions around the event of the Shoah. In the context of "the Heidegger affair," which erupted in France in 1987 and concerned the influence of Heidegger on contemporary French thought despite his role as a Nazi sympathizer, Lyotard published *Heidegger and "the jews"* (1988). He subsequently argued in "Europe, the Jews and the Book" (1990) that the disinterring and vicious violation of a Jewish body at a cemetery in Carpentras in 1990 was only the latest in a long series of attempts in the West to erase the differend dividing Jews and Europe. In *Un trait d'union (The Hyphen*, 1993), Lyotard traced the origins of this divide to the hyphen that marks the differend in the so-called Judeo-Christian tradition. Through a reading of Paul's Epistles, Lyotard explores how the *trait d'union* serves to mark the erasure of the differend between Jewish and Christian conceptions of time, memory and history, election, revelation and redemption, justice, ethics, knowledge, and language.

Lyotard's analysis of anti-Semitism was thus integrally woven into his postmodern theory, encompassing a critique of the whole Greco-Roman-Christian-Enlightenment and modern European tradition, using the figure of "the Jew" to demonstrate the West's incapacity to think heterogeneity and cultural difference. By the 1980s, "Auschwitz" came to function metonymically to indicate a series of philosophical questions about history and reference, ethics and politics that registered the break between modernity and the postmodern. "'Auschwitz' can be taken as a paradigmatic name for the tragic 'incompletion' of modernity," Lyotard stipulates, insisting that "it is the crime opening postmodernity.... How could the grand narratives of legitimation still have credibility in these circumstances?"[3] This chapter examines the key texts in which Lyotard elaborated his post-Holocaust, postmodern reflections on the underlying causes of Judeophobia.

In responding to Jaspers's reflections on guilt in light of the Nuremberg trials of leading Nazis, Lyotard signaled that the Shoah raised a host of philosophical problems previously unexamined, including an inadequate understanding of responsibility in the face of genocide. Developing this insight in his later riffs on psychoanalysis, he suggested that Jews and Judaism were the alter ego or super-ego of the West, the unconscious Other against which the Greco-Christian European tradition was defined. Akin to Bauman, Lyotard proposed that hostility toward Jews was generated by their incomprehensibility and unidentifiability. This confounded the Western desire to master through knowledge and reason, which was prioritized over ethics and responsibility toward the Other, a theme he drew from the Jewish philosopher Emmanuel Levinas. Dispersed, Judaism was founded on textuality, which challenged the emphasis on incarnation that could lead to idol worship in Christianity. Inspired by Maurice Blanchot, for Lyotard, Jews were constituted by exile and diaspora, which disrupts appeals for unity and mythic forms of identity. In agreement with Adorno, Lyotard drew upon the Jewish experience to personify the dangers of "identity thinking." Auschwitz ultimately served as a sign of the dead ends of all final solutions. In Lyotard's meditations on Heidegger, Heidegger's silence about the horror of the annihilation of European Jewry serves as a totem for the limits of all thought. The exterminatory impulse, Lyotard maintains, is generated by the refusal to recognize that all thinking forgets, represses, and marginalizes. What Lyotard terms "the jews" serve as a reminder of this forgetting, which stokes the anxiety generated toward "the Jews." In his last works, Lyotard addressed how Judeophobia was generated by the desire for mastery, incorporation, appropriation, and the assimilation of cultural difference. Lyotard's postmodernism thus understands Judeophobia as a symptom of a deep structural problem within Western philosophy and culture.

LYOTARD'S INTELLECTUAL TRAJECTORY

Born in Versailles (Seine-et-Oise) in 1924, from an early age Jean-François Lyotard (1924–1998) had an interest in cultural expression. He recalls that by eleven or twelve he "wanted either to become a monk (especially a Dominican), a painter, or historian" and three years later he "actually began to write poems, essays, short stories, and, later still, a novel."[4] After studying at the elite preparatory schools, lycées Buffon and Louis-le-Grand, he twice failed entrance to the École Normale Supérieure before he pursued advanced degrees in literature and philosophy at the Faculté des lettres de Paris (the Sorbonne), where he befriended Gilles Deleuze. He passed the *agrégation* (the examination to teach philosophy) in 1950 and began to teach at a lycée in Constantine, the capital of the French department of East Algeria, moving after two years to teach at a school for the sons of military personnel at La Flèche in the metropole until 1959.

Lyotard's engagement with Marxism began in Constantine, spurred by the burgeoning colonial conflict in Algeria, which erupted into the war of independence in 1954. From 1954 to 1964, he contributed to and served on the editorial committee of the journal *Socialisme ou barbarie* (Socialism or barbarism), along with Cornelius Castoriadis, Claude Lefort, and Pierre Souyris. After splitting with the journal over Castoriadis's new theoretical direction, he worked on the newspaper *Pouvoir ouvrier* (Worker's power). Both outlets were avant-garde venues for elaborating a Marxist critique of Stalinism and dogmatic dialectical materialism. His first articles were composed during the heat of the Franco-Algerian War but were only published together twenty-five years later as *La Guerre des Algériens: Écrits 1956–63* (The Algerian war: Texts 1956-63, 1989). They opposed the French colonial regime in Algeria while analyzing the conflict between colonizer and colonized as it unfolded. If a Marxist framework guided his analysis, by the aftermath of the war Lyotard had lost his belief in Marxism as a totalizing theory.[5]

He began to teach at the Sorbonne in 1959 and then acquired a position at the University of Paris X, Nanterre, the site of the beginnings of the student revolts that led to the massive uprisings in May-June 1968, which he energetically supported. He completed his *doctorat d'état* in 1971, after which he moved to the University of Paris VIII at Vincennes, a post that he held until his official retirement in 1989, also teaching seminars at the Centre national de la recherche scientifique. He was one of the founders of the International College of Philosophy, serving as its second director. He continued to teach in various international institutions until his death of a second bout with cancer on April 21, 1998.

Lyotard's first published book *La Phénoménologie* (1954) is still a classic introduction to the subject.[6] Searching for new theoretical orientations, Lyotard became fascinated with psychoanalysis after he attended Jacques Lacan's seminars in the mid-1960s. Intrigued with Lacan's critique of ego-psychology and his structuralist remapping of the unconscious via linguistics, Lyotard eventually published works in the late 1960s and early 1970s that challenged both the Freudian and Lacanian emphasis on the Oedipus complex and that also critiqued phenomenology and structuralism. Like many of his contemporaries, in the 1970s he contributed to the revival of Friedrich Nietzsche in France and the attention to the will to power at work in truth claims.[7] *La Condition postmoderne* (*The Postmodern Condition*, 1979) was a breakthrough text that led to his international acclaim. As Frederic Jameson describes it, *The Postmodern Condition* is "at the crossroads of many problems and books which intersect in the text."[8] Claiming in its subtitle to be "a report on knowledge," it welds together a sociological analysis of knowledge production and science and technology with a set of epistemological reflections.

Lyotard argues that the postmodern condition is constituted by a crisis of legitimation derived from the "incredulity toward metanarratives" in contemporary society.[9] By metanarratives, Lyotard means "precisely narrations with a legitimating function."[10] Grand narratives claim to provide a universal story according to which all other claims can be evaluated. The metanarratives of modernity include the natural sciences, Hegelianism and Marxism, and psychoanalysis, for these were each all-encompassing accounts of reality. The postmodern condition, Lyotard avers, is characterized by a lack of consensus about any narrative that can provide a basis for a universal explanation or a universal law that can resolve epistemological or political disputes. When he began to articulate this postmodern critique in the late 1970s and early 1980s, he demonstrated a profound interest in the work of Levinas and more generally in Judaism as a source providing a critical perspective from which to deconstruct Western thought. Lyotard's own intellectual route (Marxism, phenomenology, decolonization, psychoanalysis, May '68, Nietzsche, deconstruction) exemplifies the aggregate of influences acting on postmodern thought, which ultimately offered new insights into conceptualizing Judeophobia.

BEGINNINGS: "GERMAN GUILT"

Lyotard's very first publication was an intimation of the central role that Nazism, the Holocaust, and Judeophobia would eventually play in his thought. It was a lengthy review of *Die Schuldfrage* (*The Question of German Guilt*, 1947), the famous essay that Karl Jaspers had published on the occasion of the Nuremberg trials. In his opening line, Lyotard recognized the seminal nature of Jaspers's work, which contemplated "something that has not yet been *thought*, in the strict sense of the word: German guilt."[11] After parsing Jaspers's analysis, Lyotard leveled a powerful critique that intimated his differences with Jaspers's existentialist analysis of Nazism. He argued that the categories Jaspers developed to assess the problem individualized guilt, ultimately depoliticizing his analysis of Nazism, since it failed to recognize how individual choices operated within political structures.

To clarify the problem of German guilt, Lyotard explained, Jaspers distinguished between four different modes of responsibility: (1) legal responsibility

(*Kriminelle Schuld*), defined in terms of national or international law, for which liability rests in the courts; (2) political responsibility (*Politische Schuld*), since every people is responsible for the government that it gives itself, requiring each citizen to reflect on their role within the policies and programs carried about by their state; (3) moral responsibility (*Moralische Schuld*), defined in classic existential terms as the culpability of a free consciousness that chooses its own actions and then is judged by those undertakings; and (4) metaphysical responsibility (*Metaphysische Schuld*), which was a matter of individual conscience resting upon the metaphysical principle that each of us is coresponsible for every other human being—Jaspers asserting that this solidarity is what defines our humanity. With metaphysical guilt, Jaspers averred, only God can judge.

Jaspers recognized that these four categories interpenetrated one another. But he maintained that conceptually they ought to be kept distinct. This was important, for example, since legally one could not charge a collective in the same way one could an individual. Indeed, Jaspers argues against the notion of "collective guilt" and he uses the example of "the Jews" to demonstrate his point: the Nazi horror made evident the irresponsibility of ascribing collective guilt to the Jewish people for the death of Jesus or stabbing the Germans in the back.[12] It is dangerous and fallacious to conjure up collectivities like "the Jews" or "the Germans." Moreover, to do so was to engage in "typological" thought. To postulate *the* Germans or *the* Jews presupposed "a degradation of the individual as such: this was the basis of the profoundly abstract Nazi systematization."[13]

Still, Jaspers went on to indicate that Nazi criminal guilt was undeniable, even if the Nuremberg tribunal only established the legal precedents after the fact. Political blame, too, was evident. Germans bore political responsibility collectively for allowing a minority to act in their name. Abstention from counteracting this amounted to political guilt. While Jaspers went on to insist that there could be no collective moral culpability, certain institutional groups were also collectively accountable, including the Gestapo, the SS, and the Reichskabinett. While moral guilt was absolute and wholly individual, it took a wide diversity of forms that Jaspers outlined: from "moral masking" to "bad conscience," from "half measures" to "present acceptance of the worst with an eye to a better future," and from "omission," "inaction," and "fence-sitting" to sheer "opportunism." Its valence depended upon measuring intentions. There were also a bundle of contextual circumstances or excuses (*Entschuldigung*) that mitigated guilt. When it came to a metaphysical accounting, however, "the only good consciences were in the camps."[14]

After laying out Jaspers's arguments, Lyotard's criticisms of his conceptualization of German guilt dangled on a pointed question: "*Why* was this book written? Not to what purpose, but for what motives?"[15] According to Lyotard, Jaspers's motivations hung on the horns of a dilemma. On the one hand, he clung to the philosopher's belief that *self-awareness* could purify each German who undertook the accounting of the soul for their individual part in the machinery of destruction. "Purification (*Reinigung*) will be an action of self on the self," wrote Lyotard, summarizing Jaspers's approach.[16] Individual salvation was possible through the assumption of individual responsibility.

But the Christian theological thrust of Jaspers's assessment was misguided and built on an inherent tension. For Jaspers sought to lay out a path as well for *German* regeneration, even though he insisted that it could not be taken collectively. In contending that Germans as individuals needed to work through the past in order to purify themselves, Jaspers had consequently posed "a political problem nonpolitically."[17] Moreover, the political could not be so easily detached from the moral, and morality could not be so easily separated from the metaphysical. Nazism, Lyotard maintained, "cannot be brought to trial by any moral or metaphysical law, except in terms of its consequences."[18] To take account of these consequences and to reflect on what structured them was to assess Nazism politically. For Lyotard, the shortcoming of Jaspers's *Existenzphilosophie* was that it resulted in depoliticizing his account of German guilt. The catharsis that Jaspers sought could only have a "social form" that was "subordinate to the conditions of history."[19] Despite his criticisms, Lyotard was aware that Jaspers's "dispersal of responsibilities, remains the paradoxical defining characteristic of the book."[20] Most significant for Lyotard's later work, he also appreciated that Jaspers was attuned to how Nazism signaled the "probable failure of our Western civilization" and the need for a new conception of humanity evoked in his notion of metaphysical guilt.[21]

JEWS AND THE UNCONSCIOUS

If Lyotard's earliest work, evident in his review of Jaspers's *Die Shuldfrage*, was developed by playing a proto-Marxism off phenomenology and existentialism, then his writing in the 1960s and 1970s can be summarized in the title of his *Dérive à partir de Marx et Freud* (1973). His drift from Marx to Lacan nonetheless challenged psychoanalysis by insisting that the Lacanian conception of the unconscious as structured like a language erased the difference between consciousness and the unconscious. Like Gilles Deleuze and Felix Guattari, and congruent with the growing antipsychiatry movement of the 1970s,[22] Lyotard challenged the Freudian and Lacanian emphasis on the Oedipus complex by characterizing the unconscious as an unrepresentable, uncodifiable economy of libidinal energy that remains Other to consciousness.[23] He would explore the ramifications of this drift for Jews and Judaism in two articles, "Jewish Oedipus" (1970) and "Figure Foreclosed" (1984).[24]

In these articles, Lyotard explicitly linked the problems in psychoanalysis and philosophy he was considering by drawing a parallel between the unconscious and the figure of "the Jew" in Western culture. He depicted "the Jew" as incomprehensible and unidentifiable, the imperative alterity that the European tradition and Western metaphysics has consistently excluded, repressed, and "forgotten." From this early stage, therefore, Lyotard's work assessed the problem of anti-Semitism on its most general structural level. He critiqued the whole Greco-Roman-Christian-Enlightenment tradition of the West by suggesting how it had failed in its debt and responsibility for the Other. Both articles turn upon how Lyotard establishes Jews and Judaism as an opposing tradition to the Greco-Roman-Christian-Enlightenment. These articles thus prefigure how Lyotard later came to define the postmodern itself. Reflections on Jews and Judaism serve to deconstruct the West's hierarchies, Lyotard suggested, especially the prioritization of knowledge over ethics, and truth in opposition to art.

Lyotard made his key claims through a reading of Freud. For it was Freud, he says in the opening of "Jewish Oedipus," who distinguished between knowledge and "truth-work."[25] Lyotard goes on to correlate art and theater, maintaining that theater was a form of dream work that actually performed truth-work. This "*truth-work* operates through the mediation of the tragic scene," wrote Lyotard, and it "sets us off on an important track: Hamlet's unaccomplishment of the paternal word as modernity's difference from the Greek world."[26]

Wrapped into this pithy and enigmatic formulation, in "Jewish Oedipus," Lyotard set up a group of oppositions he sought to question: Greek/Jew, Oedipus/Hamlet, accomplishment/unaccomplishment, tragedy/ethics, embodiment/absence. To do so, Lyotard explained that a key difference between Greek and Shakespearean tragedy is that unlike *Oedipus*, *Hamlet* clearly stages a play within a play. This Lyotard reads as self-reflexive: an externalization of the problematic raised by the play within the play itself. As a result, "*we in the audience are able to see the blind spot, to see Hamlet not see.*"[27]

As Lyotard unpacked his opposition between Oedipus and Hamlet, he suggested a set of parallels that Freud established contrasting the Greek and the Jewish traditions. The Greek (Oedipus) and the Jewish Shakespearean (Hamlet) are also counterpoints between the tragic and the ethical, and between accomplishment and embodiment in contrast to nonfulfillment, absence, longing, loss, and debt, which are identified as Jewish traits. "Oedipus fulfills his fate of desire," writes Lyotard. "The fate of Hamlet," on the other hand, "is nonfulfillment of desire; this chiasma is the one that extends between what is Greek and what is Jewish, between the tragic and the ethical."[28]

Lyotard developed these suggestive contrasts through a set of formulas that he teased out of religious existentialists like Rudolf Bultmann and Levinas. From Bultmann, he took the notion that "in Hebraic ethics representation is forbidden," which demands hearing the father's word. This sets the stage for an "ethical subject" who "knows himself seized by an Other who has spoken"; as such, Hamlet is "elected."[29] This Levinasian treatment of Hamlet in opposition to Oedipus is evident in Lyotard's citations from Levinas's *Quatre lectures talmudiques*, which expressed in a Jewish lexicon the arguments he made in *Totality and Infinity* for an ethics that precedes ontology, and a rejection of dialectical totalization as one finds in Hegel and Marx, or ontological fulfillment as one finds in Christianity. Writes Lyotard, echoing Levinas, "This voice is a light, and the face, *Totality and Infinity* has taught us... the presence of the absolute Other."[30] Levinas and Lyotard thereby critiqued the Western tradition as emphasizing a form of knowledge that incorporates everything outside of it into a totalizing logic of the same, and that prioritizes epistemology and truth over ethics.

The last few paragraphs of "Jewish Oedipus" stem from a quick gloss on *Moses and Monotheism* that forms the tie between this earlier text and Lyotard's later "Figure Foreclosed." Lyotard maintains that what Freud offered in *Moses and Monotheism* was an account of the rejection of Jews, which "blocks the road of anamnesis for the Jews."[31] The Jew is thus the forgotten. Unlike other religions, Judaism refused to participate in the parricide that founds the cult. Instead, Jews acted out by killing Moses, but then foreclosed any recollection of this murder. This foreclosure distanced them from Christianity and from later models of reconciliation (read Hegelianism and dialectical thought). In an interpretation of Freud's opposition between *Oedipus* and *Hamlet*, then, Lyotard traced out the "difference between Greek fate... and Jewish kerygma."[32] In the Greek Oedipus, the tragedy is Oedipus's nonrecognition of his fatal flaw given his fixation with truth and self-knowledge. Hamlet's (Jewish) tragedy is announced by the spin the atheistic Jew Freud puts on it. Hamlet takes a detour through art (the play within the play) toward an ethics that demands "the ear that wants to hear *what* the voice of the Other says, instead of being seized and dispossessed, and this is the atheism demanded by Freud."[33] This ethics that precedes epistemology that Lyotard reworks by reading Freud with a Levinasian lens, is predicated on an epistemological break with a Western tradition defined by how it knows, classifies, structures, and orders the world in its cognitive grasp. At work in the "truth-work" of "Jewish Oedipus," then, was a wholesale critique of the Greco-Roman-Christian-Enlightenment West.

By the early 1980s, Lyotard had already explicitly developed this into his understanding of the postmodern condition. In "Figure Foreclosed," he reprised and dramatically extended his earlier flirtation with Freud's *Moses*. Like "Jewish Oedipus," "Figure Foreclosed" is a dense, layered, and complicated text that offers yet another enigmatic reading of Freud's *Moses and Monotheism*. It proved key to Lyotard's postmodern understanding of anti-Semitism.

Recall that in *Moses and Monotheism*, Freud maintained that the original Moses was a monotheistic Egyptian who sought to continue the religion of Akhenaton with a group that fled Egypt. His own people then murdered him, repressing the guilty memory of the murder. They later resurrected him as Moses the Midianite, their lawgiver. Freud thus transposed onto his account of the origins of Judaism his analysis of *Totem and Taboo*, which sought to explain the origins of religion by maintaining that the Ur-father was murdered and devoured, engendering a guilt that solidifies tribal fraternity and thus initiates the symbolic or the totemic reality, a return of the repressed, which for Freud underlies the neurosis of religion.

In "Figure Foreclosed," Lyotard extended his take on Freud's *Moses*. He claimed that in Judaism there is a complete foreclosure (as opposed to a repression) of parricide, an exclusion of the totemic meal, and a denial of magic and myth that marks Judaism as different from other totemic religions. "It is because it is different that it is important," wrote Lyotard. "And the empirical mark of its difference has always been the hatred it inspires: antisemitism."[34] In threading together his take on Judaism and Freud's *Moses*, Lyotard wove together a set of oppositions that once unwound indicate how he depicted Judaism as an alter ego to the Greco-Christian West, a ceaselessly self-interrogating Other constitutive of the West, but excluded from its logos—its superego, but denied as such.

There have been two traditions of disaggregating power and knowledge in the West, claimed Lyotard in his opening lines: Moses and Socrates, one Jewish and the other Greek. As we saw in "Jewish Oedipus," he maintained that constitutive of Judaism was a prohibition against making an image of God coupled with the compulsion of worshipping this absent deity. This ultimately privileged intellectuality over sensuality, textuality over embodiment, the reality principle over the pleasure principle, the word over the image. The Jews as a "People of the Book" are opposed to the Greco-Christian worshippers of the idolized cross. Instead, Judaism worships the command of the absolute but absent Other. "The wanderings of the Jews express the transcendence of the readable over the visible," wrote Lyotard, which severs Jews from the earth, the peasant, and the mythic.

On top of his earlier suggestions in "Jewish Oedipus," Lyotard now revised his reading of *Moses*, clearly integrating the arguments that Blanchot developed in his classic, "Être juif" ("Being Jewish"). Elizabeth Bellamy has argued, "French postmodernism's preoccupation with the figure of the Jew has its postwar origins not so much in Sartre as in Blanchot."[35] But Blanchot's text is a critique of Sartre's *Anti-Semite and Jew*. Included in *L'entretien infini* (*The Infinite Conversation*), a series of essays written between 1953 and 1965, Blanchot's "Being Jewish" reproves Sartre's negative ontology of "the Jew": the Jew as the object of the specular gaze that was central to Sartre's analysis in *Anti-Semite and Jew*.

According to Blanchot, Sartre described anti-Semitism rigorously. As we have seen, Sartre showed that the accusation drawn up against "the Jew" reveals nothing about the Jew but everything about the anti-Semite, since the anti-Semite projects the force of his injustice, his stupidity, his base meanness, and his anxiety onto his enemy. But in affirming that Jews are no more than a product of the Other's gaze and are only Jewish by the fact of being seen as such by the Other (which thereby obliges Jews to either deny or to claim their identity), Sartre tends to recognize Jewish difference, but merely as the negation of anti-Semitism.[36]

At the same time that Blanchot was critical of Sartre, he also generalized Sartre's reflections on the marginalization of Jews to forge what became an important theme of postmodern critiques of the West: "Every society, and in particular Christian society, has had its Jew in order to affirm itself against him through relations of general oppression."[37] The form of oppression visited upon the body of the Jew within the body politic thus entails "a particular relation of responsibility (a relation not yet elucidated) with this 'Other' that is the Jew."[38]

Unlike Sartre, however, Blanchot maintained that Judaism is more than just a rich cultural heritage. He asserted via riffs on the work of Albert Memmi, André Neher, and Levinas that Judaism offers positive truths that are still significant today. In particular, "being Jewish" signifies that "the idea of exodus and the idea of exile can exist as a legitimate movement."[39] On the basis of this affirmation of "uprooting," "strangeness," and "foreignness," Blanchot developed the kernels of several postmodern themes. "To be pagan is to be fixed, to plant oneself in the earth," while Judaism teaches the value of the sojourn, he wrote, of "a people without a land and bound by a word."[40] The Jewish diaspora "forbids the temptation of Unity-Identity" and "has nothing of the mythical about it."[41] Jewish dispersion is not only spatial and temporal but also epistemological, because the exile of Abraham was also a paradigm of man's exclusion "from the truth."[42] Jewish monotheism inscribes the preservation of alterity that comes from dialogue with the unknown and unknowable, the strange and distant, and bears witness "as Levinas says, to this relation with difference that the human face ... reveals to us and entrusts to our responsibility."[43] Anti-Semitism is precisely "the repulsion inspired by the Other" that takes different forms in its effort to suppress the significance of "being Jewish."

Blanchot's account of "Being Jewish" influenced Lyotard's reading of *Moses and Monotheism*. The absent father Moses pronounces the law, wrote Lyotard, establishing an ethical order that "will constitute the cultural superego specific to the Jewish people and to the West."[44] But unlike the Greco-Christian tradition, founded on repression and the return of the repressed, the Jewish relation to the father is one of foreclosure. This distinction was the axial point of Lyotard's whole argument. For while in the totemic "religion of the son" there is use of magic and images, "Judaism excluded the figure, excludes magic, excludes reconciliation, excludes the totem meal; Judaism crudely refuses to admit to parricide."[45]

Here Lyotard's "Figure Foreclosed" drifted into worrisome territory, however. For he maintained that he would show that according to Freud's own lexicology—his psychoanalytic vocabulary and form of analysis—that unlike Christianity, Judaism was not neurotic, but "psychotic." This was an advance from Christianity, although not a complete working through. As problematic as the opposition sounds, Lyotard valorized the position of the psychotic for four reasons that summed up his argument in "Figure Foreclosed." First, the Jewish detachment from myth was congruent with a detachment from reality. The result was that Jewish thought also foreclosed mediation and the dialectic constitutive of Platonism, Christianity, and Hegelianism (i.e., much of Western thought). Secondly, following Bultmann once more, Lyotard insisted that the Hebraic was not concerned with politics, but with moral demands that were worked out through what Lyotard called the "predominance of the text."[46]

Following from this and thirdly, Judaism was a religion based on the Law defined by the *Urvater* as a text to be deciphered, not a matter of blood or symbols. "The Jew" is thus understood by Lyotard as an illocutionary position—a listener to the address of God, the Other who demands, like the father Moses. As such, Judaism is a religion based on writing: the discourse of an absence that refuses the final fulfillment of meaning. This defines the final characteristic of the "Jewish son": "constant self-accusations, and worries about responsibilities."[47] The "Judaic superego" is "an ego accused, an ego which can never atone for the debt it owes its 'conscience,' its father."[48] Lyotard expressed the upshot of this set of oppositions between totemism and Judaism in a stark formula: "The Jew is to the savage, or at least to the Christian, what acting-out is to remembering."[49]

Via anamnesis, re-membering the foreclosed relation to the father—the symbol of authority and power and knowledge and truth—Lyotard suggested that Freud offered a pathway to truth-work. But this Jewish conscience and consciousness was foreclosed in defining the origins of the Greco-Christian West. The result was a form of Western rationality predicated on mastery through knowledge often at the expense of ethics. Lyotard's interpretation of Freud's *Moses* as a vehicle to reflect on what being Jewish meant for the history of Western philosophy thus constituted a deconstruction of the West: "Deconstruction is not disorder," he wrote. It is rather the expression "of an order which language lacks or which lacks language."[50]

AUSCHWITZ AND THE DIFFEREND

The effort to think the order that language lacks or which lacks language was the heart of Lyotard's masterwork, *The Differend*, written in the same period as "Figure Foreclosed." It is a series of "notices" or sketches of thought, preserving the exploratory process in thinking, judging, and reading that he sought to encourage. As noted in the chapter on Sartre's use of the term, defining the concept of the differend, Lyotard distinguished it from litigation:

> A differend [différend] would be a case of conflict, between (at least) two parties that cannot be equitably resolved for lack of a rule of judgment applicable to both arguments. One side's legitimacy does not imply the other's lack of legitimacy.... The title of this book suggests (through the generic value of the definite article) that a universal rule of judgment between heterogeneous genres is lacking in general.[51]

A differend arises because different language games[52] or regimes of phrases have different rules of formation that are linked to form different *genres* of discourse (i.e., the rules for linking phrase regimes) that come into conflict in different contexts (historical, political, ethical, aesthetic, philosophical, social). For Lyotard, conflicts over difference(s) are inevitable and the postmodern condition is such that there is no universal discourse that can provide a final arbitration of disputes.[53]

The Differend opens with an extended discussion of Auschwitz, which Lyotard, like Hannah Arendt, considered an event of such magnitude that it shatters the criteria of judgment about it since "even the authority of the tribunal that was supposed to establish the crime ... was exterminated."[54] There is not only a differend between the event and the moral seismograph that ought to measure it, there is a further differend that separates the experience of victims and perpetrators. As is the case for Alain Finkielkraut, Auschwitz signals irreparable rupture and infinite loss without the possibility of reconciliation.[55] Albeit an indeterminate situation where one cannot appeal to a universal law or agreed-upon criteria, Lyotard nevertheless insists that Auschwitz demands judgment.

Auschwitz is therefore not a mere historical event, but a limit experience, what Lyotard calls "a sign of history": an event that cannot be expressed in previous idioms. His analysis takes as its point of departure the final section of Theodor Adorno's *Negative Dialectics*, where Adorno meditates on metaphysics and what is entailed in thinking "after Auschwitz."[56] Adorno's basic project in *Negative Dialectics* was to demonstrate the totalitarian nature of "identity thinking"—thinking that demands a final reconciliation between subject and object, thinking absolutely, thought determined to stand universally and transhistorically, in short, any thought that defines itself as an absolute meaning or "the final solution."

For Adorno, Auschwitz is a sign that represents the final culmination and death of the logic of identity thinking, a sign demanding that thought not repeat the logic of Auschwitz. However, to construe a determined meaning to Auschwitz, for example, to fix its significance in terms of the equation "Auschwitz = identity thinking" repeats the logic. Auschwitz is a sign, then, for the impossibility of encapsulating its significance. Taking Adorno's ruminations on thinking "after Auschwitz" as a model, Lyotard argues that Auschwitz names an event that cannot be represented, that radically disturbs us, but that cannot be fully apprehended or expressed. He concurs with Claude Lanzmann, the director of the famous nine-hour documentary *Shoah*, that efforts to re-present Auschwitz "as it really was" banalize it and mask its abhorrence. The monstrosity of Auschwitz is sublime in the sense that we are horrified by something but the referent of that awe cannot be represented.

Lyotard thus raises the question of the adequacy of any witness to Auschwitz and the general problems of testifying to trauma. Rather than dismiss Holocaust deniers like Robert Faurisson offhand,[57] Lyotard probed the limits of historical representation that constitute their lever in demands for a "revisionist" approach to the Holocaust.[58] Even as the deniers' work is an effort to continue the Final Solution by silencing all survivor testimony about it, they have a point when they claim that there are no witnesses to the gas chambers since every true witness was exterminated in the process. What continues to burn about Auschwitz is that the process of destruction attempted to destroy even the memory of the Shoah, to eliminate even the traces of the devastation.

Faurisson claims to challenge the accuracy of witnessing to the Shoah on historical grounds alone, whereas Lyotard sought to reveal that there is always more than merely historical knowledge in survivor testimony. There is thus a differend between every representation of Auschwitz and the suffering of the victims. The task of thinkers, writers, and artists becomes not to represent Auschwitz, which is impossible, but to bear witness to this impossibility. The task of postmodern philosophy and art for Lyotard is to represent the limits of representation and to express the differend between representation and the unrepresentable. Auschwitz is a sign of the exigency to communicate this incommunicability and the need to judge where universal criteria do not exist.

HEIDEGGER AND "THE JEWS"

Heidegger and "the jews," Lyotard's intervention into the Heidegger affair in 1988, extended these reflections on the relation between history and memory, explicitly considering their implications for Jews and Judaism. The occasion for his reflections was the third wave of the Heidegger affair concerning the relationship between Heidegger's Nazism and his thought. As Dominick LaCapra notes in "Heidegger's Nazi Turn," Heidegger's "affiliation with the Nazis has been known since 1933."[59] This is because in April, shortly after Hitler's assumption of the chancellorship and amid the political restructuring of education, Heidegger maneuvered to obtain the post of rector of the University of Freiburg. He was elected to the position on April 21 and delivered his rectoral address on "The Self-Assertion of the German University," on April 27. It was replete with references to the *Führerprinzip* couched in some of his philosophical formulations.[60] In May 1933, Heidegger sent a telegram to Hitler expressing solidarity with the recent *Gleichschaltung* legislation that promised to align the university with the official policies of the Third Reich. This included enforcing the anti-Semitic laws that banned Jews from all government service, including university life. Known as the Baden Decree, it was implemented to purge the "Jewification of the Universities." It meant that Edmund Husserl, the founder of phenomenology and Heidegger's benefactor, was now removed as professor emeritus, forbidden from even using the university library. He was one among 1,600 Jewish professors expunged. Commenting on this in a letter to Karl Jaspers, Arendt noted painfully, "I cannot but regard Heidegger as a potential murderer."[61] While his reign as a Nazi official ended when he resigned as rector in April 1934, Heidegger still continued to end classes by saluting Hitler. Moreover, he proclaimed "the inner truth and greatness of the movement" in 1935, and he remained in the Nazi Party until 1945. Almost as disturbing as his direct affiliation with Nazism was Heidegger's postwar silence about the Holocaust, broken only by a few callous comments.

Heidegger's relationship to Nazism was first deliberated in France in 1946 and 1947 in *Les Temps Modernes*, and then in more scattered discussions from 1948 to 1987.[62] It became a major affair in France in the immediate aftermath of the publication of Victor Farías's dossier, *Heidegger et le nazisme*, in 1987. Farías's text was responded to between October 1987 and May 1988 with the publication of a series of books on the topic by some of France's most prominent philosophers:

Jacques Derrida, Pierre Bourdieu, Philippe Lacoue-Labarthe, Luc Ferry, and Alain Renaut, and in a flurry of subsequent radio and television programs and magazine and journal articles internationally.

Lyotard's *Heidegger and "the jews"* was his contribution to this discussion.[63] His basic thesis is that all thinking, and therefore all remembering, forgets. There are lacunae and limits to all thought. His specific target is Heidegger's philosophy because Heidegger's thought was centrally concerned with the forgetfulness of the West in its failure to think Being. Heidegger's refusal to speak about the Holocaust consequently becomes a model of thought that forgets.

Heidegger's role in the Nazi Party and, more perniciously, that he made almost no comment about the Holocaust in the postwar period, implicated him in the Nazi Final Solution—the effort to eliminate European Jewry without trace or memory. The Final Solution was the politics of absolute forgetting that resulted in a politics of extermination. Since, for Lyotard, there are two modes to the politics of forgetting—effacement and representation—the question is how one remembers this forgetting. And more generally how one remembers the limits of thought—the unrepresentable, the unthinkable in thought—that Lyotard explicitly names in this work "the jews."

Lyotard argues that there is a double obligation for any history or monument to the memory of the "the jews": (1) we must remember that in memorializing we forget; forgetting this forgetting results in effacement, and (2) in remembering "the Forgotten," we must also recognize that no history, literary work, or other memorialization of the Holocaust is capable of representing the shock of the past "as it really was." As David Carroll suggests, the obligation in remembering the Shoah should thus *not* be phrased as "Never forget" but rather "Never forget that in all memory there is 'the Forgotten.'"[64] Every history, every memorialization that wishes to remain sensitized to the memory of the victims of the Holocaust must negotiate this double bind of history and memory. Lyotard thus reminds us of our duty to remember the Forgotten, forcing us to recall that we will never come to terms with this remembering.

EUROPE, THE JEWS, AND THE BOOK

The implications of not remembering the Forgotten were splayed across the front pages of newspapers with the desecration of the tombs at Carpentras cemetery on May 10, 1990. While over thirty graves were defiled, what was most ghoulish about the incident was that "the corpse of an eighty-year-old buried two weeks earlier was removed from his grave and abused: as well as an attempted impalement, someone had laid a Star of David and a slab inscribed 'a souvenir from the neighbors,' taken from other graves on the body."[65]

To appreciate the weight of Lyotard's response, the incident at the Carpentras cemetery should be situated within its context: a slew of copycat attacks that followed; the media sensation it created, especially the way that the press linked the Carpentras moment to the rising popularity of Jean-Marie Le Pen's Far-Right Front National (FN);[66] the FN's flirtation with Holocaust denial; and generally the increase in racist, anti-immigration discourse of the extreme Right. This was countered by antiracism as a unifying theme for intellectuals on the Left, especially following the municipal elections in Dreux in 1983 when the FN achieved their first electoral victory.[67] These proximate contexts should likewise be correlated with what Henry Rousso has called "the Vichy Syndrome" in its multiple manifestations;[68] with the Franco-Israeli relationship following the Six-Day War of 1967;[69] with the response to a series of violent assaults on Jews: the massacre of Jewish athletes in Munich in 1972, the attacks on the kosher student restaurant in the Latin Quarter in March 1978, on the synagogue in rue Copernic in October 1980, and on Jo Goldenberg's deli in the "Jewish Quarter" (Marais) in August 1982;[70] as well as with the Heidegger affair. It was against this background that Lyotard intervened in the Carpentras affair with his article, "Europe, the Jews and the Book," published in *Liberation* on May 15, 1990.[71]

Transcending all these contemporary events, Lyotard situates the violation of the tombs in Carpentras within the largest possible frame: the differend dividing Europe from Jews and Judaism. Carpentras is an example of a repetitive and compulsive syndrome embedded in Western culture to efface Jews and Judaism that was now manifesting itself in the tendency to erase Jewish memory even "after Auschwitz." The profanation of the tombs and the displaying of a corpse torn out of its coffin on a stake in the Jewish cemetery of Carpentras say something specific: after the Shoah the Jews have no right to their dead or to the memory of their dead. There is a long tradition of the profanation of Jewish cemeteries in Europe. This drive to efface not only Jews and Judaism but also their memory is constitutive of the West, according to Lyotard, but denied as such. He then correlates this impetus with the image of the Jews as "the People of the Book."[72]

Provocatively, Lyotard maintains that the opposition to the "People of the Book"—and to what it says about books and readers more generally—is what animates the desecration of the tombs: "Do people have something against books, against their book, against the readers of this book that would lead them to the point of violating Jews' tombs to kill their dead? ... In fact, yes."[73] Why does Lyotard make the link between the profanation of tombs and texts? Because he regards textuality—both reading and writing—as inherently demanding and beyond instrumentality and utility: "Nothing is as slow, difficult and unprofitable as learning to read, which is an endless activity. In a society avid for performance, profit and speed, it is an exercise that has lost its value, along with the institution that trains people for it."[74] For Lyotard, the modern (it)self is organized around gaining time—circumventing the ruse of finitude inscribed in temporality—and reading is a subversion of the instrumental rationality that undergirds the modern.[75]

In "Europe, the Jews and the Book," Lyotard also condenses some of the key themes from his articles "Figure Foreclosed" and "Jewish Oedipus." He argues that the Jews as "People of the Book" constitute "the base of Europe's whole culture" but remain within "that culture as excluded from it."[76] He thus repeats, albeit with a difference, his analysis of *Moses and Monotheism*: the Book (i.e., the Hebrew Bible) which is at the base of Europe's whole culture remains within that culture only as what is denied, like the Egyptian Moses whose murder by his own people was repressed only to be later transferred onto the Midianite Moses. Hence, the Jews (as the "People of the Book") constitute a figure of the European unconscious as Lyotard, after Freud, concludes:

> Thus the annihilation of what the book of the Jews says continues in the unconscious of a permissive Europe. Thus continues the annihilation of the message that the law does not belong to us and that our reconciliation with it remains pending. This is the constitutive anti-Semitism of a Europe that has in one way or another, always thought the opposite of this message, has always thought its self-constitution.[77]

Therefore, what is at stake at Carpentras is the differend that animates Judeophobia. Jews are the Other against which European culture has defined itself. This has been foreclosed in Europe's self-understanding, resulting in the repetitive compulsion to erase Jewish history and memory. The Jewish proclivity toward textuality—the painstaking and infinite process of reading and reinterpreting that has defined Jews as "People of the Book"—provokes ire in a world evermore consumed with accomplishment, materialism, and the pursuit of power. Jewish law embodies the counterpoint to these drives that animate the pleasure principle, since it represents the mandate of an ethics whose demands are infinite but that must be maintained as first principles. Judeophobia is the organized rejection of these Jewish principles.

THE HYPHEN

Building on this set of propositions synthesized in "Europe, the Jews and the Book," Lyotard contended that the differend dividing Judaism from the West is itself an old story, one that he analyzed at much greater length in his work of 1993, *Un trait d'union* (*The Hyphen*). The hyphen Lyotard pointed to was that found in the phrase "Judeo-Christian tradition." Lyotard locates the origin of this differend in the Epistles of Saint Paul, in which the book of the Jews was designated as the "Old" Testament in order for the new work to be defined as a "New" Testament. With this began the temporal cleavage that ushered in the modern.[78]

In both *The Hyphen* and in "Europe, the Jews and the Book," Lyotard argued that Paul's Epistles marked the genesis of Jewish exclusion. Lyotard also stressed the differend dividing the Torah, where "no one ever gains access to His [God's] visible presence" and where "the law of justice and peace does not become incarnate" from Paul's insistence that in Jesus "the Voice was made manifest. It said clearly: love each other like brothers."[79] Lyotard thus emphasizes an irreducible theological and historical difference between the absent God of Judaism and Christian theology based on presence and incarnation.[80]

Lyotard also refers to the tensions immanent within freedom and emancipation—a subject that he addressed at greater length in his article, "La Mainmise" ("The Grip"), which itemized the continuities between Paul's Epistles and the modern story of the Enlightenment, stressing how both stories repress, exclude, and forget Jewish difference. Lyotard's central point in "La Mainmise," whose "grip" is an image of knowledge in the West, is that emancipation and Enlightenment in the West were both rooted in the ideal of independence and autonomy.[81] As such, Lyotard argued that emancipation was conceived as a liberation from anxiety and conscience. Freedom now meant freedom from the Other, who was externalized and "gripped." Consequently, knowledge in the West, especially since Bacon and Descartes, is determined by the desire for mastery, incorporation, appropriation, and the assimilation of difference.

Lyotard stressed a differend dividing the Greco-Roman-Christian model of emancipation, figured in the sacrifice of Jesus and later transfigured in the Enlightenment, and the Jewish model of emancipation,[82] depicted in the sacrifice of Isaac, where God will provide for emancipation. But God is not foreseeable. He has promised. How the promise will be kept, no one knows. We must scrutinize the letters of the book. Scrutinizing the letter of the book does not just mean observing the rites to the letter, as Paul ungenerously suggests. Jewish emancipation lies in the pursuit of writing, writing about writing, and writing on the occasion of the event.[83]

In "Europe, the Jews and the Book," Lyotard recapitulated this argument by picking up on the theme of fraternity:

> The Christians announce to us that finally, we are all reconciled brothers. The Jews remind us that we are always sons, blessed but insubmissive.... The Christian churches had introduced the motif of fraternity. The French Revolution extended it, by turning it on its head. We are brothers, not as sons of God but as free and equal citizens. It is not an Other who gives us the law. It is our civic community that does, that obliges, prohibits, permits. That is called emancipation from the Other, and autonomy. Our law opens citizenship to every individual, on condition of respect for republican principles. The Jews are allowed in like anyone else. That is called assimilation.[84]

This metanarrative of the West's continual dismissals, rejections, and introjections of Jewish difference confronts its own limits at the gates of Auschwitz:

> In the European unconscious, it is recognized that his [the Jew's] debt to the Other will prevail over his duties to the others, to the national community. And that he is bound to be a potential traitor. Unless he forgets himself as Jew. This is the great temptation for the "assimilated" themselves. The "final solution" will come as a monstrous reminder to them that they are always, even *despite themselves*, witnesses to something about which Europe wants to know nothing.[85]

Lyotard here echoes the Sartrean thesis in *Anti-Semite and Jew* that the gaze of gentile society will always serve as a barrier to Jewish integration.[86] For Sartre, in seeking to forget the gaze of gentile society, Jews risk inauthenticity. In Lyotardian terms, the assimilated Jew is the Jew who forgets that he is the forgotten.

Lyotard gives his own metanarrative about Jewish exclusion, repression, and victimization by the West its most sustained elaboration in the section on "the jews" in *Heidegger and "the jews."* In "Europe, the Jews and the Book," he invoked a passage that paraphrased the opening of his earlier essay on Heidegger: "The whole social, political, religious, and speculative history of Christian Europe bears witness to a permanent undertaking, using various means (inquisition, conversion, expulsion, censorship) to neutralize the Jewish message and banish the community of unbelievers."[87] Lyotard now read Carpentras as symptomatic of the West's desire to forget the European tradition of forgetting the Jews: "My claim is that the Jews represent *something that Europe does not want to or cannot know anything about*. Even when they are dead, it abolishes their memory and refuses them burial in its land. All of this takes place in the unconscious and has no right to speak. When the deed is done in full daylight, Europe is seized for an instant by the horror and the terror of *confronting its own desire*."[88] But in reprising his earlier reflections on "the jews," "Europe, the Jews and the Book" also makes evident what Geoffrey Bennington has called the "terrible ambiguity"[89] between this image of "the jews" and "real" Jews. For in his intervention in the Carpentras affair, Lyotard names "Jews" with a capital "J" while ascribing to them the same markers as "the jews." "The Jews," writes Lyotard, "are not a nation. They do not speak a language of their own. They have no roots in a *nature,* like the European nations. They claim to have their roots in a book."[90]

This conflation in Lyotard's work between what he seeks to characterize as a structure of obligation and responsibility—the debt of the West to its ("jewish") Other— and "real" Jews is made evident in his own reiteration of the argument of *Heidegger and "the jews"* on the occasion of a conference in Vienna by the same name:

> The Jews cannot manage to find their place in the systems by which thought is represented in the politics and social practices of the European West. They cannot form a "nation" in the medieval sense, nor a people in the modern sense. The Law forbids them to acquire the communitarian status of an ethnic group.... Their relation to the event of the Covenant and the Promise is

a relation of dependence, not a relation to a land and history but a relation to the letter of a book and to a paradoxical temporality. The book is not the object of a hermeneutic reading that might expose and accumulate its meaning, but of a talmudic reading that tries to get at that meaning through the screens of previous interpretations.[91]

Lyotard thus systematically correlates "the Jews" as an unconscious affect, an unrepresentable alterity, and an ethical category signifying debt, obligation, and responsibility, primarily because of the priority accorded to the Jewish relation to the text that he constantly insists upon.

This image of the "People of the Book" condenses a hypothesized, historically abstracted, aestheticized, and allegorical depiction of "the Jews" in Lyotard's texts. Lyotard's valorization of "the Jews" as nomadic, rootless, and diasporic repeats images of "the Jews" that have been so pivotal to their exclusion. Several commentators have pointed to problems with the tropes Lyotard uses to depict "the jews." Michael Weingrad has suggested that, even as Lyotard prophetically proclaims the end of grand narratives, he reinscribes "the very old narrative of the Wandering Jew."[92] Dominick LaCapra has argued that Lyotard rebaptizes "the jews" with a hyperbolic "anaesthetics" of the sublime and his own "postmodern" understanding of its analogues or accompaniments: trauma, *écriture*, alterity, nomadism, the un(re)presentable, *Nachtraglichkeit*, not-forgetting-that-there-is-the-Forgotten, and so forth.[93]

As Elizabeth Bellamy contends, these tropes turn "the Jews" from "the sublime object of ideology," in Žižek terms, into "a kind of ideological object of the sublime."[94] Max Silverman maintains that in "employing an ethnic allegory to characterize the tension between order and disorder, reason and resistance to reason, the self-constituted self and the heterogeneous self, Europe and its other(s), this postmodern theory would appear to overlap uncomfortably with the ethnic allegory employed frequently in the age of modernity."[95] These commentators thus point to the way in which Lyotard's depiction of "the jews" undermines core elements of his own project to "work through" Jews and Judaism in order to destabilize the logic of the exclusion and the repression of the Other in the history of the West.

To these criticisms I would add that Lyotard, whose work most emphatically seeks to unwork the speculative, totalizing, universalizing, and quintessentially modern philosophy of Hegel, even ends up reiterating significant elements of the Hegelian image of "the Jew."⁹⁶ Hegel's *Early Theological Writings* stress the heterogeneity in Judaism of man and God and the self-alienation of the Jews in their conception of the Law. This position is reiterated in *The Phenomenology of Spirit*, where Jews are depicted as the failure of the dialectic, as a remnant that cannot be assimilated, and as the ruin of reconciliation.⁹⁷ In *Die Religionen der geistigen Individualität*, the Jewish God is cast in the position of "sublimity" (*Erhabenheit*) and Judaism depicted as the "Religion of Sublimity."⁹⁸ Thus, whereas Hegel denigrates Jews and Judaism as essentially nondialectical, the antithesis of his union of opposites, it is precisely as such that Lyotard valorizes Judaism. Like Hegel, Lyotard's views depend upon what Gillian Rose has problematized as the "diremption"⁹⁹ (that is, the forced separation) of the Hellenic and Hebraic. Her own argument is that Athens and Jerusalem have historically been more intertwined than Lyotard's typologies (of both traditions) lead us to believe. Jonathan and Daniel Boyarin have put this critique within a larger frame, arguing that Lyotard's work reiterates the Pauline allegorization of "the Jews" and the spiritualization of history.¹⁰⁰

Therefore, what Lyotard's own work refuses to forget is not Jews, but the crimes against humanity committed by Christian and modern Europe.¹⁰¹ At the same time, however, Lyotard demonstrates a tendency to forget some of the anti-Semitic motifs of Jewish marginalization, repression, and exclusion. The repeated reference to the Jews as the "People of the Book" in Lyotard's work is a static and abstract image that results in a frozen portrait of "the Jew" as an abstracted essence that only serves a philosophical function in Lyotard's thought.

Lyotard's abstracted appropriation of "the jews" to depict the sublime Other to the West reinscribes Jews as marginalized outcasts and forgets the actual relations of the Jewish religious tradition and of Jewish history to what Lyotard calls "the Law." Nonetheless, one should not conclude from this critique of Lyotard that postmodern approaches should simply be dismissed as "irrationalism, neoconservatism, intellectual terrorism, simple minded liberalism, nihilism and cynicism" that have nothing of substance to offer beneath their jargon-laden language.¹⁰²

Lyotard's postmodern critique is important because it sensitizes us to anamnesis and the immemorial in history. Bill Readings's "Glossary" in *Introducing Lyotard* clearly defines what Lyotard means by anamnesis and the immemorial: "That which can neither be remembered (represented to consciousness) nor forgotten (consigned to oblivion). It is that which returns, uncannily. As such, the immemorial acts as a kind of *figure* for consciousness and its attempts at representing itself historically. The prime example is Auschwitz."[103] Ultimately what Lyotard's own postmodern theorization of anti-Semitism forgets actually illuminates what Lyotard theorized as the basis of anti-Semitism. For Lyotard, Jews and Judaism are the irrepressible, unknowable, inexpressible Other. Anti-Semitism is built upon a deep drive inherent in Western culture: the will to mastery and domination through knowledge of what remains ultimately ungraspable. Lyotard follows Levinas in maintaining that against this drive, Judaism posits ethics as first philosophy as a counterpoint.

As we have seen, from Lyotard's earliest work, he suggested that Nazism raised a host of epistemological, political, and ethical questions that were intertwined and that required a rethinking of Western culture and Western modernity. In the 1970s and 1980s via his readings of Freud's *Moses*, he maintained that Jews and Judaism were foreclosed from the West, but constitutive of it. Judaism was the basis of the West's own superego—its set of ethical ideals demarcated by the law of the father—but targeted precisely as such. Attention to the foreclosed Jew enabled one to unravel the binaries and hierarchies that structured Western thought and to deconstruct the conceptual arrangement that privileged knowledge over ethics and truth over art.

For Lyotard, Judeophobia is characterized by the repulsion at what Jews and Judaism ostensibly signify: ethics as prior to knowledge; refusal of mythomania and idol worship; valorization of exile and diaspora; absence as opposed to incarnation and embodiment; and importantly, textuality and interpretation that always excludes a final solution of meaning. The Holocaust revealed the full wrath of the foreclosure of Jews and Judaism from Western consciousness and the hatred or contempt this inspired. But its effort at effacement, too, could be forgotten. Carpentras, yet again, bore witness to the West's own failure to think its own limits. Lyotard's postmodern theorization of anti-Semitism thus provides not only the tools to understand his own repetition of certain allosemitic typologies, but why this repetition has been constitutive of the West from its origins. In making these claims, Lyotard drew inspiration from the popularity that Léon Poliakov's historical work on anti-Semitism began to receive just as postmodern theory was reaching its apex.

CHAPTER 6

Léon Poliakov, the Origins of Holocaust Studies, and the Long History of Judeophobia

The postmodern theories of Lyotard about the central but denied role of Judeophobia in shaping the Western tradition were given empirical flesh and blood in the work of Léon Poliakov (1910-1997). He was one of the great historians of the twentieth century, a founding father of Holocaust and genocide studies, and a forerunner of the critical history of anti-Semitism, racism, stereotyping, persecution, and demonization. Yet his groundbreaking contributions to these areas of scholarship are today often overlooked.[1] This chapter focuses on Poliakov's often-unacknowledged contributions to the establishment of Holocaust studies and explores how he understood a key engine in the machinery of the destruction of European Jewry: anti-Semitism. It also elucidates how Poliakov historicized the key role of philosophers in developing the underlying categories at work in racism. His work underscores how the major philosophers of the modern Western canon—like Kant and Hegel—actively translated theological categories into the modern idiom of philosophy and science. In doing so, philosophers and scientists imported theological tropes and axiological binaries, translating notions of good and evil, for example, into "fit" and "degenerate," laying the groundwork for modern racial thought.

While Poliakov was a great historian, he was no theorist. He spends little time in his vast oeuvre explaining how the ideas about Jews and race that he historicized came together to shape racist thinking over the long history of Western culture. Undertaking that archaeology will be the task of this chapter.

Poliakov's breakthrough book, *Bréviaire de la haine: Le IIIe Reich et les Juifs* (*Harvest of Hate: The Nazi Program for the Destruction of the Jews of Europe*) was published in 1951 with the aid of Raymond Aron.[2] It was the first overarching history of the Holocaust. In re-reading *Harvest of Hate* there are three aspects that I emphasize. First, the prescience of the volume. As a foundational survey of the Holocaust, Poliakov's work became a palimpsest that sketched key aspects of the Shoah that were developed and treated by others, but rarely with credit to their origins in his work. Second, Poliakov's interpretation of Nazi anti-Semitism was profound and merits consideration in its own right. Third, I problematize some of Poliakov's own conclusions about the causes of anti-Semitism derived from the insights of Freud, Maurice Samuel, and Jacques Maritain. At the same time, I show from reading Poliakov intertextually alongside these other authors, the beginnings of a Jewish-Christian dialogue on the significance of anti-Judaism in the wake of the Holocaust.

Underlying *Harvest of Hate* was the question of *why* Jews are denigrated and demonized. Poliakov's next book was the first volume of what became his answer to that question, the *Histoire de l'antisémitisme* (*History of Anti-Semitism*, 1955-1994), which surveys the history of Judeophobia from its origins through the post-Holocaust era in five volumes.[3] His monumental history remains the most important work on the topic. Indeed, Poliakov's footnotes helped create the archive on the subject.[4] In volume 3, *From Voltaire to Wagner* (1968), Poliakov offered a series of acute insights about the secularization of anti-Judaism, linking a set of Christian theological precepts with modern categories. He demonstrated how concepts like the great chain of being, providence, salvation, election, conversion, and evil were translated into the modern idiom of racial hierarchies, progress, emancipation, assimilation, and degeneration. Poliakov's *Le Mythe Aryen* (*The Aryan Myth*, 1971) would continue this probative appraisal of the transmission belts of anti-Judaism into modern exclusionary nationalism and racism, indicating how biblical genealogies became the basis of modern national myths of origin. In these two major studies, the focus of the second half of this chapter, Poliakov explored the role modern philosophers played in shaping modern racial thought. He shows that philosophy played a central role in the translation of theological tropes into rational, scientific ones. In short, Poliakov helps us to understand not only the paths of transferral between anti-Judaism and anti-Semitism but also the links between anti-Semitism and anti-Black racism. Moreover, he forces us to reevaluate our thinking about racism that slots different trajectories for theology, philosophy, and racial science, showing that these were all thoroughly intertwined in the development of the core ideas and institutions of Western culture.

POLIAKOV'S INTELLECTUAL DEMARCHE

While Poliakov's oeuvre was extremely wide-ranging, his great works are certainly focused on Judeophobia. "If it is true that all one does is to write the same book over and over again," Poliakov averred in his autobiography, "then my case is a blatant one."[5] His biography explains the origins of his work. As Georges Elia Sarfati put it, "It was a response to the personal question, 'why do they want to kill me?'"[6] It was a question Poliakov must have asked from an early age.

Poliakov's transnational childhood was impacted by three linguistic, cultural, and political influences: Russian, German, and French. Named for Leo Tolstoy, who had died on the eve of his birth, he was born in Saint Petersburg in 1910. The oldest son in a family of girls, he grew up with no religious or intellectual affiliation with Judaism. His father, Vladimir, was a Crimean Jew with no formal education who had made his wealth publishing leftist newspapers, but who supported the Whites in the civil war. As a result, the family fled to Paris in 1920, where Léon was enrolled in Lycée Janson, a school where he felt "isolated." His father initially had difficulty establishing a business in France and so they left for Berlin, where at eleven, Léon became an "enthusiastic German patriot."[7] The Poliakovs returned to France in 1924 when his father got a position as the head of a publicity firm. In 1934, at Léon's urging, Vladimir returned to his vocation and created a daily newspaper, *Pariser Tageblatt*, catering to the influx of primarily Jewish immigrants arriving from Germany and eastern Europe.[8] Beginning his career writing for the paper, Léon simultaneously completed his studies in law.

The chief editor of the newspaper was a dodgy character, Georg Bernhard, and the paper was thoroughly underfinanced, with the result that Bernhard was rarely paid on time. In 1936 a scandal broke when Bernhard indicated on the front page of the *Pariser Tageblatt* that the owner, Vladimir Poliakov, was a traitor in the pay of the Nazis. This was a huge shock for the readers of the paper, since its orientation was explicitly antifascist. After a long defamation trial, the Poliakovs were victorious, but Vladimir was ruined. Léon's first published book was on the *Pariser Tageblatt* affair in order to rectify his father's reputation. Interest in Léon's book came from many famous individuals who were wrapped up in this affair, like Vladimir Jabotinsky, who was a contributor to the newspaper. Jabotinsky thought enough of Léon's book to encourage him to become a writer. While in retrospect, Léon considered himself a little "anti-Semitic" at the time, this was tempered with his first injection of "a certain Zionist enthusiasm," which came when he visited his sister in 1937, who had married a settler in Palestine.[9]

The death of his father in May 1939 closely coincided with the outbreak of World War II. His mother died the following spring. Poliakov later thought this was a good thing, since two Russian Jews who spoke French with difficulty would probably not have survived the occupation of France by the Nazis.[10] With the beginning of war, despite having never been naturalized, Poliakov was called up for duty, pursuant to a law that stateless persons from Russia, Poland, and Armenia could be mobilized. Along with 1.8 million other French soldiers, he was promptly captured and interned in a camp called Domart.[11] Here his linguistic abilities gave him a distinct advantage, since he could help procure things for his captors. When he accompanied the camp commander on a trip to Paris, he escaped. Poliakov spent the rest of the war as a stateless Jew in hiding, roving across France using false papers, doing odd jobs, moving between Paris, Marseille, Nice, Grenoble, Saint-Etienne, La Ricamarie, and Tence near Le Chambon-sur-Lignon. He sometimes fabricated papers for others also surviving the Nazi occupation.

His father's death led to an important contact during this period, Rabbi Zalman Schneerson, who came from the illustrious Lubavitch line of hassids. Despite his secular upbringing, Poliakov wanted to bury his father in a religious ceremony. So he visited Rabbi Schneerson in his office near the place de la République in the appropriately named rue Dieu. Still in shock, he asked the rabbi, "What does one do to have faith in God?" In a quintessential rabbinic response, Schneerson replied, "Come to my house for thirty days and say *Kaddish*, as the tradition requires. Then, we'll speak about it seriously."[12] So as not to appear frivolous, Poliakov trekked across Paris each day. Although they never had that conversation about faith, the contact was made and it proved important when Poliakov moved to Marseille, hoping to avoid the roundups that had begun in the occupied zone in the summer of 1941. There he once more encountered Rabbi Schneerson, who offered him a job as his secretary, despite the fact that he was a nonbeliever, and he lived among the rabbi's entourage, known as the Association Israélites Pratiquants (AIP).

In Marseille, he would also often meet his friend, the philosopher Aleksandr Kozevnikov. Under his Gallicized name, Alexandre Kojève had already gained fame as a key commentator on Hegel, as a result of his famous seminar in the

1930s that served as one of the crucibles of twentieth-century French thought.[13] It was Kojève who would steep Poliakov in philosophy. Later in the war, when living near Le Chambon-sur-Lignon, he met Jacob Gordin and his wife and children.[14] Gordon was an erudite Jewish thinker who dramatically expanded Poliakov's horizons through his initiation into Jewish thought, facilitating his "intellectual conversion to Judaism."[15]

In the immediate aftermath of the war, Poliakov reconnected with another Schneerson, Isaac, a wealthy industrialist and an important personality in the Union général des israélites de France (UGIF), the representative body for Jews in France under the occupation.[16] They had first met in 1943 in the Italian occupation zone. By this time, Isaac Schneerson had already created the Centre de Documentation in Grenoble. The Centre resulted from a meeting on April 28, 1943, in Schneerson's apartment, where forty activists from across the Jewish community convened to figure out how to document the persecution of the Jews. They sought both to bear witness and hopefully to demand justice at the end of the war. The group began by creating a list of all "Aryanized" Jewish businesses with notations taken from the *Journal officiel* (the official daily of the French state that documents all legislative actions). This list constituted the origins of the first archive in the world dedicated to documenting the genocide of European Jewry. Renamed the Centre de Documentation Juive Contemporaine (Contemporary Jewish Documentation Center or CDJC), they would later also produce the first journal on the topic, *Le Monde juif.* Today this is not only a library and archive, but the site of the major Holocaust memorial in Paris, the Mémorial de la Shoah. Following the war, Schneerson proposed that Poliakov become the general secretary of the group, and shortly thereafter made him head of research.

Poliakov became the driving force in establishing the cache of archival materials at the CDJC. How he did so was a good example of the contingency of history. One day he was at the French national police headquarters poking around. He was shown a box that had just arrived from Poland. It happened to contain the archives of the Gestapo and the SS in France. It turned out that neither Police Superintendent Bergé nor the personnel of his office read German. Thus, Poliakov became the expert translator and organizer of these documents, which became the fount of the holdings at the CDJC.

With the beginning of the Nuremberg trial, the French delegation, headed by François de Menthon and many other lawyers, were in the awkward position of not really having many sources with which to indict the Nazi criminals in the dock, especially compared to the Americans and the Soviets. So Poliakov was called upon as a result of his "expertise" to accompany them to Nuremberg. There he spent most of his time immersing himself in the huge trove of documents that the chief prosecutors made the basis of the trial.

Poliakov's copies of these sources would become the archive of *Harvest of Hate* and the basis of the collection at the CDJC. *Bréviaire de la haine* would catapult Poliakov into a career as a historian of great import, if only limited renown. With the success of the book, in 1952 he was appointed as a research fellow at the Centre National de la Recherche Scientifique. In 1954, he joined the prestigious École Pratique des Hautes Études, then directed by the eminent historian Fernand Braudel, the kingpin of the Annales domination of the historical discipline in the aftermath of the war.[17] Poliakov remained marginal within the Annales school, let alone the French academy, until the 1970s. In a beautiful homage to him upon his induction into the Légion d'honneur in 1988, Dominique Schnapper, daughter of Raymond Aron and herself an important professor of sociology, summed up this transformation:

> From being marginal, you became central. In the 1970s, everyone became interested in Jews, Judaism, anti-Semitism. You were a precursor. Everyone rendered homage. You were recompensed with the first grand prize of the Fondation du judaïsme française. You came to know the joy of young university students, and to have around you young, admiring, friendly colleagues.[18]

As Schnapper highlights, and as we saw in the chapter on Lyotard's work, during the late 1970s, Jews, Judaism, the Shoah, and anti-Semitism became hot topics of discussion.[19] Poliakov had by then imbibed the ethos of the Annales school's multidisciplinary approach to history and their wide-ranging use of source material.

Never having been trained as a historian, working at the École was transformative. Poliakov's first published works with the CDJC were collections of documents and some of his later success was a result of the fact that he always quoted extensively from the sources in his books. His legal training and experience at Nuremberg are also evident in his historical works, since he often writes like a prosecuting attorney, indicting the criminal with the evidence from what they said about their own crimes. With the Annales school, he came to share a broad vision and panoramic scope, writing not only "total history" but leading the way in the *histoire des mentalités* over the *longue durée*, specifically insofar as these mental habits were shaped by Judeophobia. Poliakov's magnum opus, his monumental five volumes on *L'Histoire de l'antisémitisme*, would emerge out of the problem of anti-Semitism first posed in *Bréviaire de la haine*.

BRÉVIAIRE DE LA HAINE AND NAZI ANTI-SEMITISM

Bréviaire de la haine was the first all-encompassing survey of the genocide of European Jewry in any language. As such, it was a groundbreaking work in Holocaust studies, effectively establishing the terms of many of the debates that have defined the field. Overshadowed by Raul Hilberg's *The Destruction of the European Jews* (1961), today Poliakov's book is seldom acknowledged for the pioneering part it played. When it first appeared in 1951, however, *Bréviaire de la haine* was hailed. Across the board in the major French dailies (*Le Monde*, *L'Aurore*, *Le Parisien libéré*) and weeklies (*L'Observateur*, *Les Nouvelles littéraires*), it was heralded as a trailblazing work of scholarship. P. Grappin in *Politique étrangère* termed it a "magisterial study...a historic work of the first rank" that went further than anything before it. A. Latreille in *Le Monde* proclaimed, "M. Poliakov has painted a tableau more impressive by his objectivity than any literary reconstruction." Pierre Naville, writing under the pseudonym J. Gallois in *L'Observateur*, called it "a book...of exceptional force and truth, that must not only be read and studied but studied in the universities, especially in Germany."[20] It was soon translated into English and Spanish (in 1954), into Italian (in 1955), into Czech (in 1965), and into Portuguese (in 1988). When it came out in America, Jacques Maritain, one of the leading Catholic intellectuals of his time, lauded the English translation in *Social Research*:

> M. Poliakov's book traces, with inexorable and infallible objectivity, the stages of the business of extermination. In the face of such horror, one need not raise one's voice; it suffices to *say* it. One can barely perceive, here or there, a restrained shudder, and occasionally, concerning the hangman, something like a terrible humor, which grips the heart. This is precisely the Jewish humor, but in extreme tension of anguish and pierced by tears of blood.

R. H. S. Crossman in the *New Statesman* signaled the massive contribution Poliakov had made to the early work on the Holocaust by setting his impact against the other key work in the formative period of Holocaust studies: "I had always assumed that Mr. Reitlinger had written the last word about Hitler's extermination camps. Now Mr. Poliakov has proved me wrong. [Reitlinger's] *The Final Solution* [published in 1953] was a masterpiece of cold clinical research. *Harvest of Hate* is a bigger book with a wider sweep."[21]

Published the same year as her monumental *Origins of Totalitarianism*—and notwithstanding a line from Raymond Aron's review of *Bréviaire* when he slighted Arendt by saying that "this book [by Poliakov] has all the merits that are not those of Madame Arendt"—no one more than she recognized Poliakov's signal achievement.[22] Arendt itemized his many contributions in her review article of the French text in *Commentary*.[23] She highlighted Poliakov's elucidation of the Taylorist approach of the "death factory-technicians" (303); his recognition that "the only country on the Nazi side of the lines that resolutely and effectively shielded the Jews was Germany's one important European ally, Italy" (303);[24] his delicate balance in discussing "the terrible dilemma of the *Jüdenrate*, their despair as well as their confusion, their complicity and their sometimes pathetically ludicrous ambitions" (303);[25] and Poliakov's "deflation of the myth" about the role "the German officers' corps and the old pre-Hitler civil servants," had played in the destruction of European Jewry.[26] Most importantly, Arendt also trumpeted the landmark link that Poliakov established between the euthanasia program and the Final Solution.[27]

Beyond what Arendt emphasized, more could be said about Poliakov's innovations. Poliakov anticipated the debates about Jewish resistance, as well as the Nazi treatment of "inferior peoples" (i.e., the assault on Slavs and the Sinti and Roma), devoting a separate chapter to each issue long before these topics were integrated in the historiography on the Holocaust.[28] In addition, he antedated Marrus and Paxton on Vichy's role in the Holocaust. "Vichy anti-Semitism," wrote Poliakov, "was the product of a cross between the xenophobia so characteristic of certain sections of the French middle class, and an old, traditionally reactionary, clerical anti-Semitic doctrine. . . . *The Germans forced nothing on Vichy*; they advised, 'they made suggestions.' . . . The Vichy government went along willingly, and even with real zeal when German policy conformed to its own doctrine."[29] Poliakov also made numerous suggestive comments that prefigured Arendt's and later Bauman's arguments about the role of bureaucratic efficiency and the "banality of evil" thesis in accounting for what Poliakov called "the psychology of the executioners."[30] Predating the divide between intentionalists and functionalists, Poliakov managed to strike a balance between the positions taken up most recently in Daniel Jonah Goldhagen's argument about the "eliminationist anti-Semitism" of Hitler's willing executioners and Christopher Browning's discussion of "ordinary Germans."[31] Part of the shock of Goldhagen's account was the harrowing detail about the bloodied hands of hundreds of thousands of German killers, which Poliakov likewise discussed. At the same time, in detailing the formation and tasks of the Einsatzgruppen, Poliakov was clear those who were selected were a result of a largely random bureaucratic function. "The personnel of the action groups," he wrote, "were not sadists lusting for blood, but an average and representative selection from the German police corps of 1941."[32]

When Poliakov died in 1997, the French press made evident that his contributions to Holocaust studies should be recognized. The byline for his obituary in *Le Figaro* said it all: "One of the pioneers of the historiography of the Shoah died yesterday at the age of 87." *Bréviaire de la haine*, *Le Figaro* went on to state plainly, was "the first global analysis of the processes of Nazi annihilation."[33] In *Le Monde*, Christian Delacampagne elaborated: "He was one of the pioneers of the French research on the Shoah and on anti-Semitism in a period when these subjects did not interest his contemporaries." Moreover, Delacampagne declaimed, *Bréviaire* should today be considered "a work of reference" as "the first serious work consecrated to the study of the 'final solution.'"[34] *L'Humanité*, for its part, mourned the "death of a great witness," and indicated that *Bréviaire* had a "large echo" that was well known among specialists.[35] The *New York Times* noted a macabre version of this "echo" when their obituary pointed out that "books by Mr. Poliakov were on the prison reading list of Adolf Eichmann as he awaited trial in Jerusalem in 1961 for arranging the transport of millions of Jews to Nazi death camps."[36]

It is no wonder that Eichmann sought a measure of self-objectification in Poliakov's oeuvre, since the explanatory and affective power of *Harvest of Hate* was the way that he juggled the rational and irrational aspects of the Nazi slaughter of Jews. He maintained that the bureaucratic, managed process of the machinery of destruction and the rapacious and carnivalesque unleashing of the worst in human beings combined in the Nazi genocide. Nazi anti-Semitism was therefore a deadly combination of irrational and mystical Jew hatred—"the tragic twilight of a Wagnerian night" as Poliakov put it—and the rational, but no less brutal, anti-Semitism of many of the functionaries of the Final Solution, where

Poliakov's example was Eichmann's boss, Heinrich Himmler. It was these two alternating currents of anti-Semitism that Poliakov called "sacred" and "profane" that combined to create the cataclysmic destruction wrought by the Nazi executioners.[37]

Elaborating on the sacred dimensions of Nazism, in a section called the "Basis and Meaning of Nazi Anti-Semitism," Poliakov contended that at its core "Nazism was primarily a religion." He argued that the sacral measures that were essential to Nazi anti-Semitism were what distinguished it from other forms of anti-Semitism. "The Nazi theodicy," Poliakov explained, "demanded the existence of an Enemy, that *Gegenreich* (Anti-Reich)," which meant, as Hermann Rauschning's aphorism put it, "If the Jew did not exist, we should have to invent him."[38] The representation of "the Jew" as the "plastic demon" of decadence, as Wagner famously put it, functioned to transform the abstractions of the racial soul, blood and soil, and the antitype of the German *Volk* into a concrete antipathy "because a devil was indispensable to the Nazi religion. The Jew, principle of impurity and evil, symbolized the devil. This Manichean duality was essential."[39] Norman Cohn, in *Warrant for Genocide*, a book that Poliakov translated into French, would later argue that the myth of the world Jewish conspiracy was "a modern adaptation of... [the] ancient demonological tradition,"[40] and this notion was key to the genocidal anti-Semitism of the Nazis, as Jeffrey Herf has recently demonstrated once more in *The Jewish Enemy*.[41]

Poliakov suggested that the demonization of Jews is what distinguished Nazi anti-Semitism from Nazi racism: "If the Jew occupied Satan's place in Nazi eschatology, the non-German or 'sub-human' lacking any sacred attribute was for the most part classified among the animals; at best, he was considered, according to a contemporary definition, as a 'transitional form between the animal and Nordic man.'"[42] This was an early gloss on a theme that would long preoccupy Poliakov, who would later conclude, "Here we see another of the differences between anti-Semitism and racism: blacks [and Sinti and Roma and Slavs] were generally bestialized, whereas Jews were generally seen as diabolical."[43] In short, the road to Auschwitz was built by diabolical anti-Semitism—the sacred horror made abject in Nazi anti-Semitism—but it was paved by the profane anti-Semitism that aroused a general disrespect for Jews and Judaism.[44]

Poliakov's distinction between the sacred and profane in Nazi racism not only facilitated an insightful differentiation within Nazi ideology but also helped to account for the seemingly contradictory practices of the Nazi persecution of

Jews, which wavered between "pillage and enslavement" (discussed in chapter 3), ghettoization, (addressed in chapter 4), and deportation, concentration, and extermination (elaborated in chapters 5-8). It also enabled a useful opening toward the comparative framework of genocide pursued in the last chapters of the book (chapters 11-12).[45]

From its opening pages, Poliakov's account of Nazism as a religion plumbed the depths of the Western vilification of Jews and Judaism. Christianity was heavily implicated in this charge, as the French title of the book clearly indicates, since the breviary is the book of the daily Catholic liturgy.[46] Emphasizing the point, Poliakov proffers, "Does not the catechism teach tens of millions of modern children that the Jews were the murderers of Jesus and therefore condemned until the last judgment?"[47] While insisting upon the religious dimensions of Judeophobia as central to anti-Semitism, Poliakov knew this would ruffle the feathers of his mostly Christian readers.

This was, in fact, a major worry for Poliakov. From the start, he was particularly concerned about the Catholic response to the book and he wanted a Catholic intellectual to preface the work. He explained to Aron in a letter on October 12, 1950, that it would be a good idea, since he had cited sensitive documents about the Vatican.[48] Maritain originally agreed to write the preface but then renounced his willingness upon actually reading the manuscript, insisting in a sharply worded letter to Poliakov, "I see that you have spoken of the position of the Vatican in inexact terms (there is not a shadow of anti-Semitism in the thought of the Pope)."[49] Ten days after Maritain's refusal, Poliakov secured the agreement of François Mauriac, despite pointing out to him the lines that had so disturbed Maritain.

Mauriac was willing to do so because he thought Poliakov's book helped to explain the "inexplicable crimes" with which "all Christianity finds itself indirectly associated." Nonetheless, Mauriac and Poliakov disagreed about the role of the Jews in anti-Semitism. Mauriac reproached Poliakov for not accounting at all for the comportment of Jews themselves in causing anti-Semitism, which he maintained in no way excuses anti-Semitism, nor the Nazi infamy. But he does insist that it was a part of the problem. Poliakov countered that he had indirectly alluded to the role of Jewish behavior, pointing Mauriac to a set of pages where this was the case. But he asked Mauriac to consider whether this behavior was a cause or an effect of anti-Semitism. Poliakov also objected to Mauriac's use of the term "nature" when speaking about Jews, a point he indicated that he and

Aron agreed about, since it smacked of the language of race and could easily be exploited by unsympathetic polemicists (with Poliakov naming Maurice Bardèche as his example). These matters remained unresolved between the two thinkers when the book was published with Mauriac's preface.[50]

The concluding notes of *Bréviaire* where Poliakov attempts to name the *mysterium tremendum* that underlies anti-Semitism might well have assuaged his Christian readers, however. The passage bears citation at some length:

> The measures that they advocated, ostracism or banishment, were only symbolic murders [i.e., profane]. But when moral barriers collapsed under the impact of Nazi preaching, and the genocidal passion was free to slake itself, the hatred of God slumbering in men's hearts awoke and stood revealed in the light of day; the same anti-Semitic movement that led to the slaughter of the Jews gave scope and license to an obscene revolt against God and the moral law. An open and implacable war was declared on the Christian tradition. Hitlerism's universal iconoclasm was only the logical consequence of Nazi anti-Semitism; by an atrocious demonstration *in vivo*, it tragically confirmed the penetrating insights of such great thinkers as Sigmund Freud and Jacques Maritain, [and if you look at the footnote, the crystallization of this thesis by Maurice Samuel] who saw in original anti-Semitism a "revolt of the illbaptized" against the moral law, a frenzied and unavowed hatred of Christ and the Ten Commandments that in its furious search for satisfaction vented itself on the only object that was allowed to be fair and legal game, the baffling people of God. Here we have the *causa specifica* of anti-Semitism; and so by another route, we again find our way to the deep meaning of the Nazi explosion: Hitlerism attacked the Jews as the symbol of all established values, which it had marked down for destruction. Here one perceived the deep paradox of the Jews' Calvary: they were the first victims of the anti-Christ sacrificed, in the last analysis, for a cause that was hardly theirs.[51]

As Poliakov attempted to achieve closure on the questions his text had opened about anti-Semitism, he suggested that the *causa specifica* in Maurice Samuel's terse formulation was "Christophobia." Let us succinctly unpack this complex and troubling claim by briefly examining how Freud, Samuel, and Maritain understood anti-Semitism.

CHRISTOPHOBIA: FREUD, SAMUEL, AND MARITAIN

We have already seen the ways in which the Frankfurt School, Parsons, and Lyotard drew from Freud's psychoanalytic theories in developing their own arguments. To appreciate Poliakov's take, we would do well to discuss Freud's ideas in more detail. Aside from marginal comments that were elaborated by others, Freud wrote little on anti-Semitism until his last completed work, *Moses and Monotheism* (1939). Still, he first speculated on the origins of anti-Semitism, suggesting it was rooted in the fear of castration aroused by circumcision, in a footnote in the Case of Little Hans (1909). Wrote Freud:

> The castration complex is the deepest unconscious root [*Wurzel*] of anti-Semitism; for even in the nursery [*Kinderstube*] little boys hear that a Jew has something cut off his penis—a piece of his penis, they think—and this gives them the right to despise Jews. And there is no stronger unconscious root for the sense of superiority over women. Weininger (the young philosopher who, highly gifted but sexually deranged, committed suicide after producing his remarkable book, *Geschlecht und Charaker* [1903]), in a chapter that attracted much attention, treated Jews and women with equal hostility and overwhelmed them with the same insults. Being a neurotic, Weininger was completely under the sway of his infantile complexes; and from that standpoint what is common to Jews and women is their relation to the castration complex.[52]

As Jay Geller points out, "The note condenses many of Freud's multiple identity and theory constructions by binding gender, sexuality, and ethnicity/religion/race to the workings of the unconscious, neurosis, and the castration complex."[53]

The footnote intimated a shift in Freud's oeuvre that took shape with *Totem and Taboo* in 1912, where he moved from a focus on individual psychology to mass psychology, generalizing to groups and civilizations his exploration of identity construction as a result of the sublimation of incestuous, parricidal, and murderous wishes. With the backdrop of World War I, he began to explore the relationship to death and narcissism at work in group psychology.[54] His writing on the "Uncanny" (1919), where Freud examined the stranger who is at the same time "secretly familiar" and who might therefore be constructed as the "internal enemy" proved central to his analysis of anti-Semitism in *Moses and Monotheism*.

This set of insights about anti-Semitism were all brought together in Freud's interpretation of *Moses and Monotheism*, which was certainly the source of Poliakov's closing comments. In the work, Freud discussed the oedipal relationship between the "religion of the father" (Judaism) and the "religion of the son" (Christianity). He connected the claim of Jewish chosenness and his analysis of circumcision as the foundation of anti-Semitism. And he evoked the notion of the "narcissism of minor differences," which leads to the rigidification of group boundaries and the domination of group identity in terms of the superego. Finally, in the specific passage invoked by Poliakov, Freud suggested that anti-Semitism was the product of a culture that was never fully Christianized:

> We must not forget that all those peoples who excel today in their hatred of Jews became Christians only in late historic times, often driven to it by bloody coercion. It might be said that they are all "misbaptized." They have been left, under a thin veneer of Christianity, what their ancestors were, who worshipped a barbarous polytheism. They have not got over the grudge against the new religion which was imposed on them; but they have displaced the grudge on the source from which Christianity reached them. The fact that the Gospels tell a story which is set among Jews, and in fact deals only with Jews, has made this displacement easy for them. *Their hatred of Jews is at bottom a hatred of Christians*, and we need not be surprised that in the German National Socialist revolution this intimate relation between the two monotheistic religions finds such a clear expression in the hostile treatment of both of them.[55]

In a formula that was shared by Samuel and Maritain and many others at the time, Freud argued that Hitlerism was a barbarism, a barely disguised paganism.[56] Nazism marked a vicious revolt against the ethical ideals of monotheism, whose mandates impose a difficult set of constraints on human instincts, at the same time that they are generally recognized as ideal values. Christ was the incarnation of these values and the wrath of the Nazis found a convenient target in "the Jews" who were the source of Christianity; this helps to explain the unconscious motivations for the assault on the Jews in World War II.

No doubt, Freud's ruminations were partly the result of his inherently vexed situation as a central European Jew, an expression of the double binds of his own identity.[57] The list of epithets that have been applied to him make this evident: for Peter Gay he was a "godless Jew," for Isaac Deutscher, "a non-Jewish Jew," for Yerushalmi, "a psychological Jew," who in thus naming him derides those who have called him "an ambivalent Jew," which he was, especially as concerned the dominant Viennese Christian culture that had given birth to Hitler.[58] In *Moses and Monotheism* Freud confronted personal and political questions around the Jewish Question. As he did so, Freud hinted that Christianity constitutes a more complete working through of the sublimation of civilizing instincts. I will not linger here to consider the ways in which Freud introjected an inferiority complex in relation to Christianity or even internalized the supersessionist logic at the heart of Christian theology. Nor will I address how Freud embodied the internal colonization of the norms of the Viennese culture that he shared so much with, as Daniel Boyarin suggests.[59] This is certainly only half the story of Freud's ambivalence and a limited reading of *Moses and Monotheism*, which has proven to be a seed for deeply fruitful understandings of anti-Semitism, as we have seen. I would simply highlight the ways in which Freud's position constitutes the exact obverse of the Christian claim that "the Jews" are a deicidal people when he maintained that the root of Nazism was the wish to terminate God's principles by railing against religion's ethical demands and targeting Jews as their original spokespeople. This is echoed in Poliakov's allusion to the work of Maritain and Samuel.

It is hard to avoid the intertextual resonances of Freud's analysis with Maurice Samuel's in his once-influential account of anti-Semitism, *The Great Hatred* (1940).[60] Samuel is today a forgotten figure, but in the first half of the twentieth century he was in Milton Hindus's words, "the most popular platform personality of American Jewry."[61] "A Zionist who thinks, a wit with ideas" as Louis Fisher put it,[62] Samuel was born in Macin, Romania, in 1895, moved to Paris at five, and to Manchester a year later, finally settling in the United States in 1914. A student of and later a secretary for Chaim Weitzmann, Samuel was a prolific writer, translator, and lecturer, also appearing for almost twenty years on *The Eternal Light: The Words We Live By* radio program. He published hundreds of essays and articles, six books of fiction, twenty of nonfiction, and twenty-two translations from French, German, Yiddish, and Hebrew. He wrote and spoke on issues of general cultural interest, but most of his work deals with Jewish topics: Jewish identity, Jewish values, Zionism, the Hebrew Bible, Yiddish, and anti-Semitism.[63]

The Great Hatred sought to explain "the susceptibility of the western world to the diabolisation of the Jew."[64] As had Freud, Samuel maintained that anti-Semitism is the unleashing of primitive instincts in a world devoid of the moral restraints of what he termed "Judaeo-Christianity." As we have seen, the hyphenated construct "Judaeo-Christian" that Samuel repeatedly deployed in its contemporary sense of the shared principles of Christianity and Judaism had only begun to be used widely in the 1930s, replacing the then-common "Christian civilization" as a result of Hitler's attacks on Jews.[65] Underlying these attacks, Samuel contended, was a seething rage and resentment that Christians were fettered by the precepts of ethical monotheism, embodied in the Jew-Christ.

In lecture after lecture that made up the book, Samuel hammered home his thesis that "Christophobia" was the underlying cause of anti-Semitism: "Jews are loathed as the Christ-givers, the creators or representatives of the non-force principle in human relations."[66] Samuel maintained that liberals, who tend to dislike religion as a whole, believed that anti-Semitism was like other forms of bigotry, amenable to economic, political, or social diagnoses, and consequently failed to apprehend that diabolical anti-Semitism was a totally different form of prejudice. The churches refused to acknowledge that the Christian patina was a thin skein over a repressed paganism. Christianity was in need of a "self-purgation . . . [of the] sympathetic, superstitious dread of Christ, lying concealed within the heart of Christianity itself."[67]

Christ the Jew was the incarnation of Judeo-Christian values, which Samuel enumerated: "to do what is just and right" (Genesis 18:19). To achieve this end, "Thou shalt love thy neighbor as thyself," which entailed the "passionate emphasis on God's . . . guardianship of the human individual and the person-to-person interpretation of moral relationships."[68] Moreover, he contended Judaism was the revelation of a "permanent protest" and the "perpetual after-thought" of human conscience.[69] Incarnate in Christ the Jew there stood a "recurrent outcry" of humanity's perpetual responsibility to work to establish peace, compromise, decency, justice, and goodness.

Nazi fascism, on the other hand, was, for Samuel, a purely mechanistic and biological world view, a philosophy of nature, force, and materialism, an ethos purely guided by "survival of the fittest" and "might is right." As such, Samuel sounds at times like Emmanuel Levinas in "Reflections on the Philosophy of

Hitlerism."⁷⁰ Indeed, Samuel maintained that Nazism's attraction was "not merely the worship of power, but the worship of the worship of power."⁷¹ He spelled out the bifurcation of values between anti-Semitism and Judeo-Christianity: "Deification of the body as opposed to the mind, of force as opposed to consideration, of statistical process as opposed to the sanctity of the individual."⁷²

Nazi fascism had erupted with such vengeance when it did because modernity had enabled the "mechanical mastery over nature," engendering an unprecedented "challenge to the sense of social responsibility."⁷³ Precisely at this moment of unparalleled possibility and challenge, moral conscience was overwhelmed, and Nazi fascism triumphed. Samuel's *The Great Hatred* was a prophetic and passionate plea to liberals to appreciate the differences between racial bigotry and anti-Semitism, and an injunction to Christians to fulfill the credo of their faith by educating their followers that it is sinful and anti-Christian to hate anyone.

It is no wonder that arguably the most important Catholic intellectual of the twentieth century, Jacques Maritain, embraced wholesale Samuel's thesis that anti-Semitism is Christophobia. Samuel's argument constituted the crystallization of a position in Maritain's work that he had been ambling toward throughout the interwar period, for it offered him a formula that he developed with theological profundity and eloquence.⁷⁴ "The most impressive Christian formulas concerning the spiritual essence of anti-Semitism," Maritain wrote in October 1941, "may be found in a book recently published by a Jewish writer, who seems himself strangely unaware of their profoundly Christian meaning."⁷⁵ Arguing that Samuel, Sholem Asch, Waldo Frank, and Marc Chagall were among a number of Jewish thinkers who were converging on the profound significance of the crucifixion of Christ to explain the suffering of Jews as a result of the Nazi assault, Maritain gave a distinctly Christian reading to the propositions of Samuel and Freud.

As they had, Maritain makes clear that anti-Jewish animus is multifaceted and multicausal, partly explainable by economic and social competition, class bias, nationalist forms of exclusion, or rhetorical hyperbole. But what he called "the secret soul" of anti-Semitism was, in a word, "Christophobia," which for Maritain was "the spiritual essence of the demoniacal racism of our pagan world."⁷⁶

Maritain developed an Augustinian take on Freud's and Samuel's arguments. He elucidated how the divine eschatological Mystery of Israel, whose worldly mission as a "witness people" served both as the irritant of conscience and the goad toward emancipation, was attacked by anti-Semites who sought to avenge themselves "for the pangs of its history": the pain and suffering those Christian ideals demand. Jacques Maudaule, cited by Poliakov in the passage on the *causa specifica* of anti-Semitism, aptly summed up Maritain's argument: "There is a mystery of anti-Semitism that complements the mystery of Israel; it is the reverse, if you will, of the election of Israel, and in the last analysis is a religious problem."[77] The mystical passion of Christ was Maritain's model for the suffering of humanity. Following Pascal, who maintained, "Jesus Christ is in agony until the end of the world," Maritain argued that "Christ suffers in every innocent man who is persecuted. His agony is heard in the cries of so many human beings humiliated and tortured, in the suffering of all those images and likenesses of God treated worse than beasts. He has taken all these things upon Himself, He has suffered every wound."[78] The Holocaust that he was aware was unfolding at the time that he wrote constituted what Maritain called the "passion of Israel."[79]

But "Israel's passion" was not the mystical passion of Christ and the church; it was explicitly *not* "a co-redemptive passion" capable of "the eternal salvation of souls."[80] Rather, it was the carnal, temporal torture of God's people, who were eternally yoked as suffering servants testifying to God's call: "To persecute the house of Israel is to persecute Christ, not in His mystical body as when the Church is persecuted," wrote Maritain, "but in His fleshly lineage and in His forgetful people whom He ceaselessly loves and calls."[81] Maritain mobilized this argument not only to spur Jewish-Christian reconciliation but unequivocally to castigate the perpetrators as well as the bystanders of anti-Semitism. "It is impossible to compromise with anti-Semitism," he insisted, for "it carries in itself, as in a living germ, all the spiritual evil of Nazism. Anti-Semitism is the moral Fifth Column in the Christian conscience."[82]

While Maritain was clearly calling for a united front of Jews and Christians, his argument also makes evident the risk in Freud's and Samuel's and Poliakov's claims that the *causa specifica* of anti-Semitism is "Christophobia." Ultimately, it constitutes a Christianizing of Jewish persecution. Jewish persecution is recognized only in light of the Christian supersessionist metanarrative that reinscribes Jews within the dramaturgy of the Christian salvation story, where their role is, at best, as witnesses to the truth of Christianity.

But if this is the risk of the formula that anti-Semitism is Christophobia, unpacking Poliakov's references to Freud, Samuel, and Maritain also indicates that this was the site of an important Jewish and Christian dialogue that was beginning to emerge as the crisis of European Jewry deepened. Here Freud, the "godless Jew," Samuel, "the Zionist who thinks" and Maritain, the Catholic intellectual, proffered three permutations on a theme that opened the discussion of what Jews and Judaism shared with the Christian culture that was killing them in the name of its most sacred values.

JUDEOPHOBIA: THE WESTERN TRADITION

Poliakov would follow *Harvest of Hate* with the first volume of *The History of Anti-Semitism: From the Time of Christ to the Court Jews*. This work plumbs the depths of the Western tradition to follow the trace of Judeophobia from its dawn. After a brief discussion of anti-Jewish animus in antiquity, Poliakov details the origins of Judeophobic contempt alongside the split between Judaism and Christianity, beginning in the early second century. "For the organization of Christianity," asserted Poliakov, "it was essential that the Jews be a criminally guilty people."[83] The New Testament, not least the Gospel of Matthew and the Gospel of John, along with Paul's Epistles, adumbrated what Poliakov termed "theological anti-Semitism." These New Testament seeds were watered by Origen, and reached fruition in the works of the church fathers who took one-liners from the Gospels and transformed them into an anti-Jewish ideology that served as the antithesis of nascent Christianity. Gregory of Nyssa's hateful declaration summarizes and crystallizes this early history of the demonization of Jews: "Murderers of the Lord, assassins of the prophets, rebels and detesters of God, they outrage the Law, resist grace, repudiate the faith of their fathers. Companions of the devil, race of vipers, informers, calumniators, darkeners of the mind, pharisaic leaven, Sanhedrin of demons, accursed, detested, lapidators, enemies of all that is beautiful."[84] The panoply of anti-Jewish images was thus established, here distilled in a couple of lines. Poliakov's first volume examines how this discursive mesh was mobilized during the development of medieval Christendom, from "The Age of the Crusades" (part 2, covering the 11th-13th centuries) through "The Age of the Devil" (part 3, addressing the 14th-15th centuries), and into "The Age of the Ghetto" (part 4, 16-17th centuries).

By the time he completed volume 2, *From Mohammed to the Marranos*, Poliakov laid down his core thesis about Judeophobia. Anti-Judaism, Poliakov maintained, was wound into the core of Western civilization, since its foundations were religious and theological rivalry:[85]

> To write the history of anti-Semitism is to write the history of a persecution that, in the bosom of Western society, was linked with the highest values of this society, for it was pursued in their name.... This role is played effectively in the midst of Western culture, and ... it is linked to the relationship between Judaism and her daughter religions: anti-Semitism is only the social projection of the particular tension resulting from this relationship.[86]

Having explored the long history of anti-Judaism under the cross in volume 1, Poliakov now delves into its history under the crescent in volume 2. He first explores the world of Babylonia, North Africa, and Spain before the rise of Islam. He goes on to discuss the life of the Prophet, and Islamic customs and practices with regard to both Christians and Jews. Poliakov then focuses on interreligious relations in the "Spain of the Three Religions," which began to fall apart with the advent of the Reconquista. He locates the development of the inquisitorial system and the obsession with "purity of blood" within the religious crisis of fifteenth-century Spain. It was underpinned by the drive for religious unity, which ultimately resulted in what he terms "Iberian racism." Poliakov upholds, "In the case of Spain ... the concern with religious unification could not be divorced from the obsession with purity of the blood and hatred of the Jews."[87] But in delineating the afterlife of Iberian racism, Poliakov makes evident that this was far from the hardened distinctions of modern racism, since even when *limpieza de sangre* statutes became law, the problem of "how to track down this contagion" remained. The epistemology of modern science was not yet in place, which was central to the development of modern racism.

THE ROLE OF PHILOSOPHY IN THE SECULARIZATION OF ANTI-JUDAISM

In opening volume 3 of the *History of Anti-Semitism*, Poliakov apologetically signaled a methodological shift. Instead of a "historical sociology," as he hoped, his work had devolved into a "history of ideas" focusing too much for his liking on the concerns of "historians of philosophy." Explaining what he meant, he indicated that his study documents "habits of thought."[88] Beyond unearthing "a basic trend in Western thought," a point already proclaimed in volume 2 that he now reiterated, Poliakov paid considerable attention to the role philosophers played in secularizing a series of notions central to anti-Judaism that underpin modern racism. He would establish a parallel point in *The Aryan Myth*, published three years later.

In the account that Poliakov provides, which only clearly emerges in reading these two books side-by-side, he maintains that the separation of science from ecclesiastical authority in the seventeenth century and the abandonment of the biblical cosmogony and Christian values that began with the Enlightenment created a space for modern racist theories. Today this is well known. What is really essential is Poliakov's insistence that the Christian system of binaries was imported into racist theories—good and evil, virtue and vice, sanctity and sin, purity and contamination, beauty and ugliness—each would be grafted onto racialized bodies. Philosophers, Poliakov argues, played a key part in both of these movements.

In illuminating this process, there are three key links Poliakov establishes in the nearly one thousand pages that make up these two heavy tomes. First, in the section of *The Aryan Myth* titled "The Utopias of Reason," he maintains that, influenced by the new science and coupled to new models of what defines human nature, a "rational racism" began to develop in the philosophical canon, a dogma that began to offer a "bio-scientific" justification to racist notions. Poliakov begins his account of "rational racism" by pointing to a relationship between John Locke's work and the ideas of François Bernier, who is considered the first theorist to have developed the modern category of race.[89] In his 1684 *Nouvelle division de la terre par les différentes espèces ou races d'hommes qui l'habitent* (Division of the earth by the different species or races who inhabit it), Bernier repurposed "race" to become a catch term for separating and organizing the essential varieties of human difference.[90] Poliakov points out that Locke was Bernier's "disciple."[91] Having coupled Locke and Bernier, Poliakov goes on to cite two staggering claims in Locke's *Essay Concerning Human Understanding* about Blacks that Locke uses to establish his understanding of the nature of humanity. The negative side of his argument was his claim that naturally "a negro is not a man."[92] Indeed, Locke maintains that this notion is so basic that as soon as a child starts thinking, he will be able to distinguish between the wet nurse feeding it and the Negro who frightens it![93] Negros, not being human, are beastly and thus will naturally scare any self-aware, young, white European, according to Locke.

In Poliakov's interpretation, the upshot of the racism one finds in Locke is partly a result of his reduction of human cognition to a reflection on empirical sensations. For Poliakov, this was conjoined to the development of the new cosmology that underpinned Newton's *Principia Mathematica*, whereby a mathematically expressible view of the universe was fixed onto a mechanistic account of the body. William Harvey's model of the heart was its template. In Poliakov's telling, a key locus of this move was Descartes's famous passage in the *Discourse on Method* where man is reduced to "a machine ... having been made by the hand of God."[94] In Descartes, the divine imprint remained. But human nature, it was claimed in Descartes's shadow, could be understood through a mathematical set of laws, physico-natural in their essence, reducing being human to the same laws as physical matter. "This was a technical-mathematical concept of nature reduced to a static geometrical plane," claims Poliakov, "the concept of a totally flattened out, 'two-dimensional' world."[95] This flattening of human nature, for Poliakov, had pernicious consequences. One of its side effects was racism.

Poliakov continues his analysis by showing how philosophical reason, science, and race were soldered together in the Enlightenment. These come together in Poliakov's section on "The System Builders," in his chapter on "The Century of Enlightenment" in *The History of Anti-Semitism*. He expounds the eighteenth-century debates that resulted in the establishment of formal systems of racial classification from Linnaeus through Blumenbach. He opens this section by indicating that the origin of the word "race" is somewhat uncertain. It emerged in Europe in the sixteenth century to refer to generation or descent. Right from the start, he notes, "it implied a value judgment: 'nobility of race' as opposed to 'common race,' good race as opposed to bad."[96]

One of the first to tie together the physical nature of human beings with their mental and moral natures was Carl von Linné or Linnaeus in his *Systema Naturae* (1735), where he "postulated the existence of four varieties of the species *Homo sapiens* (Americanus, Europaeus, Asiaticus, and Asser)."[97] These four types were said to differ from one another not only in skin color and hair but also in customs and temperament. According to Poliakov, the great popularizer of the developing systems of racial classification was Buffon in his *Histoire naturelle* (1749-1788). Buffon, maintains Poliakov, was second only to Voltaire in his international celebrity during the Enlightenment. He contributed to the developing discussion his "Degeneration Theory" of racial origins. In *De la dégénération des animaux*, Buffon proposed (following the suggestion of the mathematician Maupertuis in his *Vénus physique*) that primordial humans were white Europeans who underwent alterations and degenerations as they spread over the world. Peter Camper, Christoph Meiners, Immanuel Kant, and others also each made their contributions to what they deemed rational systems of racial classification.[98]

By the end of the eighteenth century, Johann Friedrich Blumenbach's *De Generis Humane Varietate Nativa* (*On the Natural Variety of Mankind*) distilled the discussion.[99] In his 1781 edition, Blumenbach enumerated five races (up from four in 1775), and in his 1795 third edition, he introduced the term "Caucasian" to name the white faces he eulogized as primordial:

> I have given this variety, the name of Mount Caucasus because the most beautiful race of men, the Georgian, is found in its vicinity and because, if the cradle of the human race can be fixed, all physiological reasons combine to place it at that spot.... The Georgians' skin is white, and this color still appears originally to belong to the human race, but it easily degenerates into a darkish color.[100]

In Blumenbach's system, Jews were defined not as a race, but as a people; their type was, Blumenbach wrote, nonetheless "clearly evident even in the[ir] skulls."[101]

Poliakov then shows that the use of the word "race" in Enlightened society in its new scientific sense, and its spread to the Jews, occurred in the early nineteenth century, especially in Germany. Once more, philosophers played an important role. This took place in the aftermath of the French Revolution and the Napoleonic wars since race theory and the Aryan myth were each an effort to redraw borders and boundaries rent asunder by the eruption of modern politics:

> The great social and political phenomena of the nineteenth century—the rise of nationalism and racism—might have been partly due to Western man's hidden need to erect new partitions and new hierarchies after the disappearance of the old hierarchical barriers.... The anguish of no longer being differentiated from the Jew, of intermingling with him ... in a standardized world, from which God is beginning to disappear and where many Christians feel themselves adrift, would therefore be a deep-seated and specific factor in modern anti-Semitism.[102]

Nowhere in Europe were these factors as interwoven as in German lands. After a section on the German *Aufklärung*, which yearned "through its novelists and dramatists to love all men, including Jews, with equal love," Poliakov indicates that the German philosophical tide turned hostile and negative. He dates the moment to the death of Moses Mendelssohn in 1786. Thereafter, Poliakov judges, "the great philosophers, even more than the poets...were dead set against the 'Chosen People,' leaving no stone unturned to attack them."[103] In this, Lutheran theology played a central role, since German idealism, Poliakov indicates, was saturated in this Lutheran tradition, "of which it was a sort of progressive secularization."[104]

Poliakov takes up this lineage in his section on "German Philosophy and the Jews." The tradition was paved by Johann David Michaelis, the great Hebraist, who opposed Dohm's call for the emancipation of the Jews in *Über die bürgerliche Verbesserung der Juden* (*On the Civil Improvement of the Jews*, 1781).[105] However, the German *philosophical* fountainhead of this tradition who called for the "metaphysical euthanasia" of Judaism was Immanuel Kant, who claimed that Judaism as a form of heteronomy was not a religion within the bounds of reason.[106] To demonstrate Kant's negative assessment of Judaism, Poliakov turns to Kant's *Anthropologie*, where he decries Jews as "a *nation* of usurers...bound together by a superstition," thus evincing their lack of capacity for pure reason or the categorical imperative.[107] Kant's "disciple Fichte," in turn, like Luther, called for the expulsion of Jews from German lands, for as he stated, "to give them civic rights—I see no means to do that except, one night, to cut off all their heads and give them new ones in which there would not be one Jewish idea."[108] In accord with Fichte's metaphorical beheading, Poliakov also locates the genesis of the idea of the "Aryan Christ" in his work, which would be fully developed by thinkers like Houston Stewart Chamberlain.[109] Fichte held that in Paul's Epistles, "original Christianity had been corrupted by its Jewish apostle," a point that he elaborated in *Reden an die deutsche Nation* (*Addresses to the German Nation*, 1808) that Poliakov terms "the charter of pan Germanism," which contained a call for Germans to reclaim a pure and uncorrupted Christianity.[110]

The young Hegel, Poliakov shows, mined this same vein of depicting "Jewish consciousness" as "wretched and servile." Hegel's main motif was to secularize the patristic theme of the perpetual slavery of Jews so long as they clung to Mosaic law. Hegel, like Michaelis, Kant, and Fichte before him, would condemn Jews with a cruel formula. "Spirit alone recognizes spirit," he penned. But Jews "saw in Jesus only the man...something great, cannot make its home in a dunghill. The lion has no room in a nest, the infinite spirit none in the prison of a

Jewish soul."[111] Hegel's supersessionism would be echoed by Schleiermacher, who likewise wrote off Judaism: "Judaism is long since dead," he claimed. "Those who yet wear its livery are only sitting lamenting beside the imperishable mummy, bewailing its departure and its sad legacy."[112]

The lineage in German thought that Poliakov tracks continues in the thought of the Young Hegelian generation: Ludwig Feuerbach, Bruno Bauer, and Karl Marx.[113] In the decade from 1840-1850 when German metaphysicians were openly critiquing the existence of God, Poliakov illustrates how the Young Hegelian critique was conjoined to a critique of Jews and Judaism. In Feuerbach's *Das Wesen des Christentums* (*The Essence of Christianity*, 1840), he "unmasked Judaism" (thereby echoing the title of Johann Andreas Eisenmenger's notorious rant against the Talmud), identifying Judaism with egoism and materialism.[114] Bauer's *Die Judenfrage* (The Jewish Question) was not only one of the first uses of the catchphrase "the Jewish Question," but in it, he formulated his opposition to Jewish emancipation on scientific grounds. Following Hegel's line on Judaism, Bauer claimed that that Jews are an unhistorical people possessing an "oriental nature" that limited human liberty and progress.[115] In a starkly modern phrase, he insisted, "The opposition is no longer religious, it is scientific." Jewish atavism, and their "perpetual segregation from others" meant that Jews could never be equal citizens.[116]

In his famous reply, *Zur Judenfrage* ("On the Jewish Question") Marx argued *against* his one-time teacher and *for* the political emancipation of the Jewish community, but in harshly Judeophobic terms. In the first part, Marx polemicized against Bauer for his critique of the Jewish religion when the proper locus should be on the roots of society and the state. He insisted upon Jewish civil and political rights, along with the removal of all strictures to Jewish movement, residence, or professional access. The second part attacked the society of his day with vehemence, denouncing it as corrupted by Judaism, since it was entirely dominated by money. "What is the profane basis of Judaism?" Marx railed:

> *Practical* self-interest ... *huckstering* and *money*. ... The Jew has emancipated himself in a Jewish manner, not only by acquiring the power of money but also because *money* has become, through him and also apart from him, a world power, while the practical Jewish spirit has become the practical spirit of the Christian nations. The Jews have emancipated themselves in so far as the Christians have become Jews.[117]

Tracking the heartbeat of Poliakov's narrative through the canonic figures of modern thought consequently reveals the central role played by philosophers in the secularization of anti-Judaism.

FROM A CHRISTIAN ANTHROPOLOGY TO A MODERN ANTHROPOLOGY: THE THEOLOGICAL UNDERPINNINGS OF MODERN RACIAL THOUGHT

If the *heartbeat* of Poliakov's account is about the role of philosophy in the secularization of anti-Judaism, the *heart* of Poliakov's story is that philosophy worked in tandem with modern science. Philosophers developed a new account of the origins, nature, and ends of human beings in parallel with the new science's account about the world. The modern view of the human subject developed by philosophers was formulated in the shade of this new science. This is what Poliakov means when he discusses a shift from a "Christian anthropology" toward a modern, "scientific anthropology" that shows the enduring legacy of anti-Judaism in the establishment of modern anti-Semitism and anti-Black racism. According to Poliakov, with the advent of full-blown racism, the Christian theological doctrines that cursed the Jews were transformed by the new scientific anthropology, since Jewish inferiority was now defined by biological difference. "It was as if the badge or canonical hat of yore were henceforth carved, 'internalized' into their flesh," Poliakov wrote, "as if Western opinion could not dispense with a definite distinction and this distinction became an *invisible essence* once the *visible symbols* identifying the Jew had been erased."[118] This argument is explicitly developed in the second part of *The Aryan Myth* with its implications cashed out in Poliakov's volume 3 of *The History of Anti-Semitism*.

The Aryan Myth examines the trajectory of anti-Judaism into modern nationalism and racism. In the first part, Poliakov explores the origin myths of nationalism, showing that the genealogies of the Pentateuch were pivotal to these origin stories across the European continent. Sketching arguments that Anthony D. Smith would call "primordialist" accounts of nationalism,[119] Poliakov considers how in the aftermath of the Roman Empire, each nation began to forge traditions about its early ancestors that connected them with the biblical genealogies. In medieval Spain, France, England, Italy, Germany, and Russia, each culture sought to discern a putative primogenitor, tracing them back to

Noah. In almost all regions of Europe, a pivotal role was assigned to the early Germanic tribes that had conquered the Roman Empire. The aristocratic elite of most nations (except Italy) identified themselves with these Germanic precursors, thus seeding the deep soil for the later Aryan myth.

The second part of *The Aryan Myth* turns from the focus on national myths of origin to modern explanations of the diversity of mankind. Here Poliakov undertakes a study of anthropological theories, broadly understood, that is, those efforts that elaborated theories on the origin, development, and nature of human beings. Specifically, he traces the accounts that led to the development of the malicious Aryan myth. He discusses the antecedents of Aryanism in the "Pre-Adamites": writers who suggested that there were multiple creations before Adam. This tradition begins with Jewish and Islamic and then medieval Christian thought.[120] But it accelerated in the seventeenth century with the work of Isaac de la Peyrère of Bordeaux, a Marrano who influenced the theory of polygenism in Voltaire and Goethe.[121] He develops this connection in his chapter on "The Anthropology of the Enlightenment," where he offers a catalog of the *philosophes*' views on the classification of the human races and the science of race, examining how "some of the most notable champions of the Enlightenment laid the foundations of the scientific racism which was to follow in the next century."[122]

Poliakov divides the leading articulators into two groups, "The Moderate Anthropologists" who still lingered in the biblical assertion of a unity to mankind (the monogenists) and the "extreme anthropologists" who formulated polygenism (the notion of separate descents for the divergent groups of *genus homo*). The progenitors of scientific racism were the polygenists, Poliakov avers, who rejected the biblical principle of the unity of mankind for reasons that were supposed to be scientific.[123] Voltaire was Poliakov's prime exemplar.[124] The kingpin of the Enlightenment was "an enigma" since he was "the leading apostle of toleration" and yet clearly racist. In his *Traité de métaphysique* (1734), for example, he bluntly states, "Bearded whites, fuzzy negroes, the long-maned yellow races and beardless men are not descended from the same man." Blacks, he thought, were at the bottom of the racial ladder while whites were "superior to these Negroes, as the Negroes are to the apes and the apes to oysters."[125] From Voltaire, Poliakov went on to itemize David Hume's shared convictions, expressed in his famous footnote to his essay "Of National Characters,"[126] alongside those of Hume's Scottish compatriot Lord Kames, Edward Long in England, and Christoph Meiners in Germany.[127] In France, the key figure was Jean-Joseph [sic] Virey, whose ideas made their way in translation to the United States, providing new justifications for proslavery arguments.[128]

In "The Quest for the New Adam," Poliakov explores the ways in which a discursive formation emerged that posited India as the site of the genesis of mankind, the origins of European languages, and also the beginnings of culture, science, and all the higher achievements of mankind. The budding science of linguistics would name these ancestral origins as Aryan, opposing this to "the Hamites, the Mongols—and the Jews."[129]

It was the work of William Jones that established the link between Sanskrit and Greco-Roman languages. At the beginning of the nineteenth century, this connection penetrated into European culture primarily through the lectures on universal history given by Friedrich Schlegel, who immediately gave it "an anthropological twist by deducing from the relationship of language a relationship of race."[130] Schlegel not only overlay the discovery of linguistic connections with cultural archetypes but also refined the vocabulary of this developing scientific truth. After Schlegel, Poliakov concludes, "the authentic and useful science of linguists became absorbed in the crazy doctrine of 'racial anthropology.'"[131]

This point ties together the account provided by Poliakov in *The Aryan Myth* with his overview of the secularization of anti-Judaism by the philosophers in *The History of Anti-Semitism*. "The new anthropology of the Enlightenment," he avers, "provided the general framework for a semantic and sociological phenomenon which I have examined thoroughly in previous works [namely, *The History of Anti-Semitism*, volume 3] and which may be summarized in a few words: *the ineradicable feelings and resentments of the Christian West were to be expressed thereafter in a new vocabulary* [that of race and Aryanism]."[132] Poliakov shows that the Aryan myth was developed in the work of Schelling, Goethe, and Hegel, and then perfected by an army of German scholars who linked the various elements of the myth: "the emphasis on biology, the deserved triumph of the strongest, the preeminence of youth, the superiority of the Whites."[133] By far its most influential promoter was Jacob Grimm, the originator of the famous dictionary and disseminator of folktales, whose work became a source for the myth to be taught to a large educated public in Europe in the second half of the nineteenth century. In short, what Poliakov demonstrates is that the leading philosophers of the Enlightenment tore the prior biblical theory of the unity of the human race to shreds. They began the process of affiliating the European lineage to India. Friedrich Schlegel was the founder of the Aryan myth. Once it was launched,

Orientalists and German myth makers developed it until it was consolidated into a putatively valid scientific fact during the second half of the nineteenth century.

THE CATEGORIES OF RACISM

Poliakov not only provides a historical overview of the role of philosophers in secularizing Christian anti-Judaism and their role in developing Aryanism. He also suggests that that the specific set of categories that coalesced to form modern racism were repurposed from earlier Christian categories. Poliakov only drops small hints about the switch from premodern religious notions to modern concepts. But on the basis of these suggestions, we can tease out a set of transfers, translations, or exchanges that took place that were imported into the modern idiom of race.

Poliakov's analysis of anti-Semitism over the *longue durée* thus insists that racism was a recasting of Christian theological discourse. As he puts it, "If contemporaries formed an imaginary image of a Jewish race, they did so because a theologically condemned caste already existed."[134] This is well accepted today. What remains intriguing is that few locate this process of secularization and translation with precision. One surprising place where Poliakov itemizes this transfer is in his discussion of "the regenerators," that is, the key advocates for Jewish emancipation or civil equality for Jews as equal citizens of modern nation-states. Poliakov explains that those who placed hope in Jewish improvement adopted the language of "*regeneration*, which the science of Descartes and Buffon had borrowed from the language of the Church and which had first really meant the effects of baptism ('regeneration in Jesus Christ')."[135] Obviously, the term "regeneration" carried with it a lot of theological baggage. In taking up the Enlightenment position on the perfectibility of human nature, "the regenerators" reworked the terms of Christian *conversion* into the language of *assimilation* and *salvation* into the discourse of *emancipation*.

The vocabulary of regeneration reached its apex with the French Revolution, where it emerged as the key term for shaping the social contract that defined the relationship between Jews and the modern French nation.[136] As nationalisms emerged in response to the Revolutionary and Napoleonic wars, notions of religious *election* morphed in nationalist discourse into arguments for national exceptionality. Poliakov's account in *The Aryan Myth* had already indicated that biblical genealogies were the basis of national genealogies and national myths of origin. As they were, Adam as the origin and destiny of mankind ceded place to a new myth of Indo-European origins and ends, the Aryan myth. A new land of origin replaced Eden—the ur-Aryan locale supposedly at the genesis of European civilization, now cleansed of Jewish origins. For the peoples who took up this myth of origin, a new tripartite division developed between the Aryan, Shem, and Ham: "The Aryan, or real man, was defined by comparison with both brother Shem, the Jew, half-man, half-demon, and brother Ham, the black, half-animal, half-man."[137] The Aryan myth consequently defined itself in relation to both Jews and Blacks.

The hierarchies that underpinned modern systems of racial classification were themselves grafted onto the ancient and later Christian "great chain of being."[138] By the middle of the nineteenth century, race thinking supplanted the older Christian notion of providence, and anti-Semitism became "the converse of the eucharistic mystery."[139] Providence and eschatology ceded their conceptual space to conceptions of progress and the stadial view of history, which "perhaps was merely the reverse of the Christian idea of the Fall."[140] Whenever the radical reorganization of society was envisioned, Jews and Judaism were often invoked, conflating theological claims with modern racial terms. Those who had fallen from grace according to Christian theology or deviated from the true path of God according to Islam were identified with the demonic. This theological legacy of identifying Jews with evil was constitutive for their later racialization.[141] Sewing this all together, Poliakov declares that racism emerged from the confusion of races and language, history and anthropology, combined with "a philosophy choked with theological residue and science."[142]

We accordingly find buried in the vast documentation and narrative of Poliakov's tomes an explication of the specific mechanisms that designate how anti-Judaism was secularized in the development of modern racism. Poliakov's account emerged out of his own life experience and built upon the foundational role he played within Holocaust studies, where he initially sought to explain Nazi anti-Semitism. In excavating his approach to Judeophobia, this chapter makes four key points. It insists upon the trailblazing role he played as a pioneering scholar, although his work is not as well known today as it should be, especially outside of France. Second, while the role of philosophers in the elaboration of racial thought has been well developed within the critical philosophy of race—as the footnotes on Locke, Hume, Kant, and Hegel make evident—sufficient attention has not been paid to the Christian theological baggage that these thinkers imported into their philosophical works that helped to undergird modern racism. This is the key insight of Poliakov's work since it reveals how Christian anti-Judaism was the scaffolding for modern racism. Third, for Poliakov, modern racism gels in the shift from a Christian anthropology to a secular anthropology. Again, philosophers played an important role not only in the nascent discipline of physical anthropology but also in formulating influential views on the origins, nature, and destiny of human beings with important ramifications for the development of race thinking. Fourth, appreciating the role of theology in shifts from a Christian anthropology to a modern, Enlightened anthropology is important since much critical work on the history of racism and philosophical excavation of race thinking splits religion and race. Along with this split is a separation of anti-Judaism from anti-Semitism and anti-Semitism from anti-Black racism. Reading Poliakov's *History of Anti-Semitism* and *The Aryan Myth* together, we can see his argument that a set of Christian theological categories were secularized and transformed in the development of modern racism. "Race" came to name a whole constellation of categories that surround the term. Poliakov's work itemized the shifts between the great chain of being → modern racial hierarchies; from providence and eschatology → notions of progress and the stadial view of history; from baptism → regeneration; from salvation → emancipation; from religious election → national exceptionalism; from biblical genealogies → modern national myths of origin; and from the figure of Adam as the origin and destiny of mankind → the Aryan myth. The vituperative assault on the down*fall* and failure of Judaism within Christian theology marked Jews as a separate caste who were in turn castigated as a distinct race. Jews were Europe's internal enemies, twinned to other external "Semites" and their Black servile brothers. The role of these separated castes was to expiate their endemic sin if they were not to be eliminated entirely by modern social hygiene. This was done in the name of the racial systems that Poliakov's work helped to explicate.

CHAPTER 7

George Mosse on Modernity, Culture, and "the Jew"

If Léon Poliakov was one of the pioneers in understanding the history of Judeophobia over the *longue durée*, then George Mosse serves as a key figure for the historical understanding of the links between modernity and anti-Semitism. Mosse was an innovative historian who articulated the interconnections between "Jewish history and anti-Semitism; Fascism, Nazism and the Holocaust; monuments and mass politics; war and commemoration[;] ... liberalism and [its assault by] 'irrationalism'; racism, stereotypes and visual culture; [and] respectability, sexuality, and nationalism."[1] He understood how the image of "the Jew" in modern Western culture could be manipulated to manifold ends and that following its trace could provide an illuminating perspective on modernity. He historicized the links between different stereotypes, especially racial and sexual typecasting, uncovering the associative logic of prejudice. Like Poliakov, he appreciated the ongoing power of religion in modernity: that the desire to connect with the sacred has endured, not least in times of tumultuous change. As such, he explained how modern nationalism secularized religious rites and rituals. He also discerned how representations of "the Jew" served to personify the underside of modernity, especially by those who feel alienated, lost, or left behind. Finally, like Bauman, he showed that fascism, Nazism, and the Holocaust were no aberration. Rather, as Steven Ascheim puts it, these were "the culmination of deeper immanent trends, perceptions, and processes that defined Western and Central European culture."[2]

These insights were the product not only of his breadth of understanding of Western civilization but were also the result of his own existential and historical situation. Mosse was at once the quintessential insider by birth, wealth, privilege, and professional success.[3] But he was also a double outsider: as a homosexual and a Jew. As such, he was the embodiment of the respectable gentleman and a critic of bourgeois respectability. He was a victim of the events and processes that he historicized. But victimization was never a badge of pride; it was a test of character whereby his exile was experienced as revealing a path toward liberation.[4] Thus what Enzo Traverso has maintained about Horkheimer and Adorno and Arendt was also true of Mosse: "They [all] illustrated the *epistemological privilege of exile*."[5] As outsiders and refugees they perceived norms and conventions through critical eyes, were intuitively wary of nationalism and its stereotypes, and sought to reveal a path toward freedom.

Reading across Mosse's oeuvre, one can distill some of the core insights that his work generated. First, he stressed that underlying the role of religion was the need for security, stability, and community, which was created through liturgy and rites. In the modern period, especially as a part of nationalist causes, this took new forms that replaced the sacred center of society dissolved by the modern assault on the holy. Second, influenced by the Frankfurt School, he discerned a dialectic to the Enlightenment, which had two faces: (a) the culture of the eighteenth century helped to engender the politics of bourgeois respectability, which Mosse showed was inherently exclusionary; and (b) the Enlightenment commitment to classical aesthetics and to systems of classification led to the development of systemic stereotyping at the heart of modern nationalism and racism. Respectability and racism—each jointed to the Enlightenment—consequently combined to forge one causal vector undergirding fascism and Hitlerism. Third, since racism is bound to the politics of respectability—to moral norms and a sexual ethos—the antitypes to racial and sexual typologies, particularly Jews and homosexuals, always embody the opposite of these virtues. Fourth, Mosse contended that racism, which was nourished by Romanticism as much as by the Enlightenment, could be understood as an extreme form of what he termed "heightened nationalism."[6] Underpinning racism is tribalism—nationalism in a different idiom—undergirded by the same historical forces. Fifth, racism should be understood as "a visual ideology based on stereotypes."[7] Mosse ferreted out the modern representations of the Jewish body, which served as a foil for reflecting on social mores or revisions of the body politic. Sixth, like Bauman, Mosse argued that fascism and the Holocaust were not a parenthesis within modern European history, but rather were the radical fulfillment of core tendencies within modernity and bourgeois culture. These key claims emerged from Mosse's intellectual odyssey.

SCION AND OUTCAST

George Mosse was born into a life of opulence on September 20, 1918, the scion of one of the leading German Jewish families prior to the rise of the Nazis. Both his paternal and maternal grandfathers were fabulously wealthy. On his father's side, Salomon Lachmann was a Prussian grain merchant who made his fortune in the 1860s supplying the Prussian army with food during its wars against Austria and France. One of his children, Edmund Lachmann, was president of the Berlin Jewish Community for forty years and one of the first Jewish officers in the Prussian military. But this side of his family would be overshadowed by his maternal grandfather, Rudolf Mosse (1843–1920), a pioneer in the development of German advertising for the new mass market of the late nineteenth century. This business developed into a large publishing enterprise, making him one of the wealthiest men in Germany. The publishing venture was later headed by Mosse's father, which included the influential newspapers, the *Berliner Tageblatt* and the *Berliner Morgenzeitung*. Mosse's affluent upbringing was complemented by a steady diet of German liberalism, cosmopolitanism, and the ideal of *Bildung* (self-cultivation through culture). On one level, then, he was the quintessential insider within elite German culture. Except that his family were highly visible Jews. As liberals, they were also "instrumental in furthering German-French friendships ever since World War I."[8] The Nazis, accordingly, harbored a special animus toward them. As a result, they were forced into exile in 1933, with much of their property expropriated.

Mosse was also a homosexual who lived much of his life in the closet. This gave him a critical perspective on Jewish culture. He says in his autobiography, *Confronting History*, that his "double outsiderdom" provided the diagnostic optic of his work. But as important was that he was also a double insider to both German and Jewish culture. This doubled existence shaped Mosse's perspective as a "conscious pariah," (Arendt) or "connected critic" (Michael Walzer).[9] This enabled his simultaneous empathy and critical acumen in understanding both the central vectors of modern European cultural forces as well as the tensions faced by Jews and other outsiders navigating these conditions. Mosse could migrate back and forth between these viewpoints since his life was shaped at an early stage by his own migration.

Forced to flee Berlin the day after Hitler assumed power in 1933, Mosse tells a poignant anecdote about the start of his journey into exile from his lavish upbringing:

> I managed to get out only because of the German penchant for order. I don't remember the exact date but there was a new law pending according to which one had to have an exit visa. I left in a ferry across the Lake of Constance fifteen minutes before midnight, when the law was to go into effect. But instead of stopping me, the SA guards, knowing perfectly well who I was, let me go since the law did not take effect for another quarter of an hour.[10]

From Switzerland, Mosse's family went to Paris, and then to England in 1934. There he attended the Quaker Bootham School in York, where his classmates included the Earl of Houston. The school already had a strong record of producing great historians, like A. J. P. Taylor. Mosse subsequently went to Cambridge because to study history, as he put it, was a "gentleman's occupation; everybody who did not know what he wanted to do went into history."[11] Mosse tells the tale in his wonderful accent, which merged his German background, his English training, and much of his life spent in the Midwest. He would later joke about it, saying, "First I was trained to rule the German Reich, then I was taught to govern the British Empire. Alas, both vanished before my very eyes."[12] To understand him is to tune in to this wry sense of humor, delivered with his singular pronunciation, the product of his layered identity.

In August 1939, just before war broke out on the continent, he left England for the United States. He chose to remain there for the duration of the war because reentry into Britain as an enemy alien was dangerous. He was accepted into another Quaker haven, Haverford College, where he was fully initiated into the discipline of history. From there, he went on to complete his PhD at Harvard in 1946, writing a thesis on the idea of sovereignty in early modern England. While completing his dissertation, he began teaching at the University of Iowa in 1944, where he remained until 1955. In Iowa, his scholarly reputation grew with studies focused on English constitutional law and because of his popular textbooks on the Reformation. But he was especially appreciated as an outstanding lecturer, with hundreds of students clamoring to get into his classes on Western civilization, and a broader audience that listened to his occasional statewide radio broadcasts.

He moved to the University of Wisconsin-Madison in 1955 with the proviso that he specialize in the nineteenth and twentieth centuries, even though his work up to that point had concentrated on the period from the Reformation into the seventeenth century, since Madison already had a Tudor and Stuart historian. He remained there until his retirement in 1987. He also taught at the Hebrew University of Jerusalem one semester per year from 1969–1985. Within a decade of his arrival in Madison, he began to publish a series of trailblazing books, beginning with *The Crisis of German Ideology: Intellectual Origins of the Third Reich* (1964). In 1966, with Walter Laqueur, he founded the *Journal of Contemporary History*. Within the next ten years, Mosse would draw upon anthropological models and visual studies to explore the political liturgies and the mythological and symbolic forces that shaped modern nationalism and racism, most notably in *The Nationalization of the Masses* (1975) and *Toward the Final Solution: A History of European Racism* (1978). Ten years on, he was at the vanguard of gender studies with another groundbreaking book, *Nationalism and Sexuality*, which would be complemented by his history of masculinity, *The Image of Man* (1996). These pivotal texts recast the cultural and intellectual history of European modernity. This chapter focuses on how they were all linked by Mosse's multifaceted analysis of modern Judeophobia as a central thread that he explored from the variegated vantage point of each of these key studies.

MOSSE'S METHODOLOGY

To get at his approach, we should first appreciate his methodology. David Sabean rightly contends that there was always "a strong theoretical substructure to Mosse's historical practice, although it was one that he did not usually make explicit."[13] As Karel Plessini notes, "Though Mosse hardly ever systematized his theoretical beliefs, he acted as a catalyzer of many of the fundamental currents of thought of the age."[14] Reflecting on the methods that percolated in his works, Mosse wrote, "I have always approached history not as a narrative but as a series of questions and possible answers.... I believe that historical narrative must provide the framework within which problems of interest can be addressed... Theory cut loose from concrete context becomes a mere game, an amusement of no particular relevance."[15] So Mosse's theorizing remains buried in the problems he addressed and in the answers his books provide to understanding those conundrums.

Mosse's early work was all on the English Reformation and religious history. But there were some important intuitions garnered in his works on the religious conflicts of early modernity that remained central to his understanding of modernity. Not the least of these was the enduring role of religion in the modern age and the ongoing drive to connect to the sacred that he would discern in the rites and rituals of much modern political liturgy. A Mosse quip nicely sums up his point: "Most people in the West prefer catechism to [Marx's] *Kapital*."[16] This from a man who asked that God not be mentioned at his funeral and who was a self-proclaimed, "Marxist of the heart."

This one-liner intimates something important about Mosse's methodology, which was dialectical, but not in the conventional sense of historical materialism. Mosse never considered culture as an epiphenomenon of the conditions of production and exchange or material forces. Rather, he explored "the dynamic interrelationship between people's ideas and the social and political reality in which these ideas function."[17] He claimed to have digested this "Hegelian" approach to the past from George Lichtheim, whom he considered a formative intellectual influence. "There is a dialectic between myth and reality," averred Mosse," and "all of history must be viewed in a dynamic and dialectical fashion."[18] He sought to illuminate how people constructed meaning in their historical circumstances and what the consequences of these meanings entailed. Mosse insisted, for example, that to understand the social meaning of a leading anti-Semitic intellectual like Houston Stewart Chamberlain required as much reception history in "weekly and monthly magazines, the popular press, best sellers, [and] radio programs," as it did a close reading of his tome, *The Foundations of the Nineteenth Century*. In addition, it meant that key terms, like "anti-Semitism" itself, could not be presumed to mean the same thing in different contexts, or within differing national traditions.

To understand phenomena like anti-Semitism, Mosse urged a historicist bent that meant "'getting inside the heads' of historical actors."[19] As Robert Nye noted in his Festschrift in 1980, Mosse was "an intuitive sort of intellectual historian, feeling his way through his materials and reconstructing intellectual developments as they 'must' have occurred. On this view, empathy has been his most useful tool; in his hands, ideology appeals as much to deep emotional structures as to rational and cognitive ones."[20] Most illuminating of all was that Mosse often saw profound connections between seemingly opposed forces. For instance, he insisted well before his student Jeffrey Herf developed his own thesis about "reactionary modernism," that "national socialist ideology really rested on two pillars.... It combined traditionalism ... with modernity," appealing to a mythic past, but embracing aspects of modern industrial capitalism and the symbols of modern nationalism, fusing together counterrevolution and revolution.[21] Mosse also repeatedly insisted, "Any political theology grows quite naturally out of Christian theology." Therefore, any approach that treated the Nazis as quintessentially anti-Christian missed part of how the cross was bent to the purposes of the swastika.[22]

Key as well to Mosse's methodology was how he conceived of cultural history. Karel Plessini has shown that there were three phases to Mosse's development.[23] His work on the early modern period approached its topics from the purview of the history of ideas, focusing on major intellectuals and how their texts reflected the cultural aspirations and ideals of an era. This began to shift as Mosse incorporated the study of popular culture and popular piety into his research, influenced primarily by Jacob Burckhard's *The Civilization of the Renaissance* and Johan Huizinga's *The Waning of the Middle Ages*. This led him to explore the relationship between high and low culture, and to examine how the aesthetic, the mythological, and the scientific could drip into one another.

This change was discernible in the first work Mosse published on the modern period, *The Culture of Western Europe* (1961), wherein, "*culture is defined as a state or habit of mind which is apt to become a way of life intimately linked to the challenges and dilemmas of contemporary society.*"[24] To write the history of culture, for Mosse, was thus to reconstruct a system of perceptions. This was how Mosse understood "ideology" in the title of his first major work, *The Crisis of German Ideology* (1964). As such, he urged intellectual historians to "deal with popular ideas and practices, with folklore and community sentiment," an approach he termed, following H. Stuart Hughes, "retrospective cultural anthropology."[25]

The third phase of Mosse's recasting of cultural history was his focus on political liturgy and symbols. A review article published in the *American Historical Review* discussing three books on the history of anthropology, titled "History, Anthropology, and Mass Movements" (1969), served as the methodological platform that Mosse developed in his subsequent works. As Plessini notes, "The Madison historian turned the review article into a programmatic manifesto in which he fully embraced the adoption of anthropological, psychological, and aesthetic interpretative categories in order to analyze modern political liturgies."[26] The methodological program was first put into practice in *The Nationalization of the Masses* (1975). Mosse could now demonstrate how the cultural Zeitgeist of a period was interwoven with the social, political, and economic challenges of a moment, and objectified in salient images, myths, symbols, and rituals. These were often the effort to provide stability and continuity in times of change. It enabled him to move away from thinking about ideology as a form of propaganda and manipulation from above and to understand how it was incorporated into mass movements through ceremonies and festivals, shared myths, and symbols that generated mass consensus. Ultimately, Mosse's dialectical method was drawn from the German tradition, wedded to an Annales school style of cultural history, combined with a British emphasis on empiricism; these influences fused together to form Mosse's unique historical signature. It would be continued in the work of an extraordinary cohort of students who would each become leading intellectual and cultural historians.

MACHIAVELLISM, RELIGIOUS PERSECUTION, AND THE ADVENT OF MODERNITY

Key precepts in Mosse's understanding of what enabled the modern persecutory complex and its assault on Jews were laid down in his work on the early modern period. His books on early modern history included two monographs—*The Struggle for Sovereignty in England* and *The Holy Pretense*—along with his superb, short, popular book called *The Reformation* (1953), which was a standard college text for thirty years, as well as his co-authored general history with H. G. Koenigsberger, *Europe in the Sixteenth Century* (1968).[27] Despite their generally positive reception, David Sabean recounts a comment from a colleague who dismissed his writing in this period in the following terms: "How come that you yourself are so interesting and your books are so dull?"[28] Mosse's early books were exploring problems that were hardly dull. Percolating in these works was a powerful question originally posed by Machiavelli: How can a good man survive in an evil world?[29] Mosse also asked what made the world evil, and how can notions of goodness be redirected toward evil ends? These were key questions in his scholarship from the outset.

Mosse's first book, *The Struggle for Sovereignty in England* (1950), focused on the tension between the individual and the state in seventeenth-century debates about sovereignty. In the book, Mosse played this out as a battle pitting Sir Edward Coke in a losing struggle for individual rights and the preservation of common law against Thomas Hobbes's justification of absolutism. Mosse's second monograph, *The Holy Pretense: A Study in Christianity and Reason of State from William Perkins to John Winthrop* (1957), was more directly concerned with the question of political morality posed by Machiavelli, since it was he who became the most famous early defender of the notion of the "reasons of state" and realpolitik. In so doing, Machiavelli separated private from public morality, arguing that politics and the good of the state superseded ethics for political leaders. These two tensions explored in Mosse's two monographs set a baseline for how he understood the modern maltreatment of outcasts.

Thus, Mosse's early work ultimately developed a line established by the German historian of ideas Friedrich Meinecke, who defined National Socialism as "mass Machiavellism."[30] In *The Nationalization of the Masses*, Mosse made this through line clear. He explained that his work was long preoccupied with "the dignity of the individual and its challengers," alongside the ways in which Christian values were eroded by the triumph of Machiavellian "reasons of state": "The seventeenth century was an important turning point in the absorption of Christian theology by realpolitik," he opined, and the new mass politics of the nineteenth century further diminished individual worth in the face of mass man.[31]

Mosse was even more direct in the classroom than in his published work, since there he clearly laid out some important features of how early modern religious persecution contributed to the development of modern chauvinism. He did so in an unpublished series of lectures that he gave on toleration: "When the Reformation came, both Protestants and Catholics, whatever their differences, were agreed... that outside the Church there was no salvation possible, and that heresy damned souls [and]... that heresy would disintegrate society. Both believed that you should burn those who endanger men's souls as much as those who endanger men's bodies." Moreover, Mosse indicated that religious persecution was built upon two foundations: "[first], the conviction of being theologically right, of having found the Truth and therefore having to defend it; [and] (2) that heresy is also subversion [and] that the State must enforce orthodoxy[;] indeed this is one of its chief function[s]."[32] These were the axioms that justified the assault on Christian heretics, as well as the inherently damned heteropraxy of Jews, and their legacy would continue into the modern period.

RACISM, VOLKISH IDEOLOGY, AND THE ANTI-JEWISH REVOLUTION

Already an important scholar of the sixteenth and seventeenth century, Mosse's major breakthroughs would come in the field of modern European cultural history after his move to Madison. The intimations were signaled in his textbook, *The Culture of Western Europe: The Nineteenth and Twentieth Centuries* (1961), which I have noted was his first book-length foray into the modern period. In his chapters on "Racism," "Fascism," and "National Socialism and the Depersonalization of Man," he sketched arguments he would later develop into monographs.

Mosse's discussion of racism presaged *Toward the Final Solution: A History of European Racism* (1978). Racism was transnational, shared across the continent. Two key factors were crucial for the spread of these ideas. First, imperialist policies used racist arguments to justify European rule. Second, racism was fused with nationalism as a response to the problems of the industrial age, for it stressed unity and a natural order to things in a period of unprecedented change. Ultimately, racism was a hodgepodge of conflicting claims: "It came to combine its historical and occult elements with a scientific veneer designed to prove the truth of its assertions."[33] Mosse itemized the construction of systems of racial classification beginning with Linnaeus, continuing with Buffon's use of climatic theories, and cohering with the linking together of anthropological, linguistic, historical, philosophical, and occult ideas with the scientific drive toward measurement and quantification.

His most perceptive passages dealt with the racist arguments that correlated external body types with an internal racial essence. His focus on how "race manifests itself not only in physical characteristics but also in characteristics of the soul" served to explain two key points.[34] First, it offered racial theorists a solution to the vexing issue of why there were often wide differences in the outward appearance of members of ostensibly the same racial group. Racists could claim that despite these external differences, each racial group had the same internal qualities, the same soul, an identical spirit. Secondly, it completed the racial circle, correlating outer and inner qualities, tying together the racial claim that bound man and nature: "Put into a racial guise, this correspondence between man and nature led to racial stereotypes."[35] Mosse stressed the degrading implications "for the black races in Africa and for the Jews in Europe."[36]

He also anticipated adages developed in *The Crisis of German Ideology* (1964). Nationalism and Jewish emancipation were products of shared historical conjunctures. But everywhere Jews were emancipated they became a foil for nationalist racism, the antitype to the national ideal type. While core Jewish stereotypes had a much longer history, they would now be "dressed in racial garb," taking on new forms and substance for different ends, but all related to the processes of modernity.[37] In this early work, Mosse noted how the Enlightenment relegated Jews as fossils from a premodern age riddled with superstition. But he also emphasized the origins of modern anti-Semitism in the links between Romanticism and nationalism. Therein, the idealization of the peasant and the rural landscape was opposed to Jewish rootlessness, foreignness, cultural inauthenticity, urbanity, and capitalist exploitation as Europe was carved up into nation-states.

These were points developed in far greater detail in what was arguably his magnum opus, *The Crisis of German Ideology: Intellectual Origins of the Third Reich*. Albert Speer, Hitler's architect and Minister of Armaments and War Production, would say to Mosse of this book that it was the first to have understood the call of Nazism.[38] In historicizing the intellectual origins of the Third Reich, Mosse wrote against four different historiographic trends: he opposed the socialist and the liberal interpretations of Nazism, as well as the concept of totalitarianism, and most emphatically, the Luther-to-Hitler thesis.[39] All depicted Nazism in top-down terms, failing to appreciate why the German masses took to National Socialism with genuine enthusiasm. Mosse's work was a cultural history from below, thus offering something different from earlier studies like those of Paul Massing and Fritz Stern, as well as Hannah Arendt's *Origins of Totalitarianism* and *Eichmann in Jerusalem*.[40] According to Saul Friedländer, Mosse was the cultural complement to Raul Hilberg's *The Destruction of the European Jews*. As he put it, "Hilberg's own magisterial volume, published in 1961, was on all counts the most important single study of the Holocaust; yet something essential was missing: a historical background that would explain the triggering of the bureaucratic wheels of destruction. Hitler was hardly mentioned, and no ideological current was evoked, except for a list of anti-Jewish measures taken by the popes, the church councils, and other Christian institutions throughout the centuries. More historical depth was clearly needed."[41] As Friedländer notes, this is what Mosse's study provided.

To really understand Nazi ideology, Mosse claimed, we must appreciate not only what the Nazis vilified, which obviously was bound up with how they represented Jews and Judaism, but also to appreciate the ideals that they glorified, which appealed to ordinary, well-meaning, hard-working men and women. In *The Crisis of German Ideology*, Mosse set out to answer the question, "Why did millions of people respond to the Volkish call?"[42] To do so, he traces the intellectual origins of the Third Reich by examining the deep roots of volkish ideology in Romanticism, which emerged out of the maelstrom of the wars of liberation against Napoleon. He thereby demonstrates that Nazism was not a radical break with the German past: "Hitler was not... an innovator, but an adapter, a molder, who gave the prevailing Volkish theories a new edge, a more dynamic emphasis."[43] He shows how a volkish identity associated with the land, nature, and peasant virtues long marinated. It was then infused by the development of German nationalism, augmented by the rediscovery of the ancient warrior in Tacitus's *Germania*, and finally imbricated with various iterations of racism. As Friedländer acutely summarized it, "Mosse was the first, I think, to point to the necessary link in the *völkisch* imagination between blood, soil, and cosmos, body and soul, physical appearance and character—all the components, in short, of the oxymoronic 'metaphysics of rootedness.' On all counts, the rootless Jew appeared as foreign, repulsive, and dangerous. For Aryan Germandom, this antitype was the enemy per se."[44]

Mosse shows that the years between the failed liberal revolution of 1848 and German unification in 1870 set the tone. A constant hum critical of the *Rechtsstaat* and parliamentary politics as inherently agonistic was joined to a widespread concern about commercialism, industrialization, urbanism, and the rising middle classes. These all threatened a new popular hero, the peasant, associated with the organic, corporatist web of values within which he lived. The peasant personalized the folk hero and ideal German: a social type identified with simplicity, integrity, tradition, proximity to nature, honesty, family values, and heartfelt piety. The opposite of this idealized peasant was a series of urban, uprooted figures: the new proletariat, the migratory worker, journalists, and the quintessential antitype, "the Jew"—an urban dweller with a soulless religion, unethical by nature, wily and legalistic, who crowded into the unhealthy, rapidly expanding cosmopolitan cities to exploit those pure, poor peasants who were arriving with the waves of industrialization and urbanization. The volkish anthem called for a Germanic, spiritual revolution that would set the crisis of German ideology aright. It would aim not at overturning the social structure of capitalism, since class struggle divided rather than united. But it would combat the dark forces of modernity embodied by Jews. This script provided the foundation narrative and Mosse historicizes its key articulators.

He then examines the institutionalization of this volk ideology in the education system: in school textbooks, in the Youth Movement, by professors, and in university fraternities. A whole generation of young minds was raised with these ideas in schools explicitly founded on volkish blueprints and principles. They were taught these notions in state schools, where the ideas were imprinted in textbooks and curricula, and advocated by influential teachers; student organizations adopted volkish principles; and students and teachers passed through the Youth Movement, which had 60,000 members by World War I. This prepared the soil for the response to the Great War when these ideas became part of the reaction to the crisis of German defeat. This bedrock of "the anti-Jewish revolution" was already laid by the 1880s and 1890s.

Writing against the "Luther-to-Hitler hypothesis" that argued that anti-Semitism was something indigenous to German national character, instead Mosse historicizes the accretion of this idealized national narrative peopled with typecast figures, showing how it was racialized, weaponized, politicized, and widely disseminated by the end of the century. Volkish thinking existed in works of literature, popular philosophical treatises, political parties, and social movements, and it was incorporated into anti-Semitic mass movements like those of Adolf Stöcker and Otto Böckel.[45] After 1918, volk ideology permeated the Conservative Party. It became more prevalent among veterans and workers as the social, political, economic, and cultural crisis deepened. But its revolutionary avant-garde was an antibourgeois middle-class youth who "had the same goal as their predecessors: to transcend their origins through a 'spiritual revolution.' The defeat in war and the difficulties of the Weimar Republic merely heightened this quest and gave it a sharper focus toward the building of a new society."[46]

This new society was advocated in works like Möller van den Bruck's *The Third Reich* (1923), originally titled *The Third Way*. It was one of a number of works that called for "a German revolution," a third way between capitalism and Marxism, which espoused a metaphysical revolution connected to the liberation of the soul of the volk. Fascism, too, was an effort to forge such a third way. Indeed, volkish thought was the German iteration of this international movement. They all shared a critique of bourgeois parliamentary democracy as nothing but the expression of private business interests by other means and called for a true democratic revolution that would place the people in power. Giving German texture to wider fascist themes, thinkers like Carl Schmitt and Oswald Spengler advocated a corporate order between society and state welded together by nationalist myths and a *führer*. Schmitt was hardly alone in Germany when he eulogized the Aryan race as the glue that bound together the potential tensions between various corporate entities and charismatic leadership. Within this vision,

> The Jews were identifiable not only as a separate and alien people racially inferior to the Aryans but also as the source of the imbalanced, pernicious capitalism that was plaguing Germany. Anti-Semitism could conveniently encompass the charges of racial adulteration, economic sabotage, and absolute enmity to the German Volk. It could also, just as conveniently, picture the Jews as the incarnation of the inferior race, as capitalism, or as Bolshevism. In short, Jewry was the corrupting force of materialism.... Directed into the channels of anti-Semitism, the Volkish alternative of "the third way" became increasingly popular.[47]

Ultimately, Hitler proved successful because he did not rely on the narrower base of the third-way alternative. He had begun to cultivate mass support that included financiers and the haute bourgeoisie, since like other volkish thinkers, he did not want to disturb social or economic relationships in the name of his revolution. Hitler was the consummation of volkish history, redirecting the German volkish revolution into the anti-Jewish revolution. He shifted focus from real social and economic grievances, and channeled them into anti-Semitism through ingeniously splitting off German and Jewish capitalism:

> Here then was the source of Hitler's success: his ability to transform the revolutionary longings and grievances of a large sector of the populace into an anti-Jewish revolution. Not the big capitalist or the economic middleman, but the Jew, was made the incarnation of the enemy. In his deft and ingenious distinction between Jewish and German capitalism, Hitler saved the capitalist structure of Germany from sure ruin and, in effect, preserved it. Meanwhile, the Jews were eliminated as an economic force, leaving behind their investments, inventories, and wealth. In the process, they also shifted the guilt from the true source of Germany's crisis: the malfunctioning of the German capitalist structure, the lost war, and the frustrations of the past century.[48]

The anti-Jewish revolution was ultimately successful, avers Mosse, because it dramatized and personalized the volkish thought that was developed over a century. Better than any other group, the Nazis concretized and objectified a long-simmering ideology. Heinrich Treitschke's slogan that "the Jews are our misfortune" could encompass the whole of volkish ideology and the Nazis' simple promise was that order would be restored when this menace was eliminated.

RACISM AND THE NATIONALIZATION OF THE MASSES

All of Mosse's subsequent work would develop and refine and elaborate strands of *The Crisis of German Ideology*. In *The Nationalization of the Masses: Political Symbolism and Mass Movements in Germany from the Napoleonic Wars through the Third Reich* (1975), Mosse expanded upon the crucial role that political rites, modern myths, and symbols play in mass political movements. If ideological origins and their institutionalization were central in *The Crisis of German Ideology*, then in *The Nationalization of the Masses*, Mosse expanded the channels through which this ideology was objectified, personified, and disseminated. He sought to account for how the sacred center that was eroded by the dissipation of Christendom as a defining system of moral values by the seventeenth century was replaced by modern, nationalist, secular liturgies. Royal or princely dynasties gave way to the eighteenth-century concept of popular sovereignty, embodied by the general will. In modernity, in Mosse's words, "the general will became a secular religion, the people worshipping themselves, and the new politics sought to guide and formalize this worship."[49] Alongside the Machiavellian rhetoric of realpolitik and interests of state was a new aestheticization of politics, beginning in the French Revolution and developed in the nineteenth century, that incorporated and mobilized the masses as a political force through national monuments, orchestrated public festivals, flags, hymns, mythic narratives, and symbols. Mosse is explicitly interested in historicizing how nationalism rallied the masses through what he terms "the new politics," or what Carl Schorske called "politics in a new key" that was critical of liberal, representative government, since it claimed that liberalism atomized the general will into fragmented parliamentary interests rather than creating a sense of national unity.[50]

Going beyond *The Crisis of German Ideology*, *The Nationalization of the Masses* was more explicitly critical of the notion of totalitarianism or the propaganda model for explicating nationalist fervor. As Mosse put it, "'Totalitarianism' was never a system of government in which a charismatic leader beguiled his followers like the Pied Piper of Hamelin."[51] Propaganda implies a ploy that manipulated the masses, brainwashing them with values they did not share. It suggests that at the core of the Nazis were a small group of puppet masters. Instead, in focusing on nationalism as a form of religious faith that sanctified group values, Mosse sought to capture how nationalist enthusiasm was fostered, shared, and expressed by millions. He understood that the terror apparatus of the Nazi state could not explain the genuine popularity of Nazi culture: the identification with Nazi literature, art, architecture, mass rallies, and organizations. The popular zeal that underpinned the regime had a long history that accounted for its success. This was the focus of Mosse's history.

In reconstructing this past, Mosse clearly took on board the criticisms of *The Crisis of German Ideology* that it put excessive emphasis on anti-Semitism as the heartbeat of volkish ideology. The renowned scholar of political anti-Semitism, Peter Pulzer, had chided Mosse for "over-simplifying things when he refers to it [Nazism] without qualification as 'the anti-Jewish revolution.'"[52] Likewise, Oxford historian A. J. Nicholls suggested, "He exaggerates the extent to which anti-semitism was the prime factor in Hitler's appeal to the German people."[53] As Walter Laqueur, Mosse's collaborator on the *Journal of Contemporary History*, phrased it in the *New York Review of Books*, "The many millions who chose Hitler in 1933 did so for a great variety of reasons, of which the Nordic mythology was certainly not the most important."[54] Putting the Jewish negative antitype to German nationalism to one side, in *Nationalization of the Masses* Mosse sought to focus more emphatically on the positive call of National Socialism: how it channeled deep longings and popular values to create a consensus of support for Germanism. The anti-Jewish thrust is little examined, as Mosse dwells instead on the positive embodiments of German nationalism.

Once again, his teleological thrust is National Socialism as the climax of the new politics. Each chapter historicizes the elements that reached their zenith within Nazi culture. He recounts the development of the key symbols of Germanism: the sacred flame, the oak tree, folk clothing, song and dance, and the flag. He itemizes the way in which a classical Greek aesthetic melded with Roman monumentalism and German autochthonous forms to forge the aesthetic of national monuments, which were often decorated with these national symbols. These memorials became the new national churches.[55] They often entombed the ancestors to be emulated: "Ancestor worship was essential for national theology, manifested by the statues within the monument.... Past and present thus joined hands."⁵⁶ Following the first national festival in 1832, national monuments were often the sites for public festivals that developed a liturgy that included processions and speeches abounding in symbolic representations of national unity. Mosse treats the key organizations that performed their patriotism at these sites: from Friedrich Ludwig Jahn's gymnasts, to sharpshooting societies (*Schützengesellschaften*), to male choirs.

In his chapter on the role of theater in mass movements, a section concentrates on the most important cultural figure of the German nineteenth century, Richard Wagner, who encapsulates Mosse's story. Wagner's operas were conceived as a *Gesamtkunstwerk*, a synthesis of the arts intended to unite people with a higher meaning and purpose. Wagner provided a stirring soundtrack to mythic narratives of freedom and salvation from sin, exemplified by the eponymous black knight of *Lohengrin* (1850). Lohengrin "rides between Death and the Devil... an image which had played a large part in national literature ever since Albrecht Dürer's famous woodcut. The knight became a symbol of Germanic purity as against the temptations of the evil world."⁵⁷ Reworking the myth of the Holy Grail in *Lohengrin* and *Parsifal* (1882), and breathing new life into Norse mythology in *Der Ring des Nibelungen*, Wagner suffused these ancient stories with contemporary middle-class morality: the virtues of manliness, devotion to duty, and discipline. They would be staged in his opera house in Bayreuth, which combined classical and monumental architecture to form a new national monument, a pilgrimage site. In *The Nationalization of the Masses*, Mosse only includes a few lines that point to the role of anti-Semitism in these orchestrations: "Both Wagner and his wife felt that the Germanic and the Christian were exclusively German properties. Their racism and anti-Semitism is well enough known. The emphasis on salvation meant a need for a devil, easily enough found in the Jews."⁵⁸

The crescendo of the book is Mosse's chapter on "Hitler's Taste," where he once again demonstrates the deep reservoir within German culture that fed into Nazi culture. If he showed that volkish ideology encompassed the core of Nazism's ideological origins in *The Crisis of German Ideology*, in *The Nationalization of the Masses* Mosse demonstrates that Hitler's proclivity for monumental neoclassicism in architecture, his penchant for landscapes or peasant scenes in art, his partiality for sculpture that embodied the ideal German type, his love of Wagnerian opera, and his attention to staging huge festivals of national unity where the masses enacted these ideals as they did at the Nuremberg rallies, all brought together a longer tradition that gave credibility to the movement.

Mosse does account for the role of anti-Semitism within the Nazi movement, but he also suggests that it was not central to the Germanic revolution: "The 'negative,' the Jewish stereotype, was never represented in the ceremonial and its symbols, but was spread outside the cult in newspapers and pamphlets. The Jewish stereotype which was thought to typify ugliness could not be allowed to disturb the beauty which informed national worship."[59] If the ideology of Hitlerism was centered on an apocalyptic struggle between Aryan and Jew, within the national liturgy attacks on Jews were confined to the speeches, which were only a part of a greater religious ceremony centered on the salvation of the German people.

If *The Nationalization of the Masses* sidelined anti-Semitism, it did so to stress the positive values enacted in the political religion of nationalism that appealed to fascists and National Socialists. In *Toward the Final Solution: A History of European Racism* (1978, 1985), however, Mosse switches back to showing how racism emerged as a system of thought with deadly consequences in the nineteenth and twentieth centuries. Rather than world views peopled by cranks and simpletons, he demonstrates that anti-Black and anti-Jewish racism are both part of a complex genealogy wound into the sinews of the Western tradition. As Jeffrey Herf acutely put it, Mosse sought "to do for European history and the history of anti-semitism what the historian Winthrop Jordan had done for the history of white racism in American history: he situated it at the heart, not on the margins, of the history of European culture."[60]

The first part of the book traces ideas from the eighteenth to the middle of the nineteenth century that concentrate on the negative perceptions of Africans, while the second half focuses on the development of anti-Semitism. The arc of the book once again leads toward the Holocaust. For Mosse, the effort to exterminate Jews root and branch went beyond the justification of imperialism and exploitation to reveal the radical consequences of racism. Whereas *The Crisis of German Ideology* had stressed the links between Romanticism, volkish thought, and mystical racism within German modernity, *Toward the Final Solution* emphasized the ties between the Enlightenment, aesthetics, and scientific racism in a trans-European story. Citing Horkheimer and Adorno, Mosse makes this connection explicit when he writes, "The Enlightenment tended to fit all human beings into the same mold—not only by its fondness for classification and its idealization of classical beauty, but also through its assumption that all of humankind shared its goals and that its moral order was part of the natural order and thus set for all time and place."[61]

Like the aestheticization of modern mass politics that he emphasized in *The Nationalization of the Masses*, Mosse underlined the aesthetic underpinning of racism, based upon the classical ideal of beauty that was celebrated during the Enlightenment. He showed that the distinction between beauty and ugliness was crucial for visual stereotyping and the basis for systems of racial hierarchy.[62] Doing so, Mosse illuminated how central aesthetic ideals were to the history we have discussed in Poliakov's work on the Enlightenment. Mosse explains that the ideal type against which all races were judged was the white marble of the classical Greek statue. This was coupled to Enlightenment notions of rationality. The Enlightenment was about the self-cultivation of the human mind through reason. This was summarized by Kant's motto *sapere aude*, "Dare to know," in his essay "What Is Enlightenment." The faculty of reason was to be built up through the study of the classics and modern sciences to create an efficient and beautiful society based on the laws of nature. Enlightenment rationality emphasized the classification of knowledge, evident in its most famous product, the *Encyclopedié*.

As we saw in discussing Poliakov, congruent with this project was the hierarchical classification of humans, constituted by a secularization of the great chain of being. Enlightenment naturalists like Carl von Linné, Buffon, and the founder of modern anthropology, Blumenbach, constructed the first systems of racial classification. Significant as well was the part played by Protestant theologian Johann Kaspar Lavater, the inventor of physiognomy, the science of reading the human face. The artist Peter Camper, who dwelt upon measuring the facial angle, abetted him, claiming this angle was inherently different for Europeans and Blacks. Franz Joseph Gall, in turn, founded the science of phrenology, which maintained that human character was determined by the configuration of the head. For Carl Gustav Carus, it was not the skull but the whole human skeleton that told the story of innate human difference. Even the modern history of the "Jewish nose" had eighteenth-century origins in Johann Schudt's *Jewish Peculiarities* and in J. J. Winckelmann's reflections in *History of the Art of the Ancient World*. "Roman and Greek noses indicated the conqueror, the man of refinement of taste," Mosse comments, "but the Jewish nose designated a wary and suspicious character."[63]

What united all these Enlightenment thinkers, Mosse makes plain, was a "concept of beauty [that] implied the ideal of moderation and order.... Greek sculpture defined the proper anatomical proportions.... No one could claim that Negroes had faces which reflected the Greek aesthetic ideal."[64] Mosse thus underscores a dark side of the Enlightenment that was evident in the new sciences of the eighteenth century like anthropology, physiognomy, and phrenology that were responsible for classifying human beings according to their national and civilizational origins, the shape and features of their face and skull, and identifying these with moral and spiritual capacities.

Over the nineteenth century there was an infusion of race thinking into the development of history as a professional discipline, into the rise of nationalism, into linguistics (as in the distinction between Aryan and Semite), and into science (most perniciously in eugenics and social Darwinism). By the end of the nineteenth century, "race," "nation," "the people," "civilization," and "culture" were homologues. In the context of mounting militarism, aggressive nationalism, and the frenzy of European imperial conquest, the racial optic now shaped how Europeans viewed themselves and Others. It fed the rise of political anti-Semitism as a significant force on the continent, since Jews were the Others within. In *Toward the Final Solution*, then, Mosse discloses how racism was central to the systems of perception shared across Europe, even as he highlights how national and regional traditions were distinct or contributed various aspects of this trans-European ideology. The last third of the book indicates how the brutality of mass violence in World War I transformed the European order, heightening the longer anti-Semitic trends that Mosse had shown characterized the underside of European modernization, reaching its climax with the Nazi genocide.[65]

By the end of the book, Mosse makes evident how racism is a "scavenger ideology" that feeds upon the reigning ideas of each era. It annexed the writings of thinkers like Darwin or the criminologist Cesare Lombroso, who did not share a racist world view.[66] Consequently, racism is at once "banal and eclectic," he notes, gaining its power from the successful fusion of the "visual and the ideological."[67] Stereotypes, Mosse reemphasizes, were based on aesthetic notions of beauty and ugliness derived from eighteenth-century interpretations of classical aesthetics, making racism "a visually centered ideology" where outward appearance was supposed to be a reflection of inner character.[68] What accounts for the endurance of racism, he concludes, is that racist myth-making in the form of stereotypes personify abstract concepts, objectifying a narrative in periods of rapid transformation and change.

THE ANATOMY OF STEREOTYPING

Toward the Final Solution is framed by Mosse's insights about the origins, development, and durability of stereotypes, which preoccupy his subsequent work. One can glean aspects of his approach from a review article he penned about two key works by one of the most prodigious scholars of stereotyping, Sander Gilman. Mosse discussed two of Gilman's great works, *Difference and Pathology: Stereotypes of Sexuality, Race, and Madness* and *Jewish Self-Hatred: Anti-Semitism and the Hidden Language of the Jews*.[69] Mosse and Gilman clearly influenced one another's work. Mosse draws attention in particular to Gilman's sophisticated analysis of the discourse that produces stereotypes. Gilman elaborates his approach in his introduction to *Difference and Pathology*, "What Are Stereotypes and Why Use Texts to Study Them?"

Drawing upon a broadly psychoanalytic methodology, Gilman explains that the creation of stereotypes is part of how we become individuals: "We all create images of things we fear or glorify.... We assign them labels that serve to set them apart from ourselves."[70] The process of individualization and differentiation between Self and Other occurs in the earliest stages of an infant's life as we experience the anxiety over our loss of control when our needs for food, warmth, and comfort are not met immediately, as they once were in the womb. In the course of our later development, Gilman explains that "models for control are linked to structures in society which provide status and meaning for the individual."[71] When our sense of order is threatened or our drives repressed, "we project that anxiety onto the Other, externalizing our loss of control. The Other is thus stereotyped, labeled with a set of signs paralleling (or mirroring) our loss of control."

Every society has a stock "vocabulary of images" for the externalized Other that are a product of a history and culture that perpetuates them.[72] Indeed, one function of culture is to imprint a matrix of representations of Self and Others (both individual and collective) that shape our perceptions and that we integrate into our understanding of what it means to be human. These influence what we idealize and what we should avoid as dangerous.[73] They form our phobias and our fetishes.

As Mosse notes, Gilman drew upon insights he had first developed in *Seeing the Insane* to argue that we learn to see the world through what Stephen Pepper termed "*root metaphors*," which define the patterns that organize our representations of Self and Other.[74] These are structural categories that shape our perceptions. Gilman indicates that from Mosse's work he had learned that three basic categories are pivotal: "I will speak of illness, sexuality, and race, since these are labels that have been given to characteristics essential to definitions of the self at various points in history."[75] Each root metaphor is structured by a universe of negative and positive associations. One constellation of binaries is generated by the discourse around the dichotomy between the normal and the pathological. Writes Gilman, our "susceptibility to disease, pollution, corruption, and alteration, [are] things that we experience in our own bodies and observe in others. Every group has laws, taboos, and diagnoses distinguishing the 'healthy' from the 'sick.' The very concept of pathology is a line drawn between the 'good' and the 'bad.'"[76] Clearly mental illness is a significant variant of pathology, since it entails the loss of rationality, language, and thought and is often associated with violence, including sexual violence.

Pathology exemplifies the loss of order and control, and it is often associated with human sexuality and gender. As we have learned from feminism post-Beauvoir, this is another dimension of embodied human experience built around a set of bifurcations between masculinity and femininity, the normal and the deviant, reality and fantasy, strength and weakness, public and private, mind and body, independent and dependent, and reason and emotion.

The third root category of human perception shaped by binary stereotypes, according to both Gilman and Mosse, derives from racial discourse. As Mosse's work has made evident, the metalanguage of race is historically intertwined with ethnic and national identities, organized around essentialized notions of language, history, geography, and the biopolitics of populations. In racial discourse, the signs of differentiation are fixed to skin color and human physiognomy. In a work he dedicated to George Mosse, *The Jew's Body*, Gilman provides an anatomical survey of Jewish stereotypes by dissecting representations of Jewish difference fixated upon the Jewish foot, the Jewish nose, the Jewish mind, Jewish posture, and the Jewish voice. The discourse about every part of the Jew's body is dissected to show "how certain myths reflect basic cultural and psychological ways of dealing with the difference of the Jew, and become part of the generalized vocabulary of difference in Western culture."[77]

In the second text that Mosse comments upon in his review, *Jewish Self-Hatred*, Gilman focuses on how Jewish self-perceptions must navigate the standards, conventions, and norms established by the dominant Christian culture in which Jews find themselves. He examines "how Jews see the dominant society seeing them and how they project their anxiety about this manner of being seen onto other Jews as a means of externalizing their own status anxiety."[78] Every subordinate group within a culture must wrestle with this challenge.

Despite lauding Gilman's work, Mosse is still subtly critical of Gilman for failing to distinguish between stereotyping and persecution. He remarks that Gilman "exaggerates" when he argues that "persecution is inherent in a society's language."[79] Instead, Mosse thinks it is important to distinguish between what remains a myth or latent generalization about a group and how that becomes institutionalized and operant in overt discrimination. Mosse also suggests that Gilman does not adequately treat the lived experience of Jews or Blacks—their looks, gestures, body movements, or smell that makes them appear unfamiliar or frightening, which is at the root of stereotypes. Mosse intimates that this is because Gilman remains too bound to analyzing texts, insufficiently considering "the structure, needs and functions of society" that labels and defines outsiders.[80]

Beyond this criticism, neither Mosse nor Gilman places central emphasis on European imperialism nor on the colonial discourse that underpinned it. The dichotomy between metropole and colony, modern and primitive, and between civilization and savagery enters their histories of racism, but they are both fixated on the continent and primarily on Germany, which only became a colonial power late in the imperial adventure. Nonetheless, each does show what Gilman terms "the protean nature of stereotypes." To make this point, Gilman is fond of citing Fanon's *Black Skin, White Masks*. In doing so, he anticipates Homi Bhabha's exploration of the ambivalence of stereotyping, which Bhabha develops out of a reading of Fanon and Edward Said's *Orientalism*.[81] Mosse, too, ambles toward the associative logic of stereotyping that is made possible by their inherent ambiguity and by the ways in which stereotypes are always unstable metaphors or synecdoches for much broader social processes.

In the prologue and conclusion that frame *Toward the Final Solution*, it is evident that Mosse concurs on the centrality of normativity to shaping the discourse around pathology, sexuality, and race. But if Gilman stresses language and root metaphors as central to understanding stereotyping, then Mosse may be closer to Shulamit Volkov's notion of stereotypes as cultural codes.[82] Mosse also emphasizes the range of associations around nature, as opposed to the city—the dichotomy between the rural and the urban—which we have seen was so central to the development of volkish ideology. But the most important difference between Gilman's and Mosse's work is the pivotal role that Mosse ascribed to a class-based analysis of bourgeois respectability as essential for understanding the role of stereotypes in the development of modern racism.

NATIONALISM, SEXUALITY, AND THE IMAGE OF MAN

In *Nationalism and Sexuality: Middle-Class Morality and Sexual Norms in Modern Europe* (1985), Mosse hailed the importance of Gilman's work for his own.[83] This influence was clear in the book, which explored how bourgeois morality and middle-class respectability were both built upon a system of values that pivoted around notions like normality and pathology, health versus degeneracy, and insiders and outsiders, indicating how the exclusions of nationalism and sexuality were interlocked. Both modern nationalism and respectability emerged in the eighteenth century, Mosse explains, and triumphed in the nineteenth century, connected to the hegemony of the bourgeoisie and "congenial to their needs and fears," as they defined themselves against both the lower classes and the aristocracy.[84]

As we have seen with each of Mosse's monographs, the historical turning point was the French Revolution and the Napoleonic wars of liberation, which were waged in the name of patriotism, but also as a moral crusade to establish the republic of virtue in France or to wage war against it. Fired in this crucible, the era gave rise to German pietism and English evangelism, "together with the demands of mass politics and the beginnings of industrialization."[85] This maelstrom created waves of anxiety, prompting a desire for a "slice of eternity" that was found in racial and sexual stereotypes, and in the myths and symbols of the nation.[86] Replacing the earlier role of priests, educators, scientists, and doctors now became the new guardians of the borderline between normality and abnormality, sickness and health, which was a means for anchoring new historical constructs in an ostensibly unchanging nature.

Mosse would expand upon these trajectories developed in *Nationalism and Sexuality* in his last major published work, *The Image of Man* (1996), where he revisits the development of modern stereotyping by focusing on the construction of modern masculinity.[87] Here, he shows that our modern ideas of masculinity evolved from a medieval chivalric code of honor based upon the ethos of a warrior caste. In the modern period, this was sublimated into the less violent forms that define middle-class values: frugality, duty, self-sacrifice, hard work, loyalty, virtue, self-control, and independence. Key to modern bourgeois masculinity is having dependents (i.e., women and children, employees and servants) that you take care of. Women's honor was defined by maintaining her virginity, which was a guarantee of legitimate progeny. Women were excluded from public life. They were relegated to the private dominion of the home through the cult of domesticity, and confined as the trustees who "policed the boundaries between the respectable classes and the proletariat."[88] In *Nationalism and Sexuality*, Mosse highlights how women as national symbols—Marianne (in France), Germania, and Brittania—embodied these idealized images of female respectability and national purpose. They helped to fix woman's role as the helpmate and support for her husband, strengthening the gendered segregation of labor and with it the divide between the normal and abnormal.

Middle-class ideals of femininity and masculinity and national stereotypes emerged concomitantly, and they were defined against countertypes, principally "the Jew" and "the homosexual," who were the reverse of bourgeois social norms. As Bauman argued, modern society is characterized by the systematization of forms of social marginalization and exclusion, often through the creation of symbols of moral and physical disorder. Jews and homosexuals figured as these outsiders: as unsettled, as ugly, as criminal, as crazy, and as sexual deviants. They were the personification of moral and physical bedlam.

Mosse indicates once more that the same forces that accounted for the development of modern stereotypes were at work in defining the countertype. Greek aesthetic ideals influenced early anthropologists, phrenologists, physiognomists, and racial classifiers. The base was normative standards of ugliness that were the opposite of middle-class ideals of beauty, which rested upon notions of uplift, lay religion, and symbols of the sacred. Ugliness was disharmonious and out of joint. It pointed to an inner shiftiness, dishonesty, lack of control of the passions, cowardice, lustfulness, and sexual impurity. These were all signs of the countertype of virtue. In short, Jews and homosexuals represented the opposite of bourgeois virtues, as the embodiment of vice and moral deviation, as asocial and abnormal.

As we have seen from Poliakov's work, there was already a long tradition of regarding Jews not only as outsiders but also as evil. With the rise of the new sciences, their differences were now ostensibly manifest in the most visible parts of the body: on their faces (their noses, lips, ears, eyes), in their feet, and in their coloration. The Jewish nose, for example, bent at the top, jutting hawk-like from the face, was a foil for the straight nose of the Greek ideal, just as the squashed Black nose was a counterpoint to this ideal as well. The Jewish body from the feet up was an external manifestation of Jewish difference, starting with the flat feet and waddling gait of "the Jew," which was the obverse of a normative manly stride. The rotund gut, neckless body, big ears, and swarthy color of the Jewish stereotype completed the image, which was invariably old, aged, and dirty. The dirty Jew—ugly, filth-ridden, diseased—was a sign of his corruption and potential for pollution. All outsiders shared aspects of this stigmatization: they were ugly, ill proportioned, and incarnations of dis-ease. Blacks were represented as disproportionately physically powerful, overly sexual, and without self-control. They shared with Jews a dark complexion and dangerous sexual proclivities. Jews were also associated with homosexuality, habitual criminality, and, like gypsies, were perpetual wanderers. They were often figured as unmanly men, gender-benders, and, like homosexuals, were associated with devious conspiracies that sought to undermine normative society, which should be led by men of courage and probity: "Jews and homosexuals were not the only countertypes, but they were the most readily visible and frightening examples," in part because they were largely invisible as a result of assimilation.[89]

Mosse's chapter on "Racism and Sexuality" in *Nationalism and Sexuality* ties together the alliance he traces between normativity and pathology, the personification of the outsider and the stereotype of the insider, and their culmination in the bonds between racism and respectability. Racism, he argues, was nationalism intensified:

> Racism strengthened both the historical and visual thrust of nationalism.... Racism was a heightened nationalism: the differences between peoples were no longer perceived as chance variations, but as immutable, fixed in place.... As a form of heightened nationalism, racism supported bourgeois respectability.... Racism brought to a climax tendencies that had been inherent in the alliance between nationalism and respectability.[90]

Intersecting discourses were important to establish these links. The discourse of degeneration was important in drawing a line between the normal and the abnormal, resulting from the excesses of modernity. Outsiders were most at home in the city, a metaphor for what is unnatural, artificial, constantly transforming, while normality required staying in touch with the immutable and organic forces of nature: "Nationalism, racism, and bourgeois society all sought to base themselves upon nature in order to partake of its immutability," writes Mosse.[91] The potential subverters of the bourgeois order were the antitype who opposed the ideal type of youth, energy, beauty, and order. As was invariably the case with Mosse's history of modernity, Nazism marked the zenith of the forces he historicized: "National Socialism was the climax of that history which has been our concern. It contained all the bits and pieces of the past we have tried to analyze and make coherent: respectability, nationalism, manliness, the ideal of woman, the rediscovery of the human, and racism. It exemplifies the alliance of nationalism and respectability in all its intimacy and tensions."[92]

CONCLUSION: THE UNDERSIDE OF MODERNITY

If the various histories that Mosse wrote invariably culminated with the Nazis, this was because he wanted to evaluate how the intertwined elements of modernity reached their dark conclusion in the horrors wrought by National Socialism. His narrative arc was consequently teleological. Modernity's beginnings were Janus-faced. The Enlightenment and the French Revolutionary wars of liberation shaped one side. Romanticism and nationalism created the other. Into the atomic accelerator of this collision, religious beliefs and rituals were repurposed as groups and individuals refashioned modern myths and symbols that gave them a sense of place and purpose.

In historicizing these processes, Mosse helped to refashion our understanding of anti-Semitism. He challenged continuity arguments that failed to consider the profound changes within modernity between Luther and Hitler, or that located a sustained hatred from the ancient world throughout the Western world. Steven Aschheim aptly sums up Mosse's view:

> Nineteenth- and twentieth-century manifestations of antisemitism assume qualitatively different forms and substance, comprehensible only within the specific configurations and crises of modernity that produced them. As the convenient foil for a host of ideologies—*Völkish*, nationalist, and above all

the racist variety—antisemitism had to be placed against the conditioning background of the dynamics of post-emancipation bourgeois society.[93]

Mosse understood that propaganda and terror could not explain the mass appeal of political parties or modern social and political movements. To understand these entailed appreciating that racism as a "scavenger ideology" appeals to high ideals like respectability, codes of honor, and national stereotypes, even as every mythology has not only heroes but also villains. Unlike Marxists, Mosse's dialectic grasped that culture was not just the reflection of underlying social systems, even if these structures invariably recast cultural forms. Unlike liberals, he discerned that humans were not rational actors; often our most profound beliefs and ideas are shaped by myths and symbols that interpolate us.

Perhaps most importantly, Mosse refused to "ghettoize" Jewish history, including the history of anti-Jewish sentiments and persecutions, and to cut it off from the broader currents of the European experience. Anti-Semitism consequently is not unique or distinct from anti-Black racism, xenophobia, or anti-Roma sentiments. Each was entangled within European modernity. Stereotypes are woven together and stigmatized subjects can substitute for one another. The typecast figure of "the Jew" or "the homosexual" or "the woman" was a character in a script, which was at its most dangerous when the drama distilled an ideology or mythology that called its actors to violent action. Mosse sums this up in his 1988 re-edition of *The Culture of Western Europe*:

> Racism is, "a world view which relates all human behavior and character to the so-called race to which the individual or the group is said to belong. The importance of racism in modern times derives from the fact that it became a secular religion based upon science and history.... From the second half of the nineteenth century to the end of the First World War racism increased in intensity and assumed a more clearly defined direction. Between the world wars it became linked to European political mass movements like National Socialism and was able to put its theories into practice over much of the continent. Racism provides a total view of the world which besides science and history also encompasses aesthetics and morality."[94]

As Mosse wound up his history of racism in *Toward the Final Solution* in a section titled "A Conclusion That Does Not Conclude," he penned the perfect lines that give him the last word in this chapter as well:

The holocaust [sic] has passed. The history of racism which we have told has helped to explain the final solution. But racism itself has survived. As many people as ever before think in racial categories. There is nothing provisional about the lasting world of stereotypes. That is the legacy of racism everywhere. And if, under the shock of the holocaust, the postwar world proclaimed a temporary moratorium on anti-Semitism, the black on the whole remained locked into a racial posture which never varied much from the eighteenth century to our time.... Nations which had fought against National Socialism continued to accept black racial inferiority for many years after the end of the war, and did not seem to realize that all racism, whether aimed at blacks or Jews, was cut of the same cloth.[95]

Mosse's closing notes continue to resonate in our contemporary moment of racial reckoning, not least given the contemporary resurgence of Judeophobia.

CHAPTER 8

Critical Theory and Post-Holocaust Judeophobia

Post-Holocaust Judeophobia is on the rise globally. Daily we learn about assaults on individuals or Jewish institutions: about the beating of Jews in New York or Paris, about the desecration of cemeteries or Holocaust memorials, about the torching of synagogues, about threats outside of Jewish schools or threats at Jewish cultural centers. Swastikas have found their way back to walls, even dorm room doors. Most frightening is the lethal targeting of Jews since 2012: in Toulouse, Brussels, Paris, Copenhagen, and in Pittsburgh and Poway. In the background to these high-profile incidents is the regular drumbeat of denigration on social media. Judeophobic memes and conspiracy theories circulate the Internet now no longer only on the dark web; they have been normalized and mainstreamed.

This rise in post-Holocaust Judeophobia augments post-Holocaust generational trauma. A series of multinational surveys corroborate that there is a general perception among Jews of deep fear about this reprise of anti-Jewish rhetoric and violence. The FRA, the European Union Agency for Fundamental Rights, conducted a survey in twelve EU countries, interviewing 16,395 Jews: 85 percent answered that Judeophobia is by far the Jews' most serious problem.[1] CNN interviewed 7,000 Jews and non-Jews and 40 percent answered that Jews in their countries are endangered by racist violence.[2] Eurobarometer conducted 23,640 face-to-face interviews in the twenty-eight EU states and 89 percent of interviewees answered that Judeophobia has recently increased.[3] The data clearly corroborate that Jewish apprehension about the rise of Judeophobia is widely shared.

The statistics on reported violent incidents, attacks, and threats support that this fear is warranted. The best aggregator of Judeophobic incidents globally is the Center for the Study of Contemporary European Jewry (formerly the

Kantor Center) at Tel Aviv University. Since September 2000 (and the advent of the Second Intifada), there has been a huge increase in major violent attacks around the world since they started tracking these events in 1989, with high points during the Gaza War in 2008–2009 and 2015. In 2019, a new record was set for hate crimes against Jews, with little drop in 2020.[4] These numbers have skyrocketed after the October 7, 2023, Hamas terrorist attacks on Israel. In 2014 (the year of Operation Protective Edge), the Anti-Defamation League conducted the largest survey ever, covering over one hundred countries, indicating that Judeophobic stereotypes are prevalent among about 25 percent of people on the planet, and among nearly three out of four people in the Middle East.[5]

In concluding this book, I won't directly assess the phenomenon of post-Holocaust Judeophobia.[6] Nor will I simply distill the insights of the various paradigms I have considered, since each chapter opens with a summary of the key points each of these theories offer to understanding the underlying causes of Judeophobia, including the current resurgence. Instead, I will consider some of the meta-issues raised by the debates about the post-Holocaust and postcolonial Judeophobia of our present.

Each of the theorists or paradigms I consider offers key insights to contemporary discussions of post-Holocaust Judeophobia. For Sartre, what fuels Judeophobia is "bad faith," which is dialectically linked to structural racism in his anticolonial writing and what he called in his postcolonial antiracist interventions "the new racism." These conjoin in Sartre's critique of bad-faith anti-Zionism. For Hannah Arendt, core to Judeophobia is the interaction between Jews and the dominant society of which they are a part. As we saw, this risks blaming Jews for their victimization, resulting in charges that Arendt was a "self-hating Jew." I maintain, instead, that in taking this chance, Arendt inserted herself into the tradition of "conscious pariahs" that she consecrated, especially in her own prescient criticisms of Zionism. From the Frankfurt School, we can draw upon their notions of projection, personification, "secondary anti-Semitism," and "ticket thinking." For Lyotard, Jews are the alter ego of the West—the cipher of the Other: rejected, repressed, maligned, and disparaged, specifically in the Christian and post-Christian tradition initiated by Paul's Epistles. Poliakov's magisterial multivolume history of anti-Semitism puts flesh on the bones of Lyotard's speculations, historicizing the secularization from Christian and Islamic anti-Judaism into anti-Semitism and the translation of this long evolution into post-Holocaust anti-Zionism, which he was a pioneer in historicizing.

Both Lyotard and Poliakov also help to illuminate the afterlife of what we might term neo-Pauline *secularist supersessionism* articulated by a number of contemporary radical intellectuals, as we will see. Lyotard's philosophical postmodernism influenced Zygmunt Bauman's postmodern sociology that emphasized the ambivalent response to postmodernity exemplified by "neo-tribalism" as the twin of globalization—or what Bauman called "liquid modern" capitalism—producing a proliferation of stigmatized postmodern strangers. George Mosse's emphasis on fascist culture and on how populist nationalisms necessarily incorporate racism into their tribalism, abetted by the morality of bourgeois respectability, also helps us to explain the thrall of today's illiberal democracy so often abetted by Judeophobia.

Consequently, in concluding this study of major theories of anti-Semitism, I rely upon Bauman's analysis of globalization to assess the core underlying driver for contemporary Judeophobia in both its militant Islamist and white Christian nationalist forms, discussing how he understands the overlaps between Jews, immigrants, and other postmodern strangers. I draw upon George Mosse's cultural account of fascism to drill deeper into understanding white Christian nationalism and illiberal democracy. Then I consider Léon Poliakov's pioneering *De l'antisionisme à l'antisémitisme* to examine the core claims of the so-called new anti-Semitism theorists, specifically their assertions about the Left's contributions to Judeophobia. I maintain that while Poliakov offers some insights about overlaps between anti-Zionism and Judeophobia, like later maximalists or alarmists sounding warnings about leftist Judeophobia, this approach too easily collapses into the formula that anti-Zionism = anti-Semitism. To pull this apart, I draw upon the work of Judith Butler, highlighting how her critique of Zionism leads to charges that she is a "self-hating Jew." This calumny is then assessed by way of its paradigm case, looking at how Arendt was earlier dismissed as a self-hating, anti-Semitic "enemy of Israel" rather than a partisan of the tradition of "conscious pariahs" that she valorized.

Next, I argue that Sartre's dialectical critique of how some anti-Zionist activists recapitulate the racism they claim to question is more powerful than that of the new anti-Semitism theorists because of his firm commitment to multidirectional antiracism. Following Sartre's approach enables an assessment of how institutionalized discrimination against Muslims in Europe or Blacks in the United States may result in attacks on Jews who are said to embody the racism, colonialism, and white supremacy that these activists oppose at home and by extension in

Israel. The final section of the chapter draws out the Frankfurt School's conceptions of projection and personalization, secondary anti-Semitism, and what they call "ticket thinking" to assess the threats to Jews and their entangled Others in our post-Holocaust, postcolonial, transnational new world disorder.

As I navigate some of the most vitriolic claims in the debates about contemporary Judeophobia, my approach is spurred by two claims in Albert Memmi's *Racism*. First, his assertion that Judeophobia, Islamophobia, Negrophobia, and xenophobia are all entangled. This occasioned him to coin the term "heterophobia" to "designate the many configurations of fear, hate, and aggressiveness that, directed against an other, attempt to justify themselves through different psychological, cultural, social, or metaphysical means."[7] The second stimulus was Memmi's suggestion that we should think of racism as an allergy. Since an allergy is an autoimmune disorder, I link this claim to Derrida's analysis in *Philosophy in a Time of Terror* of how the war on terror functions as what Derrida called an "*autoimmunitary process*." "As we know," Derrida wrote, "an autoimmunitary process is that strange behavior where a living being, in quasi-*suicidal* fashion, 'itself' works to destroy its own protection, to immunize itself *against* its 'own' immunity."[8] An autoimmunitary process is a way to describe the work of deconstruction, or the self-implosion of certain ways of conceptualizing phenomena, explaining how they result in contradictions, tensions, or aporias. Judeophobia, like all forms of heterophobia, can usefully be considered an autoimmunitary process. Each of the critical theories I have considered illuminates a vector by which racist discourses and practices destroy themselves "in quasi-*suicidal* fashion." Racisms in all their forms are misdirected efforts to protect status, privileges, superiority, and power. But the autoimmunitary process also functions in some forms of antiracism when these recapitulate racism rather than pacifying it. As I explicate what each theory or theorist can offer to our thinking at present, I do so by examining how they elucidate the autoimmune syndromes within racism, and sometimes in misguided antiracist efforts.

ZYGMUNT BAUMAN: JEWS, IMMIGRANTS, AND OTHER POSTMODERN STRANGERS

Bauman's work is the best place to start this discussion of how Judeophobia in the present is entangled in anti-Muslim, anti-Black, and xenophobic racisms. We have seen how his postmodern sociology refuses binary thinking and urges a multidirectional critique: not only of assaults on Jews but also attacks on colonized peoples, immigrants, people of color, and the indigenous. In engaging with Bauman's reassessment of anti-Semitism, we have already considered his suggestions for how our rethinking demands a reexamination of our concepts, paying attention to the ambivalence upon which Judeophobia or allosemitism functions, and how this has changed over time.

In the conclusion to the chapter on sociological theories of anti-Semitism, we saw that Bauman argues that our postmodern or liquid present is constituted by two opposing forces: the forces of globalization on the one hand and on the other hand "the sectarian fury of neotribal self-assertion, the resurgence of violence as the principal instrument of order-building, the feverish search for home truths."[9] Bauman thus explains how the most acute threats to Jewish, Muslim, Black, and immigrant lives stem from how both militant Islamic jihadism and its twin, white Christian nationalism, are each the nightmare shadow of postmodern capitalism. Neotribalisms offer a self-fulfilling prophecy about the inherent incompatibility of cultures, or what Samuel Huntington famously called the clash of civilizations.[10] Benjamin Barber nicely summarized what Bauman analyzes in the title of his book, *McWorld vs. Jihad*.[11] If integral nationalism and authoritarianism are one face of the tribalism generated in response to McWorld, then the lethal forms of militant jihadi Judeophobia are another. Each are clearly exemplary forms of the suicidal autoimmunitary process. This much we have discussed.

Bauman would amplify his sociological analysis of the present in a raft of books that followed from his classic *Modernity and the Holocaust*. These would focus less on Jews and more on the "strangers at our door" in the liquid age defined by globalization. Few thinkers offer as acute an analysis of the underlining causes of the massive uptick in xenophobia, chauvinistic nationalism, and unfettered racism as Bauman.

Bauman is clear that the floating flux of liquid modernity has heightened our phobic responses. He follows Harmon Leon in suggesting that ours is a time of "phobophobia," a fear of fears. "It is the fear of being afraid that haunts us, the denizens of the liquid modern,"[12] he notes. We live in a time when we are haunted by dread, horror, and anxiety spurred by a world in constant flux, upheaval, change, and crisis that entails "an enhanced sensitivity, aversion or *allergy*."[13]

The underlying causes of our allergic or autoimmunitary reactions are itemized by Bauman. They are firstly economic: budget cuts, redundancies, mergers, outsourcing, offshoring, and regimes of austerity. This provokes a widespread lack of security. Not only economic downturns but also political instability, the radicalization of communal identities, and terrorism occasion distress. The world is rife with inequalities: in a world of extraordinary opulence for some, there is squalor, debasement, and ignominy for the vast majority. To account for this, Bauman replaces the Marxist idiom of the proletariat with an analysis of the "emergent 'precariat.'"[14] Donald Trump and other populist authoritarian leaders were birthed by the emergent precariat, Bauman avows. In the United States, for example, two-thirds of Americans live paycheck to paycheck. Many worry about threats to their status, social standing, and eroding privileges. Moreover, we all sit on the precipice of global environmental catastrophe, and we are all threatened by the reality of global pandemics. The inner core of our phobias is the fear of finding ourselves bereft and alone when misfortune strikes.

When we feel justifiably afraid, many focus their dread on phobogenic objects. These they believe are the culprits and they take defensive measures to protect themselves. This underpins the desire to build impenetrable walls and barbed-wire camps to keep our threats at bay. Bauman is clear, however, in explaining that the grounds of any causal connection or even a correlation between phobogenic objects and the pain they cause is dubious. In fact, writes Bauman, "paradoxically, it is the actions we undertake to save us from the torments of fear that may well turn out to be the most prolific and steady source of those fears."[15] This is the autoimmunitary process at work.

These actions have tended to place certain strangers in the crosshairs: immigrants; the ethnically, racially, and religiously different; and other vagabonds and postmodern outcasts. Strangers, explains Bauman, are symptoms of "some global, distant [pressures], ... intangible, obscure, mysterious and not easy to imagine forces."[16] Many consequently project their grievances, resentments, and fears onto these strangers. But strangers also inspire fascination, magnanimity, and hope.

The stranger is actually Janus-faced. As we saw, Bauman examined the consequences of the Jew as the primordial figure of the modern stranger; the ambivalence he analyzed there holds for postmodern strangers as well. We are consequently divided between those who embrace what Bauman terms "mixophilia" and those who adhere to "mixophobia." On the one hand, there is the temptation to embrace difference, prompted by "proteophilia." On the other hand, there are those menaced by difference, prodded by "proteophobia."

No Pollyanna, Bauman is wary about the protocols of those who claim to love diversity. In a world defined by capitalist consumption, he distinguishes between two ways of being enticed by difference. He highlights a discrepancy between *seeing* and *looking*, which he extrapolates using the metaphor of the snapshot, which he draws from Erich Fromm. Unlike a snapshot, *seeing*, writes Fromm, "is a human function, one of the greatest gifts with which man is endowed; it requires activity, inner openness, interests, patience, concentration."[17] This is different from *looking*, which is about turning a subject into an object, into a snapshot. This distinction is acute in the age of social media where we often digest news and our views through snapshots and snap judgements. This is Fromm's riff on the dialectic of the gaze and the struggle for human recognition. The snapshot is the postmodern version of cauterizing our ethical obligations, stripping human relationships of their moral significance through objectification, rendering them disposable. Bauman enjoins us to see Others in their strangeness, responding to their calls for asylum or refuge from their plight as refugees.

In *Strangers at the Door*, penned in 2016 in the midst of the migrant crisis, the debates about Brexit, and the election of Donald Trump, the proteophobia that Bauman long identified with Judeophobia was ascendant, locking onto a range of targets. In our present moment, strangers are perceived as dangers, he wrote. They are the embodied messengers of the dangerous side of globalization. Strangers stoke our fear of "the unknown, uncertain and unpredictable."[18] Our sense of any obligation or responsibility to them is annulled through our bureaucratic, corporate, tribalist, individualized, and securitized sequestration.

We are caught at present, suggests Bauman, in a moment of cognitive dissonance whose bumper sticker could read, "Thomas Hobbes is dead. Long live Thomas Hobbes." Hobbes is dead because government since the 1980s offers less and less protection and security. Indeed, we live in a state of insecurity. Privatization results in a world of *homo lupens*, a war of all against all that feels nasty, brutish, and short. But like the phoenix, Hobbes has risen again in the form of illiberal democracies led by strongmen (Trump, Orbán, Netanyahu) and strongwomen (Marine Le Pen) who promise security and law and order. However, rather than deliver this promised security (since they often intentionally spur the chaos they claim they will end), according to Bauman, these leaders only promote what he terms "securitization."

Securitization proves to be an autoimmune process, producing as self-fulfilling prophesy the violence and terrorism it claims to protect against. Bauman explains that identifying the problems in the liquid modern world with strangers who can be defended against through building walls and ramping up national and personal security produces the problem it claims to fight. It does so in three ways: (1) It enflames heterophobia in all its variants, including xenophobia, Islamophobia, Negrophobia, and Judeophobia. (2) It insists upon an unbridgeable gap between us and them, a conflict of civilizations between our culture and theirs. (3) Finally, it is a machine for stigmatization: creating negative and hostile beliefs about outsider groups, shaming and disparaging them, the outcome of which is social alienation for those groups. The impact of stigmatization is to wound the stigmatized community through humiliation and self-contempt. Since the stranger knows the stigma is undeserved, the result can be a desire for vengeance and the reinforcement of tribalism and counterviolence.

Instead, counsels Bauman, we need to foster social investment and social inclusion. We need to build bridges, not walls. We do not need strongmen, but strong people. We need the emergent precariat to understand that the cause of their downward mobility is not the empowerment of undeserving people of color led by Jewish puppet masters, as great replacement theory would have it. Rather the cause of their malaise, in the words of Joseph Schwartz, are "the corporate elites responsible for the devastation of working-class communities."[19] We need to pierce our echo chambers through the creation of frameworks for less-distorted communication. Rather than individual solutions to global problems, we have to build frameworks for a new global politics, since, as Benjamin Barber has explained, "the nation-state is failing us on a global scale."[20]

GEORGE MOSSE: WHITE NATIONALISM AND ILLIBERAL DEMOCRACY

Bauman helps us to begin to understand the underlying causes of post-Holocaust Judeophobia by drawing our attention to the ripple effects of postmodern global capitalism, particularly as a generator of neotribalisms. George Mosse's work is instructive in amplifying our understanding of one side of this: populist authoritarianism. The rise of illiberal democracies, to use Victor Orbán's term for his own regime, are not congruent with fascism.[21] But Mosse's writing on fascism can nonetheless help us to comprehend these movements. In concluding "Toward a General Theory of Fascism" Mosse makes clear that fascism belongs to a specific historical juncture, the interwar years that brought Mussolini and Hitler to power and that gave rise to fascist movements across Europe. Since his approach offers a cultural interpretation of fascism rather than a political or socioeconomic analysis, however, Mosse can help us to understand the authoritarian populism of our present. He emphasizes how the fascist synthesis built upon long-standing ideas and cultural currents that were forged into a new fusion. "Most ominously," Mosse warns, "nationalism, the basic force that made fascism possible in the first place, not only remains but is growing in strength.... Those ideals of mass politics upon which fascism built its political style are very much alive, for ours is still a visual age to which the 'new politics' of fascism were so well attuned."[22]

There are several features of the fascist synthesis that Mosse underlines that clearly do not hold in the age of illiberal democracy. Most importantly, fascism grew out of the experience of World War I and the conditions it created. Everywhere it took hold, it was a continuation of "the war experience into peacetime."[23] Fascism was a new revolution that sought to forge a third way between the materialism of Marxism and the corrosive power of finance capitalism. The revolution was founded on a vision of utopia that would bring about a fundamental reordering of society. Fascism glorified war and insisted upon the sacrifice needed to achieve the myth of the community it upheld. These facets of fascism do not much correspond to populist nationalisms today. But the features of "heightened nationalism" outlined by Mosse that underlay fascism are helpful in describing the pull of surging authoritarian nationalism.

Mosse's critique of Jacob Talmon's *The Rise of Totalitarian Democracy* is a useful place to begin in seeing how Mosse's analysis remains germane. Published in 1952, Talmon was interested in writing a genealogy that linked the Jacobin terror with the communist regimes of the Soviet era. For Mosse, however, "it was the radical right with its nationalism that was the true heir of totalitarian democracy, as exemplified through the new political style."[24] As we have seen, Mosse was generally skeptical about the notion of "totalitarianism" since it was based on two pillars he found problematic: first, a conception that terror and propaganda were everywhere necessary for disciplining the population. Second, it failed to capture the role of the masses in willing their own domination, as Wilhelm Reich averred. What is useful about Mosse's approach to fascism for understanding the thrall of authoritarian populism at present is that it was guided by the central question of how fascism drew upon what Mosse called "the nationalization of the masses" not through propaganda and terror but through mass mobilization.

As discussed, Mosse concurred with Talmon that mass politics started with the French Revolution. But he emphasized that it did not so much inaugurate totalitarian democracy as it transformed politics into a civic religion. The French Revolution consequently created a new political style that is resonant with illiberal democracies. The Revolution remade politics through increasing the use of slogans, symbols, narratives, and rituals that form the core of what Mosse termed "heightened nationalism." Party platforms and policy positions are less important to populists than an "attitude toward life." This ethos is shaped by "a largely mythical past and through easily understood symbols which could serve as rallying points."[25] These include forging or foregrounding myths of origin and a collective memory that inculcates a sense of national mission and its regenerative power. This is enhanced through rituals that feature the national flag, national monuments, or national anthems that become rallying cries for a sense of national solidarity and greatness.

"Heightened nationalism" embraces the creation of a new liturgy through ceremonies that enable the masses to feel included in politics and imbued with a sense of belonging to a community that resonates with their sensibilities. Today this is forged virtually in imagined communities on television, talk radio, and on social media, as much as in mass rallies. The liturgical element requires "the endless repetition of slogans, choruses, [and] symbols" that annex religious passion in the name of civic virtues.[26] Mosse emphasizes that religious revival—the upswing in pietism and evangelism—was important to this process, since "traditional religious enthusiasm was ... transferred to civic rites."[27] "The myths and symbols of nationalism were superimposed upon those of Christianity," he writes.[28] The religious base of heightened nationalism remains a feature of right-wing populism.

The role of a strong leader, a living symbol of the ideals of the nationalists, also remains a key to authoritarian populisms. Built upon a notion of popular sovereignty, the leader expresses the general will of those he represents, who worship an idealized and exclusionary conception of "the people." The leader is a cipher who voices the resentments and outrage of the masses in ways that cross class lines. These are directed at the enemies of the people, in accord with Carl

Schmitt's bifurcation of friends and foes. Not only is the national mystique defined in stereotypes, but so are the outsiders to the nation. These stereotypes, as we discussed at length in our overview of Mosse's oeuvre, ground a sense of "immutability and certainty in a world of rapid change, to help get one's bearing and to prove one's superiority."[29] As Bauman explained, the outcasts are a rolling list of targets: Muslims, immigrants, liberals and socialists, and Jews.

LÉON POLIAKOV: FROM ANTI-ZIONISM TO ANTI-SEMITISM AND BACK AGAIN

If Mosse helps us to understand the surge of illiberal populist authoritarianism on the Right and how this contributes to post-Holocaust Judeophobia, then the work of Poliakov helps us to appreciate shifts in the discourse of the Left following the Six-Day War in 1967 and the student uprisings in 1968. Poliakov was the key forerunner of "the new anti-Semitism" theorists, whose signature is to sound the alarm about a conjunction of leftist and Arab/Islamic stigmatization of Israel that recapitulates anti-Jewish myths.[30] He consequently located and historicized the emergence of a new epistemic and political configuration that materialized in the aftermath of June 1967–May 1968 that indicated shifts in the index of Judeophobia.[31] In *De l'antisionisme à l'antisémitisme* (From anti-Zionism to anti-Semitism), he was concerned with showing how anti-Zionism packaged in new skins the old inebriant of anti-Semitism.

Poliakov did so by tracing the history of the myth of the "Zionist plot" that first congealed in Prague in 1952 during the Slánský trial. In the last of the great show trials between 1948 and 1953, Rudolf Slánský and thirteen others, eleven of whom were Jews, were put on trial for conspiracy against the Soviet leadership. Indicative of their treachery, the defendants were condemned for their "Jewish nationalism" (i.e., Zionism) and "cosmopolitanism," themes that wedded them to Israeli and Western imperialism. These refrains were repeatedly highlighted in the persecution of Jews in the last years of Stalin's rule across the Soviet bloc. These same catchphrases would emerge again in the Doctor's Plot in 1953 and in other cases across the Eastern bloc, reaching a new crescendo in Poland in 1968, where student unrest was laid at the door of an "international Zionist mafia,"[32] leading to a purge of Jews from the party, from their jobs, and ultimately from the country, as was the case for Bauman.

Poliakov argued that the Slánský trial and the Doctor's Plot absorbed a leftist set of myths that preceded it.[33] He shows that within Marxist theory from its genesis, and explicitly developed as policy within the Soviet Union from October 1918, a principled anti-Zionism was perfectly reconciled with a strong stance opposing anti-Semitism.[34] Beginning with Stalin's persecution of Jews from 1949–1953, however, which continued after his death "under the pretext of a critical attitude toward the Jewish State and its partisans," old Jewish tropes morphed into a new discourse of anti-Zionism that was no longer opposed to Judeophobia.[35]

Concomitantly, in the Middle East, from the first Arab-Israeli war in 1948, Arab anti-Zionism was animated by a desire to contest and ultimately destroy the Jewish state. After 1968, Poliakov maintains, the revolutionary Left, committed to radically transforming all existing structures, began to introject the Arab discourse of eliminating the structures of the Jewish state.[36] Zionism was treated as coterminous with colonialism, racism, apartheid, and crimes against humanity by the "orphans of the revolution,"[37] alongside many Arabs, and those within the larger Muslim world. Associated with these evils, Zionism was deemed illegitimate and merited destruction. In *De l'antisionisme à l'antisémitisme*, Poliakov laid down the core tracks of "the new anti-Semitism" theorists: sounding the alarm about a shared anti-Zionism on the part of the radical Left and within the Islamic world that translated anti-Jewish opprobrium to target Israel.

For all the insights of Poliakov's analysis and the new anti-Semitism theory that it helped to create, this approach can falter in its own autoimmunity process, however. The new anti-Semitism theorists undermine the fight to dampen down contemporary Judeophobia when they reduce the critique of Israel to a new form of racism via the formula that anti-Zionism = anti-Semitism. Indeed, as the statistics make clear, since spikes in violence against Jews are patently connected to the cycles of violence in the Israeli/Palestinian conflict, foreclosing criticism of Israel helps fuel the fire. A problem with "the new anti-Semitism" argument advanced by Poliakov is that it fails to avoid collapsing all forms of critique of Israel or Zionism into anti-Semitism.

Evidence-based criticism of Israel does not constitute anti-Semitism. Vociferous debate within and outside Israel includes voices that decry the occupation of the West Bank, the ongoing building of settlements, the injustices by the Israeli military, and the violation of Palestinians' human rights without ever casting opprobrium on Jews as a group and without recycling classical anti-Jewish stereotypes. Indeed, "if Israel does not treat its non-Jewish citizens equally and humanely," Walter Laqueur eloquently stated, "if it persists in holding on to territories occupied in 1967 against the will of the local population, if it illegally seizes land elsewhere, if a racialist-chauvinist fringe inside Israel defies the law and elementary human rights and to considerable degree dictates its outrageous behavior to a government, if some people in Israel are unwilling to accept the rights of others, such behavior invites condemnation."[38] Criticism of Israel on these grounds certainly is not anti-Semitic. This is a distinction that Poliakov and too many of the new anti-Semitism theorists fail to adequately register. Or they pay lip service to this notion only to reproach those who criticize Israel as aiding and abetting anti-Semites or tar them as covertly or unconsciously Judeophobic. This feature of "the new anti-Semitism" theorists hollows out the charge of anti-Semitism, turning it into a shield to combat legitimate criticism of Israeli policies.

Despite this shortcoming, the virtue of Poliakov's analysis is that he framed his historicization of anti-Zionism within the *longue durée*, arguing that from Voltaire and Fichte, through Fourier, Proudhon, Marx, and Stalin, there was a long tradition of antiracist anti-Zionism that opposed Jewish particularity to universality, the carnal Jew to the spiritual humanist, and Jewish materialism, legalism, and anachronistic superstition to the true faith and reason of humanity. This tradition was clearly a secularization of Christian supersesssionism, he suggested, as did Lyotard in *The Hyphen* and other texts, as we have seen.

Poliakov's and Lyotard's critiques of supersessionism over the *longue durée* that undergirds some versions of antiracist anti-Zionism provide an important context for understanding the shortcomings with Alain Badiou, Slavoj Žižek, Georgio Agamben, and Gianni Vattimo, and their neo-Pauline critique of Zionism. Their embrace of St. Paul as a gateway to a revolutionary universalism is deployed to disparage Israel and Zionism. This places these radical thinkers in a long tradition of Christian and post-Christian anti-Judaism, since they reduplicate the leftist lexicon's series of oppositions that Poliakov traced. For Éric Marty this results in their "metaphysical antisemitism," which comes from what Bruno Chaouat terms their "Jew-splitting."[39] As Maurice Samuels explains, Badiou, for example, "accomplishes this by splitting the 'real' Jews, the ethical or spiritual or universalist Jews, from the false or ethnic or particularist Jews who are tied to the forms of Jewish identity Badiou derisively groups under the acronym SIT (for Shoah, Israel, Tradition)."[40] Jews who quake in the wake of the Holocaust when faced with surging Judeophobia, who identify with Judaism, or who support Israel because it serves as a safe haven for Jews are denigrated by Badiou and others in the name of an antiracist philosophical universalism that traps Jews for their adherence to Jewish nationalism and for their failure to uphold a radical internationalism and humanism.[41] The neo-Pauline radical intellectuals who insist in formulaic terms that "Zionism is racism" just mirror the new anti-Semitism theorists who declaim that "anti-Zionism = anti-Semitism." The ostensible antiracism on both sides throws gas on the flames more than quelling the fire, thus functioning as an autoimmune deficiency.

JUDITH BUTLER, HANNAH ARENDT, AND THE TRADITION OF THE CONSCIOUS PARIAH

Judith Butler's case against Zionism, *Parting Ways*, obliquely but intertextually locates her position within this longer tradition of the split between Judaism and Christianity.[42] Nonetheless, Butler's anti-Zionism stems not from a neo-Pauline tradition, but from stretching cultural Zionism as articulated by Martin Buber, Arendt, and Emmanuel Levinas to a breaking point. The point of rupture results from her amplification of Arab writers whom she puts into dialogue with these giants of Jewish thought to launch her criticisms of Zionism and Israel.

For her trouble, Butler's critiques have been dismissed as the missives of a "self-hating Jew" whose anti-Zionism amounts to anti-Semitism. Take, for example, Cynthia Ozick's vituperative denunciation: "It is long past time (pace ... Butler) when the duplicitous 'rift' between anti-Zionism and anti-Semitism can be logically sustained," she writes.[43] Edward Alexander, another staunch critic, places Butler at the center of what he calls "Antisemitism-Denial: The Berkeley School."[44] The most prolonged attack comes from Cary Nelson, who depicts Butler as a Pied Piper whose support of the Boycott, Sanctions, and Divestment movement (BDS) incites anti-Semitism in his article, "The Problem with Judith Butler."[45] These tirades against Butler and other dissident Jewish critics of Zionism are often just a technique for inoculating against their "principled anti-Zionism."[46]

To insist that Butler's anti-Zionism is principled is not to endorse her position. I certainly think that her spontaneous claim about "Hamas ... [and] Hezbollah as social movements that are progressive, that are on the Left, that are part of the global Left" during a teach-in at Berkeley against the war in 2006 were not only horribly misguided but could provide cover for groups whose charters are patently Judeophobic. But, as ever, context matters. Butler's statement was made in response to a question about Israel and anticolonial activism during a heated discussion. She insists that she was merely referencing Hamas and Hezbollah's anti-imperialism, even as she says unequivocally that she does not support either Hamas or Hezbollah, since she has only ever supported nonviolent resistance. Indeed, she rejects violent resistance movements just as she rebuffs state violence. What's more, her defense of aspects of the BDS movement is grounded in the fact that this is the largest nonviolent civic political movement to establish equal rights in Israel/Palestine. Still, what is most germane for our discussion here is the analysis of the charge that she is "self-hating" or anti-Semitic. This is about silencing views her opponents refuse to even consider using the tactic of demonization and stigmatization.[47]

Butler's response lays out with clarity why we need to pull apart criticisms of Israel and Zionism from anti-Semitism. She argues that those who claim that critics of Israel "are antisemitic in their effect if not their intent," as former president of Harvard University Lawrence Summers famously put it,[48] have the effect of censorship "in effect if not intent."[49] In developing her argument, she makes several salient points about why the charge of anti-Semitism against critics of Israel or Zionism backfires.

First and most importantly, it dilutes the claim when incidents like the torching of synagogues or the desecration of Jewish cemeteries or attacks on individuals as Jews occur, since all accusations of anti-Semitism are flattened. Second, it contributes to conditions in which all criticisms of Israel are deemed as hate speech. Third, and most problematically for Butler, it forecloses any distinction between Jews and Israel, Jewishness and Zionism. This failure capitulates to the anti-Semitic fantasy that all Jews are acting in a worldwide conspiracy, which we know spurs Judeophobic violence. Moreover, it disables any critical distance within the heterogeneous Jewish community whose views on Israel range across a wide gamut of positions and between Jews and the State of Israel. "In holding out for a distinction to be made between Israel and Jews," Butler insists she is "calling for a space for dissent for Jews, and non-Jews, who have criticisms of Israel to articulate" while "also opposing anti-Semitic reductions of Jewishness to Israeli interests."[50]

The paradigm of the dissident Jewish critic of Israel who was labeled as a "self-hating," anti-Semitic, "enemy of Israel" and consequently summarily "excommunicated" from the Jewish community is Hannah Arendt.[51] An overview of her case therefore provides a historical perspective on those like Butler's today. Arendt's views on Zionism shifted over time, but as Richard Bernstein notes, "her voice was always that of a dissenting critic."[52] She generally rejected any form of group affiliation, although she did insist that "if one is attacked as a Jew, one must defend oneself as a Jew." As we have also seen, her early work on Rahel Varnhagen was inspired by a Zionist critique of assimilation, which she insisted never protected Jews from anti-Semitism. These positions remained constants in her thinking.

Shortly after the Nazi seizure of power, she was denounced to the authorities by a librarian for the research she was conducting on anti-Semitism at the behest of her friend Kurt Blumenfeld, president of the German Zionist Organization. After being held for interrogation for eight days, she fled Germany for Paris. There she worked for Zionist organizations like Youth Aliyah, which helped young Jews fleeing Europe get to Palestine. During and after World War II, "Arendt had been a tireless advocate for Jewish victims and for the existence of a Jewish Homeland in Palestine," writes Daniel Maier-Katkin, "but she envisioned the homeland as a federated, pluralistic, democratic, secular state—a homeland for Palestinians and Jews coexisting peacefully as neighbors without an official state religion."[53] Some key works written during the Second World War point her way to this position.

Her February 1943 article, "The Crisis of Zionism" summed up several short pieces written in the early years of World War II.[54] Jews, and by extension Jewish politics, were splintered by multiple challenges, she argued. First was the failure of the Jewish Agency to create a Jewish army, which Arendt had maintained was an imperative, as had Revisionist Zionists. Second was the new relationship between Jews and the emerging state that was emerging in both the United States and the Soviet Union. Third, and most crucially, was the support by Judah Magnes and others (like Martin Buber, Ernest Simon, and the director of Youth Aliyah, Henrietta Szold, along with Hashomer Hatzair) urging a binational state. Binationalism was a position that strongly appealed to Arendt, but it was opposed by the leading Zionist groups of the time as "completely unrealistic, lacking in national feeling, or—more sinisterly—a disguised pathway to an Arab state."[55]

Arendt's most encompassing position paper, "Zionism Reconsidered" was penned in 1944, synthesizing her critique of the dominant forms of Jewish nationalism and offering a historical overview of how they arrived at this position.[56] It could be read as her argument that political Zionism was itself prone to an autoimmune process, whereby Zionist calls for absolute Jewish national sovereignty and homogeneity in Palestine would lead to undermining the possibility of a Jewish homeland, a protective haven for Jews. The goal of a Jewish homeland, she maintained in "To Save the Jewish Homeland," "must never be *sacrificed* to the pseudo-sovereignty of a Jewish state."[57] Investment in Jewish nationalism that refused to recognize and negotiate with Arabs, preferably in the form of citizen councils organized at the local level but based upon equal rights for all that were protected by a federation or withing a commonwealth, would be self-suicide. It could only result in supporting "a people as the rope supports for hanging," she claimed.[58] This was the case, since even if victorious, "Jews would live surrounded by an entirely hostile Arab population, secluded inside ever-threatened borders, absorbed with physical self-defense to a degree that would submerge all other interests and activities."[59]

Rather than pursue the path of binationalism, Zionists aligned with imperial powers to achieve their goal of a nation-state, Arendt asserted. This will "inevitably lead to a new wave of Jew-hatred," she maintained. She continued by prophetically stating that "the antisemitism of tomorrow will assert that Jews not only profiteered from the presence of the foreign big powers in that region but had actually plotted it and hence are guilty of the consequences."[60] The result was that "Zionists have now indeed done their best to create that insoluble 'tragic conflict'" that she predicted would result from the forms of Jewish nationalism that she opposed.[61]

The hostile, negative, and vitriolic response to the establishment of a Jewish nation-state would become a self-reinforcing logic for why it was necessary. The instrumentalization of anti-Semitism—what Arendt called the "propaganda advantage of anti-Jewish hostility"—was thus intrinsic to this mode of Zionist Jewish politics.[62] It resulted from how Zionists conceived of anti-Semitism. Arendt maintained that Zionists understood anti-Semitism "as the natural reaction of one people against another," conceiving of it as "an eternal phenomenon attending inevitably the course of Jewish history through all the Diaspora countries," which is precisely why a Jewish nation-state was necessary.[63] However, the viewpoint that a state could insulate Jews from anti-Semitism without full recognition of their Palestinian neighbors' rights and economic interests, especially when combined with imperial power politics, was doomed to backfire, she insisted.

Arendt urged not only binationalism, but a path advocated by "the great French Zionist Bernard Lazare." He had called for a national movement where Jews were aligned in "solidarity with other oppressed peoples whose cause, though historically otherwise conditioned, was essentially the same." Instead, Arendt cautioned, Zionists were opting "in the morning-dream of freedom and justice to compromise with the most evil forces of our time by taking advantage of imperialistic interests."[64] As Bernstein indicates, Arendt's admonition of mainline Zionism was vehement, using "all the rhetorical means at her command: irony, sarcasm, condemnation, scorn, and blunt denunciation."[65] The result was that *Commentary* rejected "Zionism Reconsidered" for publication since in the words of Clement Greenberg, one of the editors, it "contained too many anti-Semitic implications—not in the sense that you intend them as such, but that the unfriendly reader might intend them as such."[66]

Unfriendly readers did, indeed, malign Arendt as such. When she once more took a dissident stance on the creation of the State of Israel in 1948 in "To Save the Jewish Homeland," Ben Halpern, a self-proclaimed Zionist "partisan," charged that she was imbued with an "enfant-terrible complex" and indulged in "outrageous sensation-mongering" in her attacks on Herzl, Weizmann, and Ben-Gurion. Worst of all, he called her a "collaborationist," a horrible derision just following the Holocaust, which laid the groundwork for impugning her as a "self-hating Jew."[67]

The condemnation of Arendt ramped up exponentially with the publication of *Eichmann in Jerusalem: A Report on the Banality of Evil*. Focused on the Jerusalem trial of Nazi war criminal Adolf Eichmann, and published first as a series of articles in the *New Yorker* from February 16 to March 16, 1963, *Eichmann in Jerusalem* unleashed a firestorm epitomized in the *Jewish Spectator* headline, "Self-Hating Jewess Writes Pro-Eichmann Series for the *New Yorker*." Anson Rabinbach notes that the controversy "was certainly the most bitter public dispute among intellectuals and scholars concerning the Holocaust that has ever taken place," while Daniel Maier-Katkin described her reception as "perhaps the most vituperative literary event of the twentieth century."[68] Even more relevant for our purposes, Susan Glenn argues that it marked a "new chapter" in the charge of "self-hatred," which henceforward tended to focus on the stance of Jews toward

Israel.⁶⁹ Arendt's thesis that senseless mass slaughter like the Holocaust could be perpetrated by ordinary people not because of their fanatical anti-Semitism but as a result of the "banality of evil" was distressing. Eichmann was "neither perverted nor sadistic," she argued, but rather "terribly and terrifying normal." He spoke and thought in officialese, using stock phrases and sound bites, slogans and clichés. He was a social climber whose values were typically bourgeois: he believed in duty, law and order, and respectability. Ultimately, he was too thoughtless to understand the ethical ramifications of his actions, Arendt charged.⁷⁰

Beyond this argument, however, Arendt's analysis of Eichmann made two main claims that aroused the most vehement indignation. First was her flippant assailing of the Judenrat, the Jewish administrative bodies that the Nazis forced upon Jewish communities in many occupied countries to help carry out the Final Solution. This Arendt called, "the darkest chapter of the whole dark story" of the Holocaust, indicting these Jewish leaders "almost without exception." Second was her strong condemnation of the use of the Eichmann trial to legitimize the Jewish state, calling it a "show trial" orchestrated by the "invisible stage manager," David Ben-Gurion, in her opening pages. This was taken as wickedly anti-Zionist. The president of the World Zionist Organization maintained that she had no "reverence for the unparalleled suffering and tragedy of the 6,000,00 who perished." Another reviewer concluded that Arendt was "digging future Jewish graves to the applause of the world's unconverted anti-Semites."⁷¹ In an exchange of letters in *Encounter*, her erstwhile friend, Gershom Scholem, said that her account had "overtones of malice" and that she lacked *ahavat Israel* (love of the Jewish people). Scholem maintained that her description of Eichmann as a "convert to Zionism" could only come from someone "who had a profound dislike of everything to do with Zionism." Arendt responded to Scholem by indicating that she did not love any people or collective, but only her friends; that the only love she knew was that of persons. "I do not 'love' the Jews," she wrote, nor do I 'believe' in them; I merely belong to them as a matter of course, beyond dispute or argument."⁷²

The full debate on Arendt's *Eichmann in Jerusalem* is beyond the confines of my point here, focused as it is on the charge that the vilification of Arendt as a "self-hating Jew" and thus an anti-Semite for her views on Zionism and Israel was paradigmatic for Jewish dissidents, marking as it did a "new chapter" in the polemics on Israel, Zionism, and anti-Semitism. While there may be much to critique in their views, both Butler and Arendt, along with their kin, are better located within the tradition of "conscious pariahs," as Arendt termed them: these are internal critics of Jews and their politics who, at the same time, resist the hostile and demeaning assault on Jewishness that comes from true Judeophobes.

Arendt developed her concept of the "conscious pariah" in her early essay, "The Jew as Pariah," modeling the type on Bernard Lazare. Conscious pariahs, Arendt explained, called upon Jews to fight against their "double slavery": "dependence, on the one hand, upon the hostile elements of his environment and, on the other, on his own 'highly-placed brethren.'"[73] Or, as she put it most clearly in a short essay on "Herzl and Lazare," in which she saluted the latter, "both were to learn that the Jewish people was threatened not only by the anti-Semites from without but also by the influence of its own 'benefactors' [i.e., Jewish elites] from within."[74]

In debates about post-Holocaust Judeophobia, labeling Jews who are vociferous critics of Israel as "self-hating" is often only about dressing political disagreements in the uniform of the enemy, turning Jewish dissidents, "connected critics" (Michael Walzer), "non-Jewish Jews" (Isaac Deutscher), or what Arendt termed "conscious pariahs" into anti-Semites, since that is what the charge amounts to. In illuminating the tradition of the conscious pariah, Arendt sought to light a path that would allow for shielding Jews from the slings and arrows of anti-Semitism, while rebelling against the parvenus of the Jewish establishment, both in Israel and the diaspora, whose politics she considered a form of suicide, or self-defeating as a result of an autoimmunitary process.

JEAN-PAUL SARTRE, HOURIA BOUTELDJA, (ANTI-) ZIONISM, AND RACISM

Those who bolster the reductive claim that anti-Zionism = anti-Semitism or who write off the critics of Zionism and of Israel as "self-hating Jews" or as anti-Semites most often stoke conflicts around anti-Semitism rather than quelling them. They turn the discussion into a polemic, tarring their enemies with charged epithets rather than patiently dismantling their arguments.

As we saw, Jean-Paul Sartre, for his part, provided a powerful analysis of why the formula that "Zionism is racism" ultimately recapitulates the anti-Semitism of old when it is used as a shibboleth to forge political coalitions on the Left. He did so when he accepted an honorary degree from Hebrew University and at more length in the second volume of the *Critique of Dialectical Reason*. His analysis explained how unprincipled or bad-faith anti-Zionism suffers from an autoimmunitary process, since any antiracism that proves to be Judeophobic undercuts itself.

What makes Sartre's analysis of anti-Zionist Judeophobia different from Poliakov (and by extension the new anti-Semitism theorists who built on his insights) is that it was never segregated. Sartre's critique of what he termed *neo-antisemitisme* was part and parcel of his commitment to oppose all forms of what he dubbed "the new racism." As we saw, Sartre's last political interventions were all focused around the struggles faced by new immigrants, who were overwhelmingly Muslim, into France. For Sartre, it was clear that what antiracism entailed was a sharp confrontation not only with *neo-antisemitisme* but also with all forms of postcolonial racism, which accounts for Sartre's multidirectional antiracism. Today this means an examination of the dialectical links between the institutionalized discrimination against Muslims in the new Europe or Blacks in the United States and how far too often, in turn, the targets of their contempt are Jews, seen as embodiments of Zionism, colonialism, racism, and white supremacy.

The decolonial theorist Houria Bouteldja provides an example. She frames her book *Whites, Jews, and Us* around a critique of Sartre because of his refusal to condemn Zionism and his insistence on the legitimacy of the Israeli state, even while he sought to encourage Israelis and Palestinians to work through the differend that divided them. Contra Sartre, Bouteldja's decolonial antiracism insists that the Israeli state is inherently illegitimate, nothing but an outpost of the ongoing colonial system. Israel and Zionism also serve to summarize and epitomize all racial projects.

Bouteldja rose to prominence as the main spokesperson of the *mouvement* (today the Parti) des Indigènes de la République.[75] The group formed in 2005, a fateful year of resistance to anti-Arab, anti-African, anti-Muslim racism given the November 2005 riots in Paris. The Indigènes are an antiracist collective that initially focused on the *loi du foulard*, the laws preempting the wearing of the hijab in France. Bouteldja's first intervention drew upon the work of Frantz Fanon to highlight how contemporary French laws about the headscarf were a continuation of colonial policies. Largely a media phenomenon—on television, the Internet, and social media—rather than grassroots organizers, the Indigènes gained prominence because of their symbolically loaded provocations that have served as strategic traps sure to elicit a visceral media response that provoke larger debates about Islamophobia, racism, and the Israeli/Palestinian conflict.

From the start, there were two novel aspects to the interventions of the Indigènes: first, akin to Latin American and other transnational *decolonial* critics, they argued that the oppression they were addressing was not *postcolonial*, but a manifestation of ongoing colonial structures and discourses that required decolonizing. As they wrote in their opening salvo in 2005, "Nous sommes les Indigènes de la Republique": "France a été colonial... La France reste un Etat colonial!" (France was and remains a colonial state!).[76] Secondly, they exploded the code of colorblindness in a Republican France that refuses to directly address racism using the language of race, religion, or ethnicity since this overlaps with the Vichy and colonial discourses of the past.

Whites, Jews, and Us is the first monograph by Bouteldja and is organized around four chapters that focus on different groups—Whites, Jews, women, and indigenous people—with a coda on secularism and religion titled "Allahou Akbar!" and a prologue, "Shoot Sartre!"[77] In her chapter on whites, Bouteldja argues that white supremacy is founded on status and privilege. What Albert Memmi terms the "banality of racism" is stoked by the fear of the loss of white entitlement.[78] This is institutionally structured by a system that Fanon would term "integral racism." Bouteldja explains this clearly and succinctly to whites: "You are afraid but you hold on to your comfort. This is your dilemma. You don't want to give up on the infinite privileges of colonial domination. Your privileges are material, statutory, institutional, political, symbolic. Within the same social standing, it is always better to be white.... It is protected by your morals, your laws, your weapons.... You are the absolute, the center, the universal."[79] France, Europe, and indeed the world system are all rendered as a racial system oscillating on the axis of white supremacy. Decolonization entails a revolutionary overthrow of this whole system.

Jews tilt between "Whites" and "Us [the indigènes]" in Bouteldja's title and in her analysis. On the one hand, Jews and Arabs are cousins. Not so much because both are "People of the Book" or because of their shared Abrahamic lineage, but because of Jews' historical relationship to (white) Christians.[80] Christian anti-Judaism meant that historically Jews were not-quite-white or off-white or provisionally white. But they have been whitened by their accession to the values of the French Republic, to the halls of power, and via their unbridled support of

Israel. Jews have done so as "stakeholders in 'Judeo-Christian civilization,'" augers Bouteldja.[81]

Indeed, the book pivots on a critique of the two pillars soldered together by the hyphen in "Judeo-Christian." One pillar is the white supremacy of Christian civilization that continues into the present. But her second line of assault is aimed at those Jews—"the Zionists"—who are central to this axis of evil. Jews were chosen by the West for three ideological missions, Bouteldja claims: "to solve the white world's moral legitimacy crisis that resulted from the Nazi genocide, to outsource republican racism, and finally to be the weaponized wing of Western imperialism in the Arab world."[82] This is a pact with the devil. Within fifty years of the creation of the State of Israel, Bouteldja maintains in one of her signature phrases, Jews went from being pariahs or "*dhimmis of the Republic*" to the role of "*Senegalese riflemen* to satisfy the needs of Western imperialism."[83] Bouteldja indicts all the imperial republics who finance and bolster the Israeli state. She also homogenizes and essentializes all Jews and Israelis. As she indicates quite clearly, "all Jews are Zionists. Now, if you aren't a Zionist, you have to prove it."[84] Bouteldja is crystal clear that her thinking is Manichean on this point: "You are condemned to the binary," she writes. "West or Third World, whiteness or decolonization, Zionism or anti-Zionism."[85]

In making her case, Bouteldja's text is framed by her condemnation of Sartre, who is exemplary of leftists who falter on the issue of Zionism. Why "Shoot Sartre!," as she provocatively suggests in the title of her opening chapter, since he was a radical supporter of Algerian independence, opposed apartheid and U.S. Jim Crow segregation, and lauded the Cuban and Vietnamese revolutions, among his many stances as an ambassador to the Third World? We should shoot Sartre, says Bouteldja, for unlike Genet, whom Bouteldja admires because he "rejoiced at France's defeat to the Germans in 1940" and because "he couldn't care less about Hitler," Sartre consistently acknowledged there was legitimacy to both the Palestinian and the Israeli positions (not to mention his opposition to Nazism).[86] For Bouteldja, since Sartre was not a confirmed anti-Zionist, he was white. Shoot Sartre, *alors*.

Bouteldja's manifesto, *Whites, Jews, and Us* is a powerful indictment of white supremacy, since it names whiteness in a dogmatically colorblind France, and seeks to confront how it operates in its banality in institutional and symbolic forms, enacting a social segregation based on ethnic, religious, and skin-based color-coding that colorblindness refuses to acknowledge. As her indictment of

Sartre suggests, however, for the minority strand of the Left that Bouteldja represents, Zionism has become shorthand for whiteness, colonialism, racism, and apartheid-like segregation everywhere. Her critique of white supremacy forgets the role that anti-Jewish racism continues to play for white Christian nationalism in Europe, but also for those Arabs and Muslims oppressed by institutional racism who have found in Jews soft targets for their wrath.

In her conclusion, Bouteldja calls on us to build a new pantheon that will enable us to combat the global rise of white supremacy and racism in all its forms. The decolonial pantheon that she heralds excludes Jews and non-Jews who do not categorically reject Zionism, however. I vehemently disagree. I argue that this pantheon should herald Sartre, not Genet, and Frantz Fanon, not Josie Fanon, as Bouteldja augurs. It should resurrect Césaire: the Césaire who taught Fanon that when they say "the Jews," or "the Zionists," expressed in a collective noun, know they are coming for you next, since all racisms are entangled. My pantheon would include the Houria Bouteldja who brilliantly indicts French and European and American white supremacy and colorblindness, but not the Bouteldja whose views on Zionism are so flat, caricatured, and unnuanced. Nor the Bouteldja who tangoes with Judeophobes like the comedian Dieudonné M'bala M'bala, the national socialist Alain Soral, or the anti-Semitic murderer Mohamed Merah.[87] In a European and American context rife with racism and white supremacy ascendant, critical theorists of all stripes must unequivocally fight the entangled racisms that continue to place Jews in the crosshairs. Unlike Sartre who understood this, Bouteldja's failure to do so compromises her antiracism, undermining her powerful criticisms of racism in the name of her polemical, polarizing, and reductive anti-Zionism. In fact, her zealous anti-Zionism suffers from an autoimmunitary process that recirculates the post-Holocaust forms of racism that Sartre diligently and perceptively fought against, undermining her antiracist politics.

THE FRANKFURT SCHOOL: PERSONALIZATION, SECONDARY ANTI-SEMITISM, AND TICKET THINKING

To round out our analysis of how to think about post-Holocaust Judeophobia we turn finally to the work of the Frankfurt School. In his encompassing overview of the Frankfurt School's approach to anti-Semitism, Lars Rensmann concludes by explaining why their approach arguably offers the most comprehensive analysis of Judeophobia, including its post-Holocaust manifestations.[88] Their work has contemporary relevance because the Frankfurt School sought to explain the links between the antidemocratic forces of social domination and the social conditions that give rise to them, placing anti-Semitism at the very center of these social phenomena, even as they considered links with other racisms (anti-Black, anti-immigrant, anti-Sinti and Roma, anti-Asian) and how these racisms intersect with misogyny and homophobia. Critical theory, writes Rensmann, "is concerned about sociopolitical structures and material conditions reproducing global poverty and centralized power, authoritarian dispositions and institutions, the politics of hate and exclusion, and threats to public freedom."[89]

There are three key contributions that the Frankfurt School offer to our understanding of post-Holocaust Judeophobia. First, they help us to apprehend the ways in which shifts in modern capitalism, new mechanisms of power and control, rising inequality, and authoritarian and populist dispositions draw upon the repertoire of anti-Jewish imagery to personify and personalize fears, anxiety, and resentments generated by these global transformations. Second, their work enables the comprehension of how the politics of Holocaust memory can result in what they termed "secondary anti-Semitism." Last, they recognized that with the waning legitimacy of scientific racism that faded with the death knell of Nazism, new forms of culturally coded racism would emerge, enabling racism without racists and anti-Semitism without anti-Semites.[90]

Today, Judeophobia is a transnational, transreligious, and transcultural problem. It travels between countries, religions, and cultures in the form of memes and texts that are diffused across the planet with just a few clicks of a button. The culture industry and the new social media have proven rich veins for disseminating hate speech and channeling resentment and paranoia. Conspiracy theories, which are the signature of Judeophobia, personify the social changes that underpin the anxiety and fear generated by the shifts in global capitalism, as we discussed via Bauman's work.

The repertoire of anti-Jewish motifs stands ready to provide a vocabulary for those without the analytic frameworks to express the social forces that they know imperil their lives: financial capitalism is embodied in a flash in the image of George Soros; elite control of world governments is neatly captured in the acronym NWO (New World Order); concentrated power over the media and the economy is simply explained by the *Protocols of the Elders of Zion*; the source of global pandemics is attributed to updated versions of the myth of well-poisoning Jews. Jews are personified as the embodiment of globalization and the globalists, and "crystallized in images of cosmopolitan Jews, Jews as global 'warmongering,' 'child killers,' 'imperialists' and 'colonizers,' or as 'blood sucking,' rapacious' greedy capitalists."[91] Abstract and complex social phenomena that surely impact our everyday lives are thus objectified, concretized, and embodied using classic anti-Jewish motifs.

Adorno and other Frankfurt School theorists offered a compelling explanation of why personalization is evermore present in our global age. They explained that anti-Jewish myths, tropes, caricatures, memes, and narratives use the language provided by the anti-Semitic repertoire because those who deploy them do not have an adequate theoretical and explanatory framework to account for their social reality. These morphing anti-Jewish images serve as an inchoate code for those without the requisite tools to describe what ails them. The theory of personalization provides powerful insight into the discursive drumbeat of social denigration on social media and within the culture industry in the age of globalization.

We can add to globalization as an underlying driver of post-Holocaust Judeophobia the unintended consequences of Holocaust memorialization. The widespread dissemination of the Holocaust in memorials, film, television, memoirs, novels, and plays, alongside Holocaust education, has resulted in some inadvertent effects. I will highlight three. First, since the Holocaust more than any other single event legitimates the Zionist narrative that Jews without a state of their own are imperiled and since the Holocaust was a key factor in undergirding support for the State of Israel from its inception, Holocaust denial as a perverse shadow of Holocaust memory emerged alongside the creation of the State of Israel and spread as Holocaust memory was globalized and universalized.[92]

In addition to Holocaust denial, "secondary anti-Semitism," a term coined by Peter Schönbach while working with Adorno in the 1960s, pointed to a new type of post-Holocaust Judeophobia that resulted from the deflection of guilt for the Holocaust. The Israeli psychiatrist Zvi Rex pithily encapsulated the core idea of "secondary anti-Semitism" when he said, "The Germans will never forgive the Jews for Auschwitz." And the Germans are not alone. With the globalization of Holocaust memorialization, this claim can be generalized to non-Jews who suffer from Holocaust fatigue, but also from a deep desire not to confront the guilt for the Shoah. As Rensmann puts it, secondary anti-Semitism constitutes a new source of "antisemitic resentment: it is motivated by the wish to repress and split off Holocaust remembrance and guilt from the collective memory of a tainted nation. In a nutshell, Jews are collectively blamed by their very existence for reminding Germans [and other nations] of their nation's crimes, guilt, and responsibility... antisemitism 'after Auschwitz' can thus also be understood as antisemitism 'because of Auschwitz.'"[93]

The Frankfurt School's *Group Experiment* provided the empirical basis for their reflections on "secondary anti-Semitism." Based on 137 group discussions conducted in 1950 and 1951 with Germans from different social backgrounds, occupations, and political milieus, Adorno and his colleagues itemized and analyzed various modes of the denial of responsibility for the crimes of the Holocaust. Akin to the earlier work in *The Authoritarian Personality*, the findings of the *Group Experiment* included statistical data on individual attitudes toward anti-Semitism, guilt, and democracy, alongside Adorno's qualitative analysis published in *Guilt and Defense*.[94] This was also the empirical basis for Adorno's later famous address "The Meaning of Working Through the Past," where he discussed "the unconscious and not so unconscious defensiveness against guilt."[95]

Grappling with modes of denial like minimization, distortion, trivialization, and relativization, Adorno analyzed the "mitigating expressions" and "euphemistic circumlocutions" that enabled elements of fascist ideology to survive and percolate within democracies.[96] Different from outright denial, what the *Group Experiment* and Adorno's analysis revealed was that these forms of Holocaust deflection were not only part of the neo-Nazi extreme Right, but widespread in German society. The legacy of fascism thus leached into democratic society. Moreover, Adorno also showed that those uneasy with feelings of guilt would displace and project these feelings onto Jews who are blamed for the perpetual injunction to collective remembrance of the Holocaust and the mandate for moral responsibility. "Never forget" expressed as a prime directive of the superego or the conscience could result in projecting onto Jews the blame for guilt, recycling anti-Jewish tropes in the process. The command to remember could be dismissed by castigating the Jewish refusal to forgive as a desire for revenge. Or it could be linked to the presumption of the Jewish control over the media and the manipulation of public opinion, or to Jewish greed for reparations. As Rensmann notes, "Attributing to Jews the ruthless thirst for revenge, the threatening power of memory and the conspiratorial power to manipulate the media, or the exploitation of the Holocaust for their material interests," are each facets of secondary anti-Semitism that recycle classic anti-Semitic tropes.

A third feature of Holocaust memorialization that potentially generates anti-Jewish sentiments results from the competition for victimhood. As Michael Rothberg has discussed, when Holocaust memory is depicted as a zero-sum game with many insisting that it is unique or exceptional—unlike any other genocide or case of group persecution—this stokes postcolonial resentment and the countercharge that the Holocaust was, in Fanon's unfortunate words, nothing more than "little family quarrels" that occlude the suffering and mass murder of slavery and colonialism.[97] One case in point where this has proven particularly divisive is the Israel/Palestine conflict. As Rothberg notes, "The contemporary conflict always unfolds against the backdrop of powerful memories of death and dispossession, namely memories of the Holocaust and memories of the Nakba and ongoing occupation. In such a context, the memories at stake are often conflictual, contested, and competitive."[98]

When the complexities of Israel/Palestine are reduced to a competition over whose suffering should be recognized, abetted by a binary viewpoint on the conflict that diminishes it to a simplistic grid of oppressor and oppressed, it becomes easy to represent Israel as yet another white, colonial, evil empire that ruthlessly persecutes the indigenous Arab population. This form of postcolonial secondary anti-Semitism inverts the once persecuted into the persecutors.[99] At its most insidious, Israel is depicted as the center of a Jewish cabal that proves to be the source of much of the evil in the world.

But equally, the inability to reckon with the ongoing history of Judeophobia in the aftermath of the extreme calamity of the Holocaust disables critics of Israel from appreciating the pull of Zionism for so many Jews post-Holocaust. This is the core claim for those who argue that a sovereign state for Jews is necessary as a refuge from their experience of persecution and violence in the diaspora. In short, Holocaust memorialization has unintentionally helped to generate three vectors of post-Holocaust Judeophobia: Holocaust denial, secondary anti-Semitism, and postcolonial Judeophobic depictions of Israel and Zionism.

Beyond their understanding of personalization and secondary anti-Semitism, the Frankfurt School also offered a more expansive understanding of how the age of disinformation so facilitated by social media can help to foster Judeophobia, alongside Islamophobia, Negrophobia, and xenophobia. A particularly acute insight was developed in the last section added in 1947 to their "Elements of Anti-Semitism" that concluded the *Dialectic of Enlightenment*. It opens with a stunning line considering that it was written just after the Holocaust: "But there are no more anti-Semites."[100] In developing this point, Horkheimer and Adorno argue that anti-Semitism as such is no longer necessary when the logic of globalized capitalism replaces all thinking with stereotypes, clichés, jargon, stock phrases, dogmatic adherence to ideology, and generally to the petrification of thought, which they call "ticket thinking."[101] "In the world of mass series production," they maintain, "stereotypes replace individual categories."[102]

In a world governed by instrumental rationality when there is only *homo economicus*, they contend, individual decisions are taken over by corporate interests: large capital, trade unions, political parties, factions, and the cookie-cutter subcultures shaped by mass culture. Modern means of communication colonize all differences and humans are divided into blocs. All mediations are eliminated by the "cogwheel mechanism of industry."[103] "Ticket thinking," they continue, "is a product of industrialization and its advertising machine."[104] Judeophobia, they argue, is itself a symptom of the mass production of "ticket thinking" by the culture industry. Since this is the case, the Jews as victims could be replaced, as is evident by the rampant globalized Islamophobia, Negrophobia, and xenophobia today. And Jews themselves can easily get caught up in the cogwheels of "ticket thinking." Horkheimer and Adorno thus suggest how a frenetic, paranoid, and delusional neoconservative philosemitism on the Right serves as the shadow side of militant Islamism's Judeophobia, each a symptom of "ticket thinking" in the age of digital communication where stereotypes and sound bites stand in the place of critical thought.

Their analysis also indicates the ways in which the struggle against anti-Semitism can paradoxically feed the symptoms it seeks to alleviate since "ticket thinking" has filtered into political struggles. This means that those that seek to gain publicity to promote their positions can do so by referencing the prepackaged reservoir of anti-Jewish images and in so doing provoke an immediate response from the army of watchdog organizations whose mission is to combat anti-Semitism. The Internet, the blogosphere, and social media feed on these polemics. In the media-driven frenzied war of words, the medium is often the only message, since in many discussions in the public sphere the only thing that people have often read are the emails or blogs or posts or tweets that offer only prescripted sound bites that feed the polemics and stoke the conflicts. This global flow thus helps to publicize political causes and helps to generate funding for the next skirmish. All this leads to little more than the further stoking of the "ticket thinking" that is the very source of the Judeophobic, Islamophobic, Negrophobic, xenophobic imagination.

In the age of "ticket thinking" where so much of what people cough up as their take on a topic is nothing more than predigested narratives and talking points, our take on the world is reduced to a script with preformed roles. Living in our bubbled social realities, we fail to get outside of the caricatures that are the essence of Judeophobia. This is a world in which there are no more anti-Semites. This is the case because anti-Semitism in its racial and biological forms died in Hitler's bunker. Perhaps more importantly, however, Judeophobia, alongside other heterophobias, has taken on a new life in a world now dominated by modes of disinformation that enjoin us to think in stereotypes.

CONCLUSION: EIGHT LESSONS FOR A POST-HOLOCAUST AGE

In summing up, what then are some of the takeaways that critical theories offer us in confronting post-Holocaust Judeophobia? First, since Judeophobia is long and complicated, shifting and changing over time, we need an array of different overarching theories to recognize its core manifestations. I have reconstructed seven major critical approaches to understanding it, arguing that these constitute the major paradigms explaining its underlying causes. Second, post-Holocaust, there has been a shift in the epistemic and political configuration of Judeophobia and other heterophobias from biological toward cultural arguments. Today, as is the case with other forms of racism, we need to become more sensitized to the new coded and subtle forms that it sometimes takes, which Adorno called, "crypto-anti-Semitism." Third, even explicitly antiracist positions can repeat the logic of racism, clearly indicating an autoimmunitary deficiency. Poliakov shows how this can be the case for *unprincipled* anti-Zionism. Abetted by the analyses of Lyotard, his work enables us to understand that even principled anti-Zionism in the form of neo-Pauline theorists like Alain Badiou, for example, can repeat the logic of Christian supersessionism. Fourth, in the case of post-Holocaust Jews, like Judith Butler, who take a principled anti-Zionist position, we should understand their interventions as part of a tradition of "conscious pariahs" or Jewish dissenters that has always been intrinsic to Jewish life. Demonizing these articulations with the epithet of "self-hating Jews" is a symptom of ticket thinking. Fifth, these conscious pariahs enable us to understand that not only can anti-Zionism suffer from an autoimmune deficiency, so can the defense of Zionism, as Hannah Arendt sought to highlight. Sixth, multidirectional antiracists like Sartre help us to appreciate how the charge that "Zionism is racism" can function as *"neo-antisemitisme"* in its post-Stalinist forms, while simultaneously encouraging us to fight against the global apartheid of the new racism that targets immigrants and other disempowered, minoritized people. Seventh, Zygmunt Bauman aids us in appreciating how tribalism—whether militant jihadi Judeophobia or white Christian nationalism—is the reverse side of postmodern capitalism, while he enjoins us to see the proliferation of postmodern strangers as equally twinned to liquid modernity. Eighth and finally, the Frankfurt School provides the most fulsome diagnosis of the global rise of authoritarianism, which is made possible because rather than analyze the real causes of social malaise, authoritarians personalize social problems by demonizing weak and vulnerable populations. The Frankfurt School also highlight how political mobilization via "ticket thinking," whether by the Left or the Right, depends upon the reduction of a critical perspective to a sound bite or to a visual image. In the age of the culture industry (Horkheimer and Adorno), in the whirl of liquid modernity (Bauman), in these dark times (Arendt), critical theory thus illuminates a path beyond the reductive binaries and allows us to properly locate the global threats that we must all face together.

Notes

INTRODUCTION

1. In the case of each of these areas, the theoretical and methodological literature is so developed that there are anthologies or guides to the literature. See, for example, Les Back and John Solomos, eds., *Theories of Race and Racism: A Reader*, 3rd ed. (London: Routledge, 2022), which does include a short section on "Racism and Anti-Semitism"; Anthony D. Smith, *Nationalism and Modernism: A Critical Survey of Recent Theories of Nations and Nationalism* (London: Routledge, 1998); Robert J. C. Young, *Postcolonialism: An Historical Introduction* (Oxford: Blackwell, 2001); Susan Archer Man and Ashly Suzanne Patterson, eds., *Reading Feminist Theory: From Modernity to Postmodernity* (Oxford: Oxford University Press, 2015).
2. See David Nirenberg's *Anti-Judaism: The Western Tradition* (New York: Norton, 2013).
3. See the 2021 FBI Hate Crime Statistics: https://www.justice.gov/crs/highlights/2021-hate-crime-statistics.
4. Karen Brodkin, *How Jews Became White Folks and What That Says About Race in America* (New Brunswick, NJ: Rutgers University Press, 1999). The most important study of Jews and whiteness in the United States is Eric L. Goldstein, *The Price of Whiteness: Jews, Race and American Identity* (Princeton, NJ: Princeton University Press, 2008). See also Sander L. Gilman, "The Jewish Nose: Are Jews White? Or, the History of the Nose Job," in *The Jew's Body* (New York: Routledge, 1991), 169–93.
5. See Diane Tobin and Gary Rubin, *In Every Tongue: The Racial and Ethnic Diversity of the Jewish People* (San Francisco: Institute for Community Research, 2005); Melanie Kay/Kantrowitz, *The Colors of Jews: Racial Politics and Radical Diasporism* (Bloomington: Indiana University Press, 2007); Teshome Wagaw, *For Our Soul: Ethiopian Jews in Israel* (Detroit: Wayne State University Press, 2018); Helen Kiyong Kim and Noah Samuel Leavitt, *JewAsian: Race, Religion, and Identity for America's Newest Jews* (Lincoln: University of Nebraska Press, 2016).
6. Matthew F. Jacobson, "Looking Jewish, Seeing Jews," in Back and Solomos, *Theories of Race and Racism*, 238–39.
7. A. Dirk Moses, "'White Genocide' and the Ethics of Public Analysis," *Journal of Genocide Research* 21, no. 2 (2019): 201–13; Jason Stanley, "Buffalo Shooting: How White Replacement

Theory Keeps Inspiring Mass Murder," *Guardian*, May 15, 2022; Richard Wolin, "'The Leprosy of the Soul in Our Time': On the European Origins of the 'Great Replacement' Theory," *Los Angeles Review of Books*, August 4, 2022.

8. Tudor Parfitt, *Hybrid Hate: Conflations of Antisemitism and Anti-Black Racism from the Renaissance to the Third Reich* (New York: Oxford University Press, 2020), chaps. 9 and 10.

9. Gary A. Tobin, Aryeh K. Weinberg, and Jenna Ferer, eds., *The UnCivil University: Intolerance on College Campuses*, rev. ed. (Lanham, MD: Lexington, 2009).

10. On the spread of the theory of intersectionality, see Tom Bartlett, "The Intersectionality Wars," *Chronicle of Higher Education*, May 21, 2017, http://www.chronicle.com/article/The-Intersectionality-Wars/240095. For the accusation that "'Intersectionality' is a code word for anti-Semitism," see Alan Dershowitz's op-ed in the *Washington Examiner*, March 30, 2017, http://www.washingtonexaminer.com/alan-dershowitz-intersectionality-is-a-code-word-for-anti-semitism/article/2618871. For the most important and substantive article addressing this issue, showing the complexity of intersectional theory when it comes to Jews, see David Schraub, "WhiteABBREVIATEJews: An Intersectional Approach," *Association for Jewish Studies Review* 43, no. 2 (November 2019): 379-407.

11. For examples, see Gareth Stedman Jones, *Languages of Class: Studies in English Working Class History, 1832–1982* (Cambridge: Cambridge University Press, 1983); Joan Wallach Scott, *Gender and the Politics of History* (New York: Colombia University Press, 1988); Kwame Anthony Appiah, "Racisms," in *Anatomy of Racism*, ed. David Theo Goldberg (Minneapolis: University of Minnesota Press, 1990), 3-17; Paul C. Taylor, *Race: A Philosophical Introduction*, 2nd ed. (Cambridge: Polity, 2013); Talal Asad, *Genealogies of Religion: Discipline and Reasons of Power in Christianity and Islam* (Baltimore, MD: John Hopkins University Press, 1993); Jonathan Z. Smith, "Religion, Religions, Religious," in *Relating Religion: Essays in the Study of Religion* (Chicago: University of Chicago Press, 2004), 179-96; Anthony D. Smith, *The Nation in History: Historiographical Debates About Ethnicity and Nationalism* (Hanover, NH: University Press of New England, 2000); and for its application to our concerns, see Cynthia M. Baker, *Jew* (New Brunswick, NJ: Rutgers University Press, 2017).

12. See Yehuda Bauer, "In Search of a Definition of Antisemitism," in *Approaches to Antisemitism: Context and Curriculum*, ed. Michael Brown (New York: American Jewish Committee; International Center for University Teaching of Jewish Civilization, 1994), 10-23, 10; Robert Wistrich, *Antisemitism: The Longest Hatred* (New York: Pantheon, 1991), xvi; James Carroll, *Constantine's Sword: The Church and the Jews, A History* (Boston: Houghton Mifflin, 2001), 628-29n 17; A. Roy Eckardt, "The Nemesis of Christian Antisemitism," *Journal of Church and State* 13, no. 2 (Spring 1971): 227-44, 227; and Richard Levy, "Forget Webster," *German Studies Review* 29, no. 1 (February 2006): 145-46.

13. Shmuel Almog, "What's in a Hyphen?," *SICSA Report: The Newsletter of the Vidal Sassoon International Study of Antisemitism* (Summer 1989): 1-2 http://sicsa.huji.ac.il/hyphen.htm.

14. The most careful delineation of the origins of the concept stem word *antisemit-* and its cognates *antisemiten* and *antisemitisch* and *antisemitismus* and of the semantic inflation of the term is David Engel, "Away from a Definition of Antisemitism: An Essay in the Semantics of Historical Description," in *Rethinking European Jewish History*, ed. Jeremy Cohen and Moshe Rosman (Oxford: Littman Library of Jewish Civilization, 2009), 30-53.

15. See Moshe Zimmerman, *Wilhelm Marr: The Patriarch of Antisemitism* (Oxford: Oxford University Press, 1986), 88, 92, 95, 113.
16. On the development of the Aryan myth, see Léon Poliakov, *The Aryan Myth: A History of Racist and Nationalist Ideas in Europe*, trans. Edmund Howard (New York: Basic Books, 1974), and George Mosse, *Towards the Final Solution: A History of European Racism* (Madison: University of Wisconsin Press, 1985), 39-47.
17. Edward W. Said, *Orientalism* (New York: Pantheon, 1978), 27-28.
18. Gil Anidjar, *Semites: Race, Religion, Literature* (Stanford: Stanford University Press, 2008), 20.
19. Gil Anidjar, *The Jew, the Arab: A History of the Enemy* (Stanford: Stanford University Press, 2003). For an earlier but similar argument, see Allan Harris Cutler and Helen Elmquist Cutler, *The Jew as Ally of the Muslim: Medieval Roots of Anti-Semitism* (Notre Dame, IN: University of Notre Dame Press, 1986).
20. Ivan Davidson Kalmar, "Anti-Semitism and Islamophobia: The Formation of a Secret," *Human Architecture: Journal of the Sociology of Self-Knowledge* 7, no. 2 (2009): 134-44. See also Kalmar and Derek J. Penslar, "Orientalism and the Jews: An Introduction," in *Orientalism and the Jews* (Waltham, MA: Brandeis University Press, 2004), xiii-xl; James Pasto shows the relation but also the divergences between discourse about Judaism and Islam in "Islam's 'Strange Secret Sharer': Orientalism, Judaism, and the Jewish Question," *Comparative Studies in Society and History* 40, no. 3 (1998): 437-74. More recently, see Sophia Rose Arjana, *Muslims in the Western Imagination* (Oxford: Oxford University Press, 2015).
21. Benjamin Disraeli, *Tancred; or, The New Crusade*, 2 vols. (Leipzig: Bernhard Tauchnitz, 1847), 1:169, 259, 286.
22. Obviously, in Nazi Germany, the opposite tendency was at work. See Doris L. Bergen, *Twisted Cross: The German Christian Movement in the Third Reich* (Chapel Hill: University of North Carolina Press, 1996); Susannah Heschel, *The Aryan Jesus: Christian Theologians and the Bible in Nazi Germany* (Princeton, NJ: Princeton University Press, 2008).
23. On the development of the idea of the Judeo-Christian tradition in America, see Mark Silk, "Notes on the Judeo-Christian Tradition in America," *American Quarterly* 36, no. 1 (Spring 1984): 65-84. For the most developed account, see K. Healan Gaston, *Imagining Judeo-Christian America: Religion, Secularism, and the Redefinition of Democracy* (Chicago: University of Chicago Press, 2019).
24. See Paul Hanebrink, *A Specter Haunting Europe: The Myth of Judeo-Bolshevism* (Cambridge, MA: Harvard University Press, 2018), chap. 6.
25. Arthur A. Cohen, *The Myth of the Judeo-Christian Tradition* (New York: Harper and Row, 1971), and Marshall Grossman, "The Violence of the Hyphen in Judeo-Christian," *Social Text*, no. 22 (Spring 1989): 115-22. See also Shaul Magid, "The Judeo-Christian Tradition," in *Theologies of American Exceptionalism*, ed. Winnifred Fallers Sullivan and Elizabeth Shakman Hurd (Bloomington: Indiana University Press, 2021), 81-86, and Magid, "Jew, Christian, and the Judeo-Christian: Thinking with Cynthia Baker's *Jew*," *Marginalia*, July 5, 2017, https://marginalia.lareviewofbooks.org/jew-christian-judeo-christian-thinking-cynthia-bakers-jew/. Note also Jean-François Lyotard, "On a Hyphen," in *The Hyphen: Between Judaism and Christianity*, ed. Jean-François Lyotard and Eberhard Gruber, trans. Pascale-Anne Brault and Michael Naas (Highlands, NJ: Humanity, 1999), 13-27.

26. For a deeper consideration, see Matti Bunzl, *Anti-Semitism and Islamophobia: Hatreds Old and New in Europe* (Chicago: Prickly Paradigm, 2007); Ilan Halevi, *Islamophobie et judéophobie: L'effet miroir* (Paris: Éditions Syllepse, 2015); Nasar Meer, ed., *Racialization and Religion: Race, Culture and Difference in the Study of Antisemitism and Islamophobia* (London: Routledge, 2014); James Renton and Ben Gidley, eds., *Antisemitism and Islamophobia in Europe* (London: Palgrave, 2017); Dorian Bell, *Globalizing Race: Antisemitism and Empire in French and European Culture* (Evanston, IL: Northwestern University Press, 2018), and Ethan B. Katz, "An Imperial Entanglement: Anti-Semitism, Islamophobia, and Colonialism," *American Historical Review* 123, no. 4 (October 2018): 1190–1209.

27. As such, in this book I will consciously hyphenate anti-Semitism throughout. I will, however, maintain the orthography used by other scholars as it appears in their published works, thus not hyphenating where they have not used a hyphen.

28. See, for example, Wistrich, *The Longest Hatred*, xviii, and Robert Wistrich, *Lethal Obsession: Anti-Semitism from Antiquity to the Global Jihad* (New York: Random House, 2010), 8; Bernard Lewis, *Semites and Anti-Semites: An Inquiry into Conflict and Prejudice* (New York: Norton, 1986), 20–22; Ben-Zion Netanyahu, "Antisemitism" [in Hebrew], in *The Hebrew Encyclopedia* (Jerusalem/Tel Aviv, 1959), 4:493–508; Alvin Rosenfeld, introduction to *Resurgent Antisemitism: Global Perspectives*, (Bloomington: Indiana University Press, 2013).

29. Historical works that show how relations between Jews and Muslims have changed over time in different places include Norman Stillman, *The Jews of Arab Lands: A History and Source Book* (Philadelphia: Jewish Publication Society of America, 1979); Bernard Lewis, *The Jews of Islam* (Princeton, NJ: Princeton University Press, 1984); Mark R. Cohen, *Under Crescent and Cross: The Jews in the Middle Ages* (Princeton, NJ: Princeton University Press, 1994); Mark Mazower, *Salonica, A City of Ghosts: Christians, Muslims, and Jews, 1430–1950* (New York: Alfred A. Knopf, 2004); Mohammed Kenbib, *Juifs et musulmans au Maroc, 1859–1948* (Paris: Faculté des Lettres et des Sciences Humaines-Rabat, 1994); Michelle Campos, *Ottoman Brothers: Muslims, Christians, and Jews in Early Twentieth-Century Palestine* (Stanford: Stanford University Press, 2011); Orit Bashkin, *New Babylonians: A History of Jews in Modern Iraq* (Stanford: Stanford University Press, 2012); Maud Mandel, *Muslims and Jews in France: History of a Conflict* (Princeton, NJ: Princeton University Press, 2014); Jonathan Gribetz, *Defining Neighbors: Religion, Race and the Early Zionist-Arab Encounter* (Princeton, NJ: Princeton University Press, 2014); and Ethan B. Katz, *The Burdens of Brotherhood: Jews and Muslims from North Africa to France* (Cambridge, MA: Harvard University Press, 2015).

30. Wolfgang Benz makes this point unapologetically in "Antisemitism Research," in *The Oxford Handbook of Jewish Studies*, ed. Martin Goodman (Oxford: Oxford University Press, 2002), 943–55, 944. For various definitions see Ben Halpern, "What Is Antisemitism?," *Modern Judaism*, no. 1 (1981): 251–62; David Berger, "Anti-Semitism: An Overview," in *History of Hate: The Dimensions of Anti-Semitism* (Philadelphia: Jewish Publication Society, 1986), 3–14; Wistrich, *The Longest Hatred*, xv–xxvi; Albert Lindemann, *Anti-Semitism Before the Holocaust* (London: Routledge, 2000), 8–12; Dina Porat and Kenneth S. Stern, "Defining Antisemitism," *Antisemitism Worldwide* (2003/4): 5–28.

31. Despite acknowledging this, Yehuda Bauer writes, "Semantic struggles are bound to fail; and there is little choice but to follow the popular trend and use the unscientific, inaccurate, confusing, and misleading term 'antisemitism' as a catch-all, and to

consider 'Jew-hatred' and 'Judeophobia' its synonyms." Bauer, "In Search of a Definition of Antisemitism," 12.

32. See Sander Gilman's introduction to in *Difference and Pathology: Stereotypes of Sexuality, Race, and Madness* (Ithaca, NY: Cornell University Press, 1985). I discuss stereotyping in more detail in the section "Anatomy of a Stereotype" in chapter 8.

33. The quote is from Pierre-André Taguieff's chapter, "The Theories of Prejudice and the Meanings of Racism," in *The Force of Prejudice: On Racism and Its Doubles*, trans. and ed. Hassan Melehy (Minneapolis: University of Minnesota Press, 2001 [1987]), 145. Taguieff's extraordinary footnote 12 to this chapter provides a bibliography to this literature (356–59). The classic summa on discrimination is Gordon Allport, *The Nature of Prejudice* (Cambridge, MA: Addison-Wesley, 1954).

34. For a definition of racism and an overview of its history as a term that sets it against notions like ethnocentrism, white supremacy, and others, see George Frederickson, "The Concept of Racism in Historical Discourse," in *Racism: A Short History* (Princeton, NJ: Princeton University Press, 2002), 151–70, definition on 170.

35. For an overview of the debates about defining genocide, see Scott Straus, "Contested Meanings and Conflicting Imperatives: A Conceptual Analysis of Genocide," *Journal of Genocide Research* 3, no. 3 (2001): 349–75; Ann Curthoys and John Docker, "Defining Genocide," in *The Historiography of Genocide*, ed. Dan Stone (Basingstoke, UK: Palgrave Macmillan, 2007), 9–41; Martin Shaw, *What Is Genocide?* (Cambridge, MA: Polity, 2007).

36. Gavin Langmuir, "Towards a Definition of Antisemitism," in *Towards a Definition of Antisemitism* (Berkeley: University of California Press, 1990), 311–52.

37. Langmuir, *Towards a Definition of Antisemitism*, 328.

38. Theodor W. Adorno, "Prejudice in the Interview Material," in *The Authoritarian Personality*, ed. Theodor W. Adorno, Else Frenkel-Brunswik, Daniel J. Levinason, and R. Nevitt Sandford (New York: Harper, 1950), 622–23.

39. See Shulamit Volkov, "Antisemitism as a Cultural Code: Reflections on the History and Historiography of Antisemitism in Imperial Germany," *Leo Baeck Yearbook* 23, no. 1 (1978): 25–46, and Volkov, "The Written Matter and the Spoken Word," in *Unanswered Questions: Nazi Germany and the Genocide of the Jews*, ed. François Furet (New York: Schocken, 1989). Volkov argues against simple continuity arguments in our efforts to understand anti-Semitism, whether by suggesting that anti-Semitism is a permanent prejudice, a cyclical phenomenon, or has a uniform development and growth that culminates in Nazism. Instead, she insists that it is best understood in its specific discursive context. Moreover, she claims that late nineteenth- and early twentieth-century anti-Semitism in Germany was more like anti-Semitism in France in the same period and significantly different from Nazi anti-Semitism, since it was ideology, not oratory intended to mobilize action, ideas, not propaganda. In making this argument, she suggests that one facet of Wilhelminian anti-Semitism was that "it had gradually become *a code* for the overall *Weltanschauung* and style of the right" and likewise that opposition to anti-Semitism "identified individuals and groups in the camp of democratization, parliamentarianism, and often also with cultural and economic modernism" (43).

40. Langmuir, "Towards a Definition of Antisemitism," 334.

41. Peter Schäfer, *Judeophobia: Attitudes Toward the Jews in the Ancient World* (Cambridge, MA: Harvard University Press, 1997), 203.

42. Schäfer, *Judeophobia*, 204.
43. For an overview of this literature, see Vicki Caron, "Catholics and the Rhetoric of Antisemitic Violence in Fin-de-Siècle France," in *Sites of European Antisemitism in the Age of Mass Politics, 1880–1918*, ed. Robert Nemes and Daniel Unowsky (Waltham, MA: Brandeis University Press, 2014), 36–60, specifically 36–37.
44. Engel, "Away from a Definition of Antisemitism," 30–53, quote on 53. See also Scott Ury and Guy Miron, eds., *Antisemitism and the Politics of History* (Waltham, MA: Brandeis University Press, 2023).
45. Kenneth L. Marcus, *The Definition of Anti-Semitism* (Oxford: Oxford University Press, 2015).
46. Wistrich, *The Longest Hatred*.
47. Hannah Arendt, *The Origins of Totalitarianism* (San Diego, CA: Schocken, 1971 [1951]), 8.
48. Marcus, *Definition*, 93.
49. Marcus, *Definition*, 100 and 104–5.
50. Six core tropes have proven particularly persistent: (1) the image of Judas, who embodies the Jewish traitor and exemplar of Jewish materialism, since he was willing to sell out God for thirty pieces of silver; (2) Caiaphas and the Pharisees: key depictions of Jewish leaders who are hypocrites willing to do anything to maintain their power; (3) the charge of deicide in the course of the Christian Passion narrative, indicating a willingness to undermine ultimate values; (4) the association of Jews with the devil first put into Jesus's mouth by John (8:44); (5) the supersessionist narrative found in Paul's Epistles and intermittently throughout the New Testament; and (6) the blood libel, ritual murder, host desecration, and well-poisoning charges of the medieval era, indexing a Jewish conspiracy against Christendom, which has modern analogs in the conspiracies found in the *Protocols of the Elders of Zion*.
51. International Holocaust Remembrance Alliance, "What Is Antisemitism?," https://www.holocaustremembrance.com/resources/working-definitions-charters/working-definition-antisemitism. For an encompassing analysis of how the "new antisemitism" theory led to the development and deployment of the IHRA definition and the problems with this, see Antony Lerman, *Whatever Happened to Antisemitism? Redefinition and the Myth of the "Collective Jew"* (London: Pluto, 2022).
52. Kenneth Stern, "Written Testimony Before the United States House of Representatives Committee on the Judiciary November 7, 2017, Hearing on Examining Anti-Semitism on College Campuses." See also Kenneth Stern, *The Conflict Over the Conflict: The Israel/Palestine Campus Debate* (Toronto: University of Toronto Press, 2020), chap. 7.
53. David Feldman, "Will Britain's New Definition of Antisemitism Help Jewish People? I'm Skeptical," *Guardian*, December 28, 2016, https://www.theguardian.com/commentisfree/2016/dec/28/britain-definition-antisemitism-british-jews-jewish-people.
54. Feldman, "Britain's New Definition of Antisemitism" and Judith Butler, "The Charge of Anti-Semitism: Jews, Israel, and the Risks of Public Critique," in *Those Who Forget the Past: The Question of Antisemitism*, ed. Ron Rosenbaum (New York: Random House, 2004), 438–50, 438.
55. *The Jerusalem Declaration on Antisemitism*, https://jerusalemdeclaration.org/wp-content/uploads/2021/03/JDA-1.pdf.
56. David Schraub, "A New Definition of Antisemitism Is Out, and the Antisemites Love It," *Haaretz*, April 7, 2021.

57. Michael Walzer, "I Hope That UCL Faculty and Staff Will Defend IHRA, as I Would Do Were I with Them," *Fathom*, May 2021.
58. *The Nexus Document: Understanding Antisemitism at Its Nexus with Israel and Zionism*, https://israelandantisemitism.com/wp-content/uploads/2022/11/The-Nexus-Document-Understanding-Antisemitism-At-Its-Nexus-With-Israel-And-Zionism.pdf.
59. While "Judeophobia" was coined by Leon Pinsker in his Zionist manifesto, *Auto-Emancipation* (1882), it need not be used in Pinsker's sense of a "psychic aberration" or "inherited predisposition" of Christian civilization, which is clearly eternalist in scope and psychoneurotic in emphasis. See Leon Pinsker, *Auto-Emancipation*, trans. D. S. Blondheim (New York: Maccabaean, 1906), 3, 4. It should be clear that I am using "Judeophobia" differently from Pinsker.
60. Richard Levy, *Antisemitism in the Modern World: An Anthology of Texts* (Lexington: D. C. Heath, 1991), 4.
61. Todd M. Endelman, "Comparative Perspectives on Modern Anti-Semitism in the West," in *History and Hate: The Dimensions of Anti-Semitism*, ed. David Berger (New York: Jewish Publication Society, 1986), 95–114, quote from 105.
62. Levy, *Antisemitism*, 3.
63. "The Negro is a phobogenic object, a stimulus to anxiety." Frantz Fanon, *Black Skin White Masks*, trans. Charles Lam Markmann (New York: Grove, 1967 [1952]), 151.
64. Bryan Cheyette, *Construction of "the Jew" in English Literature and Society: Racial Representations, 1875–1945* (Cambridge: Cambridge University Press, 1993), 8.
65. Zygmunt Bauman, *Life in Fragments: Essays in Postmodern Morality* (Oxford: Blackwell, 1995), 207.
66. The Tunisian Franco-Jewish writer Albert Memmi coined the term "heterophobia" as more expansive than "racism" or "anti-Semitism," since historically these have focused on biological differences rather than cultural, social, or other differences. In doing so, he suggests, "instead of speaking of anti-Semitism, which is manifestly imprecise, one might employ the term *Judeophobia*, which clearly signifies both fear and hostility toward Jews. The same can be said for *Negrophobia* and *Arabophobia*." He also encourages using "ethnophobia" for the exclusion of whole groups as preferable to "xenophobia" since the latter tends to refer only to foreigners. See Albert Memmi, *Racism*, trans. Steve Martinot (Minneapolis: University of Minnesota Press, 2000 [original French ed., 1982]), 117–21, quote from 119.
67. Bauman here reworks and reevaluates the categories developed by Taguieff in *The Force of Prejudice*, especially chapter 1.
68. Bauman, *Life in Fragments*, 208. For a similar explanation, see A. B. Yehoshua, "An Attempt to Identify the Root Cause of Antisemitism," *Azure* (Spring 2008), http://azure.org.il/include/print.php?id=18. See also the parallels in Vladimir Jankélévitch's work discussed in Jonathan Judaken, "Vladimir Jankélévitch at the *Colloques des intellectuels juifs de langue française*," in *Vladimir Jankélévitch and the Question of Forgiveness*, ed. Alan Udoff (Lanham, MD: Lexington, 2013), 3–26.
69. See Sarah Hammerschlag, *The Figural Jew: Politics and Identity in Postwar French Thought* (Chicago: University of Chicago Press, 2010); Elizabeth Bellamy, *Affective Genealogies: Psychoanalysis, Postmodernism, and the "Jewish Question" After Auschwitz* (Lincoln: University of Nebraska Press, 1997); and Jonathan Judaken, *Jean-Paul Sartre and the Jewish Question:*

Anti-Antisemitism and the Politics of the French Intellectual (Lincoln: University of Nebraska Press, 2006), chap. 8.

70. For a different taxonomy of theories of anti-Semitism, see Theodor Adorno, "Research Project on Anti-Semitism," *Studies in Philosophy and Social Science* 9 (1941): 124-43, especially 125-26.

71. Martin Lockshin, "Sinat Yisrael (Hatred of Jews)," in *Key Concepts in the Study of Antisemitism*, ed. Sol Goldberg, Scott Ury, and Kalman Weiser (London: Palgrave Macmillan, 2021), 273-85.

72. Elaine Rose Glickman, *Haman and the Jews: A Portrait from Rabbinic Literature* (Jerusalem: Jason Aronson, 1999), xi. See also Barry Walfish, *Esther in Medieval Garb: Jewish Interpretations of the Book of Esther in the Middle Ages* (Albany: SUNY Press, 1993), 143-55.

73. While not particularly sensitive to the Jewish religious interpretation of this scenario, see Albert Lindemann's *Esau's Tears: Modern Anti-Semitism and the Rise of the Jews* (Cambridge: Cambridge University Press, 1997), 3-6.

74. As Léon Poliakov put it in the first work of his summa on the history of anti-Semitism, "From the first centuries, the various motifs of the original antagonism between Jews and Christians became interwoven, now in rivalries for proselytes, now in the effort to conciliate officialdom for its own advantage, or in the exigencies of theological thought; they are the nucleus of a strictly Christian anti-Semitism." See Léon Poliakov, *The History of Anti-Semitism*, vol. 1, *From the Time of Christ to the Court Jews*, trans. Richard Howard (London: Elek, 1965 [1955]), 21. On ambivalence, see Stephen Haynes, *Reluctant Witnesses: Jews in the Christian Imagination* (Louisville, KY: Westminster John Knox, 1995), 15-24, which gives an overview on the historiography. On Augustine, see Paula Fredriksen, *Augustine and the Jews: A Christian Defense of Jews and Judaism* (New York: Doubleday, 2008). On Chrysostom, see Robert L. Wilken, *John Chrysostom and the Jews: Rhetoric and Reality in the Late 4th Century* (Berkeley: University of California Press, 1983).

75. On the development of the construct of "the Jewish Question," see Jonathan Judaken, "Antisemitism and the Jewish Question," in *Cambridge History of Judaism*, vol. 8, *The Modern Period*, ed. Mitchell B. Hart and Tony Michels (Cambridge: Cambridge University Press, 2017), 559-88.

76. Walter Laqueur, *The Changing Face of Anti-Semitism: From Ancient Times to the Present Day* (Oxford: Oxford University Press, 2006), 24.

77. See Daniel Boyarin, "The Colonial Drag: Zionism, Gender, and Mimicry," in *The Rise of Heterosexuality and the Invention of the Jewish Man* (Berkeley: University of California Press, 1997), chap. 7, and Michael Stanislawski, *Zionism and the Fin de Siècle: Cosmopolitanism and Nationalism from Nordau to Jabotinsky* (Berkeley: University of California Press, 2001).

78. On Leon Pinsker, see Benzion Netanyahu, introduction to *Road to Freedom: Writings and Addresses by Leon Pinsker* (New York: Scopus, 1944); Shlomo Avineri, *The Making of Modern Zionism: The Intellectual Origins of the Jewish State* (New York: Basic Books, 1981), chap. 7. For a revised interpretation, see Dimitry Shumsky, "Leon Pinsker and 'Autoemancipation!': A Revaluation," *Jewish Social Studies* 18, no. 1 (Fall 2011): 33-62.

79. Pinsker, *Auto-Emancipation*, 6, 14.

80. Pinsker, *Auto-Emancipation*, 8.

81. Pinsker, *Auto-Emancipation*, 8.

82. I trace the historiography of the study of anti-Semitism in detail in Jonathan Judaken, "Historiography," in Goldberg, Ury, and Weiser, *Key Concepts in the Study of Antisemitism*, 25-38.
83. See Gavin Langmuir's genealogy in "Towards a Definition of Anti-Semitism," and George Frederickson, "Appendix: The Concept of Racism in Historical Discourse," in *Racism: A Short History*, 151-70.
84. Frederickson, *Racism*, 158-66, and Robert Bernasconi, "Where Is Xenophobia in the Fight Against Racism?," *Critical Philosophy of Race* 2, no. 1 (2014): 6-19.
85. Amy Allen, *The End of Progress: Decolonizing the Normative Foundations of Critical Theory* (New York: Columbia University Press, 2016), xi-xii, offers three different ways of understanding the notion of "critical theory": (1) narrowly construed as the German tradition of interdisciplinary studies affiliated with the Institute for Social Theory, also known as the Frankfurt School, and some of their U.S. representatives; (2) more widely defined as "any politically inflected form of cultural, social, or political theory that has critical, progressive, or emancipatory aims," including feminist, queer, race, and post- and decolonial theory; (3) the tradition in literary and cultural studies identified with French post-structuralism. I embrace the loose combination of these three strands to develop critical approaches to Judeophobia.
86. See David Norman Smith, "The Social Construction of Enemies: Jews and the Representation of Evil," *Sociological Theory* 14, no. 3 (November 1996): 203-40, 207. Several of these psychologists drew on the work of Sigmund Freud, whose approach is discussed in several chapters, but most extensively in a section of chapter 7.
87. For an analysis that highlights the inherent limits of anti-anti-Semitic theorizing, see Elad Lapidot, *Jews Out of the Question: A Critique of Anti-Anti-Semitism* (Albany: SUNY Press, 2020). Contra Lapidot, in this study I am interested in drawing out the resources, tools, and insights of the theorists that are my focus, even as I consider some of the lapses in their theorizing.

1. JEAN-PAUL SARTRE'S EXISTENTIALIST ANTIRACISM

1. In France, of the 76,000 Jews deported, only 2,500 returned from the concentration and death camps. See Michael R. Marrus and Robert O. Paxton, *Vichy France and the Jews* (Stanford: Stanford University Press, 1995 [1981]); Susan Zuccotti, *The Holocaust, the French and the Jews* (New York: Basic Books, 1993); Renée Poznanski, *Jews in France during World War II*, trans. Nathan Bracher (Hanover, NH: Brandeis University Press, 2001 [1994]).
2. Raymond Aron, *The Committed Observer: Interviews with Jean-Louis Mussika and Dominique Walton*, trans. James and Marie McIntosh (Chicago: Tegnery Gateway, 1983), 95-96.
3. Emmanuel Mounier, "Les juifs parlent aux nations," *Esprit*, September 1945, 458. François Azouvi, in *Le mythe du grand silence* (Paris: Fayard, 2012), shows that the Holocaust actually received a lot of attention in postwar France.
4. Wrote Sartre, "The newspapers devote whole columns to stories of prisoners of war and deportees. Do we say anything about the Jews? Do we give a thought to those who died in the gas chambers at Lublin? Not a word." He continues that the reason for this is "because we must not irritate the anti-Semites." Jean-Paul Sartre, *Anti-Semite and Jew*, trans. George J. Becker (New York: Schocken, 1948 [1946]), 71; Jean-Paul Sartre, *Réflexions sur la question juive* (Paris: Gallimard, 1954 [1946]), 86. Despite the specificity of this

reference to Majdanek and the death camps, Enzo Traverso expresses outrage that Sartre does not place "the genocide at the center of his reflections" (73). See Enzo Traverso, "The Blindness of the Intellectuals: Historicizing Sartre's *Anti-Semite and Jew*," *October* 87 (Winter 1999): 73–88. But this was not Sartre's focus. Maurice Samuels, *The Right to Difference: French Universalism and the Jews* (Chicago: University of Chicago Press, 2016), 143, in contrast, argues, "For Sartre, then, the goal of *Réflexions* was to break the silence surrounding Jewish suffering and to provide French Jews with a new sense of security, a new self-confidence" (143).

5. Samuels, *The Right to Difference*, 144.

6. It is important to note that *Anti-Semite and Jew* was and is more than only a theory of anti-Semitism. One way of reading my book, *Jean-Paul Sartre and the Jewish Question* (as Samuel Moyn suggested in his review in the *American Historical Review*) is that it is an examination of the *Réflexions* in a series of intersecting contexts: (1) the influence of Sartre's first reflections on Jews and Judaism in the polarized and viciously anti-Semitic 1930s when the attraction of fascism was strong for many; (2) his writings on Jews and Judaism in the Vichy period, living under the Nazi jackboot, and in the midst of the Final Solution; (3) his postwar writings that helped to shape the national consensus around the mythological, antifascist, shield-and-sword image of France; (4) his interventions into the Arab-Israeli conflict, which began with his *Réflexions*, that laid the axioms of his lifelong support of the State of Israel, even if this also meant that he supported the Palestinian national liberation struggle; (5) his reexamination of the *Réflexions* in his interviews with Benny Lévy just before his death; and (6) as a crucial reference for discussions of the Jewish Question in postwar France—indeed, much of the debate on the Jewish Question, whether by Jews or non-Jews, Marxists or Christians, anticolonial radicals or anti-Semites can be mapped around how they interpreted Sartre's famous analysis of the *Anti-Semite and Jew*. See Jonathan Judaken, *Jean-Paul Sartre and the Jewish Question: Anti-Antisemitism and the Politics of the French Intellectual* (Lincoln: University of Nebraska Press, 2006), and Samuel Moyn, review in *The American Historical Review* 112, no. 4 (October 2007): 1270–71.

7. Emmanuel Levinas, "Existentialism and Anti-Semitism," trans. Denis Hollier and Rosalind Krauss, *October* 87 (Winter 1999): 28. This text by Levinas was his introduction to Sartre's lecture at the Alliance israélite universelle and published in the June 1947 issue of *Les Cahiers de l'alliance*, the journal of the organization.

8. Bernard-Henri Lévy discusses how Sartre's existentialism provides central axioms that are a "counter-fire" (300) to racism. See Lévy, *Sartre: The Philosopher of the Twentieth Century*, trans. Andrew Brown (Cambridge: Polity, 2003), 299–301.

9. Sartre, *Anti-Semite and Jew*, 153; Sartre, *Réflexions*, 185.

10. See Ralph Schor, *L'Antisémitisme en France dans l'entre-deux-guerres: Prélude à Vichy* (Paris: Éditions Complexe, 2005 [1992]), and Pierre Birnbaum, *Anti-Semitism in France: A Political History from Léon Blum to the Present* (Oxford: Blackwell, 1992).

11. Cited in Robert Soucy, "Functional Hating: French Fascist Demonology between the Wars," *Contemporary French Civilization* 23, no. 2 (Summer/Fall 1999): 158–76, quote on 158.

12. See Eugen Weber, *Action Française: Royalism and Reaction in Twentieth-Century France* (Stanford: Stanford University Press, 1962); Sandrine Sanos, *The Aesthetics of Hate: Far-Right Intellectuals, Antisemitism, and Gender in 1930s France* (Stanford: Stanford University Press, 2013), 49–55.

13. Sartre published the "Portrait de l'antisémite" in *Les Temps Modernes* in December 1945 in the third issue of the journal. The entire text was first published by Paul Morihien in November 1946. Quickly established as a classic, new editions were published by Gallimard in 1954, 1961, and 1986. See Michel Rybalka, "Publication and Reception of *Anti-Semite and Jew*," October 87 (Winter 1999): 167.
14. Jean-Paul Sartre, *Being and Nothingness: A Phenomenological Essay on Ontology*, trans. Hazel Barnes (New York: Washington Square, 1956), 675.
15. Sartre, *Being and Nothingness*, 677.
16. Sartre's focus is not on the "redemptive anti-Semitism" (Saul Friedlander) that underpinned Nazism, but rather on the anti-Semitism at work in Vichy France's approach to the Jewish Question, which was more akin to most other governments in the same period.
17. Sartre, *Anti-Semite and Jew*, 67; Sartre, *Réflexions*, 81
18. Sartre, *Anti-Semite and Jew*, 13; Sartre, *Réflexions*, 14.
19. Sartre, *Anti-Semite and Jew*, 21; Sartre, *Réflexions*, 24.
20. Sartre, *Anti-Semite and Jew*, 19; Sartre, *Réflexions*, 21.
21. Sartre, *Anti-Semite and Jew*, 54; Sartre, *Réflexions*, 64.
22. This is not the place to treat Heidegger's own volkish anti-Semitism. I discuss this in detail in Jonathan Judaken, "Heidegger's Shadow: Levinas, Arendt, and the Magician from Messkirch," in *The Routledge Companion to Philosophy of Race*, ed. Linda Alcoff, Luvell E. Anderson, and Paul Taylor (New York: Routledge, 2017), 61–74.
23. Martin Heidegger, "What Is Metaphysics?," in *Existentialism from Dostoevsky to Sartre*, ed. Walter Kaufmann (New York: Meridian, 1975), 248. In *The Courage to Be*, Paul Tillich amplified and elucidated the distinction Heidegger had drawn between anxiety and fear.
24. Martin Heidegger, *Being and Time*, trans. John Macquarrie and Edward Robinson (New York: Harper and Row, 1962), 179–82.
25. This is one of Sartre's famous formulations in *Existentialism Is a Humanism*, trans. Carol Macomber (New Haven, CT: Yale University Press, 2007), 29.
26. Simone de Beauvoir, *The Ethics of Ambiguity*, trans. Bernard Frechtman (New York: Philosophical Library, 1948), 42.
27. Beauvoir, *Ethics*, 44.
28. Aimé Césaire, *Discourse on Colonialism*, trans. Joan Pinkham (New York: Monthly Review Press, 1972 [1955]), 42.
29. On this theme in existentialism, specifically in the work of Heidegger, see Sarah Bakewell, *At the Existentialist Café: Freedom, Being, and Apricot Cocktails* (New York: Other, 2016), 78–79.
30. Beauvoir, *Ethics*, 46.
31. Beauvoir, *Ethics*, 47.
32. Beauvoir, *Ethics*, 49.
33. Beauvoir, *Ethics*, 56.
34. Jean-Paul Sartre, "Drieu la Rochelle ou la haine de soi," *Les Lettres françaises*, April 1943, and Jean-Paul Sartre, "Qu'est-ce qu'un collaborateur?" reprinted in *Situations III* (Paris: Gallimard, 1949).
35. See Robert Soucy, *French Fascism: The Second Wave, 1933–1939* (New Haven, CT: Yale University Press, 1995), 204–79.
36. Beauvoir, *Ethics*, 57.

37. Beauvoir, *Ethics*, 56.
38. Beauvoir, *Ethics*, 58.
39. Beauvoir, *Ethics*, 60.
40. Beauvoir, *Ethics*, 59. She also says this adventurism characterized the communists in 1945.
41. Beauvoir, *Ethics*, 61.
42. Beauvoir, *Ethics*, 63.
43. Beauvoir, *Ethics*, 62.
44. Sartre, *Anti-Semite and Jew*, 55; Sartre, *Réflexions*, 65.
45. Sartre, *Anti-Semite and Jew*, 56; Sartre, *Réflexions*, 67.
46. Sartre, *Anti-Semite and Jew*, 57; Sartre, *Réflexions*, 67.
47. Samuels, *The Right to Difference*, 153.
48. Sartre, *Anti-Semite and Jew*, 57; Sartre, *Réflexions*, 68.
49. Sartre, *Anti-Semite and Jew*, 57; Sartre, *Réflexions*, 68.
50. On this period, see Judaken, *Jean-Paul Sartre and the Jewish Question*, chap. 5. Works in which Sartre does address anti-Semitism in this period were primarily fictional, including *Le Scénario Freud*, ed. J.-B. Pontalis (Paris: Gallimard, 1984) and *Les Séquestrés d'Altona* (Paris: Gallimard, 1960).
51. Cited in M. Watteau, "Situation raciales et condition de l'homme dans l'oeuvre de Jean-Paul Sartre," *Présence africaine* 2 (January 1948): 2.
52. See Jonathan Judaken, "Sartre on Racism: From Existential Phenomenology to Globalization and 'the New Racism," in *Race After Sartre: Antiracism, Africana Existentialism, Postcolonialism*, ed. Jonathan Judaken (Albany: SUNY Press, 2008), 23–53.
53. Simone de Beauvoir, *The Blood of Others*, trans. Yvonne Moyse and Roger Senhouse (London: Penguin, 1964 [1945]).
54. Karl Jaspers, *The Question of German Guilt*, trans. E. B. Ashton (New York: Fordham, 2000 [1947]), 26.
55. See Jean-Paul Sartre, "You Are Wonderful," in *Colonialism and Neo-Colonialism*, trans. Azzedine Haddour, Steve Brewer, and Terry McWilliams (London: Routledge, 2001 [1964]), 60: "False naiveté, flight, bad faith, solitude, silence, a complicity at once rejected and accepted, that is what we called in 1945, collective responsibility."
56. Sartre, *Existentialism Is a Humanism*, 23.
57. Jean-Paul Sartre, "Orphée noir," preface to Léopold Sédar Senghor, *Anthologie de la nouvelle poésie nègre et malgache de langue française* (Paris: Presses Universitaires de France, 1977); translated by John MacCombie, "Black Orpheus," *The Massachusetts Review*, Autumn 1964–65, 13–52.
58. For Sartre's reiteration of anti-Jewish stereotypes, see Judaken, *Jean-Paul Sartre and the Jewish Question*, chap. 4.
59. Stuart Zane Charmé, *Vulgarity and Authenticity: Dimensions of Otherness in the World of Jean-Paul Sartre* (Amherst: University of Massachusetts Press, 1991), 202.
60. Several critics have accused Sartre of reiterating a notion of an essential Black character. See, for example, Francis A. Joppa, "Sartre et les milieux intellectuels de l'Afrique noire," *Présence francophone*, no. 25 (1989): 7–28, 21, and Christopher L. Miller, "Theories of Africans: The Question of Literary Anthropology," in *"Race," Writing and Difference*, ed. Henry Louis Gates Jr. (Chicago: University of Chicago Press, 1986). Henry Louis

Gates, Jr. thus stipulates in "Talkin' That Talk," *Critical Inquiry* 13, no. 1 (Autumn 1986): 203–10, 207, "Sartre's fantasies of 'the being' of 'the' African in *Black Orpheus* are racialist, as is his consideration of Richard Wright's 'split' audience in *What Is Literature?*"

61. Sartre, "Black Orpheus," 14; Sartre, "Orphée noir," x.
62. Sartre, "Black Orpheus," 31; Sartre, "Orphée noir," xxv.
63. Sartre, "Black Orpheus," 46; Sartre, "Orphée noir," xxxviii.
64. Robert Bernasconi, "Situating Frantz Fanon's Account of Black Experience," in *Situating Existentialism: Key Texts in Context*, ed. Jonathan Judaken and Robert Bernasconi (New York: Columbia University Press, 2012), 336–59.
65. Frantz Fanon, *Black Skin, White Masks*, trans. Charles Lam Markmann (New York: Grove, 1967), 122.
66. Fanon, *Black Skin, White Masks*, 115.
67. Abiola Irele, "A Defence of Negritude: Apropos of *Black Orpheus* by Jean-Paul Sartre," *Transition* 13 (March–April, 1964): 9.
68. V. Y. Mudimbé, *Invention of Africa: Gnosis, Philosophy, and the Order of Knowledge* (Bloomington: Indiana University Press, 1988), 85.
69. Kelly Oliver, "Alienation and Its Double; or the Secretion of Race," in *Race and Racism in Continental Philosophy*, ed. Robert Bernasconi with Sybol Cook (Bloomington: Indiana University Press, 2003), 176–95.
70. On Sartre's role in the French-Algerian war, see James Le Sueur, *Uncivil War: Intellectuals and Identity Politics During the Decolonization of Algeria* (Philadelphia: University of Pennsylvania Press, 2001).
71. On Memmi's biography and the development of his oeuvre, see Jonathan Judaken, introduction to *The Albert Memmi Reader*, ed. Jonathan Judaken and Michael Lejman (Lincoln: University of Nebraska Press, 2020), xv–xliv.
72. Lia Brozgal, *Against Autobiography: Albert Memmi and the Production of Theory* (Lincoln: University of Nebraska Press, 2013), 142.
73. Jean-Paul Sartre, introduction to *The Colonizer and the Colonized*, by Albert Memmi (Boston: Beacon, 1965), xxv.
74. Jean-Paul Sartre, "Colonialism Is a System," in *Colonialism and Neocolonialism*, trans. Azzedine Haddour, Steve Brewer, and Terry McWilliams (London: Routledge, 2001 [1964]), 30–47.
75. Sartre, introduction to *The Colonizer and the Colonized*, xxiv.
76. Sartre, "Colonialism Is a System," 44.
77. Sartre, "Colonialism Is a System," 47.
78. Jean-Paul Sartre, *Critique de la raison dialectique* (Paris: Gallimard, 1960), 726–38 and 797–814; translated by Alan Sheridan-Smith, *Critique of Dialectical Reason*: vol. 1, *Theory of Practical Ensembles* (London: Verso, 1976), 642–54 and 716–34.
79. Martin Jay, "From Totality to Totalization: Sartre," in *Marxism and Totality: The Adventures of a Concept from Lukacs to Habermas* (Berkeley: University of California Press, 1984), 351.
80. William McBride, *Sartre's Political Theory* (Bloomington: Indiana University Press, 1991), 136.
81. Sartre, *Critique of Dialectical Reason*, 721.
82. Sartre, *Critique of Dialectical Reason*, 652.

83. Sartre, *Critique of Dialectical Reason*, 720.
84. Sartre, *Critique of Dialectical Reason*, 720.
85. Tony Judt's critique of Sartre for failing to speak out about communist Judeophobia is consequently unfounded. See *Past Imperfect: French Intellectuals, 1944–1956* (Berkeley: University of California Press, 1992), 184–86.
86. Jean-Paul Sartre, *Critique of Dialectical Reason*, vol. 2, ed. Arlette Elkaim-Sartre, trans. Quintin Hoare (London: Verso, 2006), 265, 271.
87. Sartre, *Critique of Dialectical Reason*, 2:269, 270.
88. David Myers, "Can There Be a Principled Anti-Zionism: On the Nexus Between Anti-Historicism and Anti-Zionism in Modern Jewish Thought," in *Anti-Semitism and Anti-Zionism in Historical Perspective: Convergence and Divergence*, ed. Jeffrey Herf (New York: Routledge, 2007), 20–38.
89. The text was published in *Christianisme social* 74, nos. 11-12 (1966): 623–30 and as "Ceux qui sont aux prises avec l'apartheid doivent savoir qu'ils ne sont pas seuls," *Droit et liberté*, no. 257 (December 1966): 8–9. My citations are to this text. Extracts were also cited in the short article by Jean Geoffroy, "Sartre et l'apartheid," *Le Nouvel observateur*, November 16-22, 1966, 6.
90. Jacques Derrida, "Racism's Last Word," in Gates, *"Race," Writing and Difference*, 329–38.
91. Jean-Paul Sartre, "Les Pays capitalistes et leur colonies intérieures" *Tricontinental*, 1970, reprinted as "Le Tiers-monde commence en banlieue," in *Situations VIII* (Paris: Gallimard, 1972), 305.
92. Sartre, "Les Pays capitalistes," 302.
93. Michel Contat and Michel Rybalka, supplement to *Ecrits de Sartre*, *Le Magazine littéraire*, nos. 55-56 (Summer 1971). Cited in Noureddine Lamouchi, *Jean-Paul Sartre et le tiers monde: Rhétorique d'un discours anticolonialiste* (Paris: L'Harmattan, 1996), 170.
94. Jean-Paul Sartre, "France and a Matter of Racism," *New York Times*, March 11, 1973.
95. Sartre, *Anti-Semite and Jew*, 139; Sartre, *Réflexions*, 169.
96. Albert Memmi, *The Liberation of the Jew* (New York: Orion, 1966).
97. See Judaken, *Jean-Paul Sartre and the Jewish Question*, 187–88.
98. On this point, see Menachem Brinker, "Sartre et Israël (1939-1980): 'Drôle de position,'" *Sillages*, no. 3 (October 1980): 83–87, 84.
99. Sartre, "Jean-Paul Sartre et les problèmes de notre temps: Interview recueillie par Simha Flapan," *Cahiers Bernard Lazare*, no. 4 (April 1966): 4–9.
100. Jean-François Lyotard, *The Differend: Phrases in Dispute*, trans. Georges Van Den Abbeele (Minneapolis: University of Minnesota Press, 1988), xiii. For Lyotard's conception of the postmodern intellectual as one who bears witness to the differend, see Jonathan Judaken, "Bearing Witness to the *Différend*: Jean-François Lyotard, the Postmodern Intellectual and 'the Jews,'" *Studies in Contemporary Jewry: An Annual*, vol. 16, *Jews and Gender: The Challenge to Hierarchy*, ed. Jonathan Frankel (New York: Oxford University Press, 2000), 245–64.
101. Lyotard, *The Differend*, xi.
102. Lyotard, *The Differend*, xi.
103. Michel Foucault, "Truth and Power," in *Power/Knowledge: Selected Interviews and Other Writings 1972–1977*, ed. Colin Gordon (New York: Pantheon, 1980), 126–33, and Michel Foucault, "Intellectuals and Power," in *Language, Counter-Memory, Practice: Selected Essays*

and Interviews, ed. Donald F. Bouchard (New York: Cornell University Press, 1977), 205-17.

104. Jean-Paul Sartre, "Discours de Sartre à l'ambassade d'Israël pour l'acceptation de son diplôme de docteur honoris causa de l'Université hébraïque de Jérusalem 7 novembre 1976," in *Mardi chez Sartre: Un hébreu à Paris, 1967–1980*, ed. Ely Ben-Gal (Paris: Flammarion, 1992), 313-14, 313.

105. *Le Monde*, October 17-18, 1976. See Éric Marty, *Radical French Thought and the Return of the "Jewish Question"* (Bloomington: Indiana University Press, 2015), chap. 5.

106. Josie Fanon, "À propos de Franz Fanon, Sartre, le racisme et les Arabes," *El Moudjahid*, June 10, 1967, 6. Cited in Lamouchi, *Jean-Paul Sartre et le tiers monde*, 157-58.

107. Edward Said, "Diary," *London Review of Books*, June 1, 2000, 42-43.

108. See also Yoav Di-Capua, *No Exit: Arab Existentialism, Jean-Paul Sartre and Decolonization* (Chicago: University of Chicago Press, 2018), which recounts this story in detail.

109. Jean-Paul Sartre, "À-propos de Munich," *La Cause du peuple—J'Accuse*, October 15, 1972, reprinted in Yaïr Auron, *Les juifs d'extrême gauche en Mai 68: Une génération révolutionnaire marquée par la Shoah*, trans. Katherine Werchowski (Paris: Albin Michel, 1998), 236-38.

110. See Ronald Santoni, *Sartre on Violence: Curiously Ambivalent* (University Park: Penn State University Press, 2003).

2. THE FRANKFURT SCHOOL AND THE ANTI-SEMITIC QUESTION

1. The Frankfurt School's approach to anti-Semitism, given the number of interlaced texts in which they developed their arguments, is vast. This chapter attempts to synthesize their theoretical contributions to understanding the problem, but it does so in a necessarily abridged form since whole works now treat the topic from different angles. See Lars Rensmann, *The Politics of Unreason: The Frankfurt School and Antisemitism* (Albany: SUNY Press, 2017), which assesses their theoretical approach and its significance for social and political theory; Jack Jacobs, *The Frankfurt School, Jewish Lives and Antisemitism* (Cambridge: Cambridge University Press, 2015), which focuses on the links between biography and theory and the impact on their understanding of anti-Semitism and Israel; Eva-Maria Ziega, *Antisemitismus und Gesellschaftstheorie: Die Frankfurter Schule im amerikanischen Exil* (Frankfurt: Suhrkamp, 2009), and Mark P. Worrell, *Dialectic of Solidarity: Labor, Antisemitism, and the Frankfurt School* (Boston: Brill, 2008) each concentrate on the Frankfurt School's research project among American laborers.

2. On the "spearhead theory of anti-Semitism," see Joseph W. Bendersky, "Dissension in the Face of the Holocaust: The 1941 American Debate Over Antisemitism," *Holocaust and Genocide Studies* 24, no. 1 (Spring 2010): 85-116.

3. Edward Said, *Culture and Imperialism* (New York: Vintage, 1993), 278. Cited in Amy Allen, *The End of Progress: Decolonizing the Normative Foundations of Critical Theory* (New York: Columbia University Press, 2016), 1. See also Robert J. C. Young, *White Mythologies*, 2nd ed. (New York: Routledge, 2004), 39-40.

4. Espen Hammer, *Adorno and the Political* (London: Routledge, 2006), 5. See also Nigel Gibson and Andrew Rubin, "Introduction: Adorno and the Autonomous Intellectual," in *Adorno: A Critical Reader* (Oxford: Blackwell, 2002). Cited in Allen, *The End of Progress*.

2. The Frankfurt School and the Anti-Semitic Question

5. Thomas McCarthy, *Race, Empire and the Idea of Human Development* (Cambridge: Cambridge University Press, 2009), 1.
6. Allen, *The End of Progress*, xii. See also Namita Goswami, "The Mother of All Posts: Postcolonial Melancholia in the Age of Global Warming," *Critical Philosophy of Race* 1, no. 1 (2013): 105-20.
7. On American racism, Thomas Wheatland notes in *The Frankfurt School in Exile* (Minneapolis: University of Minnesota Press, 2009): "Instead of unabashedly maintaining the integrity and Eurocentrism of its early theoretical plans, the Institute reframed both itself and the project within an American context" (235). On the Frankfurt School's approach to Israel, see Jacobs, *The Frankfurt School*, 111-48.
8. Albert Memmi makes the case in "The Colonized Jew," in *Jews and Arabs*, trans. Eleanor Levieux (Chicago: J. Philip O'Hara, 1975), 38-45. For a more developed argument, see Ethan B. Katz, Lisa Moses Leff, and Maud S. Mandel, eds., *Colonialism and the Jews* (Bloomington: Indiana University Press, 2017).
9. Martin Jay, *The Dialectical Imagination* (Boston: Little, Brown, 1973), xv, indicates that the notion of "the Frankfurt School" only appeared after the Institut was reestablished when members returned to Frankfurt in the 1950s after their years in exile. I follow Jay in using the German spelling to distinguish the Institut from other institutes and referring to it as coterminous with the Frankfurt School. See also Rolf Wiggershaus, *The Frankfurt School: Its History, Theories, and Political Significance*, trans. Michael Robertson (Cambridge, MA: MIT Press, 2007), 1.
10. On the origins of the Frankfurt School, see Jack Jacobs, "Max Horkheimer's 'Die Juden und Europa' Appears," in *Yale Companion to Jewish Writing and Thought in German Culture: 1096–1996*, ed. Sander Gilman and Jack Zipes (New Haven, CT: Yale University Press, 1997), 571, and Ehrhard Bahr, "The Antisemitism Studies of the Frankfurt School: The Failure of Critical Theory," in *Foundations of the Frankfurt School of Social Research*, ed. Judith Marcus and Zoltán Tar (New Brunswick, NJ: Transaction Books, 1984), 311. See also, Jacobs, *The Frankfurt School*, 2. Karl Korsch and György Lukács were the two central figures who laid the groundwork for Western Marxism in the 1920s. See Martin Jay, *Marxism and Totality: The Adventures of a Concept from Lukács to Habermas* (Berkeley: University of California Press, 1984), 1-149.
11. Martin Jay, "Urban Flights: The Institut of Social Research between Frankfurt and New York," in *Force Fields: Between Intellectual History and Cultural Critique* (New York: Routledge, 1993), 20.
12. This sketch of the Institut in their cultural context is totally indebted to Martin Jay's discussion in "The Institut of Social Research between Frankfurt and New York" and his *The Dialectical Imagination*. On the irony of the "New Objectivity" style for a group of thinkers concerned precisely with rethinking the objectivity of all positivisms and the relationship between objectivity and subjectivity in nonidentitarian terms, see Jay, *The Dialectical Imagination*, 10.
13. Martin Jay, "The Free Jewish School Is Founded in Frankfurt am Main Under the Leadership of Franz Rosenzweig," in Gilman and Zipes, *Yale Companion to Jewish Writing and Thought in German Culture, 1096–1996*, 395-400, and Nahum N. Glatzer, "The Frankfurt Lehrhaus," *Leo Baeck Institute Yearbook* 1 (1956): 105-22.
14. Jay, *The Dialectical Imagination*, 133. Jay paraphrases Pollock in this quotation.

15. Jay, *The Dialectical Imagination*, 32.
16. Martin Jay, "The Jews and the Frankfurt School: Critical Theory's Analysis of Anti-semitism," *New German Critique*, no. 19 (Winter 1980): 137-49, 139.
17. Max Horkheimer, "Sociological Background of the Psychoanalytic Approach," in *Anti-semitism: A Social Disease*, ed. Ernst Simmel (New York: International Universities Press, 1946), 1.
18. Jacobs, *The Frankfurt School*, 9-10, which draws on the work of Zvi Rosen, *Max Horkheimer* (Munich: C.H. Beck, 1995), and John Abromeit, *Max Horkheimer and the Foundations of the Frankfurt School* (Cambridge: Cambridge University Press, 2011).
19. Max Horkheimer, "The Jews and Europe," in *Critical Theory and Society: A Reader*, ed. Stephen Eric Bronner and Douglas MacKay Kellner (New York: Routledge, 1989), 77-94.
20. The insights of Horkheimer's analysis include his discussion of the role of advertising in fascist ideology (79); the role of trade unions and the welfare state as agents of social integration (80); the provocative suggestion that there are links between fascism and Christian missionizing (81); the reduction from Kant onward of ethics to the categorical imperative of duty (85)—this is a relatively straightforward Hegelian critique of Kant, but in this context it anticipates not only the section on Kant in the *Dialectic of Enlightenment*, but also some of Hannah Arendt's analysis of Eichmann in *Eichmann in Jerusalem: A Report on the Banality of Evil* (New York: Penguin, 1963); the suggestion that the *volksgemeinschaft* was strongly shaped by the ideology of 1914 (87); the suggestion that a bureaucratic, instrumental rationality that colonizes the lifeworld has come to inform decisions of life and death (88); and, akin to Sartre, the critique of the abstract humanism of bourgeois liberalism (93).
21. On this point, see Enzo Traverso, *The Jews and Germany: From the "Judeo-German Symbiosis" to the Memory of Auschwitz*, trans. Daniel Weissbort (Lincoln: University of Nebraska Press, 1995), 124.
22. Gerhard Scholem to Walter Benjamin, November 6-8, 1938, in *The Correspondence of Walter Benjamin and Gershom Scholem, 1932–1940* (New York: Schocken, 1989), 223. Cited in Jacobs, *The Frankfurt School*, 51.
23. Horkheimer, "The Jews and Europe," 78 and 82.
24. On socialist and Marxist responses to anti-Semitism, see George Lichtheim, "Socialism and the Jews," *Dissent*, July-August 1968, 314-42; Robert Wistrich, *Socialism and the Jews: The Dilemmas of Assimilation in Germany and Austria-Hungary* (London: Associated University Presses, 1982); Enzo Traverso, *The Marxists and the Jewish Question: The History of a Debate (1843–1943)*, trans. Bernard Gibbons (Atlantic Highlands, NJ: Humanities Press, 1990), and Jack Jacobs, *On Socialists and "the Jewish Question" after Marx* (New York: New York University Press, 1992).
25. Horkheimer, "The Jews and Europe," 90.
26. On this see, Steven Aschheim, *Brothers and Strangers: The East European Jew in German and German Jewish Consciousness, 1800–1923* (Madison: University of Wisconsin Press, 1982).
27. Horkheimer, "The Jews and Europe," 90-91.
28. Max Horkheimer, *Dawn & Decline: Notes, 1926–1931 and 1950–1969*, trans. Michael Shaw (New York: The Seabury Press, 1978), 42-43.

29. Jay, "The Jews and the Frankfurt School," 138n6. Jay also reports that apparently Horkheimer had not wanted to title the essay "Die Juden und Europa," since only the last ten pages deal with this issue, but according to Gershom Scholem, *Walter Benjamin, Die Geschichte einer Freudschaft* (Frankfurt: Suhrkamp Verlag, 2016), 278, he was persuaded to call it this by Adorno.
30. Jacobs, *The Frankfurt School*, 47.
31. Wiggershaus, *The Frankfurt School*, 275. See also, Jacobs, "Max Horkheimer's 'Die Juden und Europa' Appears," 573.
32. Theodor Adorno, "Research Project on Anti-Semitism," *Studies in Philosophy and Social Science* 9 (1941): 124–43.
33. Wheatland, *The Frankfurt School in Exile*, 229.
34. I develop this argument in more detail in Jonathan Judaken, "Blindness and Insight: The Conceptual Jew in Arendt and Adorno's Post-Holocaust Reflections on the Anti-semitic Question," in *Arendt and Adorno: Political and Philosophical Investigations*, ed. Lars Rensmann and Samir Gendesha (Stanford: Stanford University Press, 2012), 173–95.
35. Wiggershaus, *The Frankfurt School*, 276–77.
36. Max Horkheimer, preface to Adorno et al., *The Authoritarian Personality* (New York:: Harper & Row, 1950), xi.
37. Ernst Simmel, introduction to *Anti-Semitism: A Social Disease*, ed. Ernst Simmel (New York: International Universities Press, 1946).
38. Simmel, *Anti-Semitism: A Social Disease*, xxv.
39. Else Frenkel-Brunswik and R. Nevitt Sanford, "The Anti-Semitic Personality: A Research Report," in Simmel, *Anti-Semitism: A Social Disease*, 96–124.
40. Max Horkheimer, "Sociological Background of the Psychoanalytic Approach," in Simmel, *Anti-Semitism: A Social Disease*, 2–6.
41. Theodor Adorno, "Anti-Semitism and Fascist Propaganda," in Simmel, *Anti-Semitism: A Social Disease*, 126–27.
42. Adorno, "Anti-Semitism and Fascist Propaganda," 129.
43. Adorno, "Anti-Semitism and Fascist Propaganda," 132–33.
44. Adorno, "Anti-Semitism and Fascist Propaganda," 137.
45. As Wheatland, in *The Frankfurt School in Exile*, notes on 240–41, all historians of the Frankfurt School agree that the Studies in Prejudice series marked a shift from the prewar work of the Institut, but they differ in their explanations. He discusses the differences between Martin Jay's *Dialectical Imagination* that argues that the Frankfurt School became more comfortable with empirical approaches during their American sojourn; Rolf Wiggershaus's *The Frankfurt School*, who suggests that practical need led them to focus on anti-Semitism and that empirical work was a complement to their theoretical work; Helmut Dubiel, *Theory and Politics: Studies in the Development of Critical Theory*, trans. Benjamin Gregg (Cambridge, MA: MIT Press, 1985), who segregates the empirical and theoretical work; Lewis Cosier, *Refugee Scholars in America: Their Impact and Their Experiences* (New Haven, CT: Yale University Press, 1984) who suggests that they became reconciled with their bourgeois upbringing; and Peter Uwe Hohendahl, *Prismatic Thought: Theodor W. Adorno* (Lincoln: University of Nebraska Press, 1995), and Zoltan Tar, *The Frankfurt School: The Critical Theories of Max Horkheimer and Theodor W. Adorno* (New York: Wiley, 1977), who saw this as a significant departure from the socioeconomic analysis of

social phenomena toward social psychology. My own view is akin to Wiggershaus's view, with the caveat that Adorno, especially, remained cautious and progressively more critical of the reductive tendency within empirical work.

46. For a careful overview of how this unfolded between 1941 and the return of Horkheimer, Adorno, and Pollock to Frankfurt, see Wheatland, *The Frankfurt School in Exile*, 227-63.
47. On Neumann's relationship to the Frankfurt School, see Wiggershaus, *The Frankfurt School*, 223-29.
48. On Neumann's revision of the proposal and meeting at the AJC, see Jacobs, *The Frankfurt School*, 67-68. Franz Neumann, *Behemoth: The Structure and Practice of National Socialism, 1933-1944* (Chicago: Ivan R. Dee, 2009 [1942, 1944]).
49. Wiggershaus, *The Frankfurt School*, 228.
50. Peter Hayes, introduction to Neumann, *Behemoth*, xiii-xiv.
51. Hayes, introduction, xiv.
52. Neumann, *Behemoth*, 104.
53. Neumann, *Behemoth*, 107, 109.
54. Neumann, *Behemoth*, 110.
55. Neumann, *Behemoth*, 121.
56. Neumann, *Behemoth*, 122.
57. Neumann, *Behemoth*, 123.
58. Neumann, *Behemoth*, 125, 127.
59. Neumann, *Behemoth*, 125.
60. Neumann, *Behemoth*, 550-52.
61. Jacobs, *The Frankfurt School*, 67. See also Bendersky, "Dissension in the Face of the Holocaust," 109.
62. Max Horkheimer and Samuel Flowerman, foreword to Adorno et al., *The Authoritarian Personality*, vi-vii.
63. The two other works were Bruno Bettelheim and Morris Janowitz, *Dynamics of Prejudice: A Psychological and Sociological Study of Veterans* (New York: Harper, 1950), and Nathan W. Ackerman and Marie Jahoda, *Anti-Semitism and Emotional Disorder: A Psychoanalytic Interpretation* (New York: Harper, 1950).
64. See Peter Pulzer, "Third Thoughts on German and Austrian Antisemitism," *Journal of Modern Jewish Studies* 4, no. 2 (July 2005): 137-78, 138.
65. Samuel Flowerman, introduction to Paul Massing, *Rehearsal for Destruction: A Study of Political Anti-Semitism in Imperial Germany* (New York: Howard Fertig, 1967 [1949]), ix.
66. Massing, *Rehearsal*, xii.
67. Massing, *Rehearsal*, xii
68. Martin Luther Thomas was yet another of the American fascist-style demagogues of the Christian Right on the radio in the 1930s. Theodor W. Adorno, *The Psychological Technique of Martin Luther Thomas' Radio Addresses* (Stanford: Stanford University Press, 2000).
69. Leo Löwethal and Norbert Guterman, *Prophets of Deceit: A Study of the Techniques of the American Agitator* (New York: Harper, 1949), 140.
70. Löwenthal and Guterman, *Prophets of Deceit*, 15.
71. Löwenthal and Guterman, *Prophets of Deceit*, 49.

72. Löwenthal and Guterman, *Prophets of Deceit*, 88.
73. Löwenthal and Guterman, *Prophets of Deceit*, 112.
74. Horkheimer, preface to *The Authoritarian Personality*, xi.
75. Peter E. Gordon, "The Authoritarian Personality Revisited: Reading Adorno in the Age of Trump," boundary2, June 15, 2016, https://www.boundary2.org/2016/06/peter-gordon-the-authoritarian-personality-revisited-reading-adorno-in-the-age-of-trump/.
76. Adorno et al., *The Authoritarian Personality*, 1.
77. Adorno et al., *The Authoritarian Personality*, 228.
78. See Lars Rensmann, *The Politics of Unreason*, 80n32. Rensmann notes that fewer than ten years after its publication, guides on the research it had generated were published; he references Richard Christie and Peggy Cook, "A Guide to the Published Literature Relating to 'The Authoritarian Personality' through 1956," *Journal of Psychology* 45 (1958): 171-27, and also Jos Meloen, "The Fortieth Anniversary of 'The Authoritarian Personality,'" *Politics and the Individual* 1 (1991): 119-27, who notes more than two thousand published studies on authoritarianism and even more references to the original work.
79. Gordon, "The Authoritarian Personality Revisited." Gordon draws upon not only some of Adorno's comments within *The Authoritarian Personality*, which are my focus as well, but also his unpublished essay "Remarks on The Authoritarian Personality" and on Theodor Adorno's 1951 essay, "Freudian Theory and the Pattern of Fascist Propaganda," published in *Psychoanalysis and the Social Sciences* and later included in *The Essential Frankfurt School Reader*, ed. Andrew Arato and Eike Gebhardt (New York: Continuum, 1982), 118-37.
80. Horkheimer, preface to *The Authoritarian Personality*, xii.
81. Adorno et al., *The Authoritarian Personality*, 744.
82. On the confirmation bias within the study, along with other critiques raised by scholars, see Gordon, "The Authoritarian Personality Revisited."
83. Adorno et al., *The Authoritarian Personality*, 747.
84. Adorno et al., *The Authoritarian Personality*, 608.
85. Adorno et al., *The Authoritarian Personality*, 617.
86. Adorno et al., *The Authoritarian Personality*, 622-23.
87. Adorno et al., *The Authoritarian Personality*, 638.
88. Gunzelin Schmid Noerr, "The Position of 'Dialectic of Enlightenment' in the Development of Critical Theory," editor's afterword in *Dialectic of Enlightenment*, trans. Edmund Jephcott (Stanford: Stanford University Press, 2002), 217.
89. Max Horkheimer and Theodor Adorno, "Preface to the New Edition," in *Dialectic of Enlightenment* (Stanford: Stanford University Press, 1969), xi.
90. There are two English editions and I prefer different locutions in each: Max Horkheimer and Theodor W. Adorno, *Dialectic of Enlightenment*, trans. John Cumming (New York: Continuum, 2000). Citations to this edition are cited as *Dialectic of Enlightenment* (Continuum); Horkheimer and Adorno, *Dialectic of Enlightenment: Philosophical Fragments*, trans. Edmund Jephcott (Stanford: Stanford University Press, 2002). This edition, edited by Gunzelin Schmid Noerr, is the new scholarly standard edition in English, not least because Noerr includes notes that offer the alternative versions of the text from the

different German editions. Citations to this edition are cited as *Dialectic of Enlightenment* (Stanford).
91. Rensmann, *The Politics of Unreason*, 275. For the publishing history, see Jacobs, *The Frankfurt School*.
92. Martin Jay, *Force Fields*, 2.
93. Horkheimer and Adorno, *Dialectic of Enlightenment* (Continuum), 168.
94. Horkheimer and Adorno, *Dialectic of Enlightenment* (Stanford), 138.
95. Horkheimer and Adorno, *Dialectic of Enlightenment* (Continuum), 169.
96. Horkheimer and Adorno, *Dialectic of Enlightenment* (Continuum), 170.
97. Horkheimer and Adorno, *Dialectic of Enlightenment* (Continuum), 171.
98. Horkheimer and Adorno, *Dialectic of Enlightenment* (Stanford), 139.
99. Horkheimer and Adorno, *Dialectic of Enlightenment* (Continuum), 170.
100. Horkheimer and Adorno, *Dialectic of Enlightenment* (Continuum), 171.
101. Horkheimer and Adorno, *Dialectic of Enlightenment* (Stanford), 140, based on the 1944 version, which was later amended. This citation is preferred here given the list of targets itemized.
102. Horkheimer and Adorno, *Dialectic of Enlightenment* (Continuum), 172.
103. Horkheimer and Adorno, *Dialectic of Enlightenment* (Continuum), 173.
104. Jacobs, *The Frankfurt School*, 76.
105. Horkheimer and Adorno, *Dialectic of Enlightenment* (Continuum), 174.
106. Horkheimer and Adorno, *Dialectic of Enlightenment* (Continuum), 179.
107. Horkheimer and Adorno, *Dialectic of Enlightenment* (Stanford), 144.
108. Max Weber, *Ancient Judaism*, trans. and ed. Hans H. Gerth and Don Martindale (Glencoe, IL: The Free Press, 1952). For some of the critical literature on Weber, see Ephraim Schmeuli, "The 'Pariah People' and Its 'Charismatic Leadership': A Reevaluation of Max Weber's 'Ancient Judaism,'" *American Academy of Jewish Research Proceedings* 36 (1968): 167-247; c); David Ellenson, "Max Weber on Judaism and the Jews," in *After Emancipation: Jewish Religious Responses to Modernity* (Cincinnati: Hebrew Union College Press, 2004), 80-95.
109. Horkheimer and Adorno, *Dialectic of Enlightenment* (Continuum), 178.
110. The quotation is from Simon Jarvis, *Adorno: A Critical Introduction* (New York: Routledge, 1998), 31. Cited in Jacobs, *The Frankfurt School*, 77. See also Anson Rabinbach, "The Cunning of Unreason: Mimesis and the Construction of Antisemitism in Horkheimer and Adorno's *Dialectic of Enlightenment*," in *In the Shadow of Catastrophe: German Intellectuals Between Apocalypse and Enlightenment* (Berkeley: University of California Press, 1997), 166-98.
111. Horkheimer and Adorno, *Dialectic of Enlightenment* (Continuum), 181.
112. Horkheimer and Adorno, *Dialectic of Enlightenment* (Continuum), 181.
113. Horkheimer and Adorno, *Dialectic of Enlightenment* (Continuum), 184-85.
114. Horkheimer and Adorno, *Dialectic of Enlightenment* (Continuum), 186.
115. Horkheimer and Adorno, *Dialectic of Enlightenment* (Continuum), 184.
116. Horkheimer and Adorno, *Dialectic of Enlightenment* (Continuum), 185.
117. Horkheimer and Adorno, *Dialectic of Enlightenment* (Stanford), 150.
118. Horkheimer and Adorno, *Dialectic of Enlightenment* (Continuum), 187.

119. Horkheimer and Adorno, *Dialectic of Enlightenment* (Stanford), 156.
120. See Horkheimer and Adorno, *Dialectic of Enlightenment* (Continuum), 191–93.
121. See Horkheimer and Adorno, *Dialectic of Enlightenment* (Continuum), 197.
122. Horkheimer and Adorno, *Dialectic of Enlightenment* (Stanford), 163.
123. Horkheimer and Adorno, *Dialectic of Enlightenment* (Stanford), 164.
124. Horkheimer and Adorno, *Dialectic of Enlightenment* (Stanford), 165.
125. Horkheimer and Adorno, *Dialectic of Enlightenment* (Stanford), 165.
126. See Horkheimer and Adorno, *Dialectic of Enlightenment* (Continuum), 186.
127. See Horkheimer and Adorno, *Dialectic of Enlightenment* (Continuum), 186.
128. Horkheimer and Adorno, *Dialectic of Enlightenment* (Continuum), 175.

3. HANNAH ARENDT, ANTI-SEMITISM, AND HER "STORY" OF HISTORY

1. Like so many other Jewish critics, Arendt objected in particular to Sartre's contention that the Jew was a product of the anti-Semitic gaze. See Hannah Arendt, *The Origins of Totalitarianism* (San Diego, CA: Harcourt Brace Jovanovich, 1973 [1951]), xv. All references are to this edition. For a more complicated appreciation of the overlaps between Arendt's and Sartre's analyses, see Richard J. Bernstein, *Hannah Arendt and the Jewish Question* (Cambridge, MA: MIT Press, 1996), 47–48 and 195–97n2. For other Jewish critics on Sartre, see Jonathan Judaken, *Jean-Paul Sartre and the Jewish Question: Anti-Antisemitism and the Politics of the French Intellectual* (Lincoln: University of Nebraska, 2006), chap. 8.
2. On Arendt's fractious relations with the Frankfurt School and specifically Adorno, see Elisabeth Young-Bruehl, *Hannah Arendt: For Love of the World* (New Haven, CT: Yale University Press, 1982), especially 166–68. On Arendt's rejection of psychological, especially psychoanalytic explanations, see Julia Schulze Wessel and Lars Rensmann, "The Paralysis of Judgment: Arendt and Adorno on Antisemitism and the Modern Condition," in *Arendt and Adorno: Political and Philosophical Investigations*, ed. Lars Rensmann and Samir Gandesha (Stanford: Stanford University Press, 2012), 330n12.
3. Michael Rothberg, *Multidirectional Memory: Remembering the Holocaust in the Age of Decolonization* (Stanford: Sanford University Press, 2009), and Bryan Cheyette, *Diasporas of the Mind: Jewish and Postcolonial Writing and the Nightmare of History* (New Haven, CT: Yale University Press, 2013), 8–9.
4. On the tradition of the "conscious pariah" see Hannah Arendt, "The Jew as Pariah: A Hidden Tradition," in *The Jew as Pariah: Jewish Identity and Politics in the Modern Age*, ed. Ron H. Feldman (New York: Grove, 1978), 67–90.
5. The concept of "dark times" was a key notion for Arendt. See David Luban, "Explaining Dark Times: Hannah Arendt's Theory of Theory," *Social Research* 50, no. 1 (Spring 1983): 214–48.
6. Most of the biographical information on Arendt is from Young-Bruehl, *Hannah Arendt*. Arendt uses the term "a-religious" to describe her family in her interview "'What Remains? The Language Remains': A Conversation with Günter Gaus," in *Essays in Understanding, 1930–1954*, ed. Jerome Kohn (New York: Harcourt Brace, 1994), 6.
7. On Heidegger's Jewish children, see Richard Wolin, *Heidegger's Children: Hannah Arendt, Karl Löwith, Hans Jonas, and Herbert Marcuse* (Princeton, NJ: Princeton University Press, 2001).

3. Hannah Arendt, Anti-Semitism, and Her "Story" of History   271

8. Arendt, "What Remains?," 12.
9. Hannah Arendt to Karl Jaspers, *Correspondence: 1926–1969*, trans. Robert and Rita Kimber (New York: Harcourt Brace Jovanovich, 1992), 197.
10. Hannah Arendt, "We Refugees," in Feldman, *The Jew as Pariah*, 55–66, 56.
11. Hannah Arendt, *Eichmann in Jerusalem: A Report on the Banality of Evil* (New York: Penguin, 1963).
12. For the historiography that follows, see especially Richard H. King and Dan Stone, introduction to *Hannah Arendt and the Uses of History: Imperialism, Nation, Race, and Genocide* (New York: Berghahn, 2007). On the split between an early and late phase in Arendt's work, see Richard H. King, "Endings and Beginnings: Politics in Arendt's Early Thought," *Political Theory* 12, no. 2 (May 1984): 235–51.
13. Feldman, *The Jew as Pariah*, which was later incorporated and supplemented by Hannah Arendt, *The Jewish Writings*, ed. Jerome Kohn and Ron H. Feldman (New York: Schocken, 2007); Young-Bruehl, *Hannah Arendt*. On how these works began to shift the reception of Arendt, see Leon Botstein, "The Jew as Pariah: Hannah Arendt's Political Philosophy," *Dialectical Anthropology* 8, nos. 1–2 (October 1983): 47–75.
14. Shiraz Dossa, "Human Status and Politics: Hannah Arendt on the Holocaust," *Canadian Journal of Political Science* 13 (1980): 309–23.
15. Arendt, *Origins*, 185n1. See Chinua Achebe, "An Image of Africa: Racism in Conrad's *Heart of Darkness*," in *Norton Critical Edition of Joseph Conrad's Heart of Darkness*, ed. Paul B. Armstrong, 4th ed. (New York: W. W. Norton, 2006), 336–49. For a nuanced interpretation that focuses on the representation of colonialism and racism in Conrad, see Brian W. Shaffer, "Joseph Conrad: *Heart of Darkness*," in *A Companion to Modernist Literature and Culture*, ed. David Bradshaw and Kevin J. H. Dettmar (Malden, MA: Blackwell, 2006), 314–23.
16. George Kateb, *Hannah Arendt: Politics, Conscience, Evil* (Oxford: Oxford University Press, 1983), 61–63.
17. Anne Norton, "Heart of Darkness: Africa and African Americans in the Writings of Hannah Arendt," in *Feminist Interpretations of Hannah Arendt*, ed. Bonnie Honig (University Park: Penn State University Press, 1995), 247–61.
18. Hannah Arendt, "Reflections on Little Rock," in *The Portable Hannah Arendt*, ed. Peter Baehr (New York: Penguin, 2000), 231–43. Originally published in *Dissent* 6, no. 1 (Winter 1959).
19. Hannah Arendt, "A Reply to Critics," in Baehr, *The Portable Hannah Arendt*, 243–46.
20. Hannah Pitkin, *The Attack of the Blob: Hannah Arendt's Concept of the Social* (Chicago: University of Chicago Press, 1993), 293.
21. Seyla Benhabib, *The Reluctant Modernism of Hannah Arendt* (Thousand Oaks, CA: Sage, 1999), 83.
22. See Judith Shklar, "Hannah Arendt as Pariah," *Partisan Review* 1, no. 50 (1983): 64–77; Martin Jay, *Permanent Exiles: Essays on the Intellectual Migration from Germany to America* (New York: Columbia University Press, 1986), 237–56; Dagmar Barnouw, *Visible Spaces: Hannah Arendt and the German-Jewish Experience* (Baltimore, MD: Johns Hopkins University Press, 1990); Jeffrey C. Isaac, *Arendt, Camus, and Modern Rebellion* (New Haven, CT: Yale University Press, 1992); Bernstein, *Hannah Arendt and the Jewish Question*; Steven E. Aschheim, ed., *Hannah Arendt in Jerusalem* (Berkeley: University of California Press, 2001).

23. See, for example, Paul Gilroy, *Between Camps: Nations, Cultures and the Allure of Race* (London: Routledge, 2000); Richard H. King, *Race, Culture, and the Intellectuals, 1940–1970* (Washington, DC: Woodrow Wilson, 2004), 96-119; King and Stone, *Hannah Arendt and the Uses of History*; Rothberg, *Multidirectional Memory*, 33-65; Cheyette, *Jewish and Postcolonial Writing*, 6-18, and Cheyette, "Postcolonialism and the Study of Anti-Semitism," *American Historical Review* 123, no. 4 (October 2018): 1234-45; and Kathryn T. Gines, *Hannah Arendt and the Negro Question* (Bloomington: Indiana University Press, 2014).
24. Ernest Gellner, "From Königsberg to Manhattan (or Hannah, Rahel, Martin and Elfriede or Thy Neighbour's *Gemeinschaft*)," in *Culture, Identity, and Politics* (Cambridge: Cambridge University Press, 1987), 75.
25. This was the title of *The Origins of Totalitarianism* when it was published in England.
26. Hannah Arendt, *Men in Dark Times* (New York: Harcourt, Brace and World, 1968), 33.
27. Hannah Arendt, *The Human Condition* (Chicago: University of Chicago Press, 1958), 184.
28. Lisa Disch, "More Truth than Fact: Storytelling as Critical Understanding in the Writings of Hannah Arendt," *Political Theory* 21 (November 1993): 665-94, 666. See also Luban, "Explaining Dark Times."
29. On the centrality of *Origins* to Arendt's political theory, see Margaret Canovan, *Hannah Arendt: A Reinterpretation of Her Political Thought* (Cambridge: Cambridge University Press, 1995).
30. See Canovan, *Hannah Arendt*, 28-29, for a list of the elements of totalitarianism: anti-Semitism, decay of the nation-state, racism, imperialism, and the alliance between capitalism and the mob. Canovan draws on a manuscript by Arendt to itemize these elements.
31. Hannah Arendt, "A Reply," to Eric Voegelin's review of *The Origins of Totalitarianism*, by Hannah Arendt, *Review of Politics* 15, no. 6 (January 1953): 70.
32. Arendt, "A Reply," 70.
33. Arendt, *Origins*, xiv.
34. Writes Arendt, an ideology "differs from a single opinion in that it claims to possess either the key to history, or the solution to all 'riddles of the universe,' or the intimate knowledge of the hidden universal laws which are supposed to rule nature and man." In short, ideologies are encompassing world views, shaped by overarching notions like race thinking for racists. See Arendt, *Origins*, 159.
35. Voegelin, review , 68-76, 84-85.
36. Arendt, "A Reply," 76-84, 78.
37. Disch, "More Truth than Fact," 676.
38. Arendt, "Reply," 80.
39. Arendt, "Reply," 83.
40. Hannah Arendt, "Understanding and Politics," in Kohn, *Essays in Understanding*, 319.
41. See Maurizio Passerin d'Entrèves, *The Political Philosophy of Hannah Arendt* (London: Routledge, 1994), 5, and Seyla Benhabib, "Hannah Arendt and the Redemptive Power of Narrative," *Social Research* 57, no. 1 (Spring 1990): 168-96, 189.
42. Passerin d' Entrèves, *Political Philosophy*, 31.
43. Elisabeth Young-Bruehl, "Hannah Arendt's Storytelling," *Social Research* 44, no. 1 (1977): 183-90, 184.

44. Arendt, *Men in Dark Times*, 20.
45. On this point, see Bernstein, *Hannah Arendt and the Jewish Question*, 51.
46. Arendt, *Origins*, vii.
47. Hannah Arendt, "The Concept of History: Ancient and Modern," in *Between Past and Future* (New York: Penguin, 1968), 89.
48. Luban, "Explaining Dark Times," 231.
49. Arendt, "Reply," 78.
50. Arendt, "Reply," 78.
51. Arendt, "The Concept of History," 49.
52. Arendt, "The Concept of History," 51.
53. Disch, "More Truth than Fact," 666. See Donna Haraway, "Situated Knowledges: The Science Question in Feminism and the Privilege of Partial Perspective," in *Simians, Cyborgs, and Women: The Reinvention of Nature* (New York: Routledge, 1991).
54. Arendt, "The Concept of History," 51.
55. Hannah Arendt, "The Gap Between Past and Future," in *Between Past and Future*, 12.
56. Arendt, "The Concept of History," 51.
57. Hannah Arendt, "Reply," 78: "If I describe these conditions without permitting my indignation to interfere, I have lifted this particular phenomenon out of its context in human society and have thereby robbed it of part of its nature, deprived it of one of its important inherent qualities."
58. See Steven Aschheim, "Hannah Arendt and the Modern Jewish Experience," *The Times Literary Supplement*, September 26, 2007.
59. Disch, "More Truth than Fact," 674. On this point, Disch develops Benhabib, "The Redemptive Power of Narrative," 186, who argues that in Arendt, "the language of narration must match the moral quality of the narrated object."
60. Arendt, "Reply," 79.
61. Arendt, "Reply," 79.
62. Arendt, *Origins*, xi, notes: "Antisemitism, a secular nineteenth-century ideology—which in name, though not in argument, was unknown before the 1870's—and religious Jew-hatred, inspired by the mutually hostile antagonism of two conflicting creeds, are obviously not the same; and even the extent to which the former derives its arguments and emotional appeal from the latter is open to question." Her tack is quite different in *Origins* from what she wrote in her draft, "Antisemitism," where she notes "modern anti-semitism is heir to medieval antecedents and thus to the ancient hatred of the Jews as well." See Arendt, "Antisemitism," in Kohn and Feldman, *The Jewish Writings*, 65. Writing post-Holocaust in *Origins*, Arendt wanted to avoid deducing the unprecedented from precedents, and this results in her emphasizing discontinuities. As we will see, she wants to explain what was different in totalitarian anti-Semitic ideology from what came before it.
63. Kathryn T. Gines has exposed how Arendt's failure to see the continuities between these phenomena leads to the shortcomings in Arendt's understanding of racism. See "Race Thinking and Racism in Hannah Arendt's *The Origins of Totalitarianism*," in King and Stone, *Hannah Arendt and the Uses of History*, 38–53.
64. Benhabib, "The Redemptive Power of Narrative," 182. Benhabib suggests that the unity of the *Origins* can be appreciated if it is read "as Arendt herself intended it to be read"

where "the elementary structure of totalitarianism is the hidden structure of the book" and suggests that this is best accomplished by beginning with the chapter on "Total Domination" because it is the concentration camps that reveal the basic elements of totalitarian domination, terror, and ideology (174). Benhabib's hermeneutic approach is to rearticulate the unity of Arendt's work by reconfiguring the elements of totalitarianism in a way that discloses not only the hidden structure of the work but Arendt's own hidden intentions. At least initially, I think it is important to highlight the novelty of Arendt's approach through an appreciation of a structure that preserves the fragmentary, nontotalizing unity of their elements.

65. See Luban, "Explaining Dark Times," 239.
66. Young-Bruehl, "Hannah Arendt's Storytelling," 184.
67. Luban, "Explaining Dark Times," 247.
68. Passerin d'Entrèves, *Political Philosophy*, 29.
69. In making this point, I differ with Robert Bernasconi's claim that Arendt is engaged in an effort to "buffer" Western culture and specifically philosophy from its complicity with anti-Semitism, racism, and genocide. See Robert Bernasconi, "When the Real Crime Began: Hannah Arendt's *The Origins of Totalitarianism* and the Dignity of the Western Philosophical Tradition," in King and Stone, *Hannah Arendt and the Uses of History*, 54–67.
70. Young-Bruehl, "Hannah Arendt's Storytelling," 188
71. Cited in Bernstein, *Hannah Arendt and the Jewish Question*, 172.
72. Ditch, "More Truth than Fact," 677.
73. Jean-François Lyotard, *Heidegger and "the jews,"* trans. Andreas Michel and Mark Roberts (Minneapolis: University of Minnesota Press, 1990).
74. Benhabib, "The Redemptive Power of Narrative," 180.
75. Benhabib, "The Redemptive Power of Narrative," 180.
76. Ditch, "More Truth than Fact," 667.
77. Ditch, "More Truth than Fact," 667.
78. Voegelin, review, 69.
79. Voegelin, review, 69.
80. Georgio Agamben, *Homo Sacer: Sovereign Power and Bare Life*, trans. Daniel Heller-Roazen (Stanford: Stanford University Press, 1998).
81. Voegelin, review, 71.
82. Arendt, *Origins*, viii.
83. Arendt provides an acute summation of the story that she presents in part 1: "Its analyses concern Jewish history in Central and Western Europe from the time of the court Jews to the Dreyfus Affair insofar as it was relevant to the birth of anti-Semitism and influenced by it. It deals with anti-Semitic movements that were still pretty solidly grounded in factual realities characteristic of Jewish-Gentile relations, that is, in the part Jews played in the development of the nation-state on one side and in their role in non-Jewish society on the other. The emergence of the first anti-Semitic parties in the 1870s and 1880s marks the moment when the limited, factual basis of interest conflict and demonstrable experience was transcended and that road opened which ended in the 'final solution.' From then on, in the era of imperialism, followed by the period of

totalitarian movements and governments, it is no longer possible to isolate the Jewish question or the anti-Semitic ideology from issues that are actually almost completely unrelated to the realities of modern Jewish history.... Anti-Semitism itself was now being used for ulterior purposes that, though their implementation finally claimed Jews as their chief victims, left all particular issues of both Jewish and anti-Jewish interest far behind" (xiv).

84. Arendt, *Origins*, 3.
85. Arendt, *Origins*, 5.
86. Arendt, *Origins*, 6.
87. Arendt, *Origins*, xii.
88. Arendt, "Antisemitism," 48.
89. Arendt, "Antisemitism," 55.
90. Arendt, "Antisemitism," 49.
91. Arendt, *Origins*, 7.
92. Arendt, *Origins*, 8.
93. For a different version of this argument, see Dan Cohn-Sherbok, *The Paradox of Anti-Semitism* (New York: Continuum, 2006). On the more sophisticated views of this paradox by Léon Poliakov and Jean-Paul Sartre, see Jonathan Judaken, "Homo Antisemiticus: Lessons and Legacies," *Holocaust and Genocide Studies* 23, no. 3 (Winter 2009): 461–77, 463–64.
94. Arendt states emphatically, "The notion of an unbroken continuity of persecutions, expulsions, and massacres from the end of the Roman Empire to the Middle Ages, the modern era, and down to our own time, frequently embellished by the idea that modern antisemitism is no more than a secularized version of popular medieval superstitions, is... fallacious" (*Origins*, xi). On Salo Baron's critique of "lachrymose" history, see Scott Ury, "'Inseparable Companions'? Anti-Semitism, Zionism and the Fate of 'the Jews,'" *American Historical Review* 123, no. 4 (October 2018): 1151–71, 1156–60.
95. Arendt, *Origins*, 9.
96. Arendt, *Origins*, 11.
97. Zygmunt Bauman, "Allosemitism," in Bryan Cheyette and Laura Marcus, eds., *Modernity, Culture, and "the Jew"* (Stanford: Stanford University Press, 1998), 153.
98. Arendt, *Origins*, 277.
99. Arendt, *Origins*, 296. For an elaboration on this theme, see Judith Butler and Gayatri Chakravorty Spivak, *Who Sings the Nation-State? Language, Politics, Belonging* (London: Seagull, 2007), 11–55.
100. Arendt, *Origins*, 289.
101. On the image of the "Rothschild Jew," see Julie Kalman, *Rethinking Antisemitism in Nineteenth-Century France* (Cambridge: Cambridge University Press, 2010), chap. 5.
102. Arendt, *Origins*, 12.
103. Bernstein, *Hannah Arendt and the Jewish Question*, 64.
104. Arendt, *Origins*, 73.
105. Arendt, *Origins*, 15.
106. See Julia Kristeva, *Hannah Arendt*, trans. Ross Guberman (New York: Columbia University Press, 2001), 128, 131.
107. Arendt, *Origins*, 66.

108. Hannah Arendt, *Rahel Varnhagen: The Life of a Jewish Woman*, rev. ed., trans. Richard and Clara Winston (New York: Harcourt Brace Jovanovich, 1974), and Arendt, "The Jew as Pariah."
109. Arendt, *Origins*, 57.
110. Arendt, *Origins*, 56.
111. Arendt, *Origins*, 60.
112. Alain Finkielkraut has written eloquently about these dilemmas in *The Imaginary Jew*, trans. Kevin O'Neill and David Suchoff (Lincoln: University of Nebraska Press, 1994).
113. Arendt, *Origins*, 65.
114. Steven Aschheim, *Scholem, Arendt, Klemperer: Intimate Chronicles in Turbulent Times* (Bloomington: Indiana University Press, 2001), 67.
115. Arendt, *Origins*, 66.
116. Arendt, *Rahel Varnhagen*, 224.
117. Arendt, *Origins*, 83.
118. I use the language of Julia Kristeva here because she has retold the story that Arendt recounts in "Between Vice and Crime" in her chapter "Hannah Arendt, Life Is a Narrative," in *Crisis of the European Subject*, trans. Susan Fairfield (New York: Other, 2000), 47–94.
119. Arendt, *Origins*, 87.
120. Kristeva, *Hannah Arendt*, 145.
121. Arendt, *Origins*, 87.
122. Arendt, *Origins*, 80. On the interconnections between homosexuality and Jewishness at the end of the nineteenth century, see Sander Gilman, *Freud, Race, and Gender* (Princeton, NJ: Princeton University Press, 1993); George L. Mosse, *The Image of Man: The Creation of Modern Masculinity* (Oxford: Oxford University Press, 1996), especially chap. 4; Daniel Boyarin, *Unheroic Conduct: The Rise of Heterosexuality and the Invention of the Jewish Man* (Berkeley: University of California Press, 1997); Daniel Boyarin, Daniel Itzkovitz, and Ann Pellegrini, eds., *Queer Theory and the Jewish Question* (New York: Columbia University Press, 2003), and Christopher E. Forth, *Masculinity in the Modern West: Gender, Civilization, and the Body* (Basingstoke: Palgrave, 2008).
123. Eve Kosovsky Sedgwick, *The Epistemology of the Closet* (Berkeley: University of California Press, 2008 [1990]). Sedgwick also compares the Jew to the homosexual, arguing for their differences. Sedgewick is wrong to emphasize the contrast, just as Arendt is wrong to emphasize their sameness, since surely there are overlaps and connections, parallels and similarities, even if these two groups are not identical in how they were treated at the end of the nineteenth century or in other periods.
124. Arendt, *Origins*, 82.
125. Arendt, *Origins*, 93.
126. Arendt already laid out this position in 1942 in her first publication in English, where she argued that "the Dreyfus affair in its entirety offers a foreshadowing of the twentieth century." See Hannah Arendt, "From the Dreyfus Affair to France Today," *Jewish Social Studies* 4, no. 3 (July 1942): 195–240, 200.
127. Hannah Arendt and Karl Jaspers, *Correspondence 1926–1969*, 55.
128. Bernstein, *Hannah Arendt and the Jewish Question*, 66–67.
129. Arendt, *Origins*, 157.

130. Arendt, *Origins*, 159.
131. Arendt, *Origins*, 198.
132. Arendt, *Origins*, 202.
133. Arendt, *Origins*, 229.
134. Arendt, *Origins*, 233.
135. Arendt, *Origins*, 424.
136. See Gines, *Hannah Arendt and the Negro Question*.
137. Shlomo Avineri, "Where Hannah Arendt Went Wrong," *Haaretz*, March 3, 2010.
138. Leon Wieseltier, "Understanding Anti-Semitism," *New Republic*, October 7, 1981, 29-32, 31-32.
139. Bernard Wasserstein, "Blame the Victim: Hannah Arendt Among the Nazis: The Historian and Her Sources," *Times Literary Supplement*, October 9, 2009, 13-15.
140. Peter Staudenmaier, "Hannah Arendt's Analysis of Antisemitism in *The Origins of Totalitarianism*: A Critical Appraisal," *Patterns of Prejudice* 4, no. 2 (2012): 154-79.
141. Arendt, *Origins*, 84.
142. Arendt, *Origins*, 20.
143. Arendt, *Origins*, 40.
144. Arendt, *Origins*, 20.
145. Pierre Birnbaum, *Anti-Semitism in France: A Political History from Leon Blum to the Present*, trans. Miriam Kochan (Oxford: Blackwell, 1992), 7. The subtitle of one of Avineri's sections summarizes the problem in Arendt's analysis—"No Poor Jews"—which entirely ignores "the fact that most of the Jews ... were neither court Jews nor financial advisors to princes, but rather small traders and shopkeepers."
146. On Arendt's relation to Marx on these points, see Ron Feldman, introduction to *The Jew as Pariah*, 40.
147. Arendt, *Origins*, 87.
148. Arendt, "Tradition and the Modern Age," 25.

4. THE SOCIOLOGY OF MODERN ANTI-SEMITISM FROM TALCOTT PARSONS TO ZYGMUNT BAUMAN

1. Zygmunt Bauman, *Modernity and the Holocaust* (New York: Cornell University Press, 1989), cover. As he puts in his introduction on "Sociology After the Holocaust": "*The Holocaust has more to say about the state of sociology than sociology in its present shape is able to add to our knowledge of the Holocaust*" (3), a position he proposes to correct.
2. Marcel Stoetzler, ed., *Antisemitism and the Constitution of Sociology* (Lincoln: University of Nebraska Press, 2014), and Chad Alan Goldberg, *Modernity and the Jews in Western Social Thought* (Chicago: University of Chicago Press, 2017).
3. On "cultural schemas" and supersessionism as a frame through which to understand Weber, Goldberg cites Paul DiMaggio, "Culture and Cognition," *Annual Review of Sociology* 23 (1997): 263-87: "Cultural schemas are 'mental structures'... which shape the way we attend to, interpret, remember, and respond emotionally to the information we encounter and possess." See Goldberg, *Modernity and the Jews*, 46.
4. Edward S. Parsons, *The Social Message of Jesus: A Course of Twelve Lessons* (New York: YWCA, 1910), 8. Parsons states that the Social Gospel was important to the origins of

sociology in the United States in Talcott Parsons, "On Building Social Systems Theory: A Personal History," in "The Making of Modern Science: Biographical Studies," special issue, *Daedalus* 99, no. 4, (Fall 1970): 826-81, 887n23.

5. Uta Gerhardt, *Talcott Parsons: An Intellectual Biography* (Cambridge: Cambridge University Press, 2002), 3.
6. For Bauman's biography, see Izabela Wagner, *Bauman: A Biography* (Cambridge: Polity, 2020).
7. Keith Tester, *The Social Thought of Zygmunt Bauman* (New York: Palgrave Macmillan, 2004), 1.
8. Janina Bauman, *A Dream of Belonging: My Years in Postwar Poland* (London: Virago, 1988), 45.
9. Bauman, *A Dream of Belonging*, 105.
10. James H. Satterwhite, "Polish Revisionism: Critical Thinking in Poland from 1953 to 1968," in *Zygmunt Bauman: Sage Masters in Modern Social Thought*, ed. Peter Beilharz, 4 vols. (London: Sage, 2002), 288-332.
11. Dennis Smith, *Zygmunt Bauman: Prophet of Postmodernity* (Cambridge: Polity, 1999), 40.
12. Bauman, *A Dream of Belonging*, 186.
13. Peter Beilharz, "Reading Zygmunt Bauman," in *The Bauman Reader*, ed. Peter Beilharz (Oxford: Basil Blackwell, 2001), 1.
14. See Ivan Strenski, *Durkheim and the Jews of France* (Chicago: University of Chicago Press, 1997), and Pierre Birnbaum, "Émile David Durkheim: The Memory of Masada," in *Geography of Hope: Exile, the Enlightenment, Disassimilation*, trans. Charlotte Mandell (Stanford, CA: Stanford University Press, 2008), 83-122. On the other key founding figures, see the essays in Stoetzler, *Antisemitism and the Constitution of Sociology*, and Goldberg, *Modernity and the Jews*.
15. Goldberg, "The American Tradition: The City and the Jews," in *Modernity and the Jews*, 76-103.
16. William B. Helmreich, "The Sociological Study of Anti-Semitism in the United States," in *Approaches to Anti-Semitism: Context and Curriculum*, ed. Michael Brown (New York: American Jewish Committee and the International Center for University Teaching of Jewish Civilization, 1994).
17. Birnbaum, *Geography of Hope*.
18. Marcel Stoetzler, "Introduction: The Theory of Society Talks Back to Its Travesty," in *Antisemitism and the Constitution of Sociology*, 12.
19. Stoetzler, "Introduction," 2-3.
20. Goldberg, *Modernity and the Jews*, 104.
21. Marcel Stoetzler, "Anti-Semitism, Capitalism and the Formation of Sociological Theory," *Patterns of Prejudice* 44, no. 2 (2010): 161-94. Citations are from 161 and 164.
22. Isacque Graeber and Steuart Henderson Britt, eds., *Jews in a Gentile World: The Problem of Anti-Semitism* (New York: Macmillan, 1942), v.
23. Joseph W. Bendersky, "Dissension in the Face of the Holocaust: The 1941 American Debate Over Antisemitism," *Holocaust and Genocide Studies* 24, no. 1 (Spring 2010): 85-116, 87.
24. Gustav Ichheiser, review in *The American Journal of Sociology* 48, no. 1 (June 1942): 129-32, 129, and Earle M. Rauber, review, *The Journal of Politics* 5, no. 3 (August, 1943): 320-21, 320.

25. Everett R. Clinchy, review in *Political Science Quarterly* 57, no. 4 (December 1942): 620–22, 621, and Robert E. Park, review in *American Sociological Review* 9, no. 6 (December 1944): 710–11, 711.
26. Franklin Folsom, *Days of Anger, Days of Hope: A Memoir of the League of American Writers, 1937–1942* (Niwot: University Press of Colorado, 1994), 290.
27. Letter from Parsons to Ben Halpern, June 26, 1942; Parsons papers, 15.2, box 17, Harvard University Archives. Cited in Uta Gerhardt, "Introduction: Talcott Parsons's Sociology of National Socialism," in Talcott Parsons, *Talcott Parsons on National Socialism*, ed. Uta Gerhardt (New York: Aldine de Gruyter, 1993), 21.
28. Letter from Graeber to Parsons, August 16, 1941; Parsons papers, 42.41, box 2, Harvard University Archives. Cited in Gerhardt, "Introduction," 21.
29. Relative to Parsons's oeuvre, there is only a small body of commentary on his writing from 1938 to 1945. These include Rainer Baum and Frank J. Lechner, "National Socialism: Toward an Action-Theoretical Interpretation," *Sociological Inquiry* 51 (1981): 281–305; Jeffrey C. Alexander, *The Modern Reconstruction of Classical Thought: Talcott Parsons* (Berkeley: University of California Press, 1983), 46–72; William Buxton, *Talcott Parsons and the Capitalist Nation-State* (Toronto: Toronto University Press, 1985), 97–116; Jens Kaalhauge Nielsen, "The Political Orientation of Talcott Parsons: The Second World War and Its Aftermath," in *Talcott Parsons: Theorist of Modernity*, ed. Roland Robertson and Bryan S. Turner (London: Sage, 1991), 217–33.

    But it is Uta Gerhardt that has most systematically interrogated the convergence of both Parsons's political and theoretical demarche and the only one to comment much on "The Sociology of Modern Anti-Semitism." In addition to Gerhardt, "Introduction," see Gerhardt, *Talcott Parsons: An Intellectual Biography*, chap. 2. She very usefully breaks down Parsons's intellectual biography in this period into five phases: "namely a pro-intervention stance prior to Pearl Harbor, an interest in issues of propaganda and power in the year 1942, a year of crisis in the Far Eastern and European theaters of operation, and a time when postwar democratization of the Axis countries, especially Germany, was pivotal prior to VE-Day. Last but not least, under the title of 'Beyond Victory,' I wish to highlight Parsons's contribution to re-education policy planning for Germany, as consultant to the Foreign Economic Administration Enemy branch between March and October 1945" (61).
30. Gerhardt, *Talcott Parsons on National Socialism*, 68.
31. Gerhardt, *Talcott Parsons: An Intellectual Biography*, 84.
32. Talcott Parsons, "Postscript to 'the Sociology of Modern Anti-Semitism,'" *Contemporary Jewry* 5 (1980): 31–38.
33. Gerhardt, *Talcott Parsons on National Socialism*, 149.
34. Parsons's "The Sociology of Modern Anti-Semitism" fits wholly into the *monumental* intellectual biography of Gerhardt. I mean this in two senses. First is the extraordinary reconstruction of Parsons's biographical and theoretical edifice undertaken by Gerhardt. She has painstakingly gone through the whole archive of his work—published and unpublished—and does so with a monumental mastery and attention to detail. Her task is to show that Parsons wrestled with a problem inherent to modern (liberal) democratic social systems: on the one hand, their capacity for integration, but on the other hand, their propensity toward anomie, which under the right circumstances can lead

280 4. The Sociology of Modern Anti-Semitism

toward authoritarianism or totalitarianism. But this commitment to preservation and veneration, what Friedrich Nietzsche named an "antiquarian" spirit, sits alongside another sense in which Gerhardt's work is monumental: as a narrative of someone or "something exemplary and worthy of emulation—at the expense of the *causes*" (Nietzsche, 59). What I hope to do is to suggest a critical turn necessary to a full appreciation of Parsons's contributions, one that I venture is perhaps at the heart of what Parsons himself came to see as the limits of his analysis and perhaps suggests why he did not publish it again, although this claim cannot be wholly substantiated. For the senses of antiquarian, monumental ,and critical history as I am using them, see Friedrich Nietzsche, "On the Uses and Disadvantage of History for Life." in *Untimely Meditations*, trans. R. J. Hollingdale (New York: Cambridge University Press, 1997).

35. Talcott Parsons, "The Sociology of Modern Anti-Semitism," in Graeber and Britt, *Jews in a Gentile World*, 121.

36. The itemization of the sociological processes of modernization listed here actually comes from "Some Sociological Aspects of the Fascist Movement" where Parsons develops some of the points he makes in "The Sociology of Modern Anti-Semitism" at greater length, focused less on anti-Semitism and more on fascism per se. See Parsons, *Talcott Parsons on National Socialism*, 203-18.

37. Talcott Parsons elucidated the concept of anomie in *The Structure of Social Action: A Study in Social Theory with Special Reference to a Group of Recent European Writers*, vol. 1 (New York: Free Press, 1968 [1937]), 376-390.

38. Parsons, *Talcott Parsons on National Socialism*, 204.

39. Parsons, "The Sociology of Modern Anti-Semitism," 114.

40. Parsons, "The Sociology of Modern Anti-Semitism," 102.

41. Gerhardt, *Talcott Parsons: An Intellectual Biography*, 85.

42. David Ellenson, "Max Weber on Judaism and the Jews," in *After Emancipation: Jewish Religious Responses to Modernity* (Cincinnati: Hebrew Union College Press, 2004), 80-95. This whole section on Weber and the Jews is thoroughly indebted to Ellenson.

43. Max Weber, *Ancient Judaism*, trans. and ed. Hans Gerth and Don Martindale (Glencoe, IL: Free Press, 1952), 3.

44. Max Weber, *The Sociology of Religion*, trans. Ephraim Fischoff (Boston: Beacon, 1963), 109.

45. Ephraim Schmueli, "The 'Pariah People' and Its 'Charismatic' Leadership: A Reevaluation of Max Weber's 'Ancient Judaism,'" *American Academy of Jewish Research Proceedings* 36 (1968): 167-247, 181.

46. Freddy Raphael, "Max Weber et le judaïsme antique," *Archives européennes de sociologie* 11, no. 2 (1970): 330.

47. Jay Holstein, "Max Weber and Biblical Scholarship," *Hebrew Union College Annual* 46 (1975): 159-79.

48. Gary A. Abraham, *Max Weber and the Jewish Question: A Study of the Social Outlook of His Sociology* (Urbana: University of Illinois Press, 1992).

49. Ellenson, *After Emancipation*, 94-95.

50. Parsons, *The Sociology of Religion*, lxii-lxvi.

51. Parsons, "The Sociology of Modern Anti-Semitism," 105-6.

52. Parsons, "The Sociology of Modern Anti-Semitism," 106.

53. On Sombart's influence on Weber's *Ancient Judaism*, see Y. Michal Bodemann, "Coldly Admiring the Jews: Werner Sombart and Classical German Sociology on Nationalism and Race," in Stoetzler, *Antisemitism and the Constitution of Sociology*, 128. On Sombart, see, as well, Herman Lebovics, *Social Conservatism and the Middle Classes in Germany, 1914–1939* (Princeton, NJ: Princeton University Press, 1969), 49–78; Fritz K. Ringer, *The Decline of the German Mandarins: The German Academic Community, 1890–1933* (Cambridge, MA: Harvard University Press, 1969); Arthur Mitzman, *Sociology and Estrangement: Three Sociologists of Imperial Germany* (New York: Knopf, 1973), 133–264; Paul Mendes-Flohr, "Werner Sombart's 'The Jews and Modern Capitalism': An Analysis of Its Ideological Premises," *Leo Baeck Yearbook* 21 (1976): 97–107; Jerry Z. Muller, *Capitalism and the Jews* (Princeton, NJ: Princeton University Press), 56–61. On Sombart's arguments about the Jews, see Toni Oelsner, "The Place of the Jews in Economic History as Viewed by German Scholars," *Leo Baeck Yearbook* 7 (1962): 183–212; Werner Eugen Mosse, "Judaism, Jews and Capitalism: Weber, Sombart and Beyond," *Leo Baeck Yearbook* 24 (1979): 3–15; Goldberg, *Modernity and the Jews*, 60–66.
54. Parsons, "The Sociology of Modern Anti-Semitism," 107.
55. Parsons, "The Sociology of Modern Anti-Semitism," 112.
56. Parsons, "The Sociology of Modern Anti-Semitism," 121. As further evidence that all the positions advanced by Parsons in "The Sociology of Modern Anti-Semitism" were held by him, including his strong call for Jewish assimilation, see Bendersky, "Dissension in the Face of the Holocaust," especially 91–92 and 102. This important article wonderfully reconstructs the argument about anti-Semitism in the United States on the basis of an archival reconstruction of the debate generated by the pamphlet on anti-Semitism, *Nazi Poison*, produced by the Council for Democracy under the leadership of Carl Friedrich at Harvard, which included Parsons and Graeber as contributors, among a number of illustrious figures at the time, including the Frankfurt School. Parsons's contributions to the discussion amounted to restating what he argued in "The Sociology of Modern Anti-Semitism" so Graeber did not alter his basic premises at all.
57. Cited in Bendersky, "Dissension in the Face of the Holocaust," 93.
58. Isacque Graeber, "An Examination of Theories of Race Prejudice," *Social Research* 20, no. 3 (Autumn 1953): 267–81, 271 and citation 274.
59. Parsons, "The Sociology of Modern Anti-Semitism," 108.
60. Parsons, *Talcott Parsons on National Socialism*, 81.
61. Parsons, *Talcott Parsons on National Socialism*, 82.
62. Parsons, *Talcott Parsons on National Socialism*, 95.
63. See, for example, Talcott Parsons and Kenneth B. Clark, eds., *The Negro American* (Boston: Beacon, 1966).
64. Nielsen, "The Political Orientation of Talcott Parsons," 229. Nielsen's article is part of a growing body of revisionist scholarship on Parsons, attempting to correct the impression of his work created in the 1960s and 1970s, under the inspiration of the New Left, that Parsons was a conservative, reactionary, Cold Warrior who legitimated bourgeois Western values. In addition to Uta Gerhardt, this literature includes J. Loubser, et al., *Explorations in General Theory in Social Science*, 2 vols. (New York: Free Press, 1976); J. C. Alexander, *Theoretical Logic in Sociology*, vol. 4, *The Modern Reconstruction of Classical Thought: Talcott Parsons* (Berkeley: University of California Press, 1983); Jurgen Habermas,

The Theory of Communicative Action, vol. 2, *Lifeworld and System: A Critique of Functionalist Reason*, trans. Thomas McCarthy (Boston: Beacon, 1987); and the work of Brian Turner. My own effort is a postrevisionist account that seeks to understand Parsons's stance on anti-Semitism, and by extension, Nazi fascism and totalitarianism in terms of their own immanent limits, taking as a stepping off point Parsons's liberalism.

65. Parsons, *Talcott Parsons on National Socialism*, 211.
66. Parsons, *Talcott Parsons on National Socialism*, 212. For an excellent overview of these links, see Paul Hanebrink, *A Specter Haunting Europe: The Myth of Judeo-Bolshevism* (Cambridge, MA: Harvard University Press, 2018).
67. Parsons, *Talcott Parsons on National Socialism*, 237-38. See R. C. Baum and F. J. Lechner, "National Socialism: Towards an Action-Theoretical Interpretation," *Sociological Inquiry* 51, nos. 3-4 (1981): 284.
68. Parsons, *Talcott Parsons on National Socialism*, 214.
69. See Edward Y. Hartshorne, Jr., *The German Universities and National Socialism* (London: Allen and Unwin, 1937). On Hartshorne's influence on Parsons, see Gerhardt, *Talcott Parsons: An Intellectual Biography*.
70. For a fuller summation of Parsons's analysis of the historical and sociological elements that gave rise to National Socialism, see Baum and Lechner, "National Socialism."
71. Parsons, *Talcott Parsons on National Socialism*, 284.
72. Talcott Parsons, "Full Citizenship for the Negro American? A Sociological Problem," in *The Negro American*, 709-54, 720-21.
73. Parsons, "Full Citizenship," 718.
74. Parsons, "Full Citizenship," 733.
75. Parsons, "Full Citizenship," 721.
76. Parsons, "Full Citizenship," 715.
77. Parsons, "Full Citizenship," 750.
78. Zygmunt Bauman, "Allosemitism: Premodern, Modern, Postmodern," in *Modernity, Culture, and "the Jew,"* ed. Bryan Cheyette and Laura Marcus (Cambridge: Polity, 1998), 143.
79. Jean-Paul Sartre, *Anti-Semite and Jew* (New York: Schocken, 1948 [1946]), 57. For an overview on Sartre, see Jonathan Judaken, *Jean-Paul Sartre and the Jewish Question: Anti-Anti-Semitism and the Politics of the French Intellectual* (Lincoln: University of Nebraska Press, 2006).
80. It is important to remember that chapters 2 and 3 of Bauman's *Modernity and the Holocaust* are focused squarely on theorizing the role of anti-Semitism as a by-product of the modernization process.
81. Since Bauman's locus of analysis is modernity, there is, of course, more to his postmodern turn than only his theorization of social differences and deviance, although this is a useful turning point around which to understand Bauman's contributions to sociological theory. The best starting point for understanding Bauman's work as a whole is the work of Peter Beilharz, specifically his chapter, "Zygmunt Bauman," in *The Wiley-Blackwell Companion to Major Social Theorists*, ed. George Ritzer and Jeffrey Stepnisky (Malden, MA: Wiley Blackwell, 2011), 155-74. See also Barry Smart, "Zygmunt Bauman," in *Profiles in Contemporary Social Theory*, ed. Anthony Elliott and Bryan Turner (London: Sage, 2001), 327-37. For monographic treatments, see Dennis Smith, *Zygmunt Bauman: Prophet of*

Postmodernity, Key Contemporary Thinkers (Cambridge: Polity, 2000), and Peter Beilharz, *Zygmunt Bauman: Dialectic of Modernity* (London: Sage, 2000).
82. Zygmunt Bauman, "The *Telos* Interview," in Beilharz, *The Bauman Reader*, 21.
83. For a comprehensive overview on how Bauman has theorized "strangers," see Niclas Månsson, "Bauman on Strangers—Unwanted Peculiarities," in *The Sociology of Zygmunt Bauman*, ed. Michael Hviid Jacobsen and Poul Poder (Burlington, VT: Ashgate, 2008), 155-71.
84. Zygmunt Bauman, *Modernity and the Holocaust* (Ithaca, NY: Cornell University Press, 2000 [1989]).
85. Zygmunt Bauman, *Modernity and Ambivalence* (Oxford: Polity, 1991).
86. There are many critical takes on Bauman's *Modernity and the Holocaust*. Among those that specifically address the link between the modernity of the Holocaust and Bauman's understanding of modern anti-Semitism, see Ivar Oxaal, "Sociology, History and the Holocaust," *Theory, Culture and Society* 8, no. 1 (1991): 153-56. Oxaal maintains that Bauman underemphasizes the role of premodern Judeophobia, but Oxaal misunderstands the historical development of Judeophobia as Bauman itemizes it, as do several other critics. John Rex, "Race, Ethnicity and the Rational Organization of Evil," *Theory, Culture and Society* 8, no. 1 (1991): 167-74, critiques Bauman for the same thing, but less acutely. A more solid overview of Bauman's project is offered by Jack Zipes's review essay, "The Holocaust, Modernity, and Tough Jews," *Telos*, no. 86 (1990): 70-83. A full-scale and quite devastating critique of Bauman's views on the Holocaust is undertaken by Yehuda Bauer, *Rethinking the Holocaust* (New Haven, CT: Yale University Press, 2001), 68-92, but does not focus on his views on anti-Semitism.
87. A version of this section was later reprinted as "Allosemitism: Premodern, Modern, Postmodern", in Cheyette and Marcus, *Modernity, Culture, and "the Jew,"* 143-56.
88. For a comprehensive overview of Bauman's understanding of "ambivalence," see Matthias Junge, "Bauman on Ambivalence—Fully Acknowledging the Ambiguity of Ambivalence," in Jacobson and Poder, *The Sociology of Zygmunt Bauman*, 41-56.
89. Zygmunt Bauman, *Life in Fragments: Essays in Postmodern Morality* (Oxford: Blackwell, 1995), 207.
90. Bauman, *Life in Fragments*, 207.
91. Bauman here reworks and reevaluates the categories developed by Pierre-André Taguieff's *La Force du préjuge: Essai sur le racisme et ses doubles* (Paris: La Découverte, 1988), translated by Hassan Melehy as *The Force of Prejudice: On Racism and Its Doubles* (Minneapolis: University of Minnesota, 2001), especially chap. 1, "Heterophobia, Heterophilia: The Definitional Antinomy." Taguieff was in turn developing a new set of categories coined by Albert Memmi. See Memmi's *Racism*, trans. Steve Martinet (Minneapolis: University of Minnesota Press, 2000), 117-21.
92. Bauman, *Life in Fragments*, 181.
93. Bauman, *Life in Fragments*, 208.
94. Bauman, *Life in Fragments*, 181.
95. Bauman, *Modernity and Ambivalence*, chap. 2.
96. Bauman, *Modernity and Ambivalence*, 78. See also Zygmunt Bauman, "Strangers are Dangers... Are They, Indeed?," in *44 Letters from the Liquid Modern World* (Cambridge: Polity, 2010), 157-62.

97. Bauman, *Life in Fragments*, 181.
98. Bauman, *Life in Fragments*, 209.
99. Bauman, *Life in Fragments*, 209.
100. Bauman, *Life in Fragments*, 209.
101. Bauman, *Modernity and the Holocaust*, 38.
102. Bauman, *Modernity and the Holocaust*, 39.
103. Bauman, *Life in Fragments*, 213.
104. Bauman, *Life in Fragments*, 211.
105. Bauman, *Modernity and the Holocaust*, 39.
106. Bauman, *Life in Fragments*, 212.
107. Bauman, *Life in Fragments*, 179.
108. Bauman, *Life in Fragments*, 180.
109. Bauman, *Life in Fragments*, 166.
110. Bauman, *Life in Fragments*, 167.
111. For a critique of Bauman's views on the modernity of genocide, see Michael Freeman, "Genocide, Civilization and Modernity," *British Journal of Sociology* 46, no. 2 (1995): 207–23.
112. Bauman, *Life in Fragments*, 193.
113. Bauman, *Life in Fragments*, 195.
114. On the garden metaphor, see Michael Crozier, "*Inter Putatorem et Vastitatem*: The Ambivalences of the Garden Metaphor in Modernity," in *The Left in Search of a Center*, ed. Michael Crozier and P. Murphy (Urbana, IL: University of Illinois Press, 1996), 64–85.
115. Bauman, *Life in Fragments*, 199.
116. Bauman, *Life in Fragments*, 200.
117. This formulation is Helen Fein's developed in *Accounting for Genocide: National Responses and Jewish Victimization during the Holocaust* (New York: Free Press, 1979), 33.
118. Sophia Marshman, "Bauman on Genocide—Modernity and Mass Murder: From Classification to Annihilation?," in Jacobsen and Poder, *The Sociology of Zygmunt Bauman*, 81.
119. Bauman, *Modernity and the Holocaust*, 92.
120. Bauman, *Modernity and the Holocaust*, 70.
121. Bauman, *Modernity and the Holocaust*, 70.
122. Bauman, *Modernity and the Holocaust*, 72.
123. For an assessment of Bauman's views on the role of bureaucracy in nullifying moral responsibility, see Arne Johan Vetlesen, "Why Does Proximity Make a Moral Difference? Coming to Terms with a Lesson Learned from the Holocaust," *Praxis International* 12, no. 4 (1993): 371–86. For an overview of Bauman's views on ethics, see Alan Latham, "An Ethics of the Ephemeral? The Possibilities and Impossibilities of Zygmunt Bauman's Ethics: A Review of Some Recent Books by Zygmunt Bauman," *Ethics, Place and Environment* 2, no. 2 (1999): 275–85.
124. Bauman, *Modernity and the Holocaust*, 21. Bauman itemizes three conditions whereby moral inhibitions against violent atrocities are nullified: when the violence is *authorized*, actions are *routinized*, and the victims are *dehumanized*.
125. Bauman, *Life in Fragments*, 5.
126. On this point, in addition to Cheyette and Marcus, *Modernity, Culture, and "the Jew,"* see Lawrence Kritzman, ed., *Auschwitz and After: Race, Culture, and "the Jewish Question" in*

France (London: Routledge, 1995); Elizabeth J. Bellamy, *Affective Genealogies: Psychoanalysis, Postmodernism, and the "Jewish Question" after Auschwitz* (Lincoln: University of Nebraska Press, 1997); and Sarah Hammerschlag, *The Figural Jew: Politics and Identity in Postwar French Thought* (Chicago: University of Chicago Press, 2010).

127. Bauman, *Life in Fragments*, 190.
128. Bauman, *Life in Fragments*, 190.
129. Some key works on the new Judeophobia include, Matti Bunzl, *Anti-Semitism and Islamophobia: Hatreds Old and New in Europe* (Chicago: Prickly Paradigm, 2007); Jeffrey Herf, ed., *Anti-Semitism and Anti-Zionism in Historical Perspective: Convergence and Divergence* (New York: Routledge, 2007); Jonathan Judaken, "So What's New? Rethinking the 'New Anti-semitism' in a Global Age," *Patterns of Prejudice* 42, nos. 4–5 (Autumn 2008): 531–60; Pierre-André Taguieff, *Rising from the Muck: The New Anti-Semitism in Europe*, trans. Patrick Camiller (Chicago: Ivan R. Dee, 2004); and Robert Wistrich, *A Lethal Obsession: Anti-Semitism from Antiquity to the Global Jihad* (New York: Random House, 2010).
130. On the postmodern stranger, see Vince Marotta, "The Stranger and Social Theory," *Thesis Eleven*, no. 62 (2000): 121–34.
131. Månsson, "Bauman on Strangers," 164.

5. JEAN-FRANÇOIS LYOTARD, POSTMODERNISM, AND "THE JEWS"

1. In no way do I wish to suggest that all thinkers identified with postmodernism are "the same": sameness, homogeneity, and normalization are important sites of critique for postmodern thinkers and there are important differences between the various positions of Jacques Derrida, Michel Foucault, Gilles Deleuze, Julia Kristeva, Luce Irigaray, and other French poststructuralists often monolithically grouped together under the label "postmodernism." Therefore, Lyotard's work does not stand metonymically for this group of thinkers as a whole. Treating Lyotard in isolation does permit a more general understanding of the postmodern position, however, especially in relation to the Jewish Question, since he is the sole figure in this group to have elaborated a theory of the postmodern and his work constitutes one of the most extensive treatments of Jews and Judaism.
2. See Elisabeth de Fontenany, *Une tout autre histoire: Questions à Jean-François Lyotard* (Paris: Fayard, 2006).
3. Jean-François Lyotard, "Apostil on Narratives," in *The Postmodern Explained: Correspondence, 1982–1985*, trans. Julian Pefanis and Morgan Thomas et al. (Minneapolis: University of Minnesota Press, 1992 [1988]), 18, 19.
4. Jean-François Lyotard, *Peregrinations: Law, Form, Event* (New York: Columbia University Press, 1988), 1.
5. On *La Guerre des Algériens*, see Jane Hiddleston, "Lyotard's Algeria: Experiments in Theory," *Paragraph* 33, no. 1 (2010): 52–69.
6. Jean-François Lyotard, *La Phénoménologie* (Paris: Presses Universitaires de France, 1954); *Phenomenology*, trans. Brian Beakley (Albany, NY: SUNY Press, 1991).
7. See Alan Schrift, *Nietzsche's French Legacy: A Genealogy of Poststructuralism* (London: Routledge, 1995), and Vincent Descombes, *Modern French Philosophy*, trans. L. Scott-Fox and J. M. Harding (London: Cambridge University Press, 1980).

8. Fredric Jameson, forward to Jean-Francois Lyotard, *The Postmodern Condition: A Report on Knowledge*, trans. Geoff Bennington and Brian Massumi (Minneapolis: University of Minnesota Press, 1984), vii.
9. Jean-Francois Lyotard, *La Condition postmoderne: Rapport sur le savoir* (Paris: Les Éditions de Minuit, 1979); for English quote, see Lyotard, *Postmodern Condition*, xxiv.
10. Jean-Francois Lyotard, *Le Postmoderne expliqué aux enfants* (Paris: Galilée, 1988); Lyotard, "Apostil on Narratives" (1984), 19.
11. Jean-François Lyotard, "German Guilt," in *Political Writings*, trans. Bill Readings and Kevin Paul Geiman (Minneapolis: University of Minnesota Press, 1993), 127–34, 127. Originally published as "La Culpabilité allemande," in *L'Age nouveau* in 1948.
12. Karl Jaspers, *The Question of German Guilt*, trans. E. B. Ashton (New York: Fordham University Press, 2000 [1947]), 34–35.
13. Lyotard, "German Guilt," 128.
14. Lyotard, "German Guilt," 130.
15. Lyotard, "German Guilt," 133.
16. Lyotard, "German Guilt," 130.
17. Lyotard, "German Guilt," 133.
18. Lyotard, "German Guilt," 132.
19. Lyotard, "German Guilt," 131.
20. Lyotard, "German Guilt," 132.
21. Lyotard, "German Guilt," 133.
22. See Julian Bourg, *From Revolution to Ethics: May 1968 and Contemporary French Thought* (Montreal: McGill University Press, 2007).
23. For Lyotard's position, see Jean-François Lyotard, *Libidinal Economy* (Bloomington: Indiana University Press, 1993).
24. See Martin Jay's chapter, "The Ethics of Blindness and the Postmodern Sublime: Levinas and Lyotard," in his *Downcast Eyes: The Denigration of Vision in Twentieth-Century French Thought* (Berkeley: University of California Press, 1993).
25. Jean-François Lyotard, "Jewish Oedipus," in *Driftworks*, ed. Roger McKeon (New York: Semiotext(e), 1984), 35–55, 35.
26. Lyotard, "Jewish Oedipus," 39.
27. Lyotard, "Jewish Oedipus," 51.
28. Lyotard, "Jewish Oedipus," 42.
29. Lyotard, "Jewish Oedipus," 42, 43.
30. Lyotard, "Jewish Oedipus," 45.
31. Lyotard, "Jewish Oedipus," 52.
32. Lyotard, "Jewish Oedipus," 52.
33. Lyotard, "Jewish Oedipus," 53.
34. Jean-François Lyotard, "Figure Foreclosed," in *The Lyotard Reader*, ed. Andrew Benjamin (Oxford: Basil Blackwell, 1989), 69–110, 90.
35. Elizabeth Bellamy, *Affective Genealogies: Psychoanalysis, Postmodernism, and the "Jewish Question" After Auschwitz* (Lincoln: University of Nebraska Press, 1997), 29. For a treatment of the links between postmodernism and the new Jewish cultural studies, including my critique of Bellamy, see Jonathan Judaken, "Mapping 'The New Jewish Cultural Studies,'" *History Workshop Journal* 51 (Spring 2001): 269–77.

36. Maurice Blanchot, "Being Jewish," in *The Infinite Conversation*, trans. Susan Hanson (Minneapolis: University of Minnesota Press, 1993), 124.
37. Blanchot, "Being Jewish," 123.
38. Blanchot, "Being Jewish," 124.
39. Blanchot, "Being Jewish," 125.
40. Blanchot, "Being Jewish," 125.
41. Blanchot, "Being Jewish," 126.
42. Blanchot, "Being Jewish," 127.
43. Blanchot, "Being Jewish," 129.
44. Lyotard, "Figure Foreclosed," 87.
45. Lyotard, "Figure Foreclosed," 90.
46. Lyotard, "Figure Foreclosed," 96.
47. Lyotard, "Figure Foreclosed, 99.
48. Lyotard, Figure Foreclosed," 101.
49. Lyotard, "Figure Foreclosed," 103.
50. Lyotard, "Figure Foreclosed," 89.
51. Jean-François Lyotard, *The Differend: Phrases in Dispute*, trans. George van Den Abbeele (Minneapolis: University of Minnesota Press, 1988 [1983]), xi. In defining Lyotard's conception of the "differend," it is important to note that for Lyotard, the "differend" should not be reduced to a concept, since concepts are connected to a (modern) logos interested in fixing meaning. Readers should rather be attentive to the minute differences in the multiple performances of this (non)concept.
52. In "Wittgenstein 'After,'" which appears in Lyotard, *Political Writings*, 19–22, Lyotard brilliantly, in a highly condensed elucidation of Wittgenstein's philosophy of language, explains that he adopts the conception of "regimes of phrases" in order to go beyond the humanism of Wittgenstein's notion of language games: "After Wittgenstein, the first task is that of overcoming this humanist obstacle to the analysis of phrase regimes, to make philosophy inhuman. Humanity is not the user of language, nor even its guardian; there is no more one subject than there is one language" (21). What Lyotard objects to in Wittgenstein's "humanism" is his overly empiricist notion of language and his emphasis on the utilitarian, instrumental side of language in his focus on how people *use* language. The notion of language games, Lyotard explains, emerges from the problems that Wittgenstein raised in the *Tractatus logico-philosophicus*: "The reflection of the *Tractatus*, which bears on the nature of logical and mathematical language, works by means of a philosophical metaphor that is, in the final analysis, fairly classical. Language is an image of the world; the world is represented in it (but the images of events that form propositions are themselves events, and language is part of the world). Thus there is a 'mirror': the elements of language and the elements of reality are organized according to an analogous structure. Knowledge can be grounded on the basis of this presupposition. But it encounters two limits. The most immediate one is that one cannot express what makes propositions possible (the structural analogy between the world and language) by means of a logical or mathematical proposition. The other inexpressible element, at the greatest distance from the mirror, is ethical, aesthetic, or theological (perhaps political) value. *You ought* is not a proposition; it is not the image of a state of affairs. The meaning of life is not in the world: 'ethics is transcendental,' 'God does not reveal himself *in* the world'

288   5. *Jean-François Lyotard, Postmodernism, and "the jews"*

(*Tractatus*)" (20). Wittgenstein's *Philosophical Investigations* come "after" the *Tractatus*, where Wittgenstein developed the concept of language games. "In the *Tractatus*, silence protects the languages of value against the claims of knowledge. In the subsequent investigations, silence disconnects the phrases of ordinary language and reveals their import. In ordinary language, a multiplicity of phrases obey different regimes.... Each set (or family) of phrases brings specific pressures to bear on the interlocutors which push them to make phrase linkages in one way rather than another.... Rules for making linkages have been fixed and learned under the aegis of tradition. These rules may or may not be known to the participants, as in many games" (20-21). Lyotard draws an analogy between Wittgenstein's understanding of language games and Kant's critical philosophy. For Lyotard, like Kant's treatment of reason, Wittgenstein discloses that "there is no unity to language; there are islands of language, each of them ruled by a different regime, untranslatable into the others" (20) and that "translation is itself a language game" (21). In short, within language there a multiplicity of language games, each of which has its own *stakes* and its own *rules*.

53. Lyotard, *The Differend*, xiii.
54. Lyotard, *The Differend*, 56.
55. See for example, Alain Finkielkraut, *The Imaginary Jew*, trans. Kevin O'Neill and David Suchoff (Lincoln: University of Nebraska Press, 1994).
56. Theodor W. Adorno, *Negative Dialectics*, trans. E. B. Ashton (New York: Continuum, 1987 [1966]), 361-65.
57. The classic account of Holocaust denial in France is Pierre Vidal-Nacquet, *Assassins of Memory: Essays on the Denial of the Holocaust*, trans. Jeffrey Mehlman (New York: Columbia University Press, 1992), which is the source of Lyotard's musings. See also Alain Finkielkraut, *The Future of a Negation: Reflections on the Question of Genocide*, trans. Mary Byrd Kelly (Lincoln: University of Nebraska Press, 1998).
58. See Saul Friedländer, ed., *Probing the Limits of Representation: Nazism and the Final Solution* (Cambridge, MA: Harvard University Press, 1992).
59. Dominick LaCapra, "Heidegger's Nazi Turn," in *Representing the Holocaust: History, Theory, Trauma* (Ithaca, NY: Cornell University Press, 1994), 137-68, 137.
60. Martin Heidegger, *Philosophical and Political Writings*, ed. M. Stassen (New York: Continuum, 2003), 2-11.
61. Hannah Arendt, *Hannah Arendt/Karl Jaspers Correspondence, 1926–1969*, ed. Lotte Kohler and Hans Saner, trans. Robert and Rita Kimber (San Diego, CA: Harcourt Brace Jovanovich, 1992), 48.
62. Ethan Kleinberg, "The 'Letter on Humanism': Reading Heidegger in France," in *Situating Existentialism: Key Texts in Context*, ed. Jonathan Judaken and Robert Bernasconi (New York: Columbia University Press, 2012), 386-413.
63. Among the many discussions, see David Carroll, "Foreword: The Memory of Devastation and the Responsibilities of Thought: 'And Let's Not Talk About That,'" in *Heidegger and "the jews,"* by Jean-François Lyotard (Minneapolis: University of Minnesota Press, 1990); LaCapra, "Heidegger's Nazi Turn"; Richard Wolin, "The French Heidegger Debate," *New German Critique*, no. 45 (Fall 1988): 135-61; Thomas Sheehan, "Heidegger and the Nazis," *New York Review of Books*, June 16, 1988; Tom Rockmore, "On Heidegger and Contemporary French Philosophy," in *Heidegger and French Philosophy: Humanism,*

Antihumanism and Being (London: Routledge, 1995). More recently, see Emmanuel Faye, *L'Introduction du nazisme dans la philosophie: Autour des séminaires inédits de 1933–1935* (Paris: Albin Michel, 2005). The latest cascade of considerations has resulted from the publication of Heidegger's *Schwarze Hefte*, or Black Notebooks, his handwritten reflections penned in small black diaries with several passages that clearly establish his Judeophobia. See Andrew J. Mitchell and Peter Trawny, eds., *Heidegger's* Black Notebooks: *Responses to Anti-Semitism* (New York: Columbia University Press, 2017), and Ingo Farin and Jeff Malpas, eds., *Reading Heidegger's* Black Notebooks, 1931-1941 (Cambridge, MA: MIT Press, 2016).

64. David Carroll, "Memorial for the *Différend*," *Parallax* 6, no. 4 (2000): 24.
65. Nelly Hansson, "France: The Carpentras Syndrome and Beyond," *Patterns of Prejudice* 25, no. 1 (1991): 32-45, 32.
66. See Olivier Roy, "Apres Carpentras: le Front National ne perdra pas ses voix," *Esprit*, 162 (June 1990): 72-75. On the National Front more generally, see Pascal Perrineau, "Le Front national: 1972-1992," in *Histoire de l'extréme droite en France*, ed. Michel Winock (Paris: Éditions du Seuil, 1993).
67. On this last point, see Jean-François Sirinelli, *Intellectuels et passions françaises: manifestes et petitions au XXe siècle* (Paris: Fayard, 1990), 513.
68. Henry Rousso, *The Vichy Syndrome: History and Memory in France since 1944*, trans. Arthur Goldhamer (Cambridge, MA: Harvard University Press, 1991).
69. On this see, Henry Weinberg, *The Myth of the Jew in France: 1967–1982* (Oakville, ON: Mosaic, 1987); Robert Wistrich, "The Myth of the Jew in Contemporary France," in *Between Redemption and Perdition: Modern Antisemitism and Jewish Identity* (London: Routledge, 1990); and Raymond Aron, *De Gaulle, Israël et les Juifs* (Paris: Plon, 1968).
70. On these events, see Yaïr Auron, "Le Procès de Leningrad (1970), le massacre de Munich (1972), l'attentat de la rue Copernic (1980): La réaction des radicaux juifs aux manifestions antisemites," in *Les Juifs d'extréme gauche de Mai '68: Une génération révolutionnaire marquée par la Shoah*, trans. Katherine Werchowski (Paris: Albin Michel, 1998); Judith Friedlander, "Antisemitism in France, 1978-1992: Questions and Debates," in *Auschwitz and After*, ed. Lawrence Kritzman (New York: Routledge, 1995); Michael Marrus, "Are the French Antisemitic? Evidence in the 1980s," in *The Jews in Modern France*, ed. Frances Malino and Bernard Wasserstein (Hanover, NH: University Press of New England, 1985), 224-42.
71. Jean-François Lyotard, "Europe, the Jews and the Book," in *Political Writings*, 159-62.
72. Lyotard, "Europe, the Jews and the Book," 160.
73. Lyotard, "Europe, the Jews and the Book," 160.
74. Lyotard, "Europe, the Jews and the Book," 160.
75. Lyotard contrasts "reading" to both interpretation and theory. As Bill Readings explains in *Introducing Lyotard: Art and Politics* (Routledge: London, 1991), reading "shares a temporality and a positioning with aesthetic and ethical judgment. Reading is neither on the inside (interpretation) nor the outside (theory) of a text" (xix). Thus, if theory aims at a timeless account of events and *hermeneutic* interpretation aims in time to extract the meaning of a text or event, then Lyotard prioritizes reading, which he associates as *Talmudic*, which aims not at totality, but rather at an infinite process of the interpretation of interpretation.

76. Lyotard, "Europe, the Jews and the Book," 160.
77. Lyotard, "Europe, the Jews and the Book," 162.
78. There is a long tradition of defining the modern as the break with the past, which is constituted as "old" in the name of the "new." On this gesture as the signature of the modern, see Habermas, *The Philosophical Discourse of Modernity*.
79. Lyotard, "Europe, the Jews and the Book," 160.
80. On this point, see Michael Weingrad, "Jews (in Theory): Representation of Judaism, Anti-Semitism, and the Holocaust in Postmodern French Thought," *Judaism* (Winter 1996): 79-98, 85.
81. Lyotard is indebted to Emmanuel Levinas on these points. For a fuller discussion of Levinas's influence on Lyotard, see Jay, "Ethics of Blindness," and Bellamy, *Affective Genealogies*, 109-10.
82. On Lyotard's distinction between an "example" and a "model," see "Discussions, or Phrasing 'after Auschwitz,'" in *The Lyotard Reader*, 360-92, 363.
83. Jean-Francois Lyotard, "The Grip (*Mainmise*)," in *Political Writings*, 148-59, 157.
84. Lyotard, "Europe, the Jews and the Book," 161.
85. Lyotard, "Europe, the Jews and the Book," 161.
86. Jean-Paul Sartre, *Reflexions sur la question juive* (Paris: Gallimard, 1954); Sartre, *Anti-Semite and Jew*, trans. George Becker (New York: Schocken, 1948).
87. Lyotard, "Europe and the Jews," 160.
88. Lyotard, "Europe and the Jews," 159.
89. Geoffrey Bennington, "Lyotard and 'the Jews,'" in *Modernity, Culture and 'the Jew*, ed. Bryan Cheyette and Laura Marcus (Cambridge: Polity, 1998), 192.
90. Lyotard, "Europe, the Jews and the Book," 159.
91. Jean-François Lyotard, "Heidegger and 'the jews': A Conference in Vienna and Freiburg," in *Political Writings*, 143.
92. Weingrad, "Jews (in Theory)," 86.
93. LaCapra, *Representing the Holocaust*, 97.
94. Bellamy, *Affective Genealogies*, 145.
95. Max Silverman, "Re-Figuring 'the Jew' in France," in Cheyette and Marcus, *Modernity, Culture and the Jew*, 197-207, 199.
96. On Lyotard's opposition to Hegel, see Vincent Descombes, *Modern French Philosophy*, trans. L. Scott-Fox and J. M. Harding (Cambridge: Cambridge University Press, 1980), 180-86.
97. See Bellamy, *Affective Genealogies*, 147. The Jew in the *Phenomenology* is depicted as "the insurmountable cleft [*Kluft*] between the being of God and the being of men" and the Jewish experience is that of the "unhappy consciousness" an (un)consciousness which is "inwardly divided in two, disunited consciousness."
98. Nathan Rotenstreich, "Hegel's Image of Judaism," *Jewish Social Studies* 15 (1953): 33-52, 43, 47. See also Yirmiyahu Yovel, *Dark Riddle: Hegel, Nietzsche, and the Jews* (Cambridge: Polity, 1998).
99. Gillian Rose makes these points about Leo Strauss and Emmanuel Levinas in her *Judaism and Modernity: Philosophical Essays* (Oxford: Blackwell, 1993). Max Silverman extends the point to other postmodern thinkers, including Lyotard, in "Re-Figuring 'the Jew' in France."

100. Daniel Boyarin and Jonathan Boyarin, "Diaspora: Generation and the Ground of Jewish Identity," *Critical Inquiry* 19 (Summer 1993): 693-725, 701.
101. Boyarin and Boyarin, "Diaspora," 700.
102. This collection of cavalier dismissals is taken from the editors' note to *Le Postmoderne expliqué aux enfants*, where they explain that the text was published in the hopes that it might clear Lyotard of these accusations. Lyotard was skeptical, since he suggested that these attributions were the result of ad hominem attacks that were generated in the place of actual reading. See "Preface to the French Edition" in *The Postmodern Explained*.
103. Readings, *Introducing Lyotard*, xxxii.

6. LÉON POLIAKOV, THE ORIGINS OF HOLOCAUST STUDIES, AND THE LONG HISTORY OF JUDEOPHOBIA

1. Take as two symptomatic examples, Paul R. Bartrop and Steven Leonard Jacobs, *Fifty Key Thinkers on the Holocaust and Genocide* (New York: Routledge, 2011), which does not even list Poliakov among its celebrated pantheon, or David Nirenberg's important work, *Anti-Judaism: The Western Tradition* (New York: Norton, 2013), whose core argument about the centrality of anti-Judaism to the development of "habits of thought" within Western culture is similar to Poliakov's underlying claim about the centrality of Judeophobia to the Western tradition, which never cites Poliakov.
2. Léon Poliakov, *Bréviaire de la haine: Le IIIe Reich et les Juifs* (Paris: Calmann-Lévy, 1951); *Harvest of Hate: The Nazi Program for the Destruction of the Jews of Europe* (Syracuse, NY: Syracuse University Press, 1954).
3. Poliakov published *L'Histoire de l'antisémitisme* in four integrated volumes with the press Calmann-Lévy. These were translated into English as *From the Time of Christ to the Court Jews*, vol. 1 of *The History of Anti-Semitism*, trans. Richard Howard (Philadelphia: University of Pennsylvania Press, 2003); *From Mohammed to the Marranos*, vol. 2 of *The History of Anti-Semitism*, trans. Natalie Gerardi (Philadelphia: University of Pennsylvania Press, 2003); *From Voltaire to Wagner*, vol. 3 of *The History of Anti-Semitism*, trans. Miriam Kochan (Philadelphia: University of Pennsylvania Press, 2003); and *Suicidal Europe, 1870–1933*, vol. 4 of *The History of Anti-Semitism*, trans. George Klin (Philadelphia: University of Philadelphia Press, 2003). The fifth volume was collectively written and published by Seuil as Léon Poliakov, ed., *Histoire de l'antisémitisme, 1945–1993* (Paris: Seuil, 1994) and remains untranslated.
4. See Léon Poliakov and Georges Elia Sarfati, *L'Envers du destin: Entretiens avec Georges Elia Sarfati* (Paris: Editions de Fallois, 1989), 9.
5. My citation is from the interview with Elisabeth Weber in *Questioning Judaism: Interviews* (Stanford: Stanford University Press, 2004), 87.
6. The biographical information on Poliakov comes either from his interviews with Sarfati, *L'Envers du destin*, or from Poliakov's *Mémoires* (Paris: Jacques Grancher, 1999). The quote is from Sarfati, *L'Envers du destin*, 9.
7. Sarfati, *L'Envers du destin*, 19.
8. On the influx of Jewish immigrants in this period, see Vicky Caron, *Uneasy Asylum: France and the Jewish Refugee Crisis, 1933–1942* (Stanford: Stanford University Press, 1999).
9. Sarfati, *L'Envers du destin*, 24.

10. For an overview of the Vichy period, see Julian Jackson, *France: The Dark Years, 1940–1944* (Oxford: Oxford University Press, 2001). For the experience of Jews under the German occupation, see Michael Marrus and Robert Paxton, *Vichy France and the Jews* (Stanford: Stanford University Press, 1981); Susan Zuccotti, *The Holocaust, the French, and the Jews* (New York: HarperCollins, 1993); Richard Weisberg, *Vichy Law and the Holocaust in France* (New York: New York University Press, 1996); Renée Poznanski, *Jews in France During World War II*, trans. Nathan Bracher (Hanover, NH: Brandeis University Press, 2001).

11. On the general experience of the French POWs, see Yves Durand's excellent *La Captivité: Histoire des prisonniers de guerre français, 1939–1945* (Paris: Fédération nationale des combattants prisonniers de guerre et combattants d'Algérie, Tunisie, Maroc, 1982). See also Sarah Fishman, *We Will Wait: Wives of French Prisoners of War* (New Haven, CT: Yale University Press, 1991). For a more global account of POWs, see Bob Moore and Kent Fedorowich, *Prisoners of War and Their Captors in World War II* (Oxford: Berg, 1996).

12. Sarfati, *L'Envers du destin*, 33.

13. On Kojève's Hegel seminar, see Vincent Descombes, *Modern French Philosophy*, trans. L. Scott-Fox and J. M. Harding (Cambridge: Cambridge University Press, 1980); Jacques d'Hondt, *Hegel et Hégélianisme* (Paris: Presses Universitaires de France, 1982); Michael S. Roth, *Knowing and History: Appropriations of Hegel in Twentieth-Century France* (Ithaca, NY: Cornell University Press, 1988); Judith Butler, *Subjects of Desire: Hegelian Reflections in Twentieth-Century France* (New York: Columbia University Press, 1988); and Ethan Kleinberg, *Generation Existential: Heidegger's Philosophy in France, 1927–1961* (Ithaca, NY: Cornell University Press, 2005), 49–110. See also Alexandre Kojève, *Introduction to the Reading of Hegel: Lectures on the Phenomenology of Spirit*, trans. James H. Nichols, Jr., ed. Allan Bloom (Ithaca, NY: Cornell University Press, 1980).

14. On the role of Le-Chambon-sur-Lignon in the rescue of French Jews, see Philip P. Hallie, *Lest Innocent Blood Be Shed: The Story of the Village of Le Chambon, and How Goodness Happened There* (New York: Harper and Row, 1979), and Patrick Henry, *We Only Know Men: The Rescue of Jews in France during the Holocaust* (Washington, DC: Catholic University of America Press, 2007).

15. Sarfati, *L'Envers du destin*, 50. Poliakov dedicated *Harvest of Hate* "To the memory of my master and friend Jacob Gordon." On the importance of Jacob Gordon to the development of postwar French Jewish philosophy, see Léon Askénazi, "Philosophie et revelation biblique: la demarche de Jacob Gordin," *Pardès: Revue européenne d'études et de culture juives*, no. 23 (1997): 71–77.

16. On the UGIF, see Richard Cohen, *The Burden of Conscience: French Jewish Leadership during the Holocaust* (Bloomington: Indiana University Press, 1987).

17. In the revised edition of his *Mémoires*, Poliakov itemized his profound differences with Braudel over the question of anti-Semitism, Jewish identity, religion, and the State of Israel, which Poliakov suggested hampered his career. See *Mémoires*, n11, 257–58. On the Annales school and Braudel's reign over it in the postwar period, see Peter Burke, *The French Historical Revolution: The Annales School, 1929–1989* (Stanford: Stanford University Press, 1990), 32–64.

18. Dominique Schnapper to Léon Poliakov, Léon Poliakov papers, consulted in Germaine Poliakov's home, translated by Jonathan Judaken.

19. See Esther Benbassa, *Histoire des juifs de France* (Paris: Seuil, 2000), 284-90, and Michel Winock, *La France et les juifs: De 1789 à nos jours* (Paris: Seuil, 2004), 327-50.
20. A. Latreille, *Le Monde*, October 16, 1952; P. Grappin, "Politique etrangère," no. 4 (1951); J. Gallois, *L'Observateur*, July 12, 1951.
21. Jacques Maritain, *Social Research* 23 (Summer 1956); R. H. S. Crossman, *New Statesman*, July 28, 1956.
22. Raymond Aron, *Critique*, January 1954.
23. Hannah Arendt, "The History of the Great Crime," *Commentary*, March 1952, 300-304.
24. Poliakov had already developed this argument in his documentary reader, the first book he produced as head of the CDJC, *La Condition des juifs en France sous l'occupation italienne* (Paris: Éditions du Centre, 1946). For more recent historiography that has problematized the role of Italy and the Jews, see Robert Wistrich and Sergio DellaPergola, eds., *Fascist Anti-Semitism and the Italian Jews* (Jerusalem: The Vidal Sassoon International Center for the Study of Anti-Semitism, 1995); Susan Zuccotti, *The Italians and the Holocaust: Persecution, Rescue and Survival* (Lincoln: University of Nebraska Press, 1996); Joshua D. Zimmerman, ed., *The Jews of Italy under Fascist and Nazi Rule, 1922–1945* (Cambridge: Cambridge University Press, 2005); Michele Sarfatti, *The Jews in Mussolini's Italy: From Equality to Persecution* (Madison: University of Wisconsin Press, 2006).
25. This has been contentious terrain in both the scholarship and in public discussions of the Holocaust, including most famously Raul Hilberg's depiction in *The Destruction of European Jews*, and especially in the response to Arendt's *Eichmann in Jerusalem*. See Isaiah Trunk, *Judenrat: The Jewish Councils in Eastern Europe Under Nazi Occupation* (New York: Macmillan, 1972). For a more recent intervention in this discussion, see Zygmunt Bauman, "Soliciting the Co-operation of the Victims," in *Modernity and the Holocaust* (Ithaca, NY: Cornell University Press, 2000), 117-50.
26. See Poliakov's discussion on p. 132. On the historiography, see Omer Bartov, "German Soldiers and the Holocaust: Historiography, Research and Implications," in Bartov, *The Holocaust: Origins, Implementation, Aftermath* (London: Routledge, 2000), 162-84.
27. See Michael Burleigh, *Death and Deliverance: "Euthanasia" in Germany c. 1900–1945* (Cambridge: Cambridge University Press, 1994), and Henry Friedlander, *The Origins of Nazi Genocide: From Euthanasia to the Final Solution* (Chapel Hill: University of North Carolina Press, 1995).
28. On Poliakov's prescience in dealing with these topics, see Abraham Edelheit, "Historiography of the Holocaust," in *Encyclopedia of the Holocaust*, ed. Israel Gutman (New York: Macmillan, 2000), 666-72, 667. Poliakov discusses "The Jewish Resistance" in chapter 9 and "Nazi Plans for the Inferior Peoples" in chapter 11.
29. Poliakov, *Harvest of Hate*, 48-49, emphasis added. See also pp. 52-53 in *Harvest of Hate*. Michael Marrus and Robert Paxton would gain far greater acclaim for helping to rupture the Gaullist myth with the publication of *Vichy France and the Jews* with the same claims.
30. See Poliakov, *Harvest of Hate*, 127-32, 209, 215, 247.
31. Daniel Jonah Goldhagen, *Hitler's Willing Executioners* (New York: Knopf, 1996) and Christopher R. Browning, *Ordinary Men: Reserve Police Battalion 101 and the Final Solution in Poland* (New York: HarperCollins, 1992). For their debate, see Daniel Jonah Goldhagen, "The Paradigm Challenged," *Tikkun*, May-June 1988, and Christopher R.

Browning, "Ordinary Germans or Ordinary Men? A Reply to the Critics," in *The Holocaust and History: The Known, the Unknown, the Disputed, and the Reexamined*, ed. Michael Berenbaum and Abraham J. Peck (Bloomington: Indiana University Press, 1998).

32. Poliakov, *Harvest of Hate*, 119.
33. A. M. P., "Mort de l'historien Léon Poliakov," *Le Figaro*, December 9, 1997.
34. Christian Delacampagne, "Léon Poliakov: Un specialist de l'analyse de l'antisémitisme," *Le Monde*, December 10, 1997, 24.
35. A. S., *L'Humanité*, December 9, 1997. Elaborating on Poliakov's role as a witness, Patrick Girard placed him side-by-side with two other titans of the testimonial literature written in French, Claude Roy and David Rousset, who also died around the same time. See Patrick Girard, "Léon Poliakov, Claude Roy, David Rousset: Adieu à la passion de la vérité," *L'Evenement du jour*, December 18/24, 1997, 25.
36. "L. Poliakov, 87, Historian of Anti-Semitism," *New York Times*, December 10, 1997, D25. Poliakov would publish a book on the trial of Eichmann, *Le Procès de Jérusalem: Jugements, documents* (Paris: CDJC-Calmann-Lévy, 1963). Along with presenting the documentation from the trial, Poliakov wrote a long introduction (85 pages) and then in the section on "Judgments," he wrote an introduction to all of the various components of the case.
37. Poliakov's position on Nazi anti-Semitism could therefore be compared to that of Saul Friedländer. See *Nazi Germany and the Jews*, vol. 1, *The Years of Persecution, 1933–1939* and vol. 2, *1939–1945: The Years of Extermination* (New York: HarperCollins, 1997, 2007). Friedländer sees his conception of "redemptive anti-Semitism" as a way to transcend the binaries of much of the scholarship focused around the polarities of anti-Semitism versus modernity; Hitler's charisma against bureaucracy; and "ordinary men" opposed to "ordinary Germans." See Saul Friedländer, "The Extermination of the European Jews in Historiography: Fifty Years Later," in Bartov, *The Holocaust*, 79-91.
38. Poliakov, *Harvest of Hate*, 2.
39. Poliakov, *Harvest of Hate*, 5.
40. Norman Cohn, *Warrant for Genocide: The Myth of the Jewish World Conspiracy and the Protocols of the Elders of Zion* (Middlesex: Penguin, 1967). This argument was put forward as early as Joshua Trachtenburg's *The Devil and the Jews: The Medieval Conception of the Jew and Its Relation to Modern Anti-Semitism* (New Haven, CT: Yale University Press, 1943).
41. Jeffrey Herf, *The Jewish Enemy* (Cambridge, MA: Harvard University Press, 2006).
42. Poliakov, *Harvest of Hate*, 263.
43. Poliakov interview in Weber, *Questioning Judaism*, 94.
44. I am suggesting that here Poliakov anticipates Karl Schleunes, Ian Kershaw, and Saul Friedländer by suggesting that the twisted road to Auschwitz was built by "redemptive anti-Semitism" but it was paved by indifference.
45. The original title for Poliakov's book was *Génocide: Une contribution à l'étude de la haine pure*. See Poliakov, *Mémoires*, 284.
46. For this reason, Pierre Boutang, writing in the reconstituted journal of the Action Française, *Aspects de la France*, remarked that Poliakov erred with his "ambiguous and unpleasant" title. See Pierre Boutang, *Aspects de la France*, June 29, 1951.
47. Poliakov, *Harvest of Hate*, 299.
48. This communication is cited in the annex to Poliakov's *Mémoires*, 284.

49. This letter is reprinted in full in the annex to Poliakov's *Mémoires*, 287.
50. The exchange between Mauriac and Poliakov is contained in Poliakov's *Mémoires*, 288–92.
51. Poliakov, *Harvest of Hate*, 299.
52. Sigmund Freud, "Analysis of a Phobia in a Five-Year-Old Boy" (1909), in *The Standard Edition of the Complete Psychological Works of Sigmund Freud*, ed. James Strachey et al. (London: Hogarth, 1955), 36.
53. Jay Geller, "The Godfather of Psychoanalysis: Circumcision, Anti-Semitism, Homosexuality and Freud's 'Fighting Jew,'" *Journal of the American Academy of Religion* 67, no. 2 (June 1999): 355–85. The literature on Freud's Jewishness is extensive. It includes the racial interpretation of Charles Maylan, *Freuds Tragischer Komplex: Eine Analyse der Psychoanalyse* (Munich: E. Reinhardt, 1929); David Bakan's interpretation of a hidden Jewish essence to Freud that connects him to the Jewish mystical tradition, *Sigmund Freud and the Jewish Mystical Tradition* (Princeton, NJ: Van Nostrand, 1958); the argument for Freud's cultural Jewishness in John Murray Cuddihy, *The Ordeal of Civility* (New York: Basic Books, 1974); following Freud's first biographer Ernest Jones, the interpretation of Peter Gay that Freud was a "godless Jew" in *A Godless Jew: Freud, Atheism and the Making of Psychoanalysis* (New Haven, CT, and Cincinnati: Yale and Hebrew Union College, 1987); a more nuanced interpretation of the religious influences on Freud in Emanuel Rice, *Freud and Moses: The Long Journey Home* (Albany: SUNY Press, 1990). The most important recent interpretations of Freud's Jewishness along with Geller's are Yosef Hayim Yerushalmi, *Freud's Moses: Judaism Terminable and Interminable* (New Haven, CT: Yale University Press, 1991); among Sander Gilman's many publications on the topic, see *Freud, Race and Gender* (Princeton, NJ: Princeton University Press, 1993) and *The Case of Sigmund Freud: Medicine and Identity at the Fin de Siècle* (Baltimore, MD: Johns Hopkins University Press, 1993); and Daniel Boyarin, *Unheroic Conduct: The Rise of Heterosexuality and the Invention of the Jewish Man* (Berkeley: University of California Press, 1997), 189–270.
54. See "Thoughts for the Times on War and Death" (1915), *Group Psychology and the Analysis of the Ego* (1921), and *Civilization and Its Discontents* (1930).
55. See Freud, *Moses and Monotheism*, in *Standard Edition*, 23:91–92. Emphasis added.
56. There are now a slew of writers who have complicated this interpretation about the relationship between Nazism and paganism and suggested instead that Christian anti-Judaism was the font of Judeophobia, beginning with James Parkes and Jules Isaac, then Poliakov in volume 1 of the *History of Anti-Semitism*, but now including Rosemary Ruether, Roy Eckardt, Friedrich Heer, Franklin Littell, Malcolm Hay, John Gager, James Carroll, Robert Michael, Dora Bergen, and Susannah Heschel, among others.
57. See Geller, "Godfather," 358 for the double binds of Freud's situation as the summation of the new historiography on him.
58. See Jay Geller, "*Atheist* Jew or Atheist *Jew*: Freud's Jewish Question and Ours," *Modern Judaism* 26, no. 1 (February 2006): 1–14, 1.
59. Boyarin explores how Jews like Freud and Theodor Herzl found symbolic means to assimilate to the dominant norms of central European culture. See Boyarin, *Unheroic Conduct*, 226: "The ambivalence underlying wishes for Jewish assimilation, like other performances of colonial mimicry, is deeply embedded in issues of both gender and sexuality."

60. Samuel explicitly denies the influence of Freud's *Moses* in a footnote, insisting that the shared viewpoint is an expression of the fact that "an understanding of the truth is now in the air." See Maurice Samuel, *The Great Hatred* (New York: Alfred A. Knopf, 1948 [1940]), 140.
61. Milton Hindus, ed., *The Worlds of Maurice Samuel: Selected Writings* (Philadelphia: Jewish Publication Society of America, 1977), 236. See also Alan T. Levenson, *Maurice Samuel: Life and Letters of a Secular Jewish Contrarian* (Tuscaloosa: University of Alabama Press, 2022).
62. Louis Fisher, *Men and Politics* (New York: Deull, Sloan and Pearce, 1941), 243.
63. Ilan Stavans, "Thinking Aloud: The Education of Maurice Samuel," *PaknTreger*, no. 49 (Fall 2005): 15–23.
64. Samuel, *The Great Hatred*, 47.
65. While there are examples of the use of "Judeo-Christian" provided in the Oxford English Dictionary from 1899 and 1910, it is only in 1939 that the term was first used in the contemporary sense of a shared tradition of ethical values. According to Arthur A. Cohen, *The Myth of the Judeo-Christian Tradition* (New York: Harper and Row, 1957), "It was only in the late nineteenth century in Germany that the Judeo-Christian tradition, as such was first defined. It was introduced by German Protestant scholarship to account for the findings developed by the Higher Criticism of the Old Testament and achieved considerable currency as a polemical term in that period. There, quite clearly, the negative significance of the expression became primary. The emphasis fell not to the communality of the word 'tradition' but to the accented stress of the hyphen. The Jewish was Latinized and abbreviated into 'Judeo' to indicate a dimension, albeit a pivotal dimension, of the explicit Christian experience" (xviii). As such, Solomon Schechter called it "Higher Anti-Semitism." For more on the emergence of the construct "Judeo-Christian" see my discussion in the introduction.
66. Samuel, *The Great Hatred*, 168.
67. This is similar to the argument that was made by Franz Rosenzweig in *The Star of Redemption*, trans. William Hallo (Notre Dame, IN: Notre Dame Press, 1970), 413–17.
68. Samuel, *The Great Hatred*, 100, 97.
69. Samuel, *The Great Hatred*, 104.
70. Emmanuel Levinas, "Reflections on the Philosophy of Hitlerism," trans. Seán Hand, *Critical Inquiry* 17, no. 1 (Autumn 1990): 62–71.
71. Samuel, *The Great Hatred*, 113.
72. Samuel, *The Great Hatred*, 111.
73. Samuel, *The Great Hatred*, 191.
74. On Maritain's shifting position in the interwar period, see Richard Crane, "Surviving Maurras: Jacques Maritain's Jewish Question," in *Naming Race, Naming Racisms*, ed. Jonathan Judaken (New York: Routledge, 2009), 51–77. For Maritain's lifelong stance on the Jewish Question, see Richard Crane, *Passion of Israel: Jacques Maritain, Catholic Conscience, and the Holocaust* (Scranton, PA: University of Scranton Press, 2010).
75. Jacques Maritain, "On Anti-Semitism," *Christianity and Crisis*, October 6, 1941, reprinted in Jacques and Raïssa Maritain, *Oeuvres completes*, vol. 8 (Paris: Éditions Universitaires Fribourg Suisse and Éditions Saint-Paul, 1989), 564–77, 566.
76. Maritain, "On Anti-Semitism," 568, 570.

77. Poliakov, *Harvest of Hate*, 299.
78. Maritain, "On Anti-Semitism," 570, 572.
79. Maritain, "On Anti-Semitism," 572.
80. Maritain, "On Anti-Semitism," 572.
81. Maritain, "On Anti-Semitism," 572.
82. Maritain, "On Anti-Semitism," 566.
83. Poliakov, *From the Time of Christ to the Court Jews*, 25.
84. Gregory of Nyssa, "Oratio V," in vol. 46 of *Patrologiæ Cursus Completus, Series Græca*, ed. Jacques-Paul Migne (Paris: Petit-Montrouge, 1858), quoted in Poliakov, *From the Time of Christ to the Court Jews*, 25.
85. For a more recent version of this argument, see Nirenberg, *Anti-Judaism: The Western Tradition*. For my review of the work, see Jonathan Judaken, "Deconstructing Anti-Semitism and Eternal Anti-Judaism," *Marginalia: A Review of Books in History, Theology, and Religion*, December 13, 2013: http://themarginaliareview.com/archives/4981.
86. Poliakov, *From Mohammed to the Marranos*, ix, xii.
87. Poliakov, *From Mohammed to the Marranos*, 281.
88. Poliakov, *From Voltaire to Wagner*, ix.
89. On François Bernier as the first to formulate the modern conception of race, see Siep Stuurman, "François Bernier and the Invention of Racial Classification," *History Workshop Journal*, no. 50 (Autumn, 2000): 1–21. See also M. L. Dufrenoy, "A Precursor of a Modern Anthropology: François Bernier (1620–1688)," *Isis* 41, no. 1 (March 1950): 27–29.
90. For a translation of the text, see François Bernier, "A New Division of the Earth," *History Workshop Journal*, no. 51 (Spring 2001): 247–50.
91. Léon Poliakov, *The Aryan Myth: A History of Racist and Nationalist Ideas in Europe*, trans. Edmund Howard (New York: Basic Books, 1974), 145.
92. John Locke, *An Essay Concerning Human Understanding* (London: Tegg and Son, 1836), 4.7.16, quoted in Poliakov, *The Aryan Myth*, 145.
93. For the centrality of Locke to racial theory, see Robert Bernasconi, "Locke's Almost Random Talk of Man: The Double Use of Words in the Natural Law Justification of Slavery," *Perspektiven der Philosophie* 18 (1992): 293–318, and Robert Bernasconi and Anika Maaza Mann, "The Contradictions of Racism: Locke, Slavery, and the *Two Treatises*," in *Race and Racism in Modern Philosophy*, ed. Andrew Valls (Ithaca, NY: Cornell University Press, 2005). For the pushback against Bernasconi's argument, see James Farr, "Locke, Natural Law, and New World Slavery," *Political Theory* 36, no. 4 (August 2008): 495–522, and Holly Brewer, "Slavery-Entangled Philosophy," *Aeon*: https://aeon.co/essays/does-lockes-entanglement-with-slavery-undermine-his-philosophy. See also, William Uzgalis, "John Locke, Racism, Slavery, and Indian Lands," in *The Oxford Handbook of Philosophy and Race*, ed. Naomi Zack (Oxford: Oxford University Press, 2017), 21–30.
94. Réne Descartes, *Discourse on Method*, in *Discourse on Method and Meditations on First Philosophy*, trans. Donald Cress (Indianapolis: Hackett, 1998), 31.
95. Poliakov, *The Aryan Myth*, 148.
96. Poliakov, *From Voltaire to Wagner*, 128.
97. Poliakov, *From Voltaire to Wagner*, 132. For more on the creation of systems of racial classification, see chapter 8, "Hierarchies of Humanity," in Elizabeth Ewen and Stuart

Ewen, *Typecasting: On the Arts and Sciences of Human Inequality* (New York: Seven Stories Press, 2008).

98. On Peter Camper, see George Mosse, *Toward the Final Solution: A History of European Racism* (Madison: University of Wisconsin Press, 1985), 14-15, 21-26. On Christoph Meiners, see Peter K. J. Park, *Africa, Asia, and the History of Philosophy: Racism in the Formation of the Philosophical Canon, 1780–1830* (Albany: SUNY Press, 2013). Citations to the literature on Kant are below.

99. On Blumenbach, see Nell Irvin Painter, *The History of White People* (New York: Norton, 2010), 72-90.

100. Poliakov, *From Voltaire to Wagner*, 138.

101. Poliakov, *From Voltaire to Wagner*, 139.

102. Poliakov, *From Voltaire to Wagner*, 290.

103. Poliakov, *From Voltaire to Wagner*, 175.

104. Poliakov, *From Voltaire to Wagner*, 175.

105. See Jonathan M. Hess, *Germans, Jews and the Claims of Modernity* (New Haven, CT: Yale University Press, 2002), 25-89.

106. The scholarly work on Kant includes Bernard Boxill, "Kantian Racism and Kantian Teleology," in Zack, *Oxford Handbook*, 44-53; Charles Mills, "Kant and Race, Redux," *Graduate Faculty Philosophy Journal* 35, nos. 1-2 (2014): 125-57; Peter K. J. Park, "The Exclusion of Asia and Africa from the History of Philosophy: Is Kant Responsible?," in *Cultivating Personhood: Kant and Asian Philosophy*, ed. Stephen R. Palmquist (New York: Walter de Gruyter, 2010), 777-90; Mark Larrimore, "Antinomies of *Race*: Diversity and Destiny in Kant," in Judaken, *Naming Race*, 7-29; Michael Mack, *German Idealism and the Jew: The Inner Anti-Semitism of Philosophy and German Jewish Responses* (Chicago: University of Chicago Press, 2003), 23-41; Robert Bernasconi, "Who Invented the Concept of Race? Kant's Role in the Enlightenment Construction of Race," in *Race*, ed. Robert Bernasconi (Oxford: Blackwell, 2001), 9-36; Emmanuel Eze, "The Color of Reason: The Idea of 'Race' in Kant's Anthropology," in *Anthropology and the German Enlightenment: Perspectives on Humanity*, ed. Katherine M. Faull (Lewisburg, PA: Bucknell University Press, 1995), 200-235; and Paul Lawrence Rose, *German-Question, Jewish Question: Revolutionary Anti-Semitism in Germany from Kant to Wagner* (Princeton, NJ: Princeton University Press, 1990).

107. Poliakov, *From Voltaire to Wagner*, 178-79.

108. Poliakov, *From Voltaire to Wagner*, 180.

109. On Houston Stewart Chamberlain, see Geoffrey Field, *Evangelist of Race: The German Vision of Houston Stewart Chamberlain* (New York: Columbia University Press, 1981). See also, Susannah Heschel, *The Aryan Jesus: Christian Theologians and the Bible in Nazi Germany* (Princeton, NJ: Princeton University Press, 2010).

110. Poliakov, *From Voltaire to Wagner*, 181.

111. Poliakov, *From Voltaire to Wagner*, 184. On Hegel and the Jews, see Yirmiyahu Yovel, *Dark Riddle: Hegel, Nietzsche, and the Jews* (University Park: Pennsylvania State University Press, 1998). There is a much more substantive literature on Hegel's anti-Black racism that has paid little heed to his anti-Jewish racism.

112. Poliakov, *From Voltaire to Wagner*, 186. See also Leora Batnitsky, *How Judaism Became a Religion: An Introduction to Modern Jewish Thought* (Princeton, NJ: Princeton University Press, 2011), 25-27.

113. On the Young Hegelians, see Nathan Rotenstreich, "For and Against Emancipation: The Bruno Bauer Controversy," *Leo Baeck Institute Year Book* 4 (1959): 3-36.
114. On Eisenmenger's role in modern anti-Semitism, see Jacob Katz, "The Sources of Modern Anti-Semitism: Eisenmenger's Method of Presenting Evidence from Talmudic Sources," in *Proceedings of the Fifth World Congress of Jewish Studies* (Jerusalem: World Union of Jewish Studies, 1972), 2:210-11.
115. On Hegel's influence on Bauer, see Leopold Davis, "The Hegelian Anti-Semitism of Bruno Bauer," *History of European Ideas* 25 (1999): 179-206.
116. See Bruno Bauer, "The Jewish Problem," in *The Jew in the Modern World: A Documentary History*, ed. Paul Mendes-Flohr and Jehuda Reinharz (Oxford: Oxford University Press, 1995), 322-23.
117. Poliakov, *From Voltaire to Wagner*, 422. On Marx and the Jewish Question, see Julius Carlebach, *Karl Marx and the Radical Critique of Judaism* (London: Routledge and Kegan Paul, 1978); Enzo Traverso, *The Marxists and the Jewish Question: The History of a Debate, 1843-1943* (Atlantic Highlands, NJ: Humanities, 1994), 13-31; Robert Wistrich, *From Ambivalence to Betrayal: Israel, the Jews and the Left* (Lincoln: University of Nebraska Press, 2012), 70-110; and Pierre Birnbaum, *Geography of Hope: Exile, the Enlightenment, Disassimilation* (Stanford: Stanford University Press, 2008), 36-82; Robert Fine, "Rereading Marx on the 'Jewish Question': Marx as a Critic of Antisemitism?," in *Antisemitism and the Constitution of Sociology*, ed. Marcel Stoetzler (Lincoln: University of Nebraska Press, 2014), 137-59.
118. Poliakov, *From Voltaire to Wagner*, 309.
119. Anthony D. Smith, *Nationalism and Modernism: A Critical Survey of Recent Theories of Nations and Nationalism* (New York: Routledge, 1998), 151-59, and Smith, *The Nation in History: Historiographical Debates about Ethnicity and Nationalism* (Hanover, NH: University Press of New England, 2000), 20-25.
120. Poliakov, *The Aryan Myth*, 132.
121. See Richard H. Popkin, *Isaac La Peyrère* (Leiden: E. J. Brill, 1987).
122. Poliakov, *The Aryan Myth*, 169.
123. Poliakov, *The Aryan Myth*, 175.
124. On Voltaire as a synthesizer of Enlightenment thought, see also Adam Sutcliff, *Judaism and Enlightenment* (Cambridge: Cambridge University Press, 2003), 231-46.
125. Poliakov, *The Aryan Myth*, 175.
126. On Hume and race, see Emmanuel C. Eze, "Hume, Race, and Human Nature," *Journal of the History of Ideas* 61, no. 4 (October 2000): 691-98, and John Immerwahr, "Hume's Revised Racism," *Journal of the History of Ideas* 52 (1992): 1-23.
127. Poliakov, *The Aryan Myth*, 177-79.
128. Poliakov, *The Aryan Myth*, 180-81.
129. Poliakov, *The Aryan Myth*, 188.
130. Poliakov, *The Aryan Myth*, 190.
131. Poliakov, *The Aryan Myth*, 193.
132. Poliakov, *The Aryan Myth*, 194.
133. Poliakov, *The Aryan Myth*, 197.
134. Poliakov, *From Voltaire to Wagner*, 458.
135. Poliakov, *From Voltaire to Wagner*, 156.

300   6. Léon Poliakov and the History of Judeophobia

136. See Ronald Schechter, *Obstinate Hebrews: Representations of Jews in France, 1715–1815* (Berkeley: University of California Press, 2003), 77–109, and Alyssa Goldstein Sepinwall, *The Abbé Gregoire and the French Revolution: The Making of Modern Universalism* (Berkeley: University of California Press, 2005).
137. Poliakov, *From Voltaire to Wagner*, 319.
138. See Arthur O. Lovejoy, *The Great Chain of Being: A Study of the History of an Idea* (Cambridge, MA: Harvard University Press, 1936).
139. Poliakov, *From Voltaire to Wagner*, 457. On providence, Poliakov writes, "Is it surprising if 'race' was soon raised to the rank of the great mover in human development, supplanting Providence?" (320).
140. Poliakov, *The Aryan Myth*, 145.
141. Poliakov, *From Voltaire to Wagner*, 463 and 467.
142. Poliakov, *From Voltaire to Wagner*, 320.

7. GEORGE MOSSE ON MODERNITY, CULTURE, AND "THE JEW"

1. Steven Aschheim, introduction to *What History Tells: George L. Mosse and the Culture of Modern Europe*, ed. Stanley G. Payne, David J. Sorkin, and John S. Tortorice (Madison: University of Wisconsin Press), 3.
2. Aschheim, introduction, 6.
3. David Gross, "Between Myth and Reality: George L. Mosse's Confrontation with History," *Telos*, no. 119 (Spring 2001): 162–64.
4. George L. Mosse, *Confronting History: A Memoir* (Madison: University of Wisconsin Press, 2000), 5.
5. Enzo Traverso, "To Brush Against the Grain: The Holocaust and German-Jewish Culture in Exile," *Totalitarian Movements and Political Religions* 5, no. 2 (Autumn 2004): 243–70. Cited in Karel Plessini, *The Perils of Normalcy: George L. Mosse and the Remaking of Cultural History* (Madison: University of Wisconsin Press, 2014), 203. See also Jost Hermand's portrait, "German Jews Beyond Judaism: The Gerhard/Israel/George L. Mosse Case," in *The German-Jewish Dialogue Reconsidered: A Symposium in Honor of George L. Mosse*, ed. Klaus L. Berghahn (New York: Peter Lang, 1996), 233–46.
6. George Mosse, *Nationalism and Sexuality: Middle-Class Morality and Sexual Norms in Modern Europe* (Madison: University of Wisconsin Press, 1985), 133.
7. Plessini, *The Perils of Normalcy*, 106.
8. George Mosse, *Nazism: A Historical and Comparative Analysis of National Socialism* (New Brunswick, NJ: Transaction Publishers, 1978), 21.
9. Hannah Arendt, "The Jew as Pariah: A Hidden Tradition," in Hannah Arendt, *The Jewish Writings*, ed. Jerome Kohn and Ron H. Feldman (New York: Schocken, 2007), 275–97, and Michael Walzer, *Interpretation and Social Criticism* (Cambridge, MA: Harvard University Press, 1993).
10. Mosse, *Nazism*, 23.
11. University of Wisconsin-Madison Archives, Oral History Project, Interview #227, George Mosse.
12. Lawrence Baron, "The Wit of George Mosse," University of Wisconsin-Madison Archives, Personal Folder, George Mosse, 5.

13. David Warren Sabean, "George Mosse and *The Holy Pretence*," in Payne, Sorkin, and Tortorice, *What History Tells*, 17.
14. Plessini, *The Perils of Normalcy*, 40.
15. Mosse, *Confronting History*, 174.
16. Baron, "The Wit of George Mosse," 3.
17. Michael Ledeen, introduction to Mosse, *Nazism*, 19.
18. Mosse, *Nazism*, 29-30.
19. Ledeen, introduction, 20.
20. Cited in Sabean, "George Mosse and *The Holy Pretence*," 16. See also Mosse's own comments in this regard in *Confronting History*: "It is my firm belief that a historian in order to understand the past has to empathize with it, to get under its skin, as it were, to see the world through the eyes of its actors and its institutions" (53).
21. Mosse, *Nazism*, 39-40.
22. Mosse, *Nazism*, 37.
23. Plessini, *The Perils of Normalcy*, chap. 2.
24. George L. Mosse, *The Culture of Western Europe: The Nineteenth and Twentieth Centuries*, 3rd ed. (Boulder, CO: Westview, 1988 [1961]), 2.
25. Mosse, *The Culture of Western Europe*, 3.
26. Plessini, *The Perils of Normalcy*, 56.
27. George L. Mosse, *The Struggle for Sovereignty in England: From the Reign of Queen Elizabeth to the Petition of Right* (East Lansing: Michigan State University Press, 1950); Mosse, *The Holy Pretense: A Study in Christianity and Reason of State from William Perkins to John Winthrop* (Oxford: Blackwell, 1957); H. G. Koenigsberger and George L. Mosse, *Europe in the Sixteenth Century* (London: Longman, 1968); George L. Mosse, *The Reformation* (New York: Holt, Rinehart and Winston, 1953).
28. Sabean, "George Mosse and *The Holy Pretense*," 16.
29. This question is highlighted in the opening line of the Festschrift for Mosse. See Seymour Drescher, David Sabean, and Allan Sharlin, "George Mosse and Political Symbolism," in *Political Symbolism in Modern Europe: Essays in Honor of George L. Mosse*, ed. Seymour Drescher, David Sabean, and Allan Sharlin (New Brunswick, NJ: Transaction Books, 1982), 1.
30. This argument is made by Plessini, *The Perils of Normalcy*, 21. I have summarized Plessini's overview of Mosse's early works discussed in chapter 2 in this section.
31. George Mosse, *The Nationalization of the Masses: Political Symbolism and Mass Movements in Germany from the Napoleonic Wars Through the Third Reich* (New York: Meridian, 1975), vii.
32. George Mosse, "Tolerance Lectures," University of Wisconsin-Madison Archives, General Files, George L. Mosse, series # 7/16/17, box 6, folder 72, Lecture I, p. 1.
33. Mosse, *The Culture of Western Europe*, 74.
34. Mosse, *The Culture of Western Europe*, 76.
35. Mosse, *The Culture of Western Europe*, 76.
36. Mosse, *The Culture of Western Europe*, 83.
37. Mosse, *The Culture of Western Europe*, 84.
38. Stanley Payne relayed this anecdote to me on March 9, 2003. The fact that Speer felt this way was surely a result of the fact that Mosse was a close reader of Speer's memoirs, which he believed provided the single best portrait of Hitler, as well as his personal

interlocutor. On Mosse's views of Speer and its influence on his interpretation, see Mosse, *Nazism*, 68.

39. One problem with the Luther-to-Hitler thesis for Mosse was that it was nondialectical and did not appreciate discontinuities. See Mosse, *Nazism*, 33. What Mosse opposed in the totalitarian thesis was the notion that Nazism was successful because it was a form of rule by terror or propagandistic manipulation. Instead, Mosse sought to account for how Nazism provided a meaningful sense of community to millions of followers who were alienated by the crises of modernity. Also, the totalitarian thesis cannot account for how Nazism moderated its ideological agenda with pragmatic politics where necessary.
40. On these points, see Saul Friedländer, "Mosse's Influence on the Historiography of the Holocaust," in Payne, Sorkin, and Tortorice, *What History Tells*, 135.
41. Friedländer, "Mosse's Influence," 135.
42. Mosse, *The Crisis of German Ideology*, 317.
43. Mosse, *The Crisis of German Ideology*, 311.
44. Friedländer, "Mosse's Influence," 135.
45. Mosse, *The Crisis of German Ideology*, 151.
46. Mosse, *The Crisis of German Ideology*, 278.
47. Mosse, *The Crisis of German Ideology*, 286.
48. Mosse, *The Crisis of German Ideology*, 292.
49. Mosse, *The Nationalization of the Masses*, 2.
50. Mosse, *The Nationalization of the Masses*, chap. 1 and passim. Carl E. Schorske, "Politics in a New Key: An Austrian Triptych," *The Journal of Modern History* 39, no. 4 (December 1967): 343–86.
51. Mosse, *The Nationalization of the Masses*, 5.
52. Peter Pulzer, "How Nazism Grew," *Jewish Chronicle*, October 21, 1966, 20.
53. A. J. Nicholls, review of *The Crisis of German Ideology: Intellectual Origins of the Third Reich*, by George Mosse, *The English Historical Review* 82, no. 325 (October 1967): 860–61, citation 861.
54. Walter Laqueur, "The Roots of Nazism," *New York Review of Books*, January 14, 1965, 15–17, cited 16. Laqueur generally lauded both Mosse's book and Pulzer's book, *The Rise of Political Anti-Semitism in Germany and Austria* (New York: Wiley, 1964).
55. Mosse, *The Nationalization of the Masses*, 67.
56. Mosse, *The Nationalization of the Masses*, 66.
57. Mosse, *The Nationalization of the Masses*, 103.
58. Mosse, *The Nationalization of the Masses*, 108.
59. Mosse, *The Nationalization of the Masses*, 198.
60. Jeffrey Herf, "Mosse's Recasting of European Intellectual and Cultural History," *German Politics and Society* 18, no. 4 (Winter 2000): 18–29, quote on 23.
61. George Mosse, *Toward the Final Solution: A History of European Racism* (Madison: University of Wisconsin Press, 1985 [1978]), xi.
62. Mosse, *Toward the Final Solution*, chap. 2 and passim.
63. Mosse, *Toward the Final Solution*, 29.
64. Mosse, *Toward the Final Solution*, 21.
65. Mosse zeroes in on this transformation in *Fallen Soldiers: Reshaping the Memory of the World Wars* (Oxford: Oxford University Press, 1990), where he historicizes how the

brutality of war was made manageable and acceptable through sacralization and trivialization. This was his pioneering contribution to the memory studies of the 1990s that became so prominent.

66. Mosse, *Toward the Final Solution*, 234.
67. Mosse, *Toward the Final Solution*, 236.
68. Mosse, *Toward the Final Solution*, 233.
69. See George Mosse, "Anatomy of a Stereotype," *New German Critique*, no. 42 (Fall 1987): 163–68. Sander L. Gilman, *Difference and Pathology: Stereotypes of Sexuality, Race, and Madness* (Ithaca, NY: Cornell University Press, 1985), and Gilman, *Jewish Self-Hatred: Anti-Semitism and the Hidden Language of the Jews* (Baltimore, MD: Johns Hopkins University Press, 1986).
70. Gilman, *Difference and Pathology*, 15.
71. Gilman, *Difference and Pathology*, 19.
72. Gilman, *Difference and Pathology*, 20.
73. See Sander Gilman, *Stand Up Straight! A History of Posture* (London: Reaktion, 2018), 8.
74. Sander Gilman, *Seeing the Insane* (New York: John Wiley, 1982).
75. Gilman, *Difference and Pathology*, 23. In his note appended to this line, he states, "These are categories suggested by George L. Mosse in his rich work on texts that contain culturally embedded stereotyped images. See his recent essay, 'Nationalism and Respectability: Normal and Abnormal Sexuality in the Nineteenth Century,'" *Journal of Contemporary History* 17 (1982): 221–46."
76. Gilman, *Difference and Pathology*, 23.
77. Sander Gilman, *The Jew's Body* (New York: Routledge, 1991), 4. In addition to Mosse, the book is also dedicated to Elaine Showalter.
78. Sander Gilman, *Jewish Self-Hatred*, 11.
79. Mosse, "The Anatomy of a Stereotype," 163.
80. Mosse, "The Anatomy of a Stereotype," 168.
81. See Gilman's long citation of Fanon in *Difference and Pathology*, 29–30, a key work for Homi Bhabha's analysis of the duality of stereotypes in *The Location of Culture* (New York: Routledge, 1994), chaps. 3–4.
82. See Shulamit Volkov, "Antisemitism as a Cultural Code: Reflections on the History and Historiography of Antisemitism in Imperial Germany," *Leo Baeck Yearbook* 23, no. 1 (1978): 25–46.
83. George L. Mosse, *Nationalism and Sexuality: Middle-Class Morality and Sexual Norms in Modern Europe* (Madison: University of Wisconsin Press, 1985): "The importance of Sander L. Gilman's work for my own is reflected in the pages that follow," x.
84. Mosse, *Nationalism and Sexuality*, 4.
85. Mosse, *Nationalism and Sexuality*, 71.
86. Mosse, *Nationalism and Sexuality*, 9.
87. George L. Mosse, *The Image of Man: The Creation of Modern Masculinity* (Oxford: Oxford University Press, 1996).
88. Mosse, *Confronting History*, 181–82.
89. Mosse, *Image of Man*, 71.
90. Mosse, *Nationalism and Sexuality*, 133.
91. Mosse, *Nationalism and Sexuality*, 137.

92. Mosse, *Nationalism and Sexuality*, 152.
93. Steven Aschheim, "George Mosse and Jewish History," *German Politics and Society* 18, no. 4 (Winter 2000): 46–57, quote 47.
94. Mosse, *The Culture of Western Europe*, 85–86.
95. Mosse, *Toward the Final Solution*, 235–36.

8. CRITICAL THEORY AND POST-HOLOCAUST JUDEOPHOBIA

1. FRA, European Union Agency for Fundamental Rights, *Experiences and Perceptions of Antisemitism: Second Survey on Discrimination and Hate Crime Against Jews in the EU*, 11. Available at https://fra.europa.eu/sites/default/files/fra_uploads/fra-2018-experiences-and-perceptions-of-antisemitism-survey_en.pdf.
2. "CNN Poll: Anti-Semitism in Europe." Available at: https://edition.cnn.com/interactive/2018/11/europe/antisemitism-poll-2018-intl/.
3. European Union, *Special Eurobarometer Report 484—December 2018: Perceptions of Antisemitism*. Available at: https://europa.eu/eurobarometer/surveys/detail/2220.
4. *Kantor Center Worldwide Report*. Available at: https://cst.tau.ac.il/antisemitism-worldwide-report-for-2022/.
5. *The ADL Global 100: An Index of Antisemitism*. Available at: https://global100.adl.org/map.
6. I have done this work elsewhere. See, for example, Jonathan Judaken, "So What's New? Rethinking the 'New Antisemitism' in a Global Age," *Patterns of Prejudice* 42, nos. 4–5 (Autumn 2008): 531–60.
7. Albert Memmi, *Racism*, trans. Steve Martinot (Minneapolis: University of Minnesota Press, 2000), 118. See also Jonathan Judaken, "Memmi on Racism and (Post-Holocaust) Judeophobia," *H-France Salon* 13, no. 4, #6. Available at: https://h-france.net/Salon/SalonVol13no04.6.Judaken.pdf
8. Jacques Derrida, *Philosophy in a Time of Terror: Dialogues with Jürgen Habermas and Jacques Derrida* (Chicago: University of Chicago Press, 2003), 94.
9. Zygmunt Bauman, *Life in Fragments: Essays in Postmodern Morality* (Oxford: Blackwell, 1995), 190.
10. Samuel Huntington, *The Clash of Civilizations and the Remaking of World Order* (New York: Simon and Schuster, 1996).
11. Benjamin Barber, *Jihad vs. McWorld* (New York: Ballantine Books, 1996).
12. Zygmunt Bauman, *44 Letters from the Liquid Modern World* (Cambridge: Polity, 2010), 117.
13. Bauman, *44 Lessons*, 115, emphasis added.
14. Zygmunt Bauman, *Strangers at Our Door* (Cambridge: Polity, 2016), 15.
15. Bauman, *44 Letters*, 116
16. Bauman, *Strangers*, 16
17. Bauman, *Life in Fragments*, 132. Quoted from Erich Fromm, *The Anatomy of Human Destructiveness* (London: Jonathan Cape, 1974), 343.
18. Bauman, *44 Letters*, 157.
19. Bauman, *Strangers*, 49.
20. Cited in Bauman, *Strangers*, 65.
21. See Samuel Moyn's critique of talking about our present as fascism reborn in "The Trouble with Comparisons," *New York Review of Books*, May 19, 2020.

22. George Mosse, *The Fascist Revolution: Toward a General Theory of Fascism* (New York: Howard Fertig, 1999), 44.
23. Mosse, *Fascist Revolution*, xvi.
24. George Mosse, "Political Style and Political Theory: Totalitarian Democracy Revisited," in *Confronting the Nation: Jewish and Western Nationalism* (Hanover, NH: Brandeis University Press, 1993), 67.
25. Mosse, *Fascist Revolution*, xii.
26. Mosse, *Fascist Revolution*, 18.
27. Mosse, *Fascist Revolution*, 5.
28. Mosse, *Fascist Revolution*, 10.
29. Mosse, *Fascist Revolution*, xiv.
30. For an overview of the generative texts of "the new anti-Semitism" theorists, see Judaken, "So What's New?," 549.
31. Léon Poliakov, *De l'antisionisme à l'antisémitisme* (Paris: Calmann-Lévy, 1969).
32. Paul Hanebrink, *A Specter Haunting Europe: The Myth of Judeo-Bolshevism* (Cambridge, MA: Harvard University Press, 2018), 188.
33. Poliakov, *De l'antisionisme à l'antisémitisme*, 10.
34. Robert Wistrich develops Poliakov's analysis in *From Ambivalence to Betrayal: The Left, the Jews, and Israel* (Lincoln: University of Nebraska Press/SICSA, 2012), 419-47. On Marxism and the Jewish Question more generally, see Robert Wistrich, *Socialism and the Jews: The Dilemmas of Assimilation in Germany and Austria-Hungary* (East Brunswick, NJ: Associated University Presses, 1982); Jack Jacobs, *On Socialists and "the Jewish Question" After Marx* (New York: NYU Press, 1992); and Enzo Traverso, *Marxists and the Jewish Question: The History of a Debate, 1843–1943* (Atlantic Highlands, NJ: Humanities, 1994).
35. Poliakov, *De l'antisionisme à l'antisémitisme*, 11. As Wistrich notes in *From Ambivalence to Betrayal*, 425: "This was the death-knell for the Leninist tradition of anti-antisemitism to which Stalin had still paid lip service."
36. Poliakov, *De l'antisionisme à l'antisémitisme*, 167.
37. This phrase is from Pierre-André Taguieff, *Rising from the Muck: The New Anti-Semitism in Europe*, trans. Patrick Camiller (Chicago: Ivan R. Dee, 2004): "Judeophobia answer[s] with remarkable symbolic efficiency, the demand for meaning and the mobilization of causes felt by ... those orphans of 'revolution' who continue to think and find guidance in the traditional Communist element of revolutionary myth, in one of its many Marxist (Leninist, Trotskyist, Third Worldist) or anarchist (neoleftist, 'neoradical') variants. For these 'radical' milieux ... Israel is the devil incarnate, 'Zionism' is the absolute enemy" (8).
38. Walter Laqueur, *The Changing Face of Antisemitism: From Ancient Time to the Present Day* (Oxford: Oxford University Press, 2006), 6.
39. Éric Marty, *Radical French Thought and the Return of the "Jewish Question,"* trans. Alan Astro (Bloomington: Indiana University Press, 2015), 37, and Bruno Chaouat, *Is Theory Good for the Jews? French Thought and the Challenge of the New Antisemitism* (Liverpool: Liverpool University Press, 2016), xix. Chaouat borrows the term "Jew-splitting" from Gabriel Noah Brahm's unpublished paper, "What Edward Said Said: Sources of the New Antisemitism in the 'Discourse' of Postcolonial Studies." See *Is Theory Good for the Jews?*, 206.

40. Maurice Samuels, *The Right to Difference: French Universalism and the Jews* (Chicago: University of Chicago Press, 2016), 176-77.
41. Alain Finkielkraut makes this same argument in *Au nom de l'autre: Réflexions sur l'antisémitisme qui vient* (Paris: Gallimard, 2003). On Badiou, see also Sarah Hammerschlag, *The Figural Jew: Politics and Identity in Postwar French Thought* (Chicago: University of Chicago Press, 2010), conclusion.
42. Judith Butler, *Parting Ways: Jewishness and the Critique of Zionism* (New York: Columbia University Press, 2012). Since the 1990s, "parting of the ways" has served as shorthand for scholars discussing the split between Judaism and Christianity. See Timothy Gabrielson, "Parting Ways or Rival Siblings? A Review and Analysis of Metaphors for the Separation of Jews and Christians in Antiquity," *Currents in Biblical Research* 19, no. 2 (2021): 178-204. Butler also associates herself with the neo-Pauline intellectuals in works like *Deconstructing Zionism: A Critique of Political Metaphysics*, ed. Gianni Vattimo and Michael Marder (New York: Bloomsbury, 2014).
43. Cynthia Ozick, "The Modern 'Hep! Hep! Hep!,'" in *The Jewish Divide Over Israel: Accusers and Defenders*, ed. Edward Alexander and Paul Bogdanor (New Brunswick, NJ: Transaction, 2006), 6.
44. Edward Alexander, "Antisemitism-Denial: The Berkeley School," in Alexander and Bogdanor, *The Jewish Divide Over Israel*, 195-208.
45. Cary Nelson, "The Problem with Judith Butler: The Political Philosophy of BDS and the Movement to Delegitimate Israel," in *The Case Against Academic Boycotts of Israel*, ed. Cary Nelson and Gabriel Noah Brahm (Chicago: MLA Members for Scholars Rights, 2015), 164-201.
46. See David N. Myers, "Can There Be a Principled Anti-Zionism? On the Nexus between Anti-Historicism and Anti-Zionism in Modern Jewish Thought," in *Anti-Semitism and Anti-Zionism in Historical Perspective: Convergence and Divergence*, ed. Jeffrey Herf (London: Routledge, 2007), 20-37, where Myers develops the distinction between principled and unprincipled anti-Zionism. See also David N. Myers, "Against Un-Jewing: Recalling the History of Jewish Dissent," *Jewschool*, July 2, 2021: https://jewschool.com/against-un-jewing-recalling-the-history-of-jewish-dissent-173313.
47. Judith Butler, "Judith Butler Responds to Attack: 'I Affirm a Judaism That Is Not Associated with State Violence,'" *Mondoweiss*: https://mondoweiss.net/2012/08/judith-butler-responds-to-attack-i-affirm-a-judaism-that-is-not-associated-with-state-violence/.
48. Lawrence Summers, "Address at Morning Prayers," in *Those Who Forget the Past: The Question of Antisemitism*, ed. Ron Rosenbaum (New York: Random House, 2004), 57-60, 59. See also Berel Lang's "On the 'the' in 'the Jews,'" which also focuses on how the definite article "the" can be anti-Semitic in effect if not in intent in *Those Who Forget the Past*, 63-70.
49. Judith Butler, "The Charge of Antisemitism: Jews, Israel, and the Risks of Public Critique," in Rosenbaum, *Those Who Forget the Past*, 438.
50. Butler, "The Charge of Antisemitism," 449-50.
51. Framing the charges against Arendt as a form of "excommunication" akin to Spinoza's comes from Amos Elon, "The Case of Hannah Arendt," in the *New York Review of Books*, November 6, 1997, 25-29. It is repeated by Steven Aschheim in his introduction to

Arendt in Jerusalem, ed. Steven Aschheim (Berkeley: University of California Press, 2001), 1.
52. Richard Bernstein, *Hannah Arendt and the Jewish Question* (Cambridge, MA: MIT Press, 1996), 102.
53. Daniel Maier-Katkin, "How Hannah Arendt Was Labeled an 'Enemy of Israel,'" *Tikkun*, November/December 2010, 12.
54. Hannah Arendt, "The Crisis of Zionism," in *The Jewish Writings*, ed. Jerome Kohn and Ron H. Feldman (New York: Schocken, 2007), 329-37.
55. Elisabeth Young-Bruehl, *Hannah Arendt: For Love of the World* (New Haven, CT: Yale University Press, 1982), 224.
56. Hannah Arendt, "Zionism Reconsidered," in *The Jewish Writings*, 343-72.
57. Hannah Arendt, "To Save the Jewish Homeland," in *The Jewish Writings*, 388-401, quote on 401.
58. Arendt, "Zionism Reconsidered," 364.
59. Arendt, "To Save the Jewish Homeland," 396.
60. Arendt, "Zionism Reconsidered," 345.
61. Arendt, "Zionism Reconsidered," 344.
62. Arendt, "Zionism Reconsidered," 347.
63. Arendt, "Zionism Reconsidered," 358.
64. Arendt, "Zionism Reconsidered," 363.
65. Bernstein, *Hannah Arendt and the Jewish Question*, 104.
66. Young-Bruehl, *Hannah Arendt*, 223. Instead, the article was published in *Menorah Journal*, a venue with a much smaller and almost wholly Jewish readership.
67. Young-Bruehl, *Hannah Arendt*, 230. See Hannah Arendt, "To Save the Jewish Homeland," 388-401, where, as I have noted, she reiterates some of the key points from her earlier articles, in particular, the need to create a homeland based on Jewish-Arab cooperation instituted in local councils.
68. Anson Rabinbach, "Eichmann in New York: The New York Intellectuals and the Hannah Arendt Controversy," *October* 108 (Spring): 97-111, and Maier-Katkin, "How Hannah Arendt Was Labeled an 'Enemy of Israel,'" 13.
69. Susan A. Glenn, "The Vogue of Jewish Self-Hatred in Post-World War II America," *Jewish Social Studies* (Spring-Summer 2006): 95-136, 120.
70. Hannah Arendt, *Eichmann in Jerusalem: A Report on the Banality of Evil* (New York: Penguin, 1963, 1964), 276, 48, 126.
71. Maier-Katkin, "How Hannah Arendt Was Labeled an 'Enemy of Israel,'" 13.
72. These quotations are cited in Michael Ezra, "The Eichmann Polemics: Hannah Arendt and Her Critics," *Democratiya* 9 (Summer 2007): 147, who offers a full roundup of the debate.
73. Hannah Arendt, "The Jew as Pariah: A Hidden Tradition," in *The Jewish Writings*, 275-97, quote on 284.
74. Hannah Arendt, "Herzl and Lazare," in *The Jewish Writings*, 338-42, quote on 339.
75. For an overview of the Indigènes de la République, see Itay Lotem, "Anti-Racist Activism and the Memory of Colonialism: Race as Republican Critique After 2005," *Modern and Contemporary France* 24 (2016): 283-98, and Lotem, "Beyond Memory Wars: The

Indigènes de la République's Grass-Roots Anti-Racism Between the Memory of Colonialism and Antisemitism," *French History* 32, no. 4 (December 2018): 573-93.

76. Houria Bouteldja, Sadri Khiari, and Félix Boggio Ewanjé-Epée, "Appel: Nous sommes les indigènes de la république," in *Nous sommes les indigènes de la république* (Paris: Éditions Amsterdam, 2012), 20.

77. Houria Bouteldja, *Whites, Jews, and Us: Toward a Politics of Revolutionary Love*, trans. Rachel Valinsky (Pasadena, CA: Semiotext(e), 2016).

78. Albert Memmi, *Racism*, trans. Steve Martinot (Minneapolis: University of Minnesota Press, 2000), 125. I argue that Memmi's *The Colonizer and the Colonized* is one of the great treatises on privilege in Jonathan Judaken, introduction to *The Albert Memmi Reader*, ed. Jonathan Judaken and Michael Lejman (Lincoln: University of Nebraska Press, 2020).

79. Bouteldja, *Whites, Jews, and Us*, 41.
80. Bouteldja, *Whites, Jews, and Us*, 53.
81. Bouteldja, *Whites, Jews, and Us*, 57.
82. Bouteldja, *Whites, Jews, and Us*, 55.
83. Bouteldja, *Whites, Jews, and Us*, 55-56.
84. Bouteldja, *Whites, Jews, and Us*, 58.
85. Bouteldja, *Whites, Jews, and Us*, 68.
86. Bouteldja, *Whites, Jews, and Us*, 23, 24.
87. Bouteldja is critical of Dieudonné even as she is sympathetic with his provocations in *Whites, Jews, and Us*, 71-72. She plays a similar game with Mohamed Merah in "Mohamed Merah et moi," in Bouteldja, Khiari, Boggio Ewanjé-Epée, *Nous sommes les indigènes de la république*, 311-14. Merah was a jihadi terrorist who killed seven people, including three children and a rabbi, at a Jewish day school in Toulouse, which he filmed, stating as a motivation for the attack that "the Jews have killed our brothers and sisters in Palestine." While not her article, see also the article by Fatouche Ouassak, "Pourquoi je soutiens Alain Soral" (Why I follow Alain Soral), in *Nous sommes les indigènes de la république*, 420-30. On Dieudonné, see Marc Weitzmann, "Did a French Comedian Inspire the Killings at the Jewish Museum in Brussels? Links Between Dieudonné, the Belgian Anti-Semite Laurent Louis, and Iran Show How Anti-Semitism Is Spreading in Europe," *Tablet*, May 27, 2014: http://www.tabletmag.com/jewish-arts-and-culture/theater-and-dance/174215/dieudonne. See also Alexander Stille, "The Case of Dieudonné: A French Comedian's Hate," *New Yorker*, January 10, 2014: http://www.newyorker.com/news/daily-comment/the-case-of-dieudonn-a-french-comedians-hate. See, as well, Bruno Chaouat, "Postscript: Theorizing Antisemitic Laughter," in *Is Theory Good for the Jews?*, 223-38.

88. Lars Rensmann, *The Politics of Unreason: The Frankfurt School and the Origins of Modern Antisemitism* (Albany: SUNY Press, 2017), 391-420. What follows in this section is significantly indebted to what Rensmann argues in his chapter "Why Critical Theory Matters."

89. Rensmann, *The Politics of Unreason*, 417.

90. See Eduardo Bonilla-Silva, *Racism Without Racists: Color-Blind Racism and the Persistence of Racial Inequality in America* (Lanham: Rowman and Littlefield, 2014).

91. Rensmann, *The Politics of Unreason*, 409.

92. There is now a historiography on Holocaust denial globally, but the classic text on the subject remains Deborah Lipstadt, *Denying the Holocaust: The Growing Assault on Truth and Memory* (New York: Free Press, 1993).
93. Rensmann, *The Politics of Unreason*, 360.
94. Friedrich Pollock and Theodor Adorno, *Group Experiment and Other Writings: The Frankfurt School on Public Opinion in Postwar Germany*, trans. Jeffrey K. Olick and Andrew J. Perrin (Cambridge, MA: Harvard University Press, 2011); Theodor W. Adorno, *Guilt and Defense: On the Legacies of National Socialism in Postwar Germany*, trans. Jeffrey K. Olick and Andrew J. Perrin (Cambridge, MA: Harvard University Press, 2010).
95. Theodor W. Adorno, "The Meaning of Working Through the Past," in *Guilt and Defense*, 213.
96. Adorno, "The Meaning of Working Through the Past," 214.
97. See Frantz Fanon, *Black Skin, White Masks*, trans. Charles Lam Markmann (New York: Grove, 1967), 115-16, and Michael Rothberg, *Multidirectional Memory: Remembering the Holocaust in the Age of Decolonization* (Stanford: Stanford University Press, 2009), 1-3.
98. Michael Rothberg, *The Implicated Subject: Beyond Victims and Perpetrators* (Stanford: Stanford University Press, 2019), 122.
99. See Rensmann, *The Politics of Unreason*, 384-85.
100. Max Horkheimer and Theodor Adorno, *Dialectic of Enlightenment*, trans. John Cumming (New York: Continuum, 2000), 200.
101. On this point, in relation to the work of Hannah Arendt, see Jeremy Waldron, "What Would Hannah Say?," *The New York Review of Books*, March 15, 2007, 8-12, 12.
102. Horkheimer and Adorno, *Dialectic of Enlightenment*, 201.
103. Horkheimer and Adorno, *Dialectic of Enlightenment*, 204, 205.
104. Horkheimer and Adorno, *Dialectic of Enlightenment*, 205.

Select Bibliography

Abraham, Gary A. *Max Weber and the Jewish Question: A Study of the Social Outlook of His Sociology.* Urbana: University of Illinois Press, 1992.

Abromeit, John. *Max Horkheimer and the Foundations of the Frankfurt School.* Cambridge: Cambridge University Press, 2011.

Achebe, Chinua. "An Image of Africa: Racism in Conrad's *Heart of Darkness*." In *Norton Critical Edition of Joseph Conrad's Heart of Darkness*, Edited by Paul B. Armstrong, 336–49. 4th edition. New York: Norton, 2006.

Ackerman, Nathan W., and Marie Jahoda. *Anti-Semitism and Emotional Disorder: A Psychoanalytic Interpretation.* New York: Harper, 1950.

Adorno, T. W. *Guilt and Defense: On the Legacies of National Socialism in Postwar Germany.* Translated by Jeffrey K. Olick and Andrew J. Perrin. Cambridge, MA: Harvard University Press, 2010.

———. *Negative Dialectics.* Translated by E. B. Ashton. New York: Continuum, 1987 [1966].

———. "Research Project on Anti-Semitism." *Studies in Philosophy and Social Science* 9 (1941): 124–43.

Adorno, T. W., Else Frenkel-Brunswik, Daniel J. Levinson, and R. Nevitt Sanford. *The Authoritarian Personality.* New York: Harper, 1950.

Agamben, Georgio. *Homo Sacer: Sovereign Power and Bare Life.* Translated by Daniel Heller-Roazen. Stanford: Stanford University Press, 1998.

Alexander, Jeffrey C. *The Modern Reconstruction of Classical Thought: Talcott Parsons.* Berkeley: University of California Press, 1983.

Allen, Amy. *The End of Progress: Decolonizing the Normative Foundations of Critical Theory.* New York: Columbia University Press, 2016.

Allport, Gordon. *The Nature of Prejudice.* Cambridge, MA: Harvard University Press, 1954.

Anidjar, Gil. *The Jew, The Arab: A History of the Enemy.* Stanford: Stanford University Press, 2003.

———. *Semites: Race, Religion, Literature.* Stanford: Stanford University Press, 2008.

Arendt, Hannah. *Between Past and Future.* New York: Penguin, 1968.

———. *Eichmann in Jerusalem: A Report on the Banality of Evil.* New York: Penguin, 1963.

———. "From the Dreyfus Affair to France Today." *Jewish Social Studies* 4, no. 3 (July 1942): 195–240.

———. *Hannah Arendt/Karl Jaspers Correspondence, 1926–1969.* Edited by Lotte Kohler and Hans Saner. Translated by Robert and Rita Kimber. San Diego, CA: Harcourt Brace Jovanovich, 1992.

———. "The History of the Great Crime." *Commentary*, March 1952, 300-304.

———. *The Human Condition*. Chicago: University of Chicago Press, 1958.

———. *The Jewish Writings*. Edited by Jerome Kohn and Ron H. Feldman. New York: Schocken, 2007.

———. *Men in Dark Times*. New York: Harcourt, Brace and World, 1968.

———. *The Origins of Totalitarianism*. San Diego, CA: Harcourt Brace Jovanovich, 1973.

———. *Rahel Varnhagen: The Life of a Jewish Woman*. rev. ed. Translated by Richard and Clara Winston. New York: Harcourt Brace Jovanovich, 1974.

———. "Reflections on Little Rock." In *The Portable Hannah Arendt*, Edited by Peter Baehr, 231-43. New London, CT: Penguin, 2000.

———. "A Reply to Critics." In *The Portable Hannah Arendt*, Edited by Peter Baehr, 243-46. New London, CT: Penguin, 2000.

———. "A Reply" to Eric Voegelin's review of *The Origins of Totalitarianism*, by Hannah Arendt. *Review of Politics* 15, no. 6 (January 1953): 70-84.

Arjana, Sophia Rose. *Muslims in the Western Imagination*. Oxford: Oxford University Press, 2015.

Aron, Raymond. *The Committed Observer: Interviews with Jean-Louis Mussika and Dominique Walton*. Translated by James and Marie McIntosh. Chicago: Tegnery Gateway, 1983.

———. *De Gaulle, Israël et les juifs*. Paris: Plon, 1968.

Aschheim, Steven. *Brothers and Strangers: The East European Jew in German and German Jewish Consciousness, 1800–1923*. Madison: University of Wisconsin Press, 1982.

———. "George Mosse and Jewish History." *German Politics and Society* 18, no. 4 (Winter 2000): 46-57.

———. ed. *Hannah Arendt in Jerusalem*. Berkeley: University of California Press, 2001.

———. *Scholem, Arendt, Klemperer: Intimate Chronicles in Turbulent Times*. Bloomington: Indiana University Press, 2001.

Askénazi, Léon. "Philosophie et revelation biblique: la demarche de Jacob Gordin." *Pardès: Revue européenne d'études et de culture juives*, no. 23 (1997): 71-77.

Auron, Yaïr. *Les Juifs d'extrême gauche de Mai '68: Une génération révolutionnaire marquée par la Shoah*. Translated by Katherine Werchowski. Paris: Albin Michel, 1998.

Avineri, Shlomo. *The Making of Modern Zionism: The Intellectual Origins of the Jewish State*. New York: Basic Books, 1981.

Azouvi, François. *Le mythe du grand silence*. Paris: Fayard, 2012.

Bahr, Ehrhard. "The Antisemitism Studies of the Frankfurt School: The Failure of Critical Theory." In *Foundations of the Frankfurt School of Social Research*, Edited by Judith Marcus and Zoltán Tar. New Brunswick, NJ: Transaction, 1984.

Bakan, David. *Sigmund Freud and the Jewish Mystical Tradition*. Princeton, NJ: Van Nostrand, 1958.

Bakewell, Sarah. *At the Existentialist Café: Freedom, Being, and Apricot Cocktails*. New York: Other, 2016.

Barber, Benjamin. *Jihad vs. McWorld*. New York: Ballantine, 1996.

Barnouw, Dagmar. *Visible Spaces: Hannah Arendt and the German-Jewish Experience*. Baltimore, MD: Johns Hopkins University Press, 1990.

Bartov, Omer, ed. *Holocaust: Origins, Implementation, Aftermath*. London: Routledge, 2000.

Bartrop, Paul R., and Steven Leonard Jacobs. *Fifty Key Thinkers on the Holocaust and Genocide*. New York: Routledge, 2011.

Bashkin, Orit. *New Babylonians: A History of Jews in Modern Iraq*. Stanford: Stanford University Press, 2012.
Batnitsky, Leora. *How Judaism Became a Religion: An Introduction to Modern Jewish Thought*. Princeton, NJ: Princeton University Press, 2011.
Bauer, Bruno. "The Jewish Problem." In *The Jew in the Modern World: A Documentary History*, Edited by Paul Mendes-Flohr and Jehuda Reinharz. Oxford: Oxford University Press, 1995.
Bauer, Yehuda. *Rethinking the Holocaust*. New Haven, CT: Yale University Press, 2001.
Baum, Rainer, and Frank J. Lechner. "National Socialism: Toward an Action-Theoretical Interpretation." *Sociological Inquiry* 51 (1981): 281-305.
Bauman, Janina. *A Dream of Belonging: My Years in Postwar Poland*. London: Virago, 1988.
Bauman, Zygmunt. *44 Letters from the Liquid Modern World*. Cambridge: Polity, 2010.
———. *Life in Fragments: Essays in Postmodern Morality*. Oxford: Blackwell, 1995.
———. *Modernity and Ambivalence*. Oxford: Polity, 1991.
———. *Modernity and the Holocaust*. Ithaca, NY: Cornell University Press, 2000.
———. *Strangers at Our Door*. Cambridge: Polity, 2016.
Beilharz, Peter, ed. *The Bauman Reader*. Oxford: Basil Blackwell, 2001.
———. "Zygmunt Bauman." In *The Wiley-Blackwell Companion to Major Social Theorists*. Edited by George Ritzer and Jeffrey Stepnisky, 155-74. Malden, MA: Wiley Blackwell, 2011.
Bellamy, Elizabeth. *Affective Genealogies: Psychoanalysis, Postmodernism, and the "Jewish Question" after Auschwitz*. Lincoln: University of Nebraska Press, 1997.
Benbassa, Esther. *Histoire des juifs de France*. Paris: Seuil, 2000.
Bendersky, Joseph W. "Dissension in the Face of the Holocaust: The 1941 American Debate Over Antisemitism." *Holocaust and Genocide Studies* 24, no. 1 (Spring 2010): 85-166.
Benhabib, Seyla. "Hannah Arendt and the Redemptive Power of Narrative," *Social Research* 57, no. 1 (Spring 1990): 168-96.
———. *The Reluctant Modernism of Hannah Arendt*. Thousand Oaks, CA: Sage, 1999.
Benz, Wolfgang. "Antisemitism Research." In *The Oxford Handbook of Jewish Studies*, Edited by Martin Goodman, 943-55. Oxford: Oxford University Press, 2002.
Berger, David. "Anti-Semitism: An Overview." In *History and Hate: The Dimensions of Anti-Semitism*, 3-14. Philadelphia: Jewish Publication Society, 1986.
Bernasconi, Robert. "Locke's Almost Random Talk of Man: The Double Use of Words in the Natural Law Justification of Slavery." *Perspektiven der Philosophie* 18 (1992): 293-318.
———. "Situating Frantz Fanon's Account of Black Experience." In *Situating Existentialism: Key Texts in Context*, Edited by Jonathan Judaken and Robert Bernasconi, 336-59. New York: Columbia University Press, 2012.
———. "When the Real Crime Began: Hannah Arendt's *The Origins of Totalitarianism* and the Dignity of the Western Philosophical Tradition." In *Hannah Arendt and the Uses of History*, Edited by Richard H. King and Dan Stone, 54-67. New York: Berghahn, 2007.
———. "Who Invented the Concept of Race? Kant's Role in the Enlightenment Construction of Race." In *Race*, Edited by Robert Bernasconi, 9-36. Oxford: Blackwell, 2001.
Bernasconi, Robert, and Anika Maaza Mann. "The Contradictions of Racism: Locke, Slavery, and the *Two Treatises*." In *Race and Racism in Modern Philosophy*, Edited by Andrew Valls, 89-107. Ithaca, NY: Cornell University Press, 2005.
Bernier, François. "A New Division of the Earth." *History Workshop Journal*, no. 51 (Spring 2001): 247-50.

Bernstein, Richard J. *Hannah Arendt and the Jewish Question.* Cambridge, MA: MIT Press, 1996.

Bettelheim, Bruno, and Morris Janowitz. *Dynamics of Prejudice: A Psychological and Sociological Study of Veterans.* New York: Harper, 1950.

Birnbaum, Pierre. *Anti-Semitism in France: A Political History from Léon Blum to the Present.* Translated by Miriam Kochan. Oxford: Blackwell, 1992.

———. *Geography of Hope: Exile, the Enlightenment, Disassimilation.* Translated by Charlotte Mandell. Stanford: Stanford University Press, 2008.

Blanchot, Maurice. "Being Jewish." In *The Infinite Conversation.* Translated by Susan Hanson, 123-30. Minneapolis: University of Minnesota Press, 1993.

Bonilla-Silva, Eduardo. *Racism Without Racists: Color-Blind Racism and the Persistence of Racial Inequality in America.* Lanham, MD: Rowman and Littlefield, 2014.

Botstein, Leon. "The Jew as Pariah: Hannah Arendt's Political Philosophy." *Dialectical Anthropology* 8, nos. 1&2 (October 1983): 47-75.

Bourg, Julian. *From Revolution to Ethics: May 1968 and Contemporary French Thought.* Montreal: McGill University Press, 2007.

Bouteldja, Houria. *Whites, Jews, and Us: Toward a Politics of Revolutionary Love.* Translated by Rachel Valinsky. Pasadena: Semiotext(e), 2016.

Boxill, Bernard. "Kantian Racism and Kantian Teleology." In *The Oxford Handbook of Philosophy and Race*, Edited by Naomi Zack, 44-53. Oxford: Oxford University Press, 2017.

Boyarin, Daniel. *Unheroic Conduct: The Rise of Heterosexuality and the Invention of the Jewish Man.* Berkeley: University of California Press, 1997.

Boyarin, Daniel, and Jonathan Boyarin. "Diaspora: Generation and the Ground of Jewish Identity." *Critical Inquiry* 19 (Summer 1993): 693-725.

Brinker, Menachem. "Sartre et Israël (1939-1980): 'Drôle de Position.'" *Sillages*, no. 3 (October 1980): 83-87.

Brodkin, Karen. *How Jews Became White Folks and What That Says About Race in America.* New Brunswick, NJ: Rutgers University Press, 1999.

Browning, Christopher R. "Ordinary Germans or Ordinary Men? A Reply to the Critics." In *The Holocaust and History: The Known, the Unknown, the Disputed, and the Reexamined*, Edited by Michael Berenbaum and Abraham J. Peck, 252-65. Bloomington: Indiana University Press, 1998.

———. *Ordinary Men: Reserve Police Battalion 101 and the Final Solution in Poland.* New York: Harper Collins, 1992.

Brozgal, Lia. *Against Autobiography: Albert Memmi and the Production of Theory.* Lincoln: University of Nebraska Press, 2013.

Bunzl, Matti. *Anti-Semitism and Islamophobia: Hatreds Old and New in Europe.* Chicago: Prickly Paradigm, 2007.

Burke, Peter. *The French Historical Revolution: The Annales School, 1929–1989.* Stanford: Stanford University Press, 1990.

Burleigh, Michael, and Wolfgang Wippermann. *The Racial State: Germany, 1933–1945.* Cambridge: Cambridge University Press, 1991.

Butler, Judith. "The Charge of Antisemitism: Jews Israel, and the Risks of Public Critique." In *Those Who Forget the Past: The Question of Antisemitism*, Edited by Ron Rosenbaum, 238-50. New York: Random House, 2004.

———. *Parting Ways: Jewishness and the Critique of Zionism.* New York: Columbia University Press, 2012.

———. *Subjects of Desire: Hegelian Reflections in Twentieth-Century France.* New York: Columbia University Press, 1988.
Butler, Judith, and Gayatri Chakravorty Spivak. *Who Sings the Nation-State? Language, Politics, Belonging.* London: Seagull, 2007.
Buxton, William. *Talcott Parsons and the Capitalist Nation-State.* Toronto: Toronto University Press, 1985.
Campos, Michelle. *Ottoman Brothers: Muslims, Christians, and Jews in Early Twentieth-Century Palestine.* Stanford: Stanford University Press, 2011.
Canovan, Margaret. *Hannah Arendt: A Reinterpretation of Her Political Thought.* Cambridge: Cambridge University Press, 1995.
Carlebach, Julius. *Karl Marx and the Radical Critique of Judaism.* London: Routledge and Kegan Paul, 1978.
Caron, Vicki. "Catholics and the Rhetoric of Antisemitic Violence in Fin-de-Siècle France." In *Sites of European Antisemitism in the Age of Mass Politics, 1880–1918,* Edited by Robert Nemes and Daniel Unowsky, 36-60. Waltham, MA: University Press of New England, 2014.
———. *Uneasy Asylum: France and the Jewish Refugee Crisis, 1933–1942.* Stanford: Stanford University Press, 1999.
Carroll, David. "Forward: The Memory of Devastation and the Responsibilities of Thought: 'And Let's Not Talk About That.'" In *Heidegger and "the jews,"* by Jean-François Lyotard. Minneapolis: University of Minnesota Press, 1990.
Carroll, James. *Constantine's Sword: The Church and the Jews, A History.* New York: Houghton Mifflin, 2001.
Césaire, Aimé. *Discourse on Colonialism.* Translated by Joan Pinkham. New York: Monthly Review Press, 1972.
Chaouat, Bruno. *Is Theory Good for the Jews? French Thought and the Challenge of the New Antisemitism.* Liverpool: Liverpool University Press, 2016.
Charmé, Stuart Zane. *Vulgarity and Authenticity: Dimensions of Otherness in the World of Jean-Paul Sartre.* Amherst: University of Massachusetts Press, 1991.
Chazan, Robert. *Medieval Stereotypes and Modern Antisemitism.* Berkeley: University of California Press, 1997.
Cheyette, Bryan. *Construction of 'the Jew' in English Literature and Society: Racial Representations, 1875–1945.* Cambridge: Cambridge University Press, 1993.
———. *Diasporas of the Mind: Jewish and Postcolonial Writing and the Nightmare of History.* New Haven, CT: Yale University Press, 2013.
Christie, Richard, and Peggy Cook. "A Guide to the Published Literature Relating to 'The Authoritarian Personality' Through 1956." *Journal of Psychology* 45 (1958): 171-91.
Cohen, Arthur A. *The Myth of the Judeo-Christian Tradition.* New York: Harper and Row, 1971.
Cohen, Jeremy. *Living Letters of the Law: Ideas of the Jew in Medieval Christianity.* Berkeley: University of California Press, 1999.
Cohen, Mark R. *Under Crescent and Cross: The Jews in the Middle Ages.* Princeton, NJ: Princeton University Press, 1994.
Cohen, Richard. *The Burden of Conscience: French Jewish Leadership During the Holocaust.* Bloomington: Indiana University Press, 1987.
Cohn, Norman. *Warrant for Genocide: The Myth of the Jewish World Conspiracy and the Protocols of the Elders of Zion.* Middlesex: Penguin, 1967.

Cohn-Sherbok, Dan. *The Paradox of Anti-Semitism*. New York: Continuum, 2006.
Confino, Alon. *A World Without Jews: The Nazi Imagination from Persecution to Genocide*. New Haven, CT: Yale University Press, 2014.
Cosier, Lewis. *Refugee Scholars in America: Their Impact and Their Experiences*. New Haven, CT: Yale University Press, 1984.
Crane, Richard. *Passion of Israel: Jacques Maritain, Catholic Conscience, and the Holocaust*. Scranton, PA: University of Scranton Press, 2010.
———. "Surviving Maurras: Jacques Maritain's Jewish Question." In *Naming Race, Naming Racisms*, Edited by Jonathan Judaken, 51–77. New York: Routledge, 2009.
Crozier, Michael. "*Inter Putatorem et Vastitatem*: The Ambivalences of the Garden Metaphor in Modernity." In *The Left in Search of a Center*, Edited by Michael Crozier and P. Murphy, 64–85. Urbana: University of Illinois Press, 1996.
Cuddihy, John Murray. *The Ordeal of Civility*. New York: Basic Books, 1974.
Cutler, Allan Harris, and Helen Elmquist Cutler. *The Jew as Ally of the Muslim: Medieval Roots of Anti-Semitism*. Notre Dame, IN: University of Notre Dame Press, 1986.
Davis, Leopold. "The Hegelian Anti-Semitism of Bruno Bauer." *History of European Ideas* 25 (1999): 179–206.
de Beauvoir, Simone. *The Blood of Others*. Translated by Yvonne Moyse and Roger Senhouse. London: Penguin, 1964.
———. *The Ethics of Ambiguity*. Translated by Bernard Frechtman. New York: Philosophical Library, 1948.
d'Entrèves, Maurizio Passerin. *The Political Philosophy of Hannah Arendt*. London: Routledge, 1994.
Derrida, Jacques. "Racism's Last Word." In *"Race," Writing and Difference*, Edited by Henry Louis Gates, Jr., 329–38. Chicago: University of Chicago Press, 1985.
Descombes, Vincent. *Modern French Philosophy*. Translated by L. Scott-Fox and J. M. Harding. London: Cambridge University Press, 1980.
d'Hondt, Jacques. *Hegel et Hégélianisme*. Paris: Presses Universitaires de France, 1982.
Disch, Lisa. "More Truth than Fact: Storytelling as Critical Understanding in the Writings of Hannah Arendt." *Political Theory* 21 (November 1993): 665–94.
Dossa, Shiraz. "Human Status and Politics: Hannah Arendt on the Holocaust." *Canadian Journal of Political Science* 13 (1980): 309–23.
Dubiel, Helmut. *Theory and Politics: Studies in the Development of Critical Theory*. Translated by Benjamin Gregg. Cambridge, MA: MIT Press, 1985.
Dufrenoy, M. L. "A Precursor of a Modern Anthropology: François Bernier (1620–1688)." *Isis* 41, no. 1 (March 1950): 27–29.
Durand, Yves. *La Captivité: Histoire des prisonniers de guerre français, 1939–1945*. Paris: Fédération nationale des combattants prisonniers de guerre et combattants d'Algérie, Tunisie, Maroc, 1982.
Eckardt, A. Roy. "The Nemesis of Christian Antisemitism." *Journal of Church and State* 13, no. 2 (Spring 1971): 227–44.
Edelheit, Abraham. "Historiography of the Holocaust." In *Encyclopedia of the Holocaust*, Edited by Israel Gutman, 666–72. New York: Macmillan, 2000.
Ellenson, David. "Max Weber on Judaism and the Jews." In *After Emancipation: Jewish Religious Responses to Modernity*, 80–95. Cincinnati: Hebrew Union College Press, 2004.

Elon, Amos. "The Case of Hannah Arendt." *New York Review of Books*, November 6, 1997.

Engel, David. "Away from a Definition of Antisemitism: An Essay in the Semantics of Historical Description." In *Rethinking European Jewish History*, Edited by Jeremy Cohen and Moshe Rosman, 30–53. Oxford: Oxford University Press, 2009.

Ewen, Elizabeth, and Stuart Ewen. *Typecasting: On the Arts and Sciences of Human Inequality*. New York: Seven Stories, 2008.

Eze, Emmanuel. "The Color of Reason: The Idea of 'Race' in Kant's Anthropology." In *Anthropology and the German Enlightenment: Perspectives on Humanity*, Edited by Katherine M. Faull, 200–235. Lewisburg, PA: Bucknell University Press, 1995.

———. "Hume, Race, and Human Nature." *Journal of the History of Ideas* 61, no. 4 (October 2000): 691–98.

Ezra, Michael. "The Eichmann Polemics: Hannah Arendt and Her Critics." *Democratiya* 9 (Summer 2007).

Fanon, Frantz. *Black Skin, White Masks*. Translated by Charles Lam Markmann. New York: Grove, 1967.

Farin, Ingo, and Jeff Malpas, eds. *Reading Heidegger's* Black Notebooks 1931–1941. Cambridge, MA: MIT Press, 2016.

Farr, James. "Locke, Natural Law, and New World Slavery." *Political Theory* 36, no. 4 (August 2008): 495–522.

Faye, Emmanuel. *L'Introduction du nazisme dans la philosophie: Autour des séminaires inédits de 1933–1935*. Paris: Albin Michel, 2005.

Feldman, Louis H. "Anti-Semitism in the Ancient World." In *History and Hate: The Dimensions of Anti-Semitism*, Edited by David Berger, 15–42. Philadelphia: Jewish Publication Society, 1986.

Field, Geoffrey. *Evangelist of Race: The German Vision of Houston Stewart Chamberlain*. New York: Columbia University Press, 1981.

Fine, Robert. "Rereading Marx on the 'Jewish Question': Marx as a Critic of Antisemitism?" *Antisemitism and the Constitution of Sociology*, Edited by Marcel Stoetzler, 137–59. Lincoln: University of Nebraska Press, 2014.

Finkielkraut, Alain. *The Future of a Negation: Reflections on the Question of Genocide*. Translated by Mary Byrd Kelly. Lincoln: University of Nebraska Press, 1998.

———. *The Imaginary Jew*. Translated by Kevin O'Neill and David Suchoff. Lincoln: University of Nebraska Press, 1994.

Fishman, Sarah. *We Will Wait: Wives of French Prisoners of War*. New Haven, CT: Yale University Press, 1991.

Folsom, Franklin. *Days of Anger, Days of Hope: A Memoir of the League of American Writers, 1937–1942*. Niwot: University Press of Colorado, 1994.

Frederickson, George. *Racism: A Short History*. Princeton, NJ: Princeton University Press, 2002.

Fredriksen, Paula. *Augustine and the Jews: A Christian Defense of Jews and Judaism*. New York: Doubleday, 2008.

Freeman, Michael. "Genocide, Civilization and Modernity." *British Journal of Sociology* 46, no. 2 (1995): 207–23.

Friedlander, Henry. *The Origins of Nazi Genocide: From Euthanasia to the Final Solution*. Chapel Hill: University of North Carolina Press, 1995.

Friedlander, Judith. "Antisemitism in France, 1978-1992: Questions and Debates." In *Auschwitz and After*, Edited by Lawrence Kritzman. New York: Routledge, 1995.

Friedländer, Saul. *Nazi Germany and the Jews*. Vol. 1, *The Years of Persecution, 1933–1939*. New York: Harper Collins, 1997.

———. *Nazi Germany and the Jews*. Vol. 2, *1939–1945: The Years of Extermination*. New York: Harper Collins, 2007.

Fromm, Erich. *The Anatomy of Human Destructiveness*. London: Jonathan Cape, 1974.

Gates, Jr., Henry Louis. "Talkin' That Talk." *Critical Inquiry* 13, no. 1 (Autumn 1986): 203–10.

Geller, Jay. "The Godfather of Psychoanalysis: Circumcision, Anti-Semitism, Homosexuality and Freud's 'Fighting Jew.'" *Journal of the American Academy of Religion* 67, no. 2 (June 1999): 355–85.

Gellner, Ernest. "From Königsberg to Manhattan (or Hannah, Rahel, Martin and Elfriede or Thy Neighbour's *Gemeinschaft*)." In *Culture, Identity, and Politics*. Cambridge: Cambridge University Press, 1987.

Geoffroy, Jean. "Sartre et l'apartheid." *Le Nouvel observateur*, no. 105 (November 1966): 16–22.

Gerhardt, Uta. *Talcott Parsons: An Intellectual Biography*. Cambridge: Cambridge University Press, 2002.

Gibson, Nigel, and Andrew Rubin. "Introduction: Adorno and the Autonomous Intellectual." In *Adorno: A Critical Reader*. Oxford: Blackwell, 2002.

Gilman, Sander. *The Case of Sigmund Freud: Medicine and Identity at the Fin de Siècle*. Baltimore, MD: Johns Hopkins University Press, 1993.

———. *Difference and Pathology: Stereotypes of Sexuality, Race, and Madness*. Ithaca, NY: Cornell University Press, 1985.

———. *Freud, Race, and Gender*. Princeton, NJ: Princeton University Press, 1993.

———. *Jewish Self-Hatred: Anti-Semitism and the Hidden Language of the Jews*. Baltimore, MD: Johns Hopkins University Press, 1986.

———. *The Jew's Body*. New York: Routledge, 1991.

———. *Seeing the Insane*. New York: John Wiley, 1982.

———. *Stand up Straight! A History of Posture*. London: Reaktion, 2018.

Gines, Katheryn. *Hannah Arendt and the Negro Question*. Bloomington: Indiana University Press, 2014.

Glatzer, Nahum N. "The Frankfurt Lehrhaus." *Leo Baeck Institute Yearbook* 1 (1956): 105–22.

Glenn, Susan A. "The Vogue of Jewish Self-Hatred in Post-World War II America." *Jewish Social Studies* (Spring-Summer 2006): 95–136.

Glickman, Elaine Rose. *Haman and the Jews: A Portrait from Rabbinic Literature*. Jerusalem: Jason Aronson, 1999.

Goldberg, Chad Alan. *Modernity and the Jews in Western Social Thought*. Chicago: University of Chicago Press, 2017.

Goldhagen, Daniel. *Hitler's Willing Executioners: Ordinary Germans and the Holocaust*. New York: Knopf, 1997.

———. "The Paradigm Challenged." *Tikkun*, May-June 1988.

Goldstein, Eric L. *The Price of Whiteness: Jews, Race, and American Identity*. Princeton, NJ: Princeton University Press, 2006.

Goswami, Namita. "The Mother of All Posts: Postcolonial Melancholia in the Age of Global Warming." *Critical Philosophy of Race* 1, no. 1 (2013): 105–20.

Graeber, Isacque, and Steuart Henderson Britt, eds. *Jews in a Gentile World: The Problem of Anti-Semitism*. New York: Macmillan, 1942.

Gribetz, Jonathan. *Defining Neighbors: Religion, Race, and the Early Zionist-Arab Encounter*. Princeton, NJ: Princeton University Press, 2014.

Grossman, Marshall. "The Violence of the Hyphen in Judeo-Christian." *Social Text*, no. 22 (Spring 1989): 115–22.

Habermas, Jurgen. *The Theory of Communicative Action*. Vol. 2, *Lifeworld and System: A Critique of Functionalist Reason*. Translated by Thomas McCarthy. Boston: Beacon, 1987.

Halpern, Ben. "What Is Antisemitism?" *Modern Judaism*, no. 1 (1981): 251–62.

Hammer, Espen. *Adorno and the Political*. London: Routledge, 2006.

Hammerschlag, Sarah. *The Figural Jew: Politics and Identity in Postwar French Thought*. Chicago: University of Chicago Press, 2010.

Hanebrink, Paul. *A Specter Haunting Europe: The Myth of Judeo-Bolshevism*. Cambridge, MA: Harvard University Press, 2018.

Hansson, Nelly. "France: The Carpentras Syndrome and Beyond." *Patterns of Prejudice* 25, no. 1 (1991): 32–45.

Haraway, Donna. "Situated Knowledges: The Science Question in Feminism and the Privilege of Partial Perspective." In *Simians, Cyborgs, and Women: The Reinvention of Nature*, 183–201. New York: Routledge, 1991.

Hartshorne, Edward Y., Jr. *The German Universities and National Socialism*. London: Allen and Unwin, 1937.

Hayes, Peter. Introduction to *Behemoth: The Structure and Practice of National Socialism, 1933–1944*. Chicago: Ivan R. Dee, 2009.

Haynes, Stephen. *Reluctant Witnesses: Jews in the Christian Imagination*. Louisville, KY: Westminster John Knox, 1995.

Heidegger, Martin. *Being and Time*. Translated by John Macquarrie and Edward Robinson. New York: Harper and Row, 1962.

——. *Philosophical and Political Writings*. Edited by M. Stassen. New York: Continuum, 2003.

——. "What Is Metaphysics?" In *Existentialism from Dostoevsky to Sartre*, Edited by Walter Kaufmann. New York: Meridian, 1975.

Helmreich, William B. "The Sociological Study of Anti-Semitism in the United States." In *Approaches to Anti-Semitism: Context and Curriculum*, Edited by Michael Brown, 134–41. New York: American Jewish Committee and the International Center for University Teaching of Jewish Civilization, 1994.

Herf, Jeffrey. *Anti-Semitism and Anti-Zionism in Historical Perspective: Convergence and Divergence*. New York: Routledge, 2007.

——. *The Jewish Enemy: Nazi Propaganda During World War II and the Holocaust*. Cambridge, MA: Harvard University Press, 2006.

——. "Mosse's Recasting of European Intellectual and Cultural History." *German Politics and Society* 18, no. 4 (Winter 2000): 18–29.

Hermand, Jost. "German Jews Beyond Judaism: The Gerhard/Israel/George L. Mosse Case." In *The German-Jewish Dialogue Reconsidered: A Symposium in Honor of George L. Mosse*, Edited by Klaus L. Berghahn, 233–46. New York: Peter Lang, 1996.

Heschel, Susannah. *The Aryan Jesus: Christian Theologians and the Bible in Nazi Germany*. Princeton, NJ: Princeton University Press, 2010.

Hess, Jonathan M. *Germans, Jews, and the Claims of Modernity.* New Haven, CT: Yale University Press, 2002.

Hiddleston, Jane. "Lyotard's Algeria: Experiments in Theory." *Paragraph* 33, no. 1 (2010): 52–69.

Hindus, Milton, ed., *The Worlds of Maurice Samuel: Selected Writings.* Philadelphia: Jewish Publication Society of America, 1977.

Hohendahl, Peter Uwe. *Prismatic Thought: Theodor W. Adorno.* Lincoln: University of Nebraska Press, 1995.

Holstein, Jay. "Max Weber and Biblical Scholarship." *Hebrew Union College Annual* 46 (1975): 159–79.

Horkheimer, Max. *Dawn & Decline: Notes 1926–1931 and 1950–1969.* Translated by Michael Shaw. New York: Seabury, 1978.

——. "The Jews and Europe." In *Critical Theory and Society: A Reader,* Edited by Stephen Eric Bronner and Douglas MacKay Kellner, 77–94. New York: Routledge, 1989.

——. "Sociological Background of the Psychoanalytic Approach." In *Antisemitism: A Social Disease,* Edited by Ernst Simmel, 1–10. New York: International Universities Press, 1946.

Horkheimer, Max, and Theodor Adorno. *Dialectic of Enlightenment.* Translated by Edmund Jephcott. Stanford: Stanford University Press, 2002.

Huntington, Samuel. *The Clash of Civilizations and the Remaking of World Order.* New York: Simon and Schuster, 1996.

Immerwahr, John. "Hume's Revised Racism." *Journal of the History of Ideas* 52 (1992): 1–23.

Isaac, Jeffrey C. *Arendt, Camus, and Modern Rebellion.* New Haven, CT: Yale University Press, 1992.

Jackson, Julian. *France: The Dark Years, 1940–1944.* Oxford: Oxford University Press, 2001.

Jacobs, Jack. *The Frankfurt School, Jewish Lives and Antisemitism.* Cambridge: Cambridge University Press, 2015.

——. "Max Horkheimer's 'Die Juden und Europa' Appears." In *Yale Companion to Jewish Writing and Thought in German Culture: 1096–1996,* Edited by Sander Gilman and Jack Zipes, 571–76. New Haven, CT: Yale University Press, 1997.

——. *On Socialists and 'the Jewish Question' after Marx.* New York: New York University Press, 1992.

Jacobson, Matthew F. "Looking Jewish, Seeing Jews." In *Theories of Race and Racism: A Reader,* Edited by Les Back and John Solomos, 238–52. London: Routledge, 2000.

Jameson, Fredric. Forward to *The Postmodern Condition: A Report on Knowledge,* by Jean-Francois Lyotard, vii–xxi. Translated by Geoff Bennington and Brian Massumi. Minneapolis: University of Minnesota Press, 1984.

Jarvis, Simon. *Adorno: A Critical Introduction.* New York: Routledge, 1998.

Jaspers, Karl. *The Question of German Guilt.* Translated by E. B. Ashton. New York: Fordham University Press, 2000.

Jay, Martin. *The Dialectical Imagination.* Boston: Little, Brown, 1973.

——. "The Ethics of Blindness and the Postmodern Sublime: Levinas and Lyotard." In *Downcast Eyes: The Denigration of Vision in Twentieth-Century French Thought,* 543–86. Berkeley: University of California Press, 1993.

——. *Force Fields: Between Intellectual History and Cultural Critique.* New York: Routledge, 1993.

——. "The Free Jewish School Is Founded in Frankfurt am Main Under the Leadership of Franz Rosenzweig." In *Yale Companion to Jewish Writing and Thought in German Culture, 1096–1996,* Edited by Sander L. Gilman and Jack Zipes, 395-400. New Haven, CT: Yale University Press, 1997.

———. "The Jews and the Frankfurt School: Critical Theory's Analysis of Antisemitism." *New German Critique*, no. 19 (Winter 1980): 137-49.

———. *Marxism and Totality: The Adventures of a Concept from Lukács to Habermas*. Berkeley: University of California Press, 1984.

———. *Permanent Exiles: Essays on the Intellectual Migration from Germany to America*. New York: Columbia University Press, 1986.

Joppa, Francis A. "Sartre et les milieux intellectuels de l'Afrique noire." *Présence francophone*, no. 25 (1989): 7-28.

Judaken, Jonathan. "Antisemitism and the Jewish Question." In *Cambridge History of Judaism*, vol. 8, *The Modern Period*, Edited by Mitchell B. Hart and Tony Michels, 559-88. Cambridge: Cambridge University Press, 2017.

———. "Bearing Witness to the *Différend*: Jean-François Lyotard, the Postmodern Intellectual and 'the jews.'" *Studies in Contemporary Jewry: An Annual*. Vol. 16, *Jews and Gender: The Challenge to Hierarchy*, Edited by Jonathan Frankel, 245-64. New York: Oxford University Press, 2000.

———. "Blindness and Insight: The Conceptual Jew in Arendt and Adorno's Post-Holocaust Reflections on the Antisemitic Question." In *Arendt and Adorno: Political and Philosophical Investigations*. Edited by Lars Rensmann and Samir Gendesha, 173-95. Stanford: Stanford University Press, 2012.

———. "Deconstructing Anti-Semitism and Eternal Anti-Judaism." *Marginalia: A Review of Books in History, Theology, and Religion*, December 13, 2013: http://themarginaliareview.com/archives/4981.

———. "Heidegger's Shadow: Levinas, Arendt, and the Magician from Messkirch." In *The Routledge Companion to Philosophy of Race*, Edited by Linda Alcoff, Luvell E. Anderson, and Paul Taylor, 61-74. New York: Routledge, 2017.

———. "Historiography." In *Key Concepts in the Study of Antisemitism*, Edited by Sol Goldberg, Scott Ury, and Kalman Weiser, 25-38. Cham, Switzerland: Palgrave Macmillan, 2020.

———. "Homo antisemiticus: Lessons and Legacies." *Holocaust and Genocide Studies* 23, no. 3 (Winter 2009): 461-77.

———. Introduction to *The Albert Memmi Reader*, Edited by Jonathan Judaken and Michael Lejman, xv-xliv. Lincoln: University of Nebraska Press, 2020.

———. *Jean-Paul Sartre and the Jewish Question: Anti-Antisemitism and the Politics of the French Intellectual*. Lincoln: University of Nebraska Press, 2006.

———. "Mapping 'The New Jewish Cultural Studies.'" *History Workshop Journal* 51 (Spring 2001): 269-77.

———. "Memmi on Racism and (Post-Holocaust) Judeophobia." *H-France Salon* 13, no. 4, #6. https://h-france.net/Salon/SalonVol13no04.6.Judaken.pdf.

———. "Sartre on Racism: From Existential Phenomenology to Globalization and 'the New Racism." In *Race After Sartre: Antiracism, Africana Existentialism, Postcolonialism*, Edited by Jonathan Judaken, 23-53. Albany: SUNY Press, 2008.

———. "So What's New? Rethinking the 'New Antisemitism' in a Global Age." *Patterns of Prejudice* 42, nos. 4-5 (Autumn 2008): 531-60.

———. "Vladimir Jankélévitch at the *Colloques des intellectuels juifs de langue française*." In *Vladimir Jankélévitch and the Question of Forgiveness*, Edited by Alan Udoff, 3-26. Lanham, MD: Lexington, 2013.

Judt, Tony. *Past Imperfect: French Intellectuals, 1944–1956*. Berkeley: University of California Press, 1992.

Junge, Matthias. "Bauman on Ambivalence—Fully Acknowledging the Ambiguity of Ambivalence." In *The Sociology of Zygmunt Bauman*, Edited by Michael Hviid Jacobsen and Poul Poder, 41–56. Burlington, VT: Routledge, 2008.

Kalman, Julie. *Rethinking Antisemitism in Nineteenth-Century France*. Cambridge: Cambridge University Press, 2010.

Kalmar, Ivan Davidson. "Anti-Semitism and Islamophobia: The Formation of a Secret." *Human Architecture: Journal of the Sociology of Self-Knowledge* 7, no. 2 (2009): 134–44.

Kalmar, Ivan Davidson, and Derek J. Penslar. Introduction to *Orientalism and the Jews*. Waltham, MA: Brandeis University Press and University Press of New England, 2004.

Kateb, George. *Hannah Arendt: Politics, Conscience, Evil*. Oxford: Oxford University Press, 1983.

Katz, Ethan B. *The Burdens of Brotherhood: Jews and Muslims from North Africa to France*. Cambridge, MA: Harvard University Press, 2015.

Katz, Ethan B., Lisa Moses Leff, and Maud S. Mandel, eds. *Colonialism and the Jews*. Bloomington: Indiana University Press, 2017.

Katz, Jacob. "The Sources of Modern Anti-Semitism: Eisenmenger's Method of Presenting Evidence from Talmudic Sources." *Proceedings of the Fifth World Congress of Jewish Studies*, 2:210-11. Jerusalem: World Union of Jewish Studies, 1972.

King, Richard H. "Endings and Beginnings: Politics in Arendt's Early Thought." *Political Theory* 12, no. 2 (May 1984): 235–51.

King, Richard H., and Dan Stone. Introduction to *Hannah Arendt and the Uses of History: Imperialism, Nation, Race, and Genocide*, 1–18. New York: Berghahn, 2007.

Kleinberg, Ethan. *Generation Existential: Heidegger's Philosophy in France, 1927–1961*. Ithaca, NY: Cornell University Press, 2005.

——. "The 'Letter on Humanism': Reading Heidegger in France." In *Situating Existentialism: Key Texts in Context*, Edited by Jonathan Judaken and Robert Bernasconi, 386–413. New York: Columbia University Press, 2012.

Kojève, Alexander. *Introduction to the Reading of Hegel: Lectures on the Phenomenology of Spirit*. Translated by James H. Nichols, Jr. Edited by Allan Bloom. Ithaca, NY: Cornell University Press, 1980.

Kristeva, Julia. *Hannah Arendt*. Translated by Ross Guberman. New York: Columbia University Press, 2001.

——. "Hannah Arendt, Life Is a Narrative." In *Crisis of the European Subject*. Translated by Susan Fairfield, 47–94. New York: Other, 2000.

Kritzman, Lawrence, ed. *Auschwitz and After: Race, Culture, and "the Jewish Question" in France*. London: Routledge, 1995.

LaCapra, Dominick. "Heidegger's Nazi Turn." In *Representing the Holocaust: History, Theory, Trauma*, 137–68. Ithaca, NY: Cornell University Press, 1994.

Langmuir, Gavin. *Toward a Definition of Antisemitism*. Berkeley: University of California Press, 1990.

Laqueur, Walter. *The Changing Face of Anti-Semitism: From Ancient Times to the Present Day*. Oxford: Oxford University Press, 2006.

Larrimore, Mark. "Antinomies of Race: Diversity and Destiny in Kant." In *Naming Race, Naming Racisms*. Edited by Jonathan Judaken, 7–29. New York: Routledge, 2009.

Latham, Alan. "An Ethics of the Ephemeral? The Possibilities and Impossibilities of Zygmunt Bauman's Ethics: A Review of Some Recent Books by Zygmunt Bauman." *Ethics, Place and Environment* 2, no. 2 (1999): 275–85.

Le Sueur, James. *Uncivil War: Intellectuals and Identity Politics During the Decolonization of Algeria*. Philadelphia: University of Pennsylvania Press, 2001.

Levinas, Emmanuel. "Existentialism and Anti-Semitism." Translated by Denis Hollier and Rosalind Krauss. *October 87* (Winter 1999).

———. "Reflections on the Philosophy of Hitlerism." Translated by Seán Hand. *Critical Inquiry* 17, no. 1 (Autumn 1990): 62–71.

———. "The Temptation of Temptation." In *Nine Talmudic Readings*. Translated by Annette Aronowicz. Bloomington: Indiana University Press, 1990.

Lévy, Bernard-Henri. *Sartre: The Philosopher of the Twentieth Century*. Translated by Andrew Brown. Cambridge: Polity, 2003.

Levy, Richard. *Antisemitism in the Modern World: An Anthology of Texts*. Lexington, MA: D. C. Heath, 1991.

Lewis, Bernard. *The Jews of Islam*. Princeton, NJ: Princeton University Press, 1984.

———. *Semites and Anti-Semites*. New York: Norton, 1999.

Lichtheim, George. "Socialism and the Jews." *Dissent* (July–August 1968): 314–42.

Lindemann, Albert. *Anti-Semitism before the Holocaust*. London: Pearson, 2000.

———. *Esau's Tears: Modern Anti-Semitism and the Rise of the Jews*. Cambridge: Cambridge University Press, 1997.

Lockshin, Martin. "Sinat Yisrael." In *Key Concepts in the Study of Antisemitism*. Edited by Sol Goldberg, Scott Ury, and Kalman Weiser, 273–85. Cham, Switzerland: Palgrave Macmillan, 2021.

Lotem, Itay. "Anti-Racist Activism and the Memory of Colonialism: Race as Republican Critique After 2005." *Modern and Contemporary France* 24 (2016): 283–98.

Lovejoy, Arthur O. *The Great Chain of Being: A Study of the History of an Idea*. Cambridge, MA: Harvard University Press, 1936.

Lowenthal, Leo, and Norbert Guterman. *Prophets of Deceit: A Study of the Techniques of the American Agitator*. New York: Harper, 1949

Luban, David. "Explaining Dark Times: Hannah Arendt's Theory of Theory." *Social Research* (Spring 1983): 214–48.

Lyotard, Jean-François. "Apostil on Narratives." In *The Postmodern Explained: Correspondence 1982–1985*, 17–22. Translated by Julian Pefanis and Morgan Thomas. Minneapolis: University of Minnesota Press, 1992.

———. *La Condition postmoderne: Rapport sur le savoir*. Paris: Les Éditions de Minuit, 1979.

———. *The Differend: Phrases in Dispute*. Translated by Georges Van Den Abbeele. Minneapolis: University of Minnesota Press, 1988.

———. "Figure Foreclosed." In *The Lyotard Reader*, Edited by Andrew Benjamin, 69–110. Oxford: Basil Blackwell, 1989.

———. "German Guilt." In *Political Writings*. Translated by Bill Readings and Kevin Paul Geiman, 127–34. Minneapolis: University of Minnesota Press, 1993.

———. "The Grip (*Mainmise*)." In *Political Writings*. Translated by Bill Readings and Kevin Paul Geiman, 148–59. Minneapolis: University of Minnesota Press, 1993.

———. *Heidegger and "the Jews."* Translated by Andreas Michel and Mark Roberts. Minneapolis: University of Minnesota Press, 1990.

———. "Jewish Oedipus." In *Driftworks*. Edited by Roger McKeon, 35–55. New York: Semiotext(e), 1984.

———. *Libidinal Economy*. Bloomington: Indiana University Press, 1993.

———. *Peregrinations: Law, Form, Event.* New York: Columbia University Press, 1988.
———. *La Phénoménologie.* Paris: Presses Universitaires de France, 1954.
———. *Le Postmoderne explique aux enfants.* Paris: Galilée, 1988.
Mack, Michael. *German Idealism and the Jew: The Inner Anti-Semitism of Philosophy and German Jewish Responses.* Chicago: University of Chicago Press, 2003.
Man, Susan Archer, and Ashly Suzanne Patterson, eds. *Reading Feminist Theory: From Modernity to Postmodernity.* Oxford: Oxford University Press, 2015.
Mandel, Maud. *Muslims and Jews in France: History of a Conflict.* Princeton, NJ: Princeton University Press, 2014.
Marcus, Kenneth L. *The Definition of Anti-Semitism.* Oxford: Oxford University Press, 2015.
Maritain, Jacques. "On Anti-Semitism." *Christianity and Crisis,* October 6, 1941.
Marotta, Vince. "The Stranger and Social Theory." *Thesis Eleven,* no. 62 (2000): 121–34.
Marrus, Michael. "Are the French Antisemitic? Evidence in the 1980s." In *The Jews in Modern France,* Edited by Frances Malino and Bernard Wasserstein, 224–42. Hanover, NH: University Press of New England, 1985.
Marrus, Michael R., and Robert O. Paxton. *Vichy France and the Jews.* Stanford: Stanford University Press, 1995.
Marshman, Sophia. "Bauman on Genocide—Modernity and Mass Murder: From Classification to Annihilation?" In *The Sociology of Zygmunt Bauman: Challenges and Critique,* Edited by Michael Hviid Jacobsen and Poul Poder. Burlington, VT: Ashgate, 2008.
Marty, Éric. *Radical French Thought and the Return of the "Jewish Question."* Bloomington: Indiana University Press, 2015.
Mazower, Mark. *Salonica, A City of Ghosts: Christians, Muslims, and Jews, 1430–1950.* New York: Vintage, 2004.
McBride, William. *Sartre's Political Theory.* Bloomington: Indiana University Press, 1991.
McCarthy, Thomas. *Race, Empire, and the Idea of Human Development.* Cambridge: Cambridge University Press, 2009.
Meloen, Jos. "The Fortieth Anniversary of 'The Authoritarian Personality.'" *Politics and the Individual* 1 (1991): 119–27.
Memmi, Albert. *The Liberation of the Jew.* New York: Orion, 1966.
———. *Racism.* Translated by Steve Martinot. Minneapolis: University of Minnesota Press, 2000.
Miller, Christopher L. "Theories of Africans: The Question of Literary Anthropology." In *"Race," Writing and Difference,* Edited by Henry Louis Gates, Jr, 281–300. Chicago: University of Chicago Press, 1986.
Mills, Charles. "Kant and Race, Redux." *Graduate Faculty Philosophy Journal* 35, nos. 1–2 (2014): 125–57.
Mitchell, Andrew J., and Peter Trawny, eds. *Heidegger's Black Notebooks: Responses to Anti-Semitism.* New York: Columbia University Press, 2017.
Moore, Bob, and Kent Fedorowich. *Prisoners of War and their Captors in World War II.* Oxford: Berg, 1996.
Mosse, George. "Anatomy of a Stereotype." *New German Critique,* no. 42 (Fall 1987): 163–68.
———. *Confronting History: A Memoir.* Madison: University of Wisconsin Press, 2000.
———. *The Crisis of German Ideology: Intellectual Origins of the Third Reich.* New York: Grosset and Dunlap, 1981.

———. *The Culture of Western Europe: The Nineteenth and Twentieth Centuries.* Boulder, CO: Westview, 1988.
———. *Europe in the Sixteenth Century.* London: Longman, 1968.
———. *Fallen Soldiers: Reshaping the Memory of the World Wars.* Oxford: Oxford University Press, 1990.
———. *The Fascist Revolution: Toward a General Theory of Fascism.* New York: Howard Fertig, 1999.
———. *The Image of Man: The Creation of Modern Masculinity.* Oxford: Oxford University Press, 1996.
———. *Nationalism and Sexuality: Middle-Class Morality and Sexual Norms in Modern Europe.* Madison: University of Wisconsin Press, 1985.
———. *The Nationalization of the Masses: Political Symbolism and Mass Movements in Germany from the Napoleonic Wars Through the Third Reich.* New York: Meridian, 1975.
———. *Nazism: A Historical and Comparative Analysis of National Socialism.* New Brunswick, NJ: Transaction, 1978.
———. "Political Style and Political Theory: Totalitarian Democracy Revisited." In *Confronting the Nation: Jewish and Western Nationalism*, 61-69. Hanover, NH: Brandeis University Press, 1993.
———. *Towards the Final Solution: A History of European Racism.* Madison: University of Wisconsin Press, 1985.
Mounier, Emmanuel. "Les juifs parlent aux nations." *Esprit* 13, no. 114 (September 1945).
Moyn, Samuel. "The Trouble with Comparisons." *New York Review of Books*, May 19, 2020.
Mudimbé, V. Y. *Invention of Africa: Gnosis, Philosophy, and the Order of Knowledge.* Bloomington: Indiana University Press, 1988.
Myers, David. "Can There Be a Principled Anti-Zionism: On the Nexus Between Anti-Historicism and Anti-Zionism in Modern Jewish Thought." In *Anti-Semitism and Anti-Zionism in Historical Perspective: Convergence and Divergence*, Edited by Jeffrey Herf, 20-38. New York: Routledge, 2007.
Nelson, Cary. "The Problem with Judith Butler: The Political Philosophy of BDS and the Movement to Delegitimate Israel." In *The Case Against Academic Boycotts of Israel*, Edited by Cary Nelson and Gabriel Noah Brahm, 164-201. Chicago: MLA Members for Scholars Rights, 2015.
Netanyahu, Ben-Zion. "Antisemitism." In *The Hebrew Encyclopedia*, 4:493-508. Jerusalem/Tel Aviv: 1959.
———. Introduction to *Road to Freedom: Writings and Addresses by Leo Pinsker.* New York: Scopus, 1944.
Neumann, Franz. *Behemoth: The Structure and Practice of National Socialism, 1933-1944.* Chicago: Ivan R. Dee, 2009.
Nielsen, Jens Kaalhauge. "The Political Orientation of Talcott Parsons: The Second World War and Its Aftermath." In *Talcott Parsons: Theorist of Modernity*, Edited by Roland Robertson and Bryan S. Turner, 217-33. London: Sage, 1991.
Nirenberg, David. *Anti-Judaism: The Western Tradition.* New York: Norton, 2013.
———. *Communities of Violence: Persecution of Minorities in the Middle Ages.* Princeton, NJ: Princeton University Press, 1996.
Noerr, Gunzelin Schmid, ed. "The Position of 'Dialectic of Enlightenment' in the Development of Critical Theory." In *Dialectic of Enlightenment*, 217-47. Translated by Edmund Jephcott. Stanford: Stanford University Press, 2002.

Norton, Anne. "Heart of Darkness: Africa and African Americans in the Writings of Hannah Arendt." In *Feminist Interpretations of Hannah Arendt*. Edited by Bonnie Honig, 247-61. University Park: Penn State University Press, 1995.

Oliver, Kelly. "Alienation and Its Double; or the Secretion of Race." In *Race and Racism in Continental Philosophy*, Edited by Robert Bernasconi and Sybol Cook, 176-95. Bloomington: Indiana University Press, 2003.

Oxaal, Ivar. "Sociology, History, and the Holocaust." *Theory, Culture and Society* 8, no. 1 (1991): 153-56.

Ozick, Cynthia. "The Modern 'Hep! Hep! Hep!'" In *The Jewish Divide Over Israel: Accusers and Defenders*, Edited by Edward Alexander and Paul Bogdanor. New Brunswick, NJ: Transaction, 2006.

Painter, Nell Irvin. *The History of White People*. New York: Norton, 2010.

Parfitt, Tudor. *Hybrid Hate: Conflations of Antisemitism and Anti-Black Racism from the Renaissance to the Third Reich*. New York: Oxford University Press, 2020.

Park, Peter K. J. *Africa, Asia, and the History of Philosophy: Racism in the Formation of the Philosophical Canon, 1780–1830*. Albany: SUNY Press, 2013.

———. "The Exclusion of Asia and Africa from the History of Philosophy: Is Kant Responsible?" In *Cultivating Personhood: Kant and Asian Philosophy*, Edited by Stephen R. Palmquist, 777-90. New York: de Gruyter, 2010.

Parsons, Edward S. *The Social Message of Jesus: A Course of Twelve Lessons*. New York: YWCA, 1910.

Parsons, Talcott. "On Building Social Systems Theory: A Personal History." In "The Making of Modern Science: Biographical Studies." Special issue, *Daedalus* 99, no. 4 (Fall 1970): 826-81.

———. "Postscript to 'the Sociology of Modern Anti-Semitism.'" *Contemporary Jewry* 5 (1980): 31-38.

———. "The Sociology of Modern Anti-Semitism." In *Jews in Gentile World*, Edited by Isacque Graeber and Steuart Henderson Britt. New York: Macmillan, 1942.

———. *The Structure of Social Action: A Study in Social Theory with Special Reference to a Group of Recent European Writers*. Vol. 1. New York: Free Press, 1968.

———. *Talcott Parsons on National Socialism*, Edited by Uta Gerhardt. New York: Aldine De Gruyter, 1993.

Parsons, Talcott, and Kenneth B. Clark. *The Negro American*. Boston: Beacon, 1966.

Pasto, James. "Islam's 'Strange Secret Sharer': Orientalism, Judaism, and the Jewish Question." *Comparative Studies in Society and History* 40, no. 3 (1998): 437-74.

Perrineau, Pascal. "Le Front national: 1972-1992." In *Histoire de l'extrême droite en France*, Edited by Michel Winock, 243-98. Paris: Éditions du Seuil, 1993.

Pinsker, Leon. *Auto-Emancipation*. Translated by D. S. Blondheim. New York: ZOA, 1948.

Pitkin, Hannah. *The Attack of the Blob: Hannah Arendt's Concept of the Social*. Chicago: University of Chicago Press, 1993.

Poliakov, Léon. *The Aryan Myth: A History of Racist and Nationalist Ideas in Europe*. Translated by Edmund Howard. New York: Basic Books, 1974.

———. *La Condition des juifs en France sous l'occupation italienne*. Paris: Éditions du Centre, 1946.

———. *Harvest of Hate: The Nazi Program for the Destruction of the Jews of Europe*. Syracuse, NY: Syracuse University Press, 1954.

———. *The History of Anti-Semitism*. Vol. 1, *From the Time of Christ to the Court Jews*. Translated by Richard Howard. London: Elek, 1965.

———. *The History of Anti-Semitism*. Vol. 2, *From Mohammed to the Marranos*. Philadelphia: University of Pennsylvania Press, 2003.

———. *The History of Anti-Semitism*. Vol. 3, *From Voltaire to Wagner*. Philadelphia: University of Pennsylvania Press, 2003.

———. *The History of Anti-Semitism*. Vol. 4, *Suicidal Europe, 1870–1933*. Philadelphia: University of Pennsylvania Press, 2003.

———. *De l'antisionisme à l'antisémitisme*. Paris: Calmann-Lévy, 1969.

———. *Mémoires*. Paris: Jacques Grancher, 1999.

———. *Le Procès de Jérusalem: Jugements, documents*. Paris: CDJC-Calmann-Lévy, 1963.

Poliakov, Léon, and Georges Elia Sarfati. *L'Envers du destin: Entretiens avec Georges Elia Sarfati*. Paris: Editions de Fallois, 1989.

Pollock, Friedrich, and Theodor Adorno, *Group Experiment and Other Writings: The Frankfurt School on Public Opinion in Postwar Germany*. Translated by Jeffrey K. Olick and Andrew J. Perrin. Cambridge, MA: Harvard University Press, 2011.

Popkin, Richard H. *Isaac La Peyrère*. Leiden: Brill, 1987.

Porat, Dina, and Kenneth S. Stern. "Defining Antisemitism." *Antisemitism Worldwide* (2003/4): 5-28.

Poznanski, Renée. *Jews in France during World War II*. Translated by Nathan Bracher. Hanover, NH: Brandeis University Press, 2001.

Rabinbach, Anson. "Eichmann in New York: The New York Intellectuals and the Hannah Arendt Controversy." *October* 108 (Spring): 97-111.

Raphael, Freddy. "Max Weber et le judaisme antique." *Archives européenes de sociologie* 11, no. 2 (1970): 297-336.

Rensmann, Lars. *The Politics of Unreason: The Frankfurt School and Antisemitism*. Albany: SUNY Press, 2017.

Rex, John. "Race, Ethnicity and the Rational Organization of Evil." *Theory, Culture and Society* 8, no. 1 (1991): 167-74.

Rice, Emanuel. *Freud and Moses: The Long Journey Home*. Albany: SUNY Press, 1990.

Rockomore, Tom. "On Heidegger and Contemporary French Philosophy." In *Heidegger and French Philosophy: Humanism, Antihumanism and Being*, 126-47. London: Routledge, 1995.

Rose, Gillian. *Judaism and Modernity: Philosophical Essays*. Oxford: Verso, 1993.

Rose, Paul Lawrence. *German-Question, Jewish Question: Revolutionary Anti-Semitism in Germany from Kant to Wagner*. Princeton, NJ: Princeton University Press, 1990.

Rosen, Zvi. *Max Horkheimer*. Munich: C. H. Beck, 1995.

Rosenbaum, Ron, ed. *Those Who Forget the Past: The Question of Anti-Semitism*. New York: Random House, 2004.

Rosenzweig, Franz. *The Star of Redemption*. Translated by William Hallo. Notre Dame, IN: Notre Dame Press, 1970.

Rotenstreich, Nathan. "For and Against Emancipation: The Bruno Bauer Controversy." *Leo Baeck Institute Year Book* 4 (1959): 3-36.

———. "Hegel's Image of Judaism." *Jewish Social Studies* 15 (1953): 33-52.

Roth, Michael S. *Knowing and History; Appropriations of Hegel in Twentieth-Century France*. Ithaca, NY: Cornell University Press, 1988.

Rothberg, Michael. *The Implicated Subject: Beyond Victims and Perpetrators*. Stanford: Stanford University Press, 2019.

———. *Multidirectional Memory: Remembering the Holocaust in the Age of Decolonization*. Stanford: Stanford University Press, 2009.

Rousso, Henry. *The Vichy Syndrome: History and Memory in France since 1944*. Translated by Arthur Goldhamer. Cambridge, MA: Harvard University Press, 1991.

Roy, Olivier. "Apres Carpentras: le Front National ne perdra pas ses voix." *Esprit* 162 (June 1990): 72–75.

Rybalka, Michel. "Publication and Reception of *Anti-Semite and Jew*." *October* 87 (Winter 1999).

Sabean, David Warren. "George Mosse and *The Holy Pretense*." In *What History Tells: George L. Mosse and the Culture of Modern Europe*, Edited by Stanley G. Payne, David J. Sorkin, and John S. Tortorice, 15–24. Madison: University of Wisconsin Press, 2004.

Said, Edward. *Culture and Imperialism*. New York: Vintage, 1993.

———. "Diary." *London Review of Books*, June 1, 2000, 42–43.

———. *Orientalism*. New York: Penguin, 1978.

Samuel, Maurice. *The Great Hatred*. New York: Alfred A. Knopf, 1948.

Samuels, Maurice. *The Right to Difference: French Universalism and the Jews*. Chicago: University of Chicago Press, 2016.

Sanos, Sandrine. *The Aesthetics of Hate: Far-Right Intellectuals, Antisemitism, and Gender in 1930s France*. Stanford: Stanford University Press, 2013.

Santoni, Ronald. *Sartre on Violence: Curiously Ambivalent*. University Park: Penn State University Press, 2003.

Sarna, Jonathan. *American Judaism*. New Haven, CT: Yale University Press, 2004.

Sartre, Jean-Paul. *Anti-Semite and Jew*. Translated by George J. Becker. New York: Schocken, 1948.

———. *Being and Nothingness*. New York: Philosophical Library, 1984.

———. *Colonialism and Neo-Colonialism*. Translated by Azzedine Haddour, Steve Brewer, and Terry McWilliams. London: Routledge, 2005.

———. *Critique of Dialectical Reason*. Vol. 1, *Theory of Practical Ensembles*. Translated by Alan Sheridan-Smith. London: Verso, 1976.

———. *Critique of Dialectical Reason*. Vol. 2. Edited by Arlette Elkaim-Sartre. Translated by Quintin Hoare. London: Verso, 2006.

———. "Discours de Sartre à l'ambassade d'Israël pour l'acceptation de son diplôme de docteur honoris causa de l'Université hébraïque de Jérusalem 7 novembre 1976." In *Mardi chez Sartre: Un hébreu à Paris, 1967–1980*, Edited by Ely Ben-Gal, 313–14. Paris: Flammarion, 1992.

———. "Drieu la Rochelle ou la haine de soi." *Les Lettres françaises*, April 1943.

———. *Existentialism Is a Humanism*. Translated by Carol Macomber. New Haven, CT: Yale University Press, 2007.

———. Introduction to *The Colonizer and the Colonized*, by Albert Memmi. Boston: Beacon, 1965.

———. "Black Orpheus." Translated by John MacCombie. *Massachusetts Review* 6 (Autumn 1964–65): 13–52.

———. "Les Pays capitalistes et leur colonies intérieures." *Tricontinental*, Paris, 1970, reprinted as "Le tiers-monde commence en banlieue." *Situations VIII*. Paris: Gallimard, 1972.

———. "Qu'est-ce qu'un collaborateur?" *Situations III*. Paris: Gallimard, 1949.

———. *Le Scénario Freud*. Edited by J.-B. Pontalis. Paris: Gallimard, 1984.

———. *Les Séquestrés d'Altona*. Paris: Gallimard, 1960.

Satterwhite, James H. "Polish Revisionism: Critical Thinking in Poland from 1953 to 1968." In *Zygmunt Bauman: Sage Masters in Modern Social Thought*. 4 vols. Edited by Peter Beilharz, 288-332. London: Sage, 2002.

Schäfer, Peter. *Judeophobia: Attitudes Toward the Jews in the Ancient World*. Cambridge, MA: Harvard University Press, 1997.

Schechter, Ronald. *Obstinate Hebrews: Representations of Jews in France, 1715–1815*. Berkeley: University of California Press, 2003.

Schmeuli, Ephraim. "The 'Pariah People' and Its 'Charismatic Leadership': A Reevalution of Max Weber's 'Ancient Judaism.'" *American Academy of Jewish Research Proceedings* 36 (1968): 167-247.

Schor, Ralph. *L'Antisémitisme en France dans l'entre-deux-guerres: Prélude à Vichy*. Paris: Éditions Complexe, 2005.

Schorske, Carl E. "Politics in a New Key: An Austrian Triptych." *The Journal of Modern History* 39, no. 4 (December 1967): 343-86.

Schrift, Alan. *Nietzsche's French Legacy: A Genealogy of Poststructuralism*. London: Routledge, 1995.

Sedgwick, Eve. *The Epistemology of the Closet*. Berkeley: University of California Press, 2008.

Sepinwall, Alyssa Goldstein. *The Abbé Gregoire and the French Revolution: The Making of Modern Universalism*. Berkeley: University of California Press, 2005.

Shaffer, Brian W. "Joseph Conrad: *Heart of Darkness*." In *A Companion to Modernist Literature and Culture*, Edited by David Bradshaw and Kevin J. H. Dettmar, 314-23. Malden, MA: Blackwell, 2006.

Sheehan, Thomas. "Heidegger and the Nazis." *The New York Review of Books*, June 16, 1988.

Shklar, Judith. "Hannah Arendt as Pariah." *Partisan Review* 1, no. 50 (1983): 64-77.

Shumsky, Dimitry. "Leon Pinsker and 'Autoemancipation!': A Revaluation." *Jewish Social Studies* 18, no. 1 (Fall 2011): 33-62.

Silk, Mark. "Notes on the Judeo-Christian Tradition in America." *American Quarterly* 36, no. 1 (Spring 1984): 65-84.

Simmel, Ernst, ed. *Anti-Semitism: A Social Disease*. New York: International Universities Press, 1946.

Smart, Barry. "Zygmunt Bauman." In *Profiles in Contemporary Social Theory*, Edited by Anthony Elliott and Bryan Turner, 327-37. London: Sage, 2001.

Smith, Anthony D. *The Nation in History: Historiographical Debates About Ethnicity and Nationalism*. Hanover, NH: University Press of New England, 2000.

———. *Nationalism and Modernism: A Critical Survey of Recent Theories of Nations and Nationalism*. New York: Routledge, 1998.

Smith, David Norman. "The Social Construction of Enemies: Jews and the Representation of Evil." *Sociological Theory* 14, no. 3 (November 1996): 203-40.

Smith, Dennis. *Zygmunt Bauman: Prophet of Postmodernity*. Cambridge: Polity, 1999.

Soucy, Robert. *French Fascism: The Second Wave, 1933–1939*. New Haven, CT: Yale University Press, 1995.

Stanislawski, Michael. *Zionism and the Fin de Siècle: Cosmopolitanism and Nationalism from Nordau to Jabotinsky*. Berkeley: University of California Press, 2001.

Staudenmaier, Peter. "Hannah Arendt's Analysis of Antisemitism in *The Origins of Totalitarianism*: A Critical Appraisal." *Patterns of Prejudice* 4, no. 2 (2012): 154–79.

Stille, Alexander. "The Case of Dieudonné: A French Comedian's Hate." *New Yorker*, January 10, 2014: http://www.newyorker.com/news/daily-comment/the-case-of-dieudonn-a-french-comedians-hate.

Stillman, Norman. *The Jews of Arab Lands: A History and Source Book*. Philadelphia: Jewish Publication Society of America, 1979.

Stoetzler, Marcel. *Antisemitism and the Constitution of Sociology*. Lincoln: University of Nebraska Press, 2014.

——. "Anti-Semitism, Capitalism and the Formation of Sociological Theory." *Patterns of Prejudice* 44, no. 2 (2010): 161–94.

Strenski, Ivan. *Durkheim and the Jews of France*. Chicago: University of Chicago Press, 1997.

Stuurman, Siep. "François Bernier and the Invention of Racial Classification." *History Workshop Journal*, no. 50 (Autumn 2000): 1–21.

Sutcliff, Adam. *Judaism and Enlightenment*. Cambridge: Cambridge University Press, 2003.

Taguieff, Pierre-André. *The Force of Prejudice: On Racism and Its Doubles*. Translated by Hassan Melehy. Minneapolis: University of Minnesota Press, 2001.

——. *Rising from the Muck: The New Anti-Semitism in Europe*. Translated by Patrick Camiller. Chicago: Ivan R. Dee, 2004.

Tar, Zoltan. *The Frankfurt School: The Critical Theories of Max Horkheimer and Theodor W. Adorno*. New York: Wiley, 1977.

Tester, Keith. *The Social Thought of Zygmunt Bauman*. New York: Palgrave Macmillan, 2004.

Tobin, Gary A., Aryeh K. Weinberg, and Jenna Ferer, eds. *The UnCivil University: Intolerance on College Campuses*, rev. ed. Lanham, MD: Lexington, 2009.

Traverso, Enzo. "The Blindness of the Intellectuals: Historicizing Sartre's *Anti-Semite and Jew*." *October* 87 (Winter 1999): 73–88.

——. *The Jews and Germany: From the 'Judeo-German Symbiosis' to the Memory of Auschwitz*. Translated by Daniel Weissbort. Lincoln: University of Nebraska Press, 1995.

——. *The Marxists and the Jewish Question: The History of a Debate (1843–1943)*. Translated by Bernard Gibbons. Atlantic Highlands, NJ: Humanities, 1990.

Trunk, Isaiah. *Judenrat: The Jewish Councils in Eastern Europe Under Nazi Occupation*. New York: Macmillan, 1972.

Uzgalis, William. "John Locke, Racism, Slavery, and Indian Lands." In *The Oxford Handbook of Philosophy and Race*, Edited by Naomi Zack, 21–30. Oxford: Oxford University Press, 2017.

Vetlesen, Arne Johan. "Why Does Proximity Make a Moral Difference? Coming to Terms with a Lesson Learned from the Holocaust." *Praxis International* 12, no. 4 (1993): 371–86.

Voegelin, Eric. "The Origins of Totalitarianism." *Review of Politics* 15, no. 6 (January 1953).

Volkov, Shulamit. "Antisemitism as a Cultural Code: Reflections on the History and Historiography of Antisemitism in Imperial Germany." *Leo Baeck Yearbook* 23, no. 1 (1978): 25–46.

——. "The Written Matter and the Spoken Word." In *Unanswered Questions: Nazi Germany and the Genocide of the Jews*, Edited by François Furet, 33–53. New York: Schocken, 1989.

Walfish, Barry. *Esther in Medieval Garb: Jewish Interpretations of the Book of Esther in the Middle Ages*. Albany: SUNY Press, 1993.

Wasserstein, Bernard. "Blame the Victim: Hannah Arendt Among the Nazis: The Historian and Her Sources." *Times Literary Supplement*, October 9, 2009, 13-15.
Weber, Eugen. *Action Française: Royalism and Reaction in Twentieth-Century France*. Stanford: Stanford University Press, 1962.
Weber, Max. *Ancient Judaism*. Translated and edited by Hans H. Gerth and Don Martindale. Glencoe: Free Press, 1952.
———. *The Sociology of Religion*. Translated by Ephraim Fischoff. Boston: Beacon, 1963.
Weinberg, Henry. *The Myth of the Jew in France: 1967-1982*. Oakville, ON: Mosaic, 1987.
Weingrad, Michael. "Jews (in Theory): Representation of Judaism, Anti-Semitism, and the Holocaust in Postmodern French Thought." *Judaism* (Winter 1996): 79-98.
Weisberg, Richard. *Vichy Law and the Holocaust in France*. New York: New York University Press, 1996.
Wessel, Julia Schulze, and Lars Rensmann. "The Paralysis of Judgment: Arendt and Adorno on Antisemitism and the Modern Condition." In *Arendt and Adorno: Political and Philosophical Investigations*, Edited by Lars Rensmann and Samir Gandesha, 197-228. Stanford: Stanford University Press, 2012.
Wheatland, Thomas. *The Frankfurt School in Exile*. Minneapolis: University of Minnesota Press, 2009.
Wiggershaus, Rolf. *The Frankfurt School: Its History, Theories, and Political Significance*. Translated by Michael Robertson. Cambridge, MA: MIT Press, 2007.
Wilken, Robert L. *John Chrysostom and the Jews: Rhetoric and Reality in the Late Fourth Century*. Berkeley: University of California Press, 1983.
Winock, Michel. *La France et les juifs: De 1789 à nos jours*. Paris: Seuil, 2004.
Wistrich, Robert. *Antisemitism: The Longest Hatred*. New York: Schocken, 1991.
———. *From Ambivalence to Betrayal: Israel, the Jews, and the Left*. Lincoln: University of Nebraska Press, 2012.
———. *A Lethal Obsession: Anti-Semitism from Antiquity to the Global Jihad*. New York: Random House, 2010.
———. "The Myth of the Jew in Contemporary France." In *Between Redemption and Perdition: Modern Antisemitism and Jewish Identity*. London: Routledge, 1990.
———. *Socialism and the Jews: The Dilemmas of Assimilation in Germany and Austria-Hungary*. London: Associated University Presses, 1982.
Wistrich, Robert, and Sergio DellaPergola, eds. *Fascist Anti-Semitism and the Italian Jews*. Jerusalem: The Vidal Sassoon International Center for the Study of Anti-Semitism, 1995.
Wolin, Richard. "The French Heidegger Debate." *New German Critique*, no. 45 (Fall 1988): 135-61.
———. *Heidegger's Children: Hannah Arendt, Karl Löwith, Hans Jonas, and Herbert Marcuse*. Princeton, NJ: Princeton University Press, 2001.
Worrell, Mark P. *Dialectic of Solidarity: Labor, Antisemitism, and the Frankfurt School*. Leiden: Brill, 2008.
Yerushalmi, Yosef Hayim. *Freud's Moses: Judaism Terminable and Interminable*. New Haven, CT: Yale University Press, 1991.
Young, Robert J. C. *Postcolonialism: An Historical Introduction*. Oxford: Wiley Blackwell, 2001.
———. *White Mythologies*, 2nd ed. New York: Routledge, 2004.
Young-Bruehl, Elisabeth. *Hannah Arendt: For Love of the World*. New Haven, CT: Yale University Press, 1982.

———. "Hannah Arendt's Storytelling." *Social Research* 44, no. 1 (1977): 183–90.
Yovel, Yirmiyahu. *Dark Riddle: Hegel, Nietzsche, and the Jews*. University Park: Penn State University Press, 1998.
Zimmerman, Moshe. *Wilhelm Marr: The Patriarch of Antisemitism*. Oxford: Oxford University Press, 1986.
Zipes, Jack. "The Holocaust Modernity, and Tough Jews." *Telos*, no. 86 (1990): 70–83.
Zuccotti, Susan. *The Holocaust, the French and the Jews*. New York: Basic Books, 1993.

Index

Abraham, Gary, 114
"Academic Freedom" (T. Parsons), 117
Addresses to the German Nation (*Reden an die deutsche Nation*) (Fichte), 181
Adorno, Theodor W., 7, 47, 243, 246, 247; "Anti-Semitism and Fascist Propaganda" by, 53-54, 59; Arendt anticipated by, 70; basic dialectical principles of argument of, 71; *Dialectic of Enlightenment* by, 65-71; "Freudian Theory and the Pattern of Fascist Propaganda" by, 268n79; *Guilt and Defense* by, 244; "The Meaning of Working Through the Past" by, 244; *Negative Dialectics* by, 146; "Remarks on *The Authoritarian Personality*" by, 268n79; "Research Project on Anti-Semitism" by, 51-52; *Studies on Authority and the Family* diverged from by, 63; "Types and Syndromes" by, 63
advertising, fascism and, 265n20
aesthetics, 204, 207-9
agitators, 59-61
AIP. *See* Association Israélites Pratiquants
AJC. *See* American Jewish Committee
Alexander, Edward, 231
Algerian conflict, 37
Allen, Amy, 47
allosemitism, 124-28; of T. Parsons, 122-23; postmodern, 130-32; Sandauer developing, 15
Almog, Shmuel, 4

Althusser, Louis, 128
ambivalence, 14-15, 126-27
America, civil rights struggle in, 120-22
American Jewish Committee (AJC), 46, 55
American Negro, The (T. Parsons and Clark), 120-21
Ancient Judaism (Weber), 68, 113
angst, 27
Anidjar, Gil, 4
Annales school, 163-64
anomie, anti-Semitism as product of, 103, 112
Anthology of African and West Indian poets writing in French (*Anthologie de la nouvelle poésie nègre et malgache de langue française*) (Senghor), 33
Anthropologie (Kant), 181
anthropology, 183-86
anti-Black racism, 32
anti-Jewish motifs, 242-43
anti-Jewish racism, volkish ideology and, 197-203
anti-Jewish tropes, leftist, 50
anti-Judaism, 1, 4, 291n1; anti-Semitism turned into by, 7; history of, 177; philosophy secularizing, 177-83; racism secularizing, 187-88
Anti-Judaism (Nirenberg), 291n1
antiracism, multidirectional, 32-36, 42-43
antisemit- (stem word), 250n14

Anti-Semite and Jew (*Réflexions sur la question juive*) (Sartre), 21–22, 26–27, 32, 43, 122, 143; on bad faith, 24; Israel championed in, 40–41; Judaken reviewing, 258n6
anti-Semitism. *See specific topics*
"Antisemitism" (Arendt), 87
"Anti-Semitism and Fascist Propaganda" (Adorno), 53–54, 59
Antisemitism and the Constitution of Sociology (Stoetzler), 107
Anti-Semitism: A Social Disease (Simmel), 53–55
"Antisemitism-Denial" (Alexander), 231
"'Antisemitism' Reassessed" (Bauman), 124, 130
"*Antisemitismus*" (German term), 4
anti-Zionism, 1, 22–23, 105–6, 230; anti-Semitism and, 9, 237–38; of Butler, 231–32; Stalinist, 38
anxiety, 27–28, 131
apartheid, in South Africa, 38–39
Arab/Israeli conflict, 32, 40–42, 229
Archimedean thinking, 83
Arendt, Hannah, 95, 148, 165, 219–20, 231–32, 247–48, 275n94; Adorno anticipating, 70; "Antisemitism" by, 87; Archimedean thinking critiqued by, 83; Bauman rearticulating, 89; binationalism supported by, 233–35; Blacks depreciated by, 76–77; "The Concept of History" by, 81; contradictions of, 100; "The Crisis of Zionism" of, 233; "Decline of the Nation-State and the End of the Rights of Man" by, 89; on Dreyfus affair, 276n126; *Eichmann in Jerusalem* by, 76, 77, 235–37, 265n20; eternal anti-Semitism skewered by, 9, 88; "excommunication" of, 233, 306n51; Frankfurt School contrasted with, 270n2; *The Human Condition* by, 76, 77; on ideology, 272n34; interactionist approach of, 74, 86, 88; "The Jew as Pariah" by, 91–92, 237; on Jewish problem, 97–99; on Jewish rights, 89–90; *The Life of the Mind* by, 83; *Love and St. Augustine* by, 75; *Men in Dark Times* by, 77; by "No Poor Jews," 277n145; objectivity dismissed by, 81; *The Origins of Totalitarianism* by, 19, 74–76, 78, 84–85, 97, 273nn62–64; philosophy buffered by, 274n69; politicization of memory criticized by, 83–84; on pre-imperialist racialism, 95–96; on Proust, 93; "Reflections on Little Rock" by, 76–77; *On Revolution* by, 76; Sartre contrasted with, 270n1; scapegoat theories refuted by, 87; stereotypes reinscribed by, 98; storytelling by, 73–74, 78–84; "To Save the Jewish Homeland" by, 234, 235, 307n67; traditional historical narrators differentiated by, 82; "Understanding and Politics" by, 79; Voegelin replied to by, 78–79; "We Refugees" by, 75; "Zionism Reconsidered" by, 234–35
Aron, Raymond, 21, 158
Aryan Myth, The (*Le Mythe Aryen*) (L. Poliakov), 159, 178, 183–87
Ascheim, Steven, 189, 215–16, 306n51
assimilation, 92; inclusion distinguished from, 121–22; by Jews, 295n59; politics of, 31
Association Israélites Pratiquants (AIP), 161
Augustine (church father), 17
Auschwitz camp, 7, 134, 145–47, 153, 233–34
authoritarianism, 63, 225–26
Authoritarian Personality, The (Frankfurt School), 58, 244, 268nn78–79
Auto-Emancipation (Pinsker), 17–18, 266n59
Avineri, Shlomo, 97, 277n145
"Awake, My People!" ("*Hakitzah ami*") (J. Gordon), 92

bad faith (*mauvaise foi*), 25; anti-Semitism embodying, 26; Judeophobia as, 219; *Anti-Semite and Jew* on, 24
Bakan, David, 295n53
Bartrop, Paul R., 291n1
Bauer, Bruno, 182
Bauer, Yehuda, 253n31
Bauman, Zygmunt, 15, 19, 102–4, 220–21, 223–25, 248; "'Antisemitism' Reassessed"

by, 124, 130; Arendt rearticulated by, 89; conditions nullifying moral inhibitions against violent atrocities itemized by, 284n124; Judeophobia reconceptualized by, 132; *Life in Fragments* by, 128; Marshman on, 129; *Modernity and Ambivalence* by, 125, 126; *Modernity and the Holocaust* by, 101, 106, 129, 222, 283n86; T. Parsons contrasted with, 105; "Sociology After the Holocaust" by, 277n1; sociology contributing to, 282n81; on strangers, 127–28
BDS movement. *See* Boycott, Sanctions, and Divestment
Beauvoir, Simone de, 22, 28, 29–30, 32, 42
Behemoth (Neumann), 45-46, 55-57
Being and Nothingness (Sartre), 22, 24, 37
Being and Time (Heidegger), 27
being-for-others (*être-pour-autrui*), 24
"Being Jewish" (Blanchot), 143
Bellamy, Elizabeth, 155
Ben-Gurion, David, 236
Benhabib, Seyla, 77, 83–84, 273n64
Benjamin, Walter, 79–80
Bennington, Geoffrey, 154
Berkeley Public Opinion Study Group, 62
Berliner Morgenzeitung (newspaper), 191
Berliner Tageblatt (newspaper), 191
Berlin Jewish Community, 191
Bernasconi, Robert, 274n69
Bernhard, Georg, 160
Bernier, François, 178, 297n89
Bernstein, Richard, 95, 233, 235
Bhabha, Homi, 211
binationalism, 233–35
Birnbaum, Pierre, 98, 106–7
Black Notebooks (*Schwarze Hefte*) (Heidegger), 288n63
"Black Orpheus" (Sartre), 33
Blacks, 32, 35, 178, 211; Arendt depreciating, 76–77; primitivism associated with, 34; racial oppression of, 33
Black Skin, White Masks (F. Fanon), 35, 211
Blanchot, Maurice, 135, 143–44
Blood of Others, The (Beauvoir), 32

Blücher, Heinrich, 75
Blum, Léon, 23
Blumenbach, Johann Friedrich, 180, 207
Blumenfeld, Kurt, 75
Bouteldja, Houria, 237–41, 308n87
Boyarin, Daniel, 156, 295n59
Boyarin, Jonathan, 156
Boycott, Sanctions, and Divestment (BDS) movement, against Israel, 9, 231
Braudel, Fernand, 163, 292n17
Bréviaire de la haine. *See Harvest of Hate*
Britt, Steuart Henderson, 108
Browning, Christopher, 166
Brozgal, Lia, 35–36
Bruck, Möller van den, 201
Buffon, Comte de, 179–80
Bultmann, Rudolf, 141
Butler, Judith, 11, 220, 231–33, 247

Camelots du roi (extreme-Right incubator), 23
Camper, Peter, 207
Camus, Albert, 27
capitalism: financial, 95, 98–100, 242–43; German split off from Jewish, 202; global, 72; Jews within, 50
capitalist countries, interior colonies of, 39
Carpentras cemetery, desecration of tombs at, 149–52
Carroll, David, 149
Carus, Carl Gustav, 207
"Caucasian" (term), 180
Cause du peuple-J'Accuse, La (Sartre), 43
CDJC. *See* Contemporary Jewish Documentation Center
Center for the Study of Contemporary European Jewry, at Tel Aviv University, 219
Centre de Documentation Juive Contemporaine. *See* Contemporary Jewish Documentation Center
Césaire, Aimé, 29, 34, 241
Chamberlain, Houston Stewart, 181, 194
Charmé, Stuart Zane, 33
Cheyette, Bryan, 14–15, 74

"Childhood of a Leader, The" (*L'Enfance d'un chef*) (Sartre), 23, 26-28
chimerical hostility, against Jews, 7-8
Christianity, 5, 168, 172, 182, 240, 296n65; anti-Semitism and, 169; in Europe, 154; Judaism split from, 176, 306n42; Judeophobia and, 126-27, 129-30; philosophy influenced by, 188
Christian theological discourse, racism recasting, 186-87
Christophobia, 169, 170-76
Chrysostom (church father), 17
citizenship, Jewish emancipation and, 89
Civilization and Its Discontents (Freud), 68
Civil Rights Bill (1964), American, 120
civil rights struggle, in America, 120-22
Clark, Kenneth B., 120-21
Cohen, Arthur A., 5, 296n65
Cohen-Solal, Annie, 43
Cohn, Norman, 167
Coke, Edward, 196
Cold War, 5
collective guilt, 138
colleges, Title VI lawsuits against, 2
colonialism, 32, 35-38, 271n15
Colonizer and the Colonized, The (*Portrait du colonisé, précédé du portrait du colonisateur*) (Memmi), 35-36
Committed Observer, The (*Spectateur engagé, Le*) (Aron), 21
communism, 41, 85-86
Communist Party, French, 41
Comte, Auguste, 107
"Concept of History, The" (Arendt), 81
Condition des juifs en France sous l'occupation italienne, La (Poliakov), 293n24
Confronting History (G. Mosse), 301n20
conscious pariahs, 74, 219, 231-37, 247
conspiracy narrative, 60-61
Contat, Michel, 39
Contemporary Jewish Documentation Center (*Centre de Documentation Juive Contemporaine*) (CDJC), 162
Contemporary Jewish Record (Graeber), 55-56
contestant enmity, 126

Coon, Carleton Stevens, 108
Coughlin, Charles, 59
Council for Democracy, 281n56
countertypes, to stereotypes, 213
Crisis of German Ideology, The (G. Mosse and Laqueur), 193, 195, 198-200, 206-7
"Crisis of Zionism, The" (Arendt), 233
critical theories. *See specific topics*
Critique of Dialectical Reason (*Critique de la raison dialectique*) (Sartre), 37-38, 238
Crossman, R. H. S., 165
cultural schemas, 277n3
Culture of Western Europe, The (G. Mosse), 195, 198, 216

death camps, 20, 21, 82, 257n4
"Decline of the Nation-State and the End of the Rights of Man, The" (Arendt), 89
decolonizing, 239, 241
Decree, Baden, 148
definition, of anti-Semitism, 6-13
Definition of Anti-Semitism, The (Marcus), 9
definitions, of critical theory, 257n85
De Generis Humane Varietate Nativa. *See On the Natural Variety of Mankind*
Delacampagne, Christian, 166
"De l'antisionisme à l'antisémitisme" (L. Poliakov), 229
Deleuze, Gilles, 135
Dérive à partir de Marx et Freud (Lyotard), 139-40
Derrida, Jacques, 39, 221
Descartes, René, 179
Destruction of the European Jews, The (Hilberg), 164, 199
Diab, Mohamad, 40
Dialectical Imagination, The (Jay), 266n45
Dialectic of Enlightenment (Frankfurt School), 245-46
Dialectic of Enlightenment (Horkheimer and Adorno), 65-71
Difference and Pathology (G. Mosse), 209
Differend, The (Lyotard), 145-47, 287n51
Discourse on Colonialism (Cesaire), 29
Discourse on Method (Descartes), 179

discrimination, 6, 36, 91
disinformation, Judeophobia fostered by, 245-46
Disraeli, Benjamin, 5
Ditsch, Lisa, 81-82
Division of the earth by the different species or races who inhabit it (*Nouvelle division de la terre par les différentes espèces ou races d'hommes qui l'habitent*) (Bernier), 178
Doctor's Plot case, 228-29
Doriot, Jacques, 23
Dreyfus affair, 9, 31, 274n83, 276n126
Drieu La Rochelle, Pierre, 29-30
Durkheim, Émile, 102

Early Theological Writings (Hegel), 156
Eichmann, Adolf, 166, 235-36
Eichmann in Jerusalem (Arendt), 76, 77, 235-37, 265n20
"Elements of Anti-Semitism" (Frankfurt School), 245-46
"Elements of a Psychoanalytic Theory of Anti-Semitism" (Fenichel), 53-54
Ellenson, David, 113
Elon, Amos, 306n51
emancipation, Jewish, 89, 153
Empty Suitcase, The (Drieu La Rochelle), 30
End of Progress, The (Allen), 47
"*Enfance d'un chef, L'*" (Sartre). *See* "Childhood of a Leader, The"
Engel, David, 8-9
England, religious history of, 193-94
English Reformation, 193-94
Enlightenment, 65-71, 179, 184, 190, 245-46; anti-Semitism and, 22; French liberalism based in, 31; G. Mosse criticizing, 207-8; race during, 180
Esprit (journal), 34
Essay Concerning Human Understanding (Locke), 178
Essence of Christianity, The (*Wesen des Christentums*) (Feuerbach), 182
eternal anti-Semitism, 7, 18, 73, 86; Arendt skewering, 9, 88; cyclical, 9-10; rabbis as, 16-17

Eternal Light, The (radio program), 172-73
Ethics of Ambiguity, The (Beauvoir), 22, 28
être-pour-autrui. *See* being-for-others
Eurocentrism, Frankfurt School reframing, 264n7
Europe, 149-53, 164, 195-99, 216; Christianity in, 154; crimes against humanity committed by, 156; Jewish history in, 216, 274n83; self-constructions in, 4-5. *See also* France; Germany
"Europe, the Jews and the Book" (Lyotard), 149-53
European culture, Jews as basis of, 150
Europe in the Sixteenth Century (Koenigsberger), 196
"Examination of Theories of Race Prejudice, An" (Graeber), 116
Existentialism Is a Humanism (*L'Existentialisme est un humanisme*) (Sartre), 33

Falk, Richard, 12
Fallen Solders (G. Mosse), 302n65
Fanon, Frantz, 14, 34-35, 42
Fanon, Josie, 42
fascism, 85-86, 225-26; advertising and, 265n20; Jews opposed by, 66, 70-71; Nazi, 173
fascist anti-Semite, 54
Faurrison, Robert, 147
fear, 27-28, 222-23
Feldman, David, 10
femininity, middle-class ideals of, 213
Fenichel, Otto, 53-54
Feuerbach, Ludwig, 182
Fifty Key Thinkers on the Holocaust and Genocide (Bartrop and Jacobs), 291n1
"Figure Foreclosed" (Lyotard), 140-45
Final Solution, 149
financial capitalism, 95, 98-100, 242-43
Finkielkraut, Alain, 146
Fisher, Louis, 172
Flowers, Samuel, 58
FN. *See* Front national
Force of Prejudice, The (*La Force du préjuge*) (Taguieff), 283n91

Foucault, Michel, 41, 128
Foundations of the Nineteenth Century, The (Chamberlain), 194
France, 293n24; anti-Semitism in, 253n39; the Holocaust and, 165-66; Jews deported by, 257n1; Nazis occupying, 161; Vichy government in, 165-66, 259n16, 293n29
Frankfurter Zeitung, 48
Frankfurt School. *See* Institute for Social Research
Frankfurt School, The (Wiggershaus), 266n45
Free Jewish School (*Freie Jüdische Lehrhaus*), 48
Freie Jüdische Lehrhaus. See Free Jewish School
French Communist Party, 41
French liberalism, Enlightenment as basis for, 31
French Republicanism, 22
French Revolution, 186-87, 227
Frenkel-Brunswik, Else, 62
Freud, Sigmund, 67, 268n79; *Civilization and Its Discontents* by, 68; double binds in identity of, 172; Jewishness of, 295n53; Lyotard on, 139-40, 145; *Moses and Monotheism* by, 52, 141-44, 151, 157, 170-72; *Totem and Taboo* by, 142, 170-71
"Freudian Theory and the Pattern of Fascist Propaganda" (Adorno), 268n79
Friedländler, Saul, 294n37
Friedrich, Carl, 108, 281n56
"From anti-Zionism to anti-Semitism" ("*De l'antisionisme à l'antisémitisme*") (L. Poliakov), 228
Fromm, Erich, 62
From Mohammed to the Marranos (L. Poliakov), 176-77
From Voltaire to Wagner (L. Poliakov), 159
Front national (FN), 150
"Full Citizenship for the Negro American?" (T. Parsons), 121

Gall, Franz Joseph, 207
Gaza War, 219
Geller, Jay, 170
Gellner, Ernst, 77
gender, pathologizing of, 210
general will, as religion, 203
generational trauma, 218-19
genocide, 128
Geography of Hope (Birnbaum), 106-7
Gerhardt, Uta, 101, 279n29, 279n34; on Graeber, 110-11
German culture, Nazi culture fed into by, 205
Germany, 133, 137, 148, 193-95, 198-202, 205-7; anti-Semitism in, 253n39; lineage of thought in, 182; "metaphysical guilt" of, 32-33; philosophy in, 181; *Sonderweg* thesis on, 58-59; volkish ideology influencing, 197-204
Gilles (Drieu La Rochelle), 30
Gilman, Sander, 209, 210, 212
Gines, Kathryn T., 273n63
Girard, Patrick, 294n35
Glenn, Susan, 235
Glickman, Elaine Rose, 16
global capitalism, 72
globalization, Judeophobia driven by, 243
Goering, Hermann, 28
Goldberg, Chad Alan, 102
Goldhagen, Daniel Jonah, 166
Gordin, Jacob, 162
Gordon, Judah Leib, 92
Gordon, Peter, 63
Graeber, Isacque: *Contemporary Jewish Record* by, 55-56; "An Examination of Theories of Race Prejudice" by, 116; Gerhardt on, 110-11; *Jews in a Gentile World* by, 108-10; T. Parsons in conflict with, 109-11, 116; "The Sociology of Modern Anti-Semitism" by, 101, 110-12, 122
Grappin, P., 164
great chain of being, 187-88, 207
Great Hatred, The (Samuel), 172-74
Greenberg, Clement, 235
Grimm, Jacob, 185
"Grip, The" ("*La Mainmise*") (Lyotard), 152-53
Grossman, Marshall, 5

Group Experiment (Frankfurt School), 244
Grünberg, Carl, 48
Guilt and Defense (Adorno), 244
Guterman, Norbert, 54, 58

"Hakitzah ami" (J. Gordon). *See* "Awake, My People!"
Halpern, Ben, 109, 235
Hamlet (play), *Oedipus* contrasted with, 140–41
Hammer, Espen, 47
Haraway, Donna, 81–82
Hartshorne, Edward Y., 119
Harvest of Hate (*Bréviaire de la haine*) (L. Poliakov), 158–59, 163–67, 169
Harvey, William, 179
Haverford College, 192
Hazal. *See* Jewish sages
Hebrew University of Jerusalem, 42
Hegel, Georg, 155–56, 181–82
Heidegger, Martin, 80, 135, 154, 259nn22–23; *Being and Time* by, 27; *Black Notebooks* by, 288n63; Nazism and, 148–49; "The Self-Assertion of the German University" by, 148; "What Is Metaphysics?" by, 27
Heidegger and "the jews" (Lyotard), 148–49, 154
"Heidegger's Nazi Turn" (LaCapra), 148
heightened nationalism, 227
Helmreich, William, 106
Herf, Jeffrey, 167, 194, 206
Hertzler, J. O., 108
heterophobia, 221, 255n66; anti-Semitism treated as, 124–25; Judeophobia as, 15; secularization inflamed by, 225
Hilberg, Raul, 164, 199
Hindus, Milton, 172
Histoire de l'antisémitisme (L. Poliakov). *See History of Anti-Semitism*
historical event, limit experience contrasted with, 146–47
history, of anti-Semitism, 91, 256n74
"History, Anthropology, and Mass Movements" (G. Mosse), 195

History of Anti-Semitism, The (*Histoire de l'antisémitisme*) (L. Poliakov), 159, 176–79, 185
History of the Art of the Ancient World (Winckelmann), 207
Hitler, Adolf, 23, 128–29, 148, 199–201, 302n39
Hitlerism, 56, 117, 171, 206
"Hitler's Taste" (G. Mosse), 205
Hobbes, Thomas, 196
Hobson, J. A., 95
Holocaust, the, 1, 101, 128, 293n25; France and, 165–66; Judeophobia after, 218–19, 237, 241–42, 247–48; sociology and, 277n1
Holocaust deniers, Lyotard probing, 147
Holy Pretense, The (G. Mosse), 196
homosexuality, 191, 276n123
Horkheimer, Max, 45, 49–51, 65–71, 246, 265n20
Human Condition, The (Arendt), 76, 77
Hume, David, 184
Husserl, Edmund, 148
hyphen, in anti-Semitism, 4–6, 252n27
Hyphen, The (*Un trait d'union*) (Lyotard), 152

ideological racism, anti-Semitism developing into, 97
ideology: Arendt on, 272n34; political, 94–97; volkish, 197–204
IHRA. *See* International Holocaust Remembrance Alliance
illiberal democracy, 225–26
Illuminations (Benjamin), 79–80
Image of Man, The (G. Mosse), 193, 212
impartiality, 81–82
imperialism, anti-Semitism and, 95
imperialist racism, Frankfurt School ignoring, 46–47
inclusion, assimilation distinguished from, 121–22
Indigènes de la République (movement), 238–39
Inside Nazi Germany (Peukert), 129

Institute for Social Research "Frankfurt School" (*Institut für Sozialforschung*), 19, 45, 219–21, 241–44, 247, 264n9; anti-Semitism not directly analyzed by, 49; Arendt contrasted with, 270n2; *The Authoritarian Personality* of, 58, 244; *Dialectic of Enlightenment* by, 245–46; "Elements of Anti-Semitism" by, 245–46; Eurocentrism reframed by, 264n7; first generation of, 48–49; *Group Experiment* by, 244; imperialist racism ignored by, 46–47; Nazis targeting, 49; new approaches pioneered by, 72; New Objectivity style of, 264n12; racialization as understood by, 47–48; *Studies in Philosophy and Social Science* by, 109; Studies in Prejudice series by, 46, 55, 266n45; *Studies on Authority and the Family* by, 62; texts developing arguments of, 263n1; ticket thinking highlighted by, 248
interior colonies, of capitalist countries, 39
International Holocaust Remembrance Alliance (IHRA), 10–11
Irele, Abiola, 35
Islamophobia, 6
Israel, 40–42, 43, 174–75, 232, 234–35; *Anti-Semite and Jew* championing, 40–41; BDS movement against, 9, 231; criticism against, 11–12, 229–30
Israeli/Arab conflict, 32, 40–42, 229
Israeli-Palestinian conflict, 1–2, 40, 44, 245

Jabotinsky, Vladimir, 160
Jacobs, Steven Leonard, 291n1
Jacobson, Matthew, 2
Jaspers, Karl, 32, 133–34, 138
Jay, Martin, 37, 48, 264n12, 266n45
JDA. *See* Jerusalem Declaration on Antisemitism
Jean-Paul Sartre and the Jewish Question (Judaken), 258n6
Jerusalem Declaration on Antisemitism (JDA), 11–13
Jew, the Arab, The (Anidjar), 4
"Jew as Pariah, The" (Arendt), 91–92, 237
Jewish community, the state in relation to, 90

Jewish emancipation, citizenship and, 89
Jewish Enemy, The (Herf), 167
Jewish history, in Europe, 216, 274n83
Jewish huckster businessman myth, 115–16
Jewish identity, race as basis of, 93
Jewish nation-state, 234–35
Jewishness: of Freud, 295n53; Judaism contrasted with, 92; queerness of, 98
Jewish nomadism, 52
"Jewish Oedipus" (Lyotard), 140–43, 141–43
Jewish Peculiarities (Schudt), 207
Jewish Question, The (*Die Judenfrage*) (B. Bauer), 182
Jewish rights, Arendt on, 89–90
Jewish sages (*Hazal*), 16
Jewish Self-Hatred (G. Mosse), 209, 211
Jews, 112, 154, 290n97; ambivalence embodied by, 126–27; anti-Semites in relation to, 26–27; assimilation by, 295n59; within capitalism, 50; chimerical hostility against, 7–8; demonization of, 167–68; European culture based on, 150; fascism opposing, 66, 70–71; financial capitalism and, 95, 98–100; France deporting, 257n1; Hegel condemning, 181–82; history of, 74; homosexuality compared with, 276n123; Lyotard valorizing, 155; modernity and, 128–30; Nazism abstracting, 129; as outsiders, 213–14; as "pariah people," 113–14; postmodernism and, 133–34; problems with modern order identified with, 118–19; as symbol, 96; tropes used against, 254n50; the West rejecting, 153; whiteness of, 2–3, 239–40, 249n4
"Jews and Europe, The" (Horkheimer), 45, 49–51
Jew's Body, The (Gilman), 210
Jews in a Gentile World (Graeber and Britt), 108–10
Jones, William, 185
Jordan, Winthrop, 206
Judaism, 181; Christianity split from, 176, 306n42; Jewishness contrasted with, 92; the West divided from, 152. *See also* anti-Judaism

Judaken, Jonathan, *Jean-Paul Sartre and the Jewish Question* by, 258n6
Judenfrage, Die. See *Jewish Question, The*
"Judeo-Christian" (term), 5, 240, 296n65
Judeophobia, 1, 6, 151-52, 157, 305n37; after the Holocaust, 218-19, 237, 241-42, 247-48; anti-Semitism differentiated from, 13-14; anxiety influencing, 131; attitudes toward, 17; as bad faith, 219; Bauman reconceptualizing, 132; Christianity and, 126-27, 129-30; disinformation fostering, 245-46; globalization driving, 243; as heterophobia, 15; Negrophobia connected with, 34; paradigms for explaining, 16-20; phobogenic objects linked to, 14-15; L. Poliakov focusing on, 160; racism tangled in, 221-22; on the Right, 23; stereotypes and, 219; in Western tradition, 176-77
Judeophobia (Schäfer), 8
Judt, Tony, 262n85

Kalmar, Ivan, 5
Kant, Immanuel, 181, 207, 265n20
Koenigsberger, H. G., 196
Kozevnikov, Aleksandr "Alexandre Kojève," 161-62
Kristeva, Julia, 93

Lacan, Jacques, 136-37
LaCapra, Dominick, 148, 155
Lachmann, Edmund, 191
Lachmann, Salomon, 191
Langmuir, Gavin, 7
language, philosophy of, 287n52
Laqueur, Walter, 193, 204, 230
Latreille, A., 164
Lavater, Kaspar, 207
Lazare, Bernard, 91, 235, 237
leaders, populism idealizing, 227-28
Lefebvre, Henri, 37
Left, the, 50, 228-29, 240
leftist anti-Jewish tropes, 50
Le Pen, Jean-Marie, 150

Lerman, Antony, 254n51
Levinas, Emmanuel, 135, 173-74, 258n7
Levinson, Daniel J., 62
Lévy, Benny, 43
Levy, Richard, 14
liberalism: anti-Semitism contrasted with, 122-23; French, 31; Horkheimer and Adorno critiquing, 66, 67; Parsons and, 102, 107, 111, 117-19; radical extreme within, 17; Sartre critiquing, 31-32
Lichtheim, George, 194
Liebesbegriff bei Augustin, Der. See *Love and St. Augustine*
Life in Fragments (Bauman), 128
Life of the Mind, The (Arendt), 83
limit experience, historical event contrasted with, 146-47
Linné, Carl von "Linnaeus," 179-80
"Lived Experience of the Black, The" (F. Fanon), 34
Locke, John, 178
Lohengrin (Wagner), 205
Lombroso, Cesare, 208
London Review of Books, 43
Love and St. Augustine (*Der Liebesbegriff bei Augustin*) (Arendt), 75
Löwenthal, Leo, 54, 58
Luban, David, 83
Luther-to-Hitler thesis, 199, 201, 302n39
Luzzatto, Sergio, 12
Lyotard, Jean-François, 19, 41, 220, 262n100, 285n1, 287n52; Blanchot influencing, 144; *Dérive à partir de Marx et Freud* by, 139-40; *The Differend* by, 145-47, 287n51; "Europe, the Jews and the Book" by, 149-53; "Figure Foreclosed" by, 140-45; on Freud, 139-40, 145; "The Grip" by, 152-53; Hegel reiterated by, 155-56; *Heidegger and "the jews"* by, 148-49, 154; Holocaust deniers probed by, 147; *The Hyphen* by, 152; intellectual trajectory of, 135-37; Jaspers reviewed by, 133-34; "Jewish Oedipus" by, 140-43; Jews valorized by, 155; on Marx, 135-36; *La Phénoménologie* by, 136-37; *The Postmodern Explained* by, 291n102; on reading, 289n75

Machiavellism, 196–97
Maier-Katkin, Daniel, 233, 235
"*Mainmise, La*" (Lyotard). *See* "Grip, The"
Marcus, Kenneth L., 9
Marcuse, Herbert, 37
Maritain, Jacques, 164, 174–75
Marr, Wilhelm, 4
Marrus, Michael, 293n29
Marshman, Sophia, 129
Marx, Karl, 49, 139–40; Lyotard on, 135–36; "On the Jewish Question" by, 182; *Sur Judenfrage* by, 99
masculinity, stereotypes of, 212–13
Massing, Paul, 58
mass movements, theater influencing, 205
mass society, 85–86
Maudaule, Jacques, 175
Mauriac, François, 168
mauvaise foi. *See* bad faith
Max Weber and the Jewish Question (Abraham), 114
McBride, William, 37
McCarthy, Thomas, 47
"Meaning of Working Through the Past, The" (Adorno), 244
Meinecke, Friedrich, 197
Melehy, Hassan, 283n91
Memmi, Albert, 35, 36, 221, 255n66
Mémorial de la Shoah (Holocaust memorial), 162
Mendelssohn, Moses, 181
Men in Dark Times (Arendt), 77
Menthon, François de, 162–63
Merah, Mohamed, 308n87
metanarratives, 137
Michaelis, Johann David, 181
mimesis, anti-Semitism as, 68–69
Misrahi, Robert, 40
mob, the, anti-Semitism and, 66–67
modernism: post-, 133–34, 285n1
modernity, 106, 196–97, 290n78; anti-Semitism linked with, 189; fear heightened by, 222–23; Jews and, 128–30; liberal, 103–4, 117–19; nationalism and, 119; National Socialism as conclusion of, 215; T. Parsons guided by, 117–18; social dislocations of, 119; sociology bolstering, 103–4; underside of, 215–17
Modernity and Ambivalence (Bauman), 125, 126
Modernity and the Holocaust (Bauman), 101, 106, 129, 222, 283n86
modernization, sociological processes of, 280n36
Monde juif Le (journal), 162
Moses and Monotheism (Freud), 52, 141–44, 151, 157, 170–72
Mosse, George L., 19, 189, 192, 220, 225, 301n38, 303n75; Ascheim on, 215–16; *Confronting History* by, 301n20; *The Crisis of German Ideology* of, 193, 195, 198–200, 206–7; culture not considered an epiphenomenon by, 194; *The Culture of Western Europe* by, 195, 198, 216; *Difference and Pathology* by, 209; Enlightenment criticizing, 207–8; *Fallen Solders* by, 302n65; "History, Anthropology, and Mass Movements" by, 195; "Hitler's Taste" by, 205; *The Holy Pretense* by, 196; homosexuality impacting, 191; *The Image of Man* by, 193, 212; Luther-to-Hitler thesis opposed by, 199, 201, 302n39; methodology, 193–96; *Nationalism and Sexuality* of, 193, 212, 214; *Nationalization of the Masses* by, 195, 197, 203–9; on Nazi movement, 206; on racism, 198; *The Reformation* by, 196; *Seeing the Insane* by, 210; *The Struggle for Sovereignty in England* by, 196–97; Talmon critiqued by, 226–28; "Toward a General Theory of Fascism" by, 226; *Toward the Final Solution* by, 198, 206, 208–9, 211–12, 216–17
Mosse, Rudolf, 191
Mounier, Emmanuel, 21
Mudimbé, V. Y., 35
multidirectional antiracism, 32–36, 42–43
Mythe Aryen, Le (L. Poliakov). *See Aryan Myth, The*
Myth of the Judeo-Christian Tradition, The (Cohen), 296n65

National Conference of Christians and Jews, 5
nationalism, 190; bi-, 233-35; heightened, 227; modernity and, 119; Poliakov exploring, 183-84; racism strengthening, 214
Nationalism and Sexuality (G. Mosse), 193, 212, 214
Nationalization of the Masses, The (G. Mosse), 195, 197, 203-9
National Socialism, 197, 204-5, 215
nation-state, mass society contrasted with, 85
Naville, Pierre "J. Gallois," 164
Nazi culture, German culture feeding into, 205
Nazi fascism, 173
Nazi movement, G. Mosse on, 206
Nazi Poison (Council for Democracy), 281n56
Nazis, 129, 130, 138, 167-68, 204-5; anti-Semitism of, 164, 166, 253n39; France occupied by, 161; Frankfurt School targeted by, 49
Nazism, 45, 67-68, 117-19, 157; anti-Semitism distinguished from, 56-57; Heidegger and, 148-49; Jews abstracted by, 129; paganism and, 295n56; as religion, 167-68; serious men supporting, 29
Negative Dialectics (Adorno), 146
Negrophobia, Judeophobia connected with, 34
Nelson, Cary, 231
Neumann, Franz, 45-46, 55-57
New Objectivity style, of Frankfurt School, 264n12
"New Racism, The" ("*Le Nouveau racisme*") (Sartre), 38-40
Newton, Isaac, 179
New World Order (NWO), 242
Nicholls, A. J., 204
Nielsen, Jens Kaalhauge, Parsons reframed by, 281n64
Nietzsche, Friedrich, 279n34
nihilistic man, 29-30
Nirenberg, David, 291n1

Nizan, Paul, 23
Noerr, Gunzelin Schmid, 65, 268n90
nomadism, Jewish, 52
"No Poor Jews" (Arendt), 277n145
Norton, Anne, 76-77
"*Nouveau racisme, Le*" (Sartre). *See* "New Racism, The"
Nouvelle division de la terre par les différentes espèces ou races d'hommes qui l'habitent. *See* Division of the earth by the different species or races who inhabit it
Nuremberg trials, 134-35, 137-39, 162-63
NWO. *See* New World Order
Nye, Robert, 194-95
Nyssa, Gregory of, 176

objectivity, Arendt dismissing, 81
Oedipus (play), *Hamlet* contrasted with, 140-41
"Of National Characters" (Hume), 184
On Revolution (Arendt), 76
On the Civil Improvement of the Jews (*Über die bürgerliche Verbesserung der Juden*) (Dohm), 181
"On the Jewish Question" ("*Zur Judenfrage*") (Marx), 182
On the Natural Variety of Mankind (*De Generis Humane Varietate Nativa*) (Blumenbach), 180
Orientalism (Said), 4
Origins of Totalitarianism, The (Arendt), 19, 74-76, 78, 84-85, 97, 273nn62-64
Other, the Self differentiated from, 209
Oxaal, Ivar, 283n86
Ozick, Cynthia, 231

paganism, 171, 295n56
Palestinian-Israeli conflict, 1-2, 40, 44, 245
Pariser Tageblatt (newspaper), 160
Parsons, Edward, 104
Parsons, Talcott, 19, 101-3, 107, 112, 277n4, 280n36; "Academic Freedom" by, 117; allosemitism of, 122-23; *The American Negro* by, 120-21; anti-Semitism decried by, 111; Bauman contrasted with, 105;

Parsons, Talcott (*continued*)
"Full Citizenship for the Negro American?" by, 121; Gerhardt on, 279n29, 279n34; Graeber in conflict with, 109-11, 116; modernity guiding, 117-18; J. Nielsen reframing, 281n64; pluralism emphasized by, 121-22; "Racial and Religious Differences as Factors in Group Tensions" by, 120-21; on racism, 119-21; *The Social Message of Jesus* by, 104; "The Sociology of Anti-Semitism" by, 102, 281n56; "Some Sociological Aspects of the Fascist Movements" by, 118; stereotypes and, 115; *Structure of Social Action* by, 102, 104-5; Weber and, 113-15

Parting Ways (Butler), 231
Paxton, Robert, 293n29
Payne, Stanley, 301n38
"People of the Book," 143, 150-52, 155
Pepper, Stephen, 210
persecution, stereotypes contrasted with, 211
Peukert, Detlev, 129
Peyrère, Isaac de la, 184
Phénoménologie, La (Lyotard), 136-37
Phenomenology of Spirit, The (Hegel), 156
philosophy, 109, 221; anti-Judaism secularized by, 177-83; Arendt buffering, 274n69; Christianity influencing, 188; in Germany, 181; of language, 287n52
Philosophy in a Time of Terror (Derrida), 221
phobophobia, 222-23
Pinsker, Leon, 18, 266n59
Pitkin, Hannah, 77
Plessini, Karel, 193
pluralism, T. Parsons emphasizing, 121-22
Poliakov, Léon, 19, 213-14, 219-20, 230-31, 256n74, 291n1; *The Aryan Myth* by, 159, 178, 183-87; Braudel differentiated from, 292n17; *La Condition des juifs en France sous l'occupation italienne* by, 293n24; *De l'antisionisme à l'antisémitisme* by, 229; Friedländler compared with, 294n37; "From anti-Zionism to anti-Semitism" by, 228; *From Mohammed to the Marranos* by, 176-77; *From Voltaire to Wagner* by, 159;

Girard on, 294n35; *Harvest of Hate* by, 158-59, 163-67, 169; *The History of Anti-Semitism* by, 159, 176-79, 185; indifference anticipated by, 294n44; innovations of, 165-66; Judeophobia focused on by, 160; nationalism explored by, 183-84; *Le Procès de Jérusalem* by, 294; "The Quest for the New Adam" by, 185

Poliakov, Vladimir, 160
Polish Sociological Association, 105
political ideology, anti-Semitism as, 94-97
politicization of memory, Arendt criticizing, 83-84
politics, religion transformed into by, 227
politics of assimilation, 31
Pollock, Friedrich, 49, 65
Popular Front (antifascist group), 23
populism, leaders idealized by, 227-28
Portrait du colonisé, précédé du portrait du colonisateur. See *Colonizer and the Colonized, The*
"Portrait Of The Anti-Semite" (*Portrait de l'antisémite*) (Sartre), 23-24, 259n13
postcolonialism, 40-42
Postmodern Explained, The (Lyotard), 291n102
postmodernism, 133-34, 285n1
prejudice, 6, 58
primitivism, Blacks associated with, 34
Principia Mathematica (Newton), 179
"Problem with Judith Butler, The" (Nelson), 231
Procès de Jérusalem, Le (L. Poliakov), 294
propaganda, 54-55, 203-4, 234-35
Prophets of Deceit (Löwenthal and Guterman), 58, 59-61
proteophobia, 15, 125-26, 127
Proust, Marcel, Arendt on, 93
Prussian State Library, 75
psychoanalysis, 54, 136-37
psychology, 69-70
Pulzer, Peter, 204

Quaker Bootham School, 192
queerness, of Jewishness, 98

"Qu'est-ce qu'un collaborateur?" (Sartre). See "What is a collaborator?"
"Quest for the New Adam, The" (L. Poliakov), 185
Question of German Guilt, The (*Die Schuldfrage*) (Jaspers), 32, 133, 137

rabbis, as eternal anti-Semitism, 16–17
Rabinbach, Anson, 235
race, 47, 297n89; during Enlightenment, 180; infusion of, 208; Jewish identity based in, 93
Race, Empire and the Idea of Human Development (McCarthy), 47
"Racial and Religious Differences as Factors in Group Tensions" (T. Parsons), 120–21
racial discourse, stereotypes and, 210
racialization, Frankfurt School understanding, 47–48
racial oppression, of Blacks, 33
racism, 95–96, 183–84, 239–41, 271n15; aesthetics and, 206–7; anti-Black, 32; anti-Jewish, 197–203; anti-Judaism secularizing, 187–88; categories of, 186–87; Christian theological discourse recast into, 186–87; ideological, 97; imperialist, 46–47; Judeophobia tangled in, 221–22; G. Mosse on, 198; multidirectional anti-, 32–36, 42–43; nationalism strengthened by, 214; *Nationalization of the Masses* and, 203–9; T. Parsons on, 119–21; rational, 178; respectability and, 190; as "scavenger ideology," 208, 216; seriality of, 37; volkish ideology and anti-Jewish racism and, 197–203; Zionism and, 237–38
Racism (Memmi), 221
Radio Frankfurt, 48
Raphael, Freddy, 114
rational racism, 178
Rauschning, Hermann, 167
Readings, Bill, 156–57, 289n75
Reden an die deutsche Nation. See *Addresses to the German Nation*
"Reflections on Little Rock" (Arendt), 76–77

Réflexions sur la question juive. See *Anti-Semite and Jew*
Reformation, The (G. Mosse), 196
Rehearsal for Destruction (Massing), 58–59
religion, 113–14; ambivalence regulated by, 127; general will as, 203; Nazism as, 167–68; politics transforming, 227
religious history, of England, 193–94
religious origin, of anti-Semitism, 67–68
religious persecution, 196–97
"Remarks on The Authoritarian Personality" (Adorno), 268n79
Remembrance of Things Past (Proust), 93
Rensmann, Lars, 241–42
Republicanism, French, 22
"Research Project on Anti-Semitism" (Adorno), 51–53
respectability, racism and, 190
responsibility, four modes of, 137–38
Rex, Zvi, 243–44
Ridley, Yvonne, 12
Rise of Totalitarian Democracy, The (Talmon), 226–28
Rose, Gillian, 156
Rosenzweig, Franz, 48
Rothberg, Michael, 74, 245
Rousso, Henry, 150
Rybalka, Michel, 39

Sabean, David, 193, 196
Said, Edward, 4, 42, 46–47
Samuel, Maurice, 172–74
Sandauer, Artur, 15, 124
Sanford, R. Nevitt, 53, 62
San Francisco Psychoanalytic Society, 53
Sartre, Jean-Paul, 18, 44, 219–21, 237–41, 257n4, 258n6; Arendt contrasted with, 270n1; *Being and Nothingness* by, 22, 24, 37; "Black Orpheus" by, 33; Blanchot criticizing, 143–44; *La Cause du peuple-J'Accuse* by, 43; "The Childhood of a Leader" by, 23, 27–28; colonialism focused on by, 32, 35–36; *Critique of Dialectical Reason* by, 37–38, 238; *Existentialism Is a Humanism* by, 33;

Sartre, Jean-Paul (*continued*)
F. Fanon criticizing, 34–35; Judt critiquing, 262n85; key axiom of, 21–23; liberalism critiqued by, 31–32; multidirectional antiracism of, 32–36, 42–43; "The New Racism" by, 38–40; "Portrait Of The Anti-Semite" of, 23–24, 259n13; *Les Temps Modernes* by, 34, 41; "The third world begins in the suburbs" by, 39; Vichy government focused on by, 259n16; *The Wall* by, 23; "What is a collaborator?" by, 30. *See also Anti-Semite and Jew*
scapegoat theories, 73, 86, 87, 120
Schäfer, Peter, 8
Schlegel, Friedrich, 185
Schmitt, Carl, 201, 227–28
Schmueli, Ephraim, 114
Schnapper, Dominique, 163
Schneerson, Isaac, 162
Schneerson, Zalman, 161
Scholem, Gershom, 50, 236
Schönbach, Peter, 243–44
Schorske, Carl, 203
Schraub, David, 12
Schudt, Johann, 207
Schuldfrage, Die. See Question of German Guilt, The
Schwartz, Joseph, 225
Schwarze Hefte. See Black Notebooks
secondary anti-Semitism, 243–44
secularization, heterophobia inflaming, 225
Sedgwick, Eve Kosovsky, 93–94
Seeing the Insane (G. Mosse), 210
"Self-Assertion of the German University, The" (Heidegger), 148
self-hating Jew label, 219, 220, 231–33, 236
"Semites" (term), 5
Senghor, Léopold Sédar, 33, 34
seriality of racism, 37
sexuality, pathologizing of, 210
Shylock Jew myth, 115–16
Silverman, Max, 155, 290n99
Simmel, Ernst, 53
Simmel, Georg, 103
Six-Day War, 41, 228

Slánský, Rudolf, 228
Slánský trial case, 228–29
Smith, Anthony D., 183–84
Smith, Gerald L. K., 59
social disaggregation, anti-Semitism resulting from, 112
social engineering, by Hitler, 128–29
social justice, 51
social malaise, 60
Social Message of Jesus, The (T. Parsons), 104
"Sociological Background of the Psychoanalytic Approach" (Horkheimer), 53–54
"Sociological Study of Anti-Semitism in the United States, The" (Helmreich), 106
sociology, 53–54, 101–2, 110–14, 122, 132, 281n56; anti-Semitism and, 103, 106–7, 123; Bauman contributing to, 282n81; the Holocaust and, 277n1; liberal modernity bolstered by, 103–4
"Sociology after the Holocaust" (Z. Bauman), 277n1
"Sociology of Anti-Semitism, The" (T. Parsons), 102, 281n56
"Sociology of Modern Anti-Semitism, The" (Graeber and Britt), 101, 110–12, 122
Sociology of Religion, The (Weber), 113–14
"Some Sociological Aspects of the Fascist Movements" (T. Parsons), 118
Sonderweg thesis, on Germany, 58–59
Soros, George, 242–43
South Africa, 38–39, 95–96
Spectateur engagé, Le. See Committed Observer, The
Speer, Albert, 199, 301n38
Spengler, Oswald, 201–2
Stalinist anti-Zionism, 38
stereotypes, 6, 46, 189; aesthetics as basis of, 208–9; anatomy of, 209–12; Arendt reinscribing, 98; countertypes to, 213; internal contradictions externalized through, 64–65; Judeophobia and, 219; of masculinity, 212–13; T. Parsons and, 115; persecution contrasted with, 211;

projection driving, 64; racial discourse and, 210
Stern, Kenneth, 10
Stoetzler, Marcel, 102, 107
storytelling, by Arendt, 73-74, 78-84
strangers, 103, 123-25, 127, 131, 223-24
Strauss, Claude-Levi, 127
Structure of Social Action, The (T. Parsons), 102, 104-5
Struggle for Sovereignty in England, The (G. Mosse), 196-97
Studies in Philosophy and Social Science (Frankfurt School), 109
Studies in Prejudice series, by Frankfurt School, 46, 55, 266n45
Studies on Authority and the Family (Frankfurt School), 62-63
sub-men, 28-29
Summers, Lawrence, 232
Sur Judenfrage (Marx), 99
Systema Naturae (Linné), 179-80

Taguieff, Pierre-André, 127, 283n91
Talcott Parsons (Gerhardt), 110
Talcott Parsons on National Socialism (Gerhardt), 101, 110
Talmon, Jacob, 226-28
Tancred (Disraeli), 5
Temps modernes, Les (Sartre), 34, 41
Tester, Keith, 105
theater, mass movements influenced by, 205
Third Reich, The (Bruck), 201
"third world begins in the suburbs, The" ("*Tiers-monde commence en banlieue*") (Sartre), 39
Thomas, Martin Luther, 267n68
ticket thinking, 246-47, 248
"*Tiers-monde commence en banlieue, Le*" (Sartre). *See* "third world begins in the suburbs, The"
Tillich, Paul, 259n23
Title VI lawsuits, against colleges, 2
Tolstoy, Leo, 160
Tönnies, Ferdinand, 112
Torah, 152

"To Save the Jewish Homeland" (Arendt), 234, 235, 307n67
totalitarianism, 50, 69-70, 85-86, 203-4, 272n30
Totem and Taboo (Freud), 142, 170-71
"Toward a General Theory of Fascism" (G. Mosse), 226
"Towards a Definition of Antisemitism" (Langmuir), 7
Toward the Final Solution (G. Mosse), 198, 206, 208-9, 211-12, 216-17
Tractatus logico-philosophicus (Wittgenstein), 287n52
Trait d'union, Un. *See* Hyphen, The
Traité de métaphysique (Voltaire), 184
Traverso, Enzo, 190, 257n4
Treitschke, Heinrich, 203
Tristes tropiques (Strauss), 127
Trump, Donald, 59
"Types and Syndromes" (Adorno), 63

Über die bürgerliche Verbesserung der Juden. *See* On the Civil Improvement of the Jews
UGIF. *See* Union général des israélites de France
"Understanding and Politics" (Arendt), 79
Union général des israélites de France (UGIF), 162
University of Iowa, 192
University of Paris, 136
University of Warsaw, 105-6
University of Wisconsin-Madison, 192-93
UN Resolution 3379, Zionism condemned by, 42

Van Leer Institute, 11
Varnhagen, Rahel, 75, 91, 92, 233
Vichy France and the Jews (Marrus and Paxton), 293n29
Vichy government, in France, 165-66, 259n16, 293n29
"Vichy Syndrome," 150
victimhood, competition for, 245
Voegelin, Eric, 78-79, 84-85
volkish ideology, 197-204

Volkov, Shulamit, 7, 253n39
Voltaire (writer), 184

Wagner, Richard, 205
Wall, The (Sartre), 23
Warrant for Genocide (Cohn), 167
Weber, Max, 68, 91, 102, 113–15
Weil, Felix, 48
Weil, Hermann, 48
Weingrad, Michael, 155
"We Refugees" (Arendt), 75
Wesen des Christentums, Das. See Essence of Christianity, The
West, the, 17, 65–66, 68–69, 152–54, 157
Western tradition, Judeophobia in, 176–77
"What is a collaborator?" ("*Qu'est-ce qu'un collaborateur?*") (Sartre), 30
"What Is Enlightenment" (Kant), 207
"What Is Metaphysics?" (Heidegger), 27
Wheatland, Thomas, 52
"Where Hannah Arendt Went Wrong" (Avineri), 97
whiteness, of Jews, 2–3, 239–40, 249n4

Whites, Jews, and Us (Bouteldja), 238–41
Wiggershaus, Rolf, 266n45
wish-fulfillment, 54–55
Wistrich, Robert, 9
Wittgenstein, Ludwig, 287n52
World War I, 18, 170–71
World War II, 49, 65, 105, 161, 233

Yitzhaki, Shlomo "Rashi," 16
Youth Aliyah (Zionist organization), 233

Zionism, 40, 43–44, 240; anti-Semitism and, 234–35; binationalism contrasted with, 234; criticism of, 12; decolonizing and, 241; racism and, 237–38; UN Resolution 3379 condemning, 42. *See also* anti-Zionism; Israel
"Zionism Reconsidered" (Arendt), 234–35
Zionist manifestos, anti-Semitism responded to, 18
Zionist plot, myth of, 228
Zionists, anti-Semitism by, 17–18
"*Zur Judenfrage*" (Marx). *See* "On the Jewish Question"

GPSR Authorized Representative: Easy Access System Europe, Mustamäe tee 50, 10621 Tallinn, Estonia, gpsr.requests@easproject.com